Edith Fowke, Professor, Department of English, York University, is a member of the Order of Canada and a Fellow of the American Folklore Society. She is the author of many books and articles on Canadian folk songs and children's lore, and editor of Folklore of Canada and the Canadian Folk Music Journal.

Carole Henderson Carpenter, Associate Professor, Division of Humanities, York University, has a doctorate in Folklore-Folklife Studies. She is the author of Many Voices: A Study of Folklore Activities in Canada and Their Role in Canadian Culture and many articles on Canadian folklore, and edits Canadian Folklore Canadien.

This book is the only comprehensive bibliography of Canadian folklore in English. The 3877 different items are arranged by genres: folktales; folk music and dance; folk speech and naming; superstitions, popular beliefs, folk medicine, and the supernatural; folklife and customs; folk art and material culture; and within genres by ethnic groups: Anglophone and Celtic, Francophone, Indian and Inuit, and other cultural groups. The items include reference books, periodicals, articles, records, films, biographies of scholars and informants, and graduate theses. Each item is annotated through a coding that indicates whether it is academic or popular, its importance to the scholar, and whether it is suitable for young people. The introduction includes a brief survey of Canadian folklore studies, putting this work into academic and social perspective.

The book covers all the important items and most minor items dealing with Canadian folklore published in English up to the end of 1979. It is concerned with legitimate Canadian folklore - whether transplanted from other countries and preserved here, or created here to reflect the culture of this country. It distinguishes between authentic folklore presented as collected and popular treatments in which the material has been rewritten by the authors.

Intended primarily for scholars of folklore, international as well as Canadian, the book will also be of use to scholars in anthropology, cultural geography, oral history, and other branches of Canadian culture studies, as well as to librarians, teachers, and the general public.

A Bibliography of Canadian Folklore in English

Compiled by Edith Fowke
and
Carole Henderson Carpenter

University of Toronto Press
Toronto   Buffalo   London

© University of Toronto Press 1981
Toronto   Buffalo   London
Printed in Canada
ISBN 0-8020-2394-0

Canadian Cataloguing in Publication Data

Fowke, Edith, 1913-
  A bibliography of Canadian folklore in English

  Includes index.
  ISBN 0-8020-2394-0

  1. Folk-lore - Canada - Bibliography.
  I. Carpenter, Carole Henderson, 1944-   II. Title.

  Z5984.C2F68 1981   016.390'00971   C81-094187-2

This book has been published with the assistance of
the Multiculturalism Program, Government of Canada

Contents

Introduction

The history of Canadian folklore is a surprisingly long one, yet few Canadians other than folklorists appreciate its true nature, its significance, and its role in our culture. This results from social and political circumstances within Canada and from misconceptions about folklore, as well as from the kind of work done by most Canadian folklorists and the differences within the international discipline of folklore studies concerning what folklore is and how it ought to be studied.

There are many definitions of folklore, a number of different schools of folklorists, and considerable interaction with other disciplines. If our work is to be meaningful to many people besides folklore specialists, we must define our subject and the scope of the study. To be most useful, a bibliography should be both broad and specific; hence we have adopted a rather broad and general definition of folklore. Our approach is that folklore is material handed on in tradition whether by word of mouth or by custom and practice. At the same time we have tried to restrict our listings to items properly belonging under folklore rather than under anthropology, sociology, or linguistics. Nevertheless, some overlapping is inevitable, and we have included a small number of items that might otherwise be classified within these and other disciplines such as geography, history, or architecture.

As our title indicates, this bibliography deals only with "Canadian Folklore in English." The very extensive French-Canadian lore is amply documented by Francophone scholars, and we have not attempted to cover languages other than English and French which are little known in Canada except by native speakers and a small number of specialized scholars. We have, however, listed any material from French-Canadian or other language groups that is printed in translation, or where the discussion of it is in English, or where it includes a significant number of English items. We should also note that by "Canadian folklore" we mean folklore that is found in Canada; we do not list titles dealing exclusively with non-Canadian folklore even if written by Canadians or published in Canada.

A Bibliography of Canadian Folklore in English

A bibliography such as this is more meaningful when seen in the context of the discipline and the nation it concerns. This is especially true of a folklore work since folklorists have become increasingly interested in contextual studies during recent years. It is therefore important to outline the extent and nature of Canadian folklore activities and to place them in the perspective of Canadian concerns and international folklore studies.

For several centuries now folklore in Canada has been collected, preserved, and interpreted by a disparate group of persons--explorers and travellers, scholars and amateurs, foreigners and Canadians, writers and performers--who have produced work varying greatly in nature, quality, and importance. By far the majority of the works are collections rather than analyses. Until recently Canadian activities have been largely isolated from international trends and theories in folklore studies, and have contributed little to the development of the discipline. However, the Canadian work has been closely related to the sociopolitical milieu of the country and has had a certain importance as a result (see item 191 in this bibliography). Past activities have had a strong formative effect on current Canadian folklore work which promises to be of considerable international importance.

In effect, folklore was collected in Canada as early as the first missionary reports on the aboriginal people's beliefs, tales, and customs. The Jesuit Relations, first published in 1616 and annually between 1632 and 1673, are the most important of such documents (see item 326). A number of explorers' accounts are also of considerable value to folklorists: for example, Henry Kelsey's Journal (2520), which contains an important record of native beliefs and superstitions, and Sir John Franklin's records of his nineteenth-century northern voyages which include considerable ethnographic information on the Inuit (2472, 2473). Many are the travellers' journals and settlers' diaries or memoirs noteworthy for their folkloric content. W. E. Cormack's Narrative of a Journey across the Island of Newfoundland in 1822 (2419), Paul Kane's Wanderings of an Artist among the Indians of North America (2519), Anna Jameson's Winter Studies and Summer Rambles in Canada (2057), and Susanna Moodie's Roughing It in the Bush (2281) are good examples. Such works frequently contain excellent folklife and contextual information as well as an occasional story or song text, as do a number of early fictional works such as Philippe-Aubert de Gaspé's important novel Les anciens canadiens (542). In recording or portraying life in early Canada, many authors wove considerable folklore into the fabric of their works--not expressly because they intended to do so, but rather because it was a main thread of the lifestyles they were documenting.

Introduction

After the first quarter of the nineteenth century, a nationaliste movement developed in Quebec which fostered interest in the preservation of the French-Canadian language and traditions (202). The products of this interest were mostly literary like Joseph-Charles Taché's Forestiers et voyageurs (Québec, 1863), W. H. Drummond's dialect poems, and Henri Beaugrand's La Chasse-Galerie and Other Canadian Stories (532). Nonetheless, the first true folklore collection in Canada (and one of the first of its kind in the world) also appeared at this time: Ernest Gagnon's seminal work, Chansons populaires du Canada (Québec, 1865).

Truly "scientific" interest in Canadian folklore was not evident until the closing years of the last century when Franz Boas began his monumental work on the native people, especially the Northwest Coast Indians. He was the first of many prominent scholars to devote a career to studying Canadian native traditions and, as the leading figure in North American anthropology, he contributed significantly to making these traditions the most thoroughly studied of any aspect of Canadian folklore.

It is one thing to be studied by outsiders and quite another to study one's own traditions. Until recently the native people of Canada had neither the means nor the inclination to collect, analyze, or publish their heritage since they were struggling simply to preserve it in the face of cultural contact. It was the French Canadians, of all the peoples of Canada, who showed the earliest scholarly interest in their own traditions. This interest has persisted and developed to a much greater extent than among Anglo-Canadians. As a result French-Canadian folklore activities far outshadow those of the other major cultural group in Canada except in specific regional and ethnic enclaves such as Newfoundland.

The roots of French-Canadian studies can be traced to popular movements and cultural concerns in the history of French Canada, but modern folklore actually began with Marius Barbeau's extensive collecting and profuse publications after he joined the staff of the National Museum of Canada in 1911. Barbeau revived the Montreal Branch of the American Folklore Society which had been founded in 1892, and gathered about him a group of ardent collectors and enthusiasts like Marcel Rioux and E.-Z. Massicotte, who helped amass the National Museum's impressive French-Canadian folklore holdings and produce the eight Canadian numbers of the Journal of American Folklore (vols. 29, 30, 32, 33, 39, 44, 53, and 62). The most important Canadian-born folklorist to date, Barbeau was encouraged and assisted by various foreign scholars, especially Franz Boas, Raoul and Marguerite d'Harcourt, and Edward Sapir. He also had many influential friends in Canada who helped him in his efforts to popularize folk traditions, particularly folk music. For instance, Barbeau's friend, the composer and conductor Sir Ernest MacMillan, arranged folk songs for choral performances and incorporated folk themes in his compositions largely to promote a national music for Canada. Such interest in and applied use of folklore is common in Canadian folklore activities (190, 191).

By the early 1900s, various people were concerning themselves with folk traditions in the Atlantic provinces. George Lyman Kittredge influenced two Harvard students to return to their native Maritime region to collect folk songs: W. Roy Mackenzie in Nova Scotia (1175-1177), and Cyrus Macmillan to Prince Edward Island (3809). Then Mary Fraser published her doctoral dissertation on Folklore of Nova Scotia (268) in 1932, the same year that Helen Creighton--destined to become one of Canada's foremost collectors--published her first book (1071). Actual collecting did not begin in New Brunswick until later, although there were a few popular publications dealing with folklore early in this century. Prompted by Lord Beaverbrook, Louise Manny started recording folk songs after World War II. She went on to establish the important Miramichi Folk Festival and to publish (with J. R. Wilson) her valuable collection, Songs of Miramichi (1189).

In addition to these Canadian collectors, numerous foreign folksong specialists gravitated to Atlantic Canada in the hope of finding in that relatively isolated and underdeveloped area the oldest songs in their most unadulterated forms. Such fieldworkers include Elisabeth Greenleaf and Grace Mansfield (1134) as well as Maud Karpeles (1158-1160) who visited Newfoundland in 1929-30, Sidney Robertson Cowell and Laura Boulton who collected in Cape Breton in the 1940s and 1950s (1059, 3318), and the more scholarly MacEdward Leach (192, 1167), and Edward D. Ives (1142-1155) who worked in several Atlantic areas in later years. Additionally, various Gaelic scholars have focussed attention on Nova Scotia's Scots traditions, especially those of the Highland descendants on Cape Breton Island.

Early interest in folklore outside the Maritimes and French Canada led to the establishment of the Canadian Folk-Lore Society in Toronto in 1908, involving such prominent figures as the major Canadian archaeologists David Boyle and W. J. Wintemberg. The main products of that unfortunately short-lived society were Wintemberg's collection of German-Canadian traditions, Folk-Lore of Waterloo County, Ontario (334), and a number of articles in the Journal of American Folklore.

Anglo-Canadian traditions in Ontario were little studied until one of the editors became interested in folklore in the 1950s. She has since produced several books and records from her own collecting as well as the first national surveys of folksongs, collections of Canadian children's lore, and an anthology of Canadian folklore (267, 956, 960, 1111, 1116, 1122, 1712).

Until quite recently, foreign scholars have shown little interest in studying central or western Canadian folklore apart from the native peoples' traditions. In fact, folklore in the west has been little studied at all except for the intensive work on Indian material. Some limited studies of minority groups, place-name collections, numerous articles, pamphlets, and books pertaining to pioneer life and characters, and the products of the Alberta Folklore and Local History Project directed by Robert Gard in the early 1940s (18, 181) constitute most of the non-native folklore works from the four western provinces up to the 1960s. The past two decades have seen more activity, primarily concerning minority-cultural groups and oral history (such as the periodical, Sound Heritage, produced since 1972 by the British Columbia Provincial Archives), although a little Anglo-Canadian lore has also been collected.

Minority-culture studies have gained considerable prominence in recent times as a result of the Royal Commission on Bilingualism and Biculturalism in the late sixties. Its recommendations led to the federal government's policy of multiculturalism within a bilingual framework. Much of the work on minority cultures has emanated from the Canadian Centre for Folk Culture Studies, the national folklore centre which grew out of the Folklore Division founded by Marius Barbeau within the National Museum. Such important scholars and collectors as Jan H. Brunvand, Linda Dégh, Ban Seng Hoe, Barbara Kirshenblatt-Gimblett, Robert Klymasz, and Kenneth Peacock have contributed to the Centre's minority-culture studies. Others who have done research on minority groups include Arthur Huff Fauset on the Nova Scotia blacks in the late twenties (662), J. B. Rudny'ckyj on Ukrainians (313, 314), and Mark Mealing on Doukhobors (2724).

Meanwhile the French-Canadian work has continued to develop and to expand into various centres including the Centre d'études acadiennes at the Université de Moncton, the Centre d'études franco-ontariennes (formerly the Institut de Folklore) at Laurentian University/Université de Sudbury, and the Centre d'études franco-terreneuviennes at Memorial University. It was a French Canadian (and a protegé of Marius Barbeau), Luc Lacourcière, who first developed academic folklore studies at a Canadian university after securing a chair in Folklore at Laval in 1944. He established Les Archives de Folklore there which, through his prodigious efforts and those of dedicated scholars he trained and/or gathered around him, evolved into an internationally-renowned folklore studies centre which is now part of CELAT (the Centre d'études sur la langue, les arts et les traditions populaires des francophones en Amerique du Nord).

The one other folklore studies programme in Canada, at Memorial University of Newfoundland, is likewise the product of a particularly fine scholar--Herbert Halpert. After coming from the United States to join the university in 1961, Halpert gradually developed graduate and undergraduate folklore programmes, an impressive archive comprised substantially of student collections, and various important publication series.

Today folklore is taught at a number of post-secondary institutions in Canada, but the discipline has yet to achieve the broad academic acceptance it enjoys in the United States and other countries. The recent creation of a national folklore society, the Folklore Studies Association of Canada (incorporated December 1975) and the establishment of its journal, Canadian Folklore Canadien (Vol. 1, 1979), will help to bring about greater popular and academic awareness of the nature and value of folklore studies in Canada.

Canadian folklore activities have a number of decided strengths and weaknesses. By far the most thoroughly studied genre is folk song, and the best-studied groups are the native peoples and the French Canadians. The scholarship concerning these materials and groups is commendable, though by no means exhaustive. Anglo-Canadian folklore has been neglected, especially in recent years when minority-culture studies have acquired perhaps too much prominence. Material culture has commanded the attention of numerous scholars and the public to such an extent that various important folklife museums have developed across the nation: for example, Upper Canada Village at Morrisburg, Ontario; Black Creek Pioneer Village in Toronto; King's Landing near Fredericton, New Brunswick; the Acadian Village at Caraquet, New Brunswick; and the Ukrainian Cultural Heritage Village near Edmonton. Eastern traditions have been far better studied than western ones, and, until very recently, urban traditions have been almost totally neglected in favour of rural ones. Much more can and should be done on occupational and pioneer lore, on urban and children's lore, on the minor genres, and on Anglo-Canadian lore generally. Too frequently members of Canada's majority group have considered folklore to be the property of others, not themselves, with the sad consequence that many Canadians neither realize nor respect their folk heritage.

There is a decided emphasis on local and regional studies in Canadian folklore. Scarce indeed are works national in perspective, dealing with Canadian oral traditions as a whole. Most Canadian folklorists have been, and still are, specialists in the study of a distinct group, whether that group be linguistic, regional, or ethnic. Few scholars who focus on genres of folklore engage in cross-group research on that particular material. Rather, song specialists, for instance, tend to concentrate on Anglo-Canadian _or_ French-Canadian folk songs. More common is the scholar who studies various traditions, but within a given group.

Canadian folklore work is particularly weak in theoretical and analytical scholarship. Cross-cultural comparisons and adaptation-assimilation studies would be particularly fruitful, yet are scarcely to be found in the literature. Folklore studies in this country must move increasingly away from being mere "butterfly collections" toward providing meaningful insights into Canadian culture. The present scholarship offers considerable hope for the future. While pursuing directions established in the past and thereby capitalizing on its strengths, it may well overcome the weaknesses of that past.

This short summary has given a bare outline of the extent and nature of Canadian folklore work. For a more extensive description and analysis, see Many Voices: A Study of Folklore Activities in Canada and Their Role in Canadian Culture (169).

This project began when we recognized the need for a comprehensive bibliography of Canadian folklore to overcome the deficiencies of the existing inadequate, inaccurate, or purely regional or ethnic works. The present bibliography grew out of two others: one prepared for English 430, "Canadian Folklore," at York University, and the other for a doctoral dissertation (2784). To the items in these, various other titles were added from some of the bibliographies listed in our first section, and from first-hand research in the periodicals listed in the second section. Two research assistants, Judith Brooks and Diane Vipond, York graduate students, helped to search the journals and check publication data and paging, and we kept adding new items as they appeared and older ones reaped from obscure sources or located in out-of-the-way places. When we realized that it was going to take considerable time to produce a bibliography of Canadian folklore fit for publication, we issued a preliminary draft in 1976: a privately published photo-offset edition of some 450 copies. Since then we have added a great many titles, corrected inaccurate details, and devised a system of annotation by coding that we hope will make the bibliography more valuable. Our coverage generally goes to the end of 1979, a good cut-off date at the beginning of a new decade.

The initial sections on bibliographies, checklists, and periodicals are somewhat selective. They do not include every bibliography or periodical that contains some items of Canadian folklore, but only those devoted entirely to, or containing a substantial amount of, Canadian lore. The most relevant periodicals have been indexed completely except for the Alberta Folklore Quarterly and Canadian German Folklore: the material in them is primarily historical, geographical, or biographical, and much of it is presented in very brief items which are not suitable for indexing. Both the Beaver and the Canadian Geographical Journal contain numerous articles dealing to some extent with folklore, but we have included only those that are somewhat more specific. Also some more popular journals (e.g., Cape Breton's Magazine, Decks Awash, Them Days, The Canadian Antiques Collector, The Newfoundlander) contain a great many brief or borderline items which do not merit individual listing. Nor have we covered newspapers or popular magazines except for a few items of special interest.

The arrangement is basically by genre, with subdivisions for the major ethnic groups. Some subdividing is necessary if an extensive bibliography is to be useful, and in Canada a regional division does not work, largely because collecting has been uneven in different regions. Also, as many folklorists specialize in one particular genre, the arrangement we have chosen will probably serve researchers best.

The attempted subdivision into four ethnic groups: Anglophone and Celtic, Francophone, native peoples, and others, created some classification problems. One difficulty concerned material from people of mixed blood. With the Métis, for example, their songs seem to belong in the French-Canadian section as they used French tunes and were sung in French, but works relating to their culture fit better in the native peoples section. Arthur Huff Fauset's Folklore of Nova Scotia is particularly difficult to classify as many of his informants were blacks or of mixed blood, but the material itself is similar to Anglo-Canadian rather than to black lore; consequently we have reluctantly included it under Anglo-Canadian. However, it should be noted that this is the major work dealing with the folklore of black Canadians.

It was also difficult to decide where some items covering a number of genres belonged. We have tried to list each one where its major emphasis lies: for example, books containing a few French items within a largely Anglo-Canadian collection go under "Anglophone and Celtic," and items that include some information about material culture may go under "Folklife and Customs." If the emphasis is not clearly on one genre, the items appear in 3B: "General: Containing More Than One Genre," and if they deal with one genre but the emphasis is not clearly on one ethnic group, they appear in the "General" sections preceding the subsections on cultural groups under folktales, folk songs, etc. A special problem is the overlapping between sections 4 and 8 regarding belief legends. These are one form of folktale, but they are also folk beliefs, and we have listed them as the latter. Some items are listed in more than one section where their material on different genres seems particularly important. To avoid too many such repetitions we have added numerical references to other relevant items at the end of the sections.

Introduction

Apart from the limits already mentioned, we have had to restrict some of the sections that come within our pattern. In particular, those sections dealing with "Folklife and Customs" and "Folk Arts and Material Culture" cannot be exhaustive. These topics are so broad that they would require extensive bibliographies of their own. Practically everything written on pioneer times and thousands of local histories could be included under "Folklife and Customs." "Folk Speech and Naming" is also hard to limit: here we are in danger of overlapping with linguistics and onomastics. In such sections we have tried to give the major books and articles, emphasizing those that seem most closely related to folklore studies, but these sections are obviously incomplete. Another area closely related to folklore is that of oral, or aural, history, and here we have listed only a few significant items.

Similarly, almost everything written about the Indians and Inuit might be considered folklore as their culture was entirely unwritten and traditional until recent times. However, modern folklore theory holds that pre-Contact native cultures cannot legitimately be classified as folk cultures because folk cultures are little traditions, that is, small groups within larger cultures. The pre-Contact native cultures were not little traditions for they constituted the larger cultures. Undoubtedly there were folk groups within the various pre-Contact Canadian native groups, but the documentation of these is not available (except as a folklore scholar might be able to discern it in general works included in the bibliography). Only now, with the development of the various "ethnostudies" such as ethnohistory is such distinction between folk and the larger native cultures prior to Contact becoming truly feasible. Since Contact, the native cultures have obviously been little traditions within the larger culture, making their traditions the legitimate province of folklorists. Hence, we have limited entries to the post-Contact era as the soundest way of isolating folkloric information from the vast amount of anthropological data concerning our native peoples, and we have emphasized the oral traditions to a greater extent than the voluminous material on customs and artifacts.

Within the more specific areas of folktales, folk songs, proverbs, riddles, children's lore, and popular beliefs, we have tried to be as complete as possible. We have listed all the first-hand traditional material we could locate, along with most secondary items based fairly directly on Canadian folklore. However, we have included only a selection of the many so-called "Canadian folktales" for children consisting of rewritten, bowdlerized, or fictionalized Indian or Inuit stories. We have also omitted most anthologies and songbooks that include a few familiar Canadian items, and most choral or instrumental arrangements of folk songs, for nearly all of these are based on primary sources already listed. Nor have we attempted to list the many fictional, dramatic, and poetic works that incorporate some folklore material. Most Canadian literature includes some folklore--at least folklife descriptions, if not more specific folklore items--but a bibliography of folklore in Canadian literature is beyond the scope of this work and the subject for a separate study.

In general the style follows the <u>MLA Style Sheet</u>. We have used short forms of publishers' names and omitted some sub-headings if the main title was self-explanatory. Where the title is not descriptive we have added an identifying word or phrase in parentheses. No provincial or state designation is given for well known places of publication; for places that may be confusing or difficult to identify the designation is given the first time the publisher is listed. Foreign publication places are identified except when obvious. London cited alone is the British capital; London, Ontario, is identified. We have generally included reprint information when it came to our attention, but such information is not complete. We usually give the original printing data as well as reprint details for books published in the last fifty years, and wherever possible we have added the number of pages as a guide to the publication's size.

In 1968 the source of many items, the National Museum of Canada, became the National Museums, with the folklore items issued by the National Museum of Man. Despite this change we have kept to a standard listing of National Museum, adding where appropriate the designation for the distinct divisions of the National Museum of Man such as the Canadian Centre for Folk Culture Studies or the Canadian Ethnology Service.

We have kept abbreviations of periodical and series titles to a minimum so readers will not have to keep referring back to a code list. Only a few abbreviations appear, for periodicals that are cited frequently and for those with particularly lengthy titles. We have normally abbreviated such words as association, transactions, proceedings, and have used standard abbreviations for provinces and states except where these appear in book or periodical titles.

We have tried to standarize the listing of authors' names, using one given name and initial(s) unless the author always used a full name or only initials, and we have omitted all titles such as Rev., Dr., or Sir except for Mrs. when a woman used it with her husband's name. Occasionally the same author may be listed in more than one way when the form of the name varies on different articles or books, but the fullest form is given in the index.

Introduction

The emphasis is on published material: only a few important mimeographed items and manuscripts are listed, except for theses and dissertations which are in a separate section. In addition to the normal coverage of books and articles we have added sections on films and records.

When some authors published articles and later incorporated the material into books we have commonly omitted the articles. However, we have tried to list all the publications of renowned folklore scholars, and we have given even very minor items in some popular magazines if they present authentic folklore texts not published elsewhere. On the other hand, we have not included all the many journalistic pieces on certain popular topics such as Oak Island and the Sasquatch.

To annotate a bibliography of this size would have required far more time than we were prepared to give it. As a substitute we have devised a letter code to give some basic information about the various items. The main division is between authentic and popular folklore. By authentic we mean material stemming directly from the folk and presented as nearly as possible as collected. By popular we mean re-written or more generalized material. Authentic folklore is indicated by capitals A, B, or C, and popular by P, plus in some cases small a, b, or c where entries include some valuable folklore. Similarly, capital letters are added to F to indicate the value of the Canadian material in foreign items, and small letters are added to G to indicate the value of the folklore in general items.

The quality judgments implicit in the A, B, C notations are necessarily subjective and tentative, but they indicate the value of the various items to the best of our ability. In establishing the grade we have weighed such factors as date of publication, reputation of the author, length, type of publication, and number of publications on the same subject. For example, early items are rated somewhat higher than later ones when the items are more authentic because they were collected earlier; on the other hand, later items are rated higher when they reflect the more scholarly approach of an evolving discipline. Articles in academic journals are usually rated higher than those in popular journals; and items whose quality might normally merit an A or B rating are sometimes rated lower in sections where a great deal of material is available. We realize that this coding system is not perfect, but we believe it will be useful as a general guide to the type and value of the various items.

We wish to thank our many colleagues who assisted us by offering suggestions and drawing to our attention items for inclusion and sources to search for such items. In particular we are grateful to Professor Herbert Halpert, bibliographer par excellence, for his invaluable assistance. We also wish to thank Secretarial Services of York University for preparation of the typescript.

We know that in a bibliography of this size some errors will undoubtedly surface despite our best efforts, and that a work like this is never really finished for it is out of date before it is published. Recognizing its limitations, we nonetheless hope that it will prove a useful tool for Canadian and international folklorists, for scholars in related disciplines, and for librarians and teachers. We also hope that it will make more accessible to many people the extensive, varied, and fascinating literature on this important and enduring aspect of our culture.

Edith Fowke and Carole Henderson Carpenter
York University
Downsview, Ontario

Abbreviations

Periodicals and Institutes

BFSSNE:	Bulletin of the Folksong Society of the Northeast
CanAntC:	Canadian Antiques Collector
CCFCS:	Canadian Centre for Folk Culture Studies
CFMJ:	Canadian Folk Music Journal
CFMSN:	Canadian Folk Music Society Newsletter
CGJ:	Canadian Geographical Journal
ISER:	Institute of Social and Economic Research
JAF:	Journal of American Folklore
JIFMC:	Journal of the International Folk Music Council
TRSC:	Transactions of the Royal Society of Canada

Other Abbreviations

Assoc.	Association	pb.	paperback
Can. ed.	Canadian edition	Pub.	Publishing
comp.	compiler	Proc.	Proceedings
Dept.	Department	Prov.	Provincial
ed.	editor	rev. ed.	revised edition
Gov't.	Government	rpt.	reprinted
illus.	illustrator	trans.	translator
pamp.	pamphlet	Trans.	Transactions

Code

A   Most important items dealing with authentic folklore.

B   Good items of somewhat less importance.

C   Valid items of minor importance.

F   Foreign items with some Canadian content.

G   General items with some folklore content.

P   Items designed for a popular audience, usually rewritten or adapted.

Y   Items designed or especially suitable for young people.

R   Reference works.

When used alone, A, B, and C refer to the whole work; when used with F they indicated that the Canadian folklore content is significant.

With G and P items we have sometimes added small letters to indicate that they contain significant amounts of authentic folklore.

Further letters are added to some of the preceding to indicate:
(1) Literary presentation of authentic material.
(r) Rewritten texts based on authentic material.
(s) Secondary works: reprinted texts.

In sections 1, 2, 11, 12, and 13, where our grading system is inappropriate, we have used asterisks to indicate items likely to be most useful.

A Bibliography of Canadian Folklore in English

1 Reference Materials: Bibliographies and checklists

*F   1   Aarne, Antti, and Stith Thompson. The Types of the
          Folktale. Helsinki: Scientiarum Fennica, 1961. 588 pp.

 G   2   Abler, Tom, Douglas Saunders, and Sally Weaver. A Can-
          adian Indian Bibliography, 1960-1970. Toronto: Univ. of
          Toronto Press, 1974. 732 pp.

 G   3   About Indians: A Listing of Books. Ottawa: Indian and
          Northern Affairs, 4th ed., 1977. 135 pp.

 G   4   Aitken, Barbara B. Local Histories of Ontario Muni-
          cipalities; 1957-1977. Toronto: Ont. Library Assoc.,
          1978. 120 pp.

      5   Alexandrin, Barbara, and Robert Bothwell. Bibliography
          of the Material Culture of New France. Ottawa: National
          Museum, History Division Series 4, 1970. 32 pp.

 F   6   Andrews, H. A., et al. 'Bibliography of Franz Boas.'
          In Franz Boas 1885-1962. Eds. A. L. Kroeber et al.
          American Anthropological Assoc. Memoirs, 61(1943),
          67-109.

 G   7   Armstrong, Jill, and Lynda Lankin. The Canadian Review
          of Sociology and Anthropology: Decennial Index 1964-
          1973. Montreal: Canadian Sociology and Anthropology
          Assoc., 1974. 20 pp.

 G   8   Artibase, Alan F. J. Western Canada Since 1870: A
          Select Bibliography and Guide. Vancouver: Univ. of
          B.C. Press, 1978. 312 pp.

 G   9   Atlantic Provinces Check-List. Halifax: Atlantic Prov-
          inces Economic Council, 1957--.

 G   10   Avis, Walter S. A Bibliography of Writings on Cana-
          dian English (1857-1965). Toronto: Gage, 1965. 17 pp.

     11   Barter, Geraldine. A Critically Annotated Bibliography
          of Works Published and Unpublished Relating to the

3

Culture of French Newfoundlanders. St. John's: Memorial
Univ., 1977. 54 pp. Mimeo.

F   12   Baughman, Ernest W. Type and Motif Index of the Folktales of England and North America. The Hague: Mouton,
1966. 606 pp.

G   13   Boucher, Thérèse. Anthropologica Vicennial Index 1955-
1974. Ottawa: St. Paul Univ., 1975. 44 pp.

     14   Bradley, Ian L. 'A Bibliography of Indian Musical Cul-
ture in Canada.' Northian News, 40 (1974), 14-20.

     15   -- 'Bibliography of the Arts and Crafts of Northwest
Coast Indians.' B.C. Studies, 21(Spring 1975), 78-124.

G   16   -- A Selected Bibliography of Musical Canadiana.
1974; rev. ed., Agincourt, Ont.: GLC Publishers, 1976.
177 pp.

     17   Bradley, Ian L., and Patricia B. Bradley. A Bibliog-
raphy of Canadian Native Arts. Victoria: GLC Publishers, 1977. 109 pp.

     18   Cameron Library. The Alberta Folklore and Local History
Collection. Edmonton: Univ. of Alberta, 1966. 33 pp.

G   19   Canadian Museums and Related Institutions. Ottawa: Canadian Museums Assoc.,1968. 138 pp.

     20   Cardin, Clarisse. 'Bio-bibliographie de Marius Bar-
beau.' Archives de Folklore, 2(1947), 17-72.

G   21   Careless, Virginia. Bibliography for the Study of
British Columbia's Domestic Material History. Ottawa:
National Museum, History Division Mercury Series 20,
1976. 77 pp.

     22   Cavanagh, Beverley. 'Annotated Bibliography: Eskimo
Music.' Ethnomusicology, 16(1972), 479-87.

F   23   Check-list of recorded songs in the English language
in the Archive of American Folk Song to July, 1940.
3 vols. Washington: Music Division, Library of Congress, 1942.

F   24   Clements, William M. The Types of the Polack Joke.
Bloomington, IN: Folklore Forum. Bibliographic and
Special Series No. 3, 1969. 45 pp.

F   25   Cleveland Public Library, John G. White Department.
Catalogue of Folklore and Folk Songs. 2 vols., folio.
Boston: Hall, 1964.

F 26 Coffin, Tristram P. An Analytical Index to the Journal of American Folklore. Philadelphia: American Folklore Society, 1958. 384 pp.

27 Cormier, Charlotte. 'Partial Inventory of Father Anselme Chiasson's Collection of Folksongs, Tales, and Legends in the Archives Acadiennes of l'Université de Moncton.' CFMSN, 4(1969), 41-64.

G 28 Cuddy, Mary Lou, and James J. Scott. British Columbia in Books: An Annotated Bibliography. Vancouver: Douglas, 1974. 144 pp.

G 29 Dickie, Gordon. 'Culture Origins in Colonial Life.' Dalhousie Review, 37(1957), 41-51, 165-74.

G 30 Duff, Wilson, and Michael Kew. 'A Select Bibliography of Anthropology of British Columbia.' B.C. Studies, 19(Autumn 1973), 73-121.

31 Dyck, Ruth. 'Ethnic Folklore in Canada: A Preliminary Survey.' Canadian Ethnic Studies, 7:2(1975), 90-101.

32 Fowke, Edith. '"Old Favourites": A Selective Index.' CFMJ, 7(1979), 29-56.

33 [Fowke, Edith.] 'A Reference List on Canadian Folk Music.' CFMJ, 6(1978), 41-56.

34 Fowke, Edith, and Carole Henderson [Carpenter]. 'A Bibliography of Canadian Folklore in English.' Communiqué: Canadian Studies, 3(Aug. 1977), 2-72.

F 35 'Frances Densmore: Bibliography.' Ethnomusicology Newsletter, 1(Apr. 1956), 14-29; 1(May 1957), 15; Ethnomusicology, 2(1958), 26; 131-32.

36 Fraser, Ian F. 'The French-Canadian Folk Song.' Bibliography of French-Canadian Poetry. New York: Columbia Univ., 1935. Pp. 102-5.

37 Gedalof, Robin. An Annotated Bibliography of Canadian Inuit Literature. Ottawa: Indian and Northern Affairs Canada, 1979. 108 pp.

F 38 Gillis, Frank J., and Alan P. Merriam. Ethnomusicology and Folk Music: An International Bibliography of Dissertations and Theses. Pub. for the Society for Ethnomusicology. Middleton, CT: Wesleyan Univ. Press, 1966. 148 pp.

G 39 Gregorovich, Andrew. Canadian Ethnic Groups Bibliography. Toronto: Dept. of Citizenship, 1972. 208 pp.

F 40 Griffin, William J. 'A Survey of U.S. and Canadian Folklore Serials.' Tennessee Folklore Society Bulletin, 30(1964), 26-32; 31(1965), 129-39; 32 (1966), 13-17; 33(1967), 121-24.

41 Guédon, Marie-Françoise. 'Canadian Indian Ethnomusicology: Selected Bibliography and Discography.' Ethnomusicology, 16(1972), 465-78.

G 42 Hall, Frederick A., et al. A Basic Bibliography of Musical Canadiana. Toronto, 1970, Pp. 20-32. Mimeo.

F 43 Haywood, Charles. A Bibliography of North American Folklore and Folksong. 2 vols. New York: Greenberg, 1951; rpt. New York: Dover, 1961.

G 44 Heinrich, Albert C. 'University Research on Canada's Eskimos: A Preliminary Check-List of Theses.' Canadian Ethnic Studies, 2:1(1970), 31-34.

45 Herrison, Michael. An Evaluative Ethno-Historical Bibliography of the Malecite Indians. Ottawa: National Museum, Ethnology Service Mercury Series 16, 1974. 260 pp.

F 46 Hickerson, Joseph C. 'A List of Folklore and Folk Music Archives and Related Collections in the United States and Canada.' JAF Supplement, 1972, pp. 17-24.

G 47 Horvath, Maria (Krisztinkovich). A Doukhobor Bibliography. Vancouver: Univ. of B.C. Library, 1968. 22 pp.

F 48. Ireland, Florence. 'The Northeast Archives of Folklore and Oral History.' Northeast Folklore, 13(1972), 1-86.

F 49 [Ives, Edward D., and Bacil F. Kirtley.] 'Bibliography of New England-Maritimes Folklore.' Northeast Folklore, 1(1958), 19-28; 2(1959), 19-23; 3(1960), 20-23.

F 50 [-- and --] 'Selected Bibliography of New England-Maritimes Folklore Prior to 1950.' Northeast Folklore, 1(1958), 29-31.

51 Jitodai, Kinuye. Bibliography of the Arts and Crafts of Northwest Coast Indians. Seattle: Univ. of Washington, 1954. 74 pp.

52 Katz, Israel J. 'Marius Barbeau, 1883-1969' (with 'Bibliography of Ethnomusicological Works'). Ethnomusicology, 14(1970), 129-42.

G 53 Klinck, Carl F., ed. Literary History of Canada. Toronto: Univ. of Toronto Press, 1965; 2nd ed. 1976. Vol. I, Bibliography and Notes, pp. 493-504.

54 Klymasz, Robert B. Bibliography of Ukrainian Folklore in Canada, 1902-64. Ottawa: National Museum, Anthropology Paper 21, 1969. 53 pp.

55 Kusnerz, Peggy Ann. Art of the Inuit: A Bibliography. Ottawa: National Museum of Man, 1979. 5 pp. Mimeo.

56 Landry, Renée. 'Archival Sources: A List of Selected Manuscript Collections at the Canadian Centre for Folk Culture Studies, National Museum of Man, Ottawa.' Canadian Ethnic Studies, 7:2(1975), 73-89.

57 -- Bibliographie de Marius Barbeau, complétant celle de Clarisse Cardin. Ottawa: CCFCS, 1969. 16 pp. Mimeo.

*F 58 Leach, Maria, ed. Funk & Wagnalls Standard Dictionary of Folklore, Mythology, and Legend. 2 vols. New York: Funk & Wagnalls, 1949. 1196 pp.

F 59 List of Publications of the Bureau of American Ethnology. With Index to Authors and Titles. Washington, D.C.: Smithsonian Institution, 1971. 134 pp.

G 60 'Living History: From Sea to Sea.' Conservation Canada, 5:1(1979), 3-10. [National Historic Parks and Sites.]

G 61 McGee, Harold F. "Ethnographic Bibliography of Northeastern North America." In Three Atlantic Bibliographies. Comps. H. F. McGee, Jr., S. A. Davis, and M. Taft. Halifax: St. Mary's Univ., 1975. Pp. 1-69.

G 62 McIlwraith, T. F. Bibliography of Canadian Anthropology. Ottawa: National Museum, Bulletins 142, 147, 173, 190, 194, and 204, 1956-67.

63 [Magee, Eleanor E., and Margaret Fancy.] Catalogue of Canadian Folk Music in the Mary Mellish Archibald Library and Other Special Collections. Sackville, N.B.: Ralph Pickard Bell Library, Mt. Allison Univ., 1974. 88 pp. Mimeo.

G 64 Mandryka, M. I. Bio-bibliography of J. B. Rudnyc'kyj. Winnipeg: Ukrainian Free Academy of Arts and Sciences, 1961. 72 pp.

65 Mattfield, Julius. The Folk Music of the Western Hemisphere: A List of References in the N.Y.P.L. New York: New York Public Library, 1925. 74 pp. (Canadian folk music, pp. 7-9; Eskimo, pp. 11-13; North American Indian, pp. 13-28.)

G 66 Matthews, William. Canadian Diaries and Autobiographies. Berkeley & Los Angeles: Univ. of California Press, 1950. 130 pp.

7

G   67   Maxwell, Janet, et al. Resource List for a Multicul-
          tural Society. Toronto: Ministry of Govt. Services,
          1977. 626 pp.

F   68   Mendelson, Michael, comp. 'A Bibliography of Fiddling
          in North America.' JEMF Quarterly, 11(1975), 104-11,
          153-60, 201-4; 12(1976), 9-14, 158-65; 13(1977),
          88-95.

G   69   Mercer, Paul. Newfoundland Songs and Ballads in Print
          1842-1974: A Title and First-Line Index. St. John's:
          Memorial Univ., 1979. 343 pp.

G   70   -- 'A Supplementary Bibliography on Newfoundland
          Music.' CFMJ, 2(1974), 52-56.

F   71   Merriam, Alan P. 'Annotated Bibliography of Theses
          and Dissertations in Ethnomusicology and Folk Music
          Accepted at American and Foreign Universities.'
          Ethnomusicology, 4(1960), 21-38.

G   72   Morley, William F. E. The Atlantic Provinces. Vol. 1:
          Canadian Local Histories to 1950, A Bibliography.
          Toronto: Univ. of Toronto Press, 1967. 137 pp.

F   73   Murdock, George P. Ethnographic Bibliography of North
          America. 4th ed. 5 vols. New Haven, CT: Human Rela-
          tions Area Files, 1975.

G   74   'Museum Resources.' Communiqué: Canadian Studies, 2
          (May 1976), pp. 1-130.

F   75   Odarchenko, Petro. 'A Survey of Publications on Uk-
          rainian Ethnology and Folklore in the Years 1957-
          1962.' Annals of the Ukrainian Academy of Arts and
          Sciences in the U.S., 10:1-2(1962-1963), 92-110.

G   76   Ontario Historic Sites, Museums, Galleries and Plaques.
          Toronto: Ont. Ministry of Culture and Recreation.
          1978. 160 pp.

G   77   Paine, Robert, ed. Third Report, September 1, 1965-
          March 31, 1971. ISER. St. John's: Memorial Univ.,
          1971. 54 pp.

G   78   -- Fourth Report and Bibliography, April 1, 1971
          to March 31, 1974. ISER. St. John's: Memorial Univ.,
          1974. 56 pp.

     79   Parr, Richard T. A Bibliography of the Athapaskan
          Languages. Ottawa: National Museum, Ethnology Service
          Mercury Series 14, 1974. 330 pp.

G 80 Peel, Bruce B. A Bibliography of the Prairie Provinces to 1953. Toronto: Univ. of Toronto Press, 1956; 1973. 780 pp.

G 81 People of Native Ancestry: A Resource Guide for the Intermediate Division. Toronto: Ont. Ministry of Education, 1977. 61 pp.

G 82 Proctor, George A. Sources in Canadian Music: A Bibliography of Bibliographies. Sackville, N.B.: Mt. Allison Univ., 1975. 38 pp.

G 83 Rogers, Helen, ed. Indian-Inuit Authors: An Annotated Bibliography. Ottawa: Information Canada, 1974. 108 pp.

G 84 Rudnyc'kyj, Jaroslav B. 'Ukrainian and Other Slavic Recordings in Canada in 1949-1956.' Institut de Phonétique et Archives Phonographiques (Publications de la Commission d'Enquête Linguistique 7), 1956, pp. 155-59.

G 85 Sealock, Richard B., and Pauline A. Seely. Bibliography of Place-Name Literature, United States, Canada, Alaska, and Newfoundland. Chicago: American Library Assoc., 1967. 352 pp.

F 86 Smith, Dwight L., ed. The American and Canadian West. Santa Barbara, CA: American Bibliographical Center-Clio Press, [1979]. 558 pp.

G 87 Sterns, Maurice A., Philip Hiscock, and Bruce Daley, eds. Newfoundland and Labrador: A Social Science Bibliography. ISER. St. John's: Memorial Univ., 1975. 70 pp.

G 88 Story, Norah. The Oxford Companion to Canadian History and Literature. Toronto: Oxford, 1967. 935 pp.

  *89 Taft, Michael. 'A Bibliography for Folklore Studies in Nova Scotia.' In Three Atlantic Bibliographies. Comps. H. F. McGee, Jr., S. A. Davis, and M. Taft. Halifax: St. Mary's Univ., 1975. Pp. 105-205.

*F 90 Taylor, Archer. English Riddles from Oral Tradition. Berkeley and Los Angeles: Univ. of California Press, 1951. 959 pp.

*F 91 Thompson, Stith. Motif Index of Folk Literature. 6 vols. Bloomington: Indiana Univ. Press, 1966.

G 92 Toye, William, ed. Supplement to The Oxford Companion to Canadian History and Literature. Toronto: Oxford, 1973. 318 pp.

F 93 Ullom, Judith. Folklore of the North American Indians: An Annotated Bibliography. Washington: Library of Congress, 1969. 126 pp.

F 94 Wallace, A. F. C. 'The Frank G. Speck Collection.' Proc. of the American Philosophical Society, 45(June 1951), 286-89.

95 Wardwell, Allen, and Lois Lebov. Annotated Bibliography of Northwest Coast Indian Art. New York: Museum of Primitive Art, Library, 1970. 25 pp.

*G 96 Watters, Reginald E. A Check List of Canadian Literature and Background Materials, 1628-1960. Toronto: Univ. of Toronto Press, rev. 1972. 1085 pp.

97 Zimmerly, David W. Museocinematography: Ethnographic Film Programs of the National Museum of Man, 1913-1973. Ottawa: National Museum, Ethnology Service Mercury Series 11, 1974. 103 pp.

See also items 1046, 1057, 1165, 1166, 1341, 1679, 1680, 2633, 3786, 3873, and 3876.

2 Periodicals

F   98   <u>Abstracts of Folklore Studies</u>. American Folklore Society, 1963-1975.

    99   <u>Alberta Folklore Quarterly</u>. Edmonton: Univ. of Alberta, 1945-1946.

G 100   <u>Alberta Historical Review</u>. Historical Society of Alberta, 1953-1974.

G 101   <u>Alberta History</u>. Quarterly. Historical Society of Alberta, 1975--.

F 102   <u>American Indian Art Magazine</u>. Quarterly. Scottsdale, AR, 1975--.

G 103   <u>The Beaver: Magazine of the North</u>. Quarterly. Winnipeg: Hudson's Bay Company, 1921--.

G 104   <u>Bulletin of the Association for Preservation Technology</u>. Quarterly. 1969--.

  105   <u>Bulletin of the Folklore Studies Association of Canada</u>. Quarterly. 1976--.

F 106   <u>Bulletin of the Folksong Society of the Northeast</u>. Cambridge, MA, 1930-1937; rpt. Philadelphia: American Folklore Society, 1960. (BFSSNE)

P 107   <u>Canada Folk Bulletin</u>. Bimonthly. Vancouver: Vancouver Folk Song Society, 1978-1980.

P 108   <u>Canada West Magazine</u>. Quarterly. Langley, B.C.: Stagecoach, 1969--.

G 109   <u>Canadian Antiques Collector</u>. Bimonthly. Toronto: Canadian Antiques and Fine Arts Society, 1966--. (<u>CanAntC</u>)

P 110   <u>The Canadian Collector</u>. Bimonthly. Toronto: Denmount Pub. Co., 1966--.

G 111   <u>Canadian Ethnic Studies</u>. Biannual. Calgary: Canadian Ethnic Studies Assoc., 1969--.

11

112 Canadian Folk Music Society Newsletter. Quarterly. 1969--. (CFMSN)

*113 Canadian Folk Music Journal. Annual. Canadian Folk Music Society, 1973--. (CFMJ)

*114 Canadian Folklore Canadien. Biannual. Folklore Studies Assoc. of Canada, 1979--.

G 115 Canadian Frontier. Quarterly. New Westminster, B.C., 1972--.

G 116 Canadian Geographical Journal. Monthly. Ottawa: Royal Canadian Geographical Society. 1930--. (Published as Canadian Geographic since 1978.) (CGJ)

G 117 Canadian-German Folklore. Occasional. Pennsylvania German Folklore Society of Ontario, 1961--.

G 118 Canadian Indian Artcrafts. Quarterly. Ottawa: National Indian Arts and Crafts Corporation, 1976--.

P 119 The Canadian Log House. Annual. Prince George, B.C., 1974--.

G 120 Canadian Oral History Association Journal. Annual. 1975--.

G 121 Canadiana. Monthly. Ottawa: National Library, 1950--.

GP 122 Cape Breton's Magazine. Monthly. Skir Dhu, Cape Breton, 1972--.

P 123 Come All Ye. Vancouver: Vancouver Folk Song Society, 1972-1977.

*124 Culture & Tradition. Annual. St. John's: Memorial Univ., and Quebec: Laval Univ., 1976--.

GP 125 Decks Awash. Bimonthly. St. John's: Extension Service, Memorial Univ., 1963--.

GP 126 Early Canadian Life. Monthly. Oakville, Ont.: Golden-glow, 1977--.

F 127 Ethnomusicology. Three times a year. Society for Ethno-musicology, 1953--.

F 128 Folk-Lore. Biannual. London: Folk-Lore Society, 1890--. (Published as Folklore since 1958, by the Folklore Society since 1969.)

F 129 The Folklore and Folk Music Archivist. Bloomington: Indiana Univ., 1958-1968.

F 130 Folklore Forum. Quarterly. Bloomington: Indiana Univ., 1968--.

12

G   131   <u>Hand Made</u>. Quarterly. Packenham, Ont.: Standing Oak, 1977--.

GP 132   <u>Harrowsmith</u>. 8 times a year. Camden East, Ont.: Camden House Publishing, 1977--.

G   133   <u>Heritage Canada</u>. Bimonthly. Ottawa: Heritage Canada, 1974--.

G   134   <u>Inuit Today</u> (formerly <u>Inuit Monthly</u>). Monthly. Ottawa: Tapirisat of Canada, 1975--.

G   135   <u>Inuktitut</u> (formerly <u>Inuttituut</u>). Quarterly. Ottawa: Dept. of Indian Affairs and Northern Development, 1977--.

GP 136   <u>The Island Magazine</u>. Biannual. Charlottetown: P.E.I. Heritage Foundation, 1976--.

*F 137   <u>Journal of American Folklore</u>. Quarterly. American Folklore Society, 1888--. (<u>JAF</u>)

F   138   <u>Journal of the Folklore Institute</u>. 3 times a year. Bloomington: Indiana Univ., 1963--.

F   139   <u>Journal of the International Folk Music Council</u>. Annual. 1949--. (JIFMC)

G   140   <u>Journal of the New Brunswick Museum</u>. Annual. 1977--.

G   141   <u>Lighthouse</u>. Quarterly. Halifax: Atlantic Institute of Education, 1973--.

F   142   <u>Lore and Language</u>. Biannual. Sheffield, U.K.: Centre for English Cultural Tradition and Language, 1969--.

P   143   <u>Newfoundland Stories and Ballads</u>. Quarterly. St. John's, 1954--.

GP 144   <u>The Newfoundlander</u>. Published as <u>The Barrelman</u>, June 1940-May 1942; <u>Newfoundlander</u>, July 1952-Dec. 1954.

F   145   <u>Northeast Folklore</u>. Annual. Orono: Univ. of Maine, 1958--.

GP 146   <u>Northern Mosaic</u>. Bimonthly. Thunder Bay, 1975--.

P   147   <u>Ontario Folkdancer</u>. 10 times a year. Toronto: Ontario Folk Dance Assoc., 1979--.

G   148   <u>Ontario History</u>. Quarterly. Published as <u>Papers and Records of the Ontario Historical Society</u>, 1899-1951; <u>Ontario History</u>, Toronto, 1952--.

G   149   <u>Quebec</u>. London, 1926-1936.

13

150 RLS. Regional Language Studies...Newfoundland. Occasional. St. John's: Memorial Univ., 1968--.

G 151 Saskatchewan History. 3 times a year. Saskatoon: Saskatchewan Archives Board, 1948--.

G 152 Sound Heritage. Quarterly. Victoria: Aural History, Provincial Archives of B.C., 1972--.

G 153 Tawow: Canadian Indian Cultural Magazine. Ottawa: Indian and Northern Affairs, 1970--.

GP 154 Them Days. Stories of Early Labrador. Quarterly. Happy Valley: Labrador Heritage and Old Timer's [sic] League, 1975--.

G 155 Transactions and Proceedings of the Royal Society of Canada. Annual. Ottawa, 1882--. (TRSC)

P 156 The/Le Troubadour. Quarterly. Montréal/Toronto: Canadian Folk Arts Council, 1976--.

See also item 40.

14

3 General

3A Historical, Descriptive, Overviews

C 157 'Alberta Folklore Project.' School and Society, 57
       (1943), 699-700.

C 158 Alcock, F. J. 'Folklore Studies at the National Museum
       of Canada.' JAF, 67(1954), 99-101.

C 159 Barbeau, C. Marius. 'Canadian-English Folk-Lore.' JAF,
       31(1918), 1-3.

B 160 -- Canadian Folklore. New York: French Folklore
       Society, 1946; rpt. from French Folklore Bulletin
       (New York), Nov. 1945; Feb.-Mar. 1946; June 1946.
       16 pp.

C 161 -- 'The Field of European Folk-Lore in America.' JAF,
       32(1919), 185-89.

C 162 -- 'Folk-Lore: Acquisitions; Totals (1914-1926).'
       Report of the Dept. of Mines for the Fiscal Year
       Ending March 31, 1926. Ottawa: King's Printer, 1926.
       Pp. 40-41.

C 163 -- 'Folk-Lore (1914-1920); Folk-Lore Collections' [in
       the National Museum]; Publications. Report of the
       Dept. of Mines for the Fiscal Year Ending March 31,
       1921. Ottawa: King's Printer, 1921 Pp. 292-94.

C 164 -- 'Folk-Lore (1921-22); Folk-Lore Collections.'
       Report of the Dept. of Mines for the Fiscal Year
       Ending March 31, 1922. Ottawa: King's Printer, 1922.
       Pp. 25-26.

C 165 -- 'Folk-Lore: Folk-Lore Collections.' Report of the
       Dept. of Mines for the Fiscal Year Ending March 31,
       1924. Ottawa: King's Printer, 1925. P. 40.

C 166 -- 'The Folk-Lore Movement in Canada.' JAF, 56(1943),
       166-68.

C 167 Canadian Folk-Lore Society. First Annual Report. Toronto, 1911.

Gb 168 Carpenter, Carole Henderson. 'Canadian Children's Literature: A Cultural Mirror.' Children's Literature Assoc. Newsletter, 2:3(1977), 3-6.

A 169 -- Many Voices: A Study of Folklore Activities in Canada and Their Role in Canadian Culture. Ottawa: National Museum, CCFCS Mercury Series 26, 484 pp.

C 170 -- 'The Folklore Studies Association of Canada: Its Formation and Activities.' Troubadour, 2(Jan.-Apr. 1978), 12-13.

F 171 Carrière, Joseph M. 'The Present State of French Folklore Studies in North America.' Southern Folklore Quarterly, 10(1946), 219-26.

Gb 172 Cosbey, Robert C. 'Proposal for a Saskatchewan Oral History Project.' Folklore Forum, Bibliographic and Special Series 12, pp. 36-55.

C 173 Creighton, Helen. 'Capturing Folklore on Tape.' Canadian Author & Bookman, 46(Spring 1971), 3, 12.

C 174 -- 'Teachers as Folklorists.' Journal of Education [N.S.], 14:7(1943), 1022-25.

G 175 Driedger, Leo, ed. The Canadian Ethnic Mosaic: A Quest for Identity. Toronto: McClelland & Stewart, 1978. 352 pp.

P 176 Egoff, Sheila. Canadian Folklore. Ottawa: Canadian Library Assoc., 1967. 11 pp. Mimeo.

P 177 -- 'Reflections and Distortions: Canadian Folklore as Portrayed in Children's Literature.' International Library Review, 4(1972), 265-79.

C 178 Fowke, Edith. 'Anglo-Canadian Folk Songs for Education.' B.C. Music Educator, 22(Spring 1979), 21-25.

A 179 -- 'Folktales and Folk Songs.' In the Literary History of Canada. Vol. I. Ed. Carl Klinck. Toronto: Univ. of Toronto Press, rev. ed., 1975. Pp. 177-87.

GY 180 Frederickson, M. 'Folk History of Nova Scotia.' Lighthouse, 2 (Winter 1975), 20-21.

C 181 Gard, Robert E. 'The Alberta Folklore and Local History Project.' JAF, 59(1946), 480-81.

Gc 182 Godard, Barbara. 'The Oral Tradition and Contemporary Fiction.' Essays on Canadian Writing, 7/8(Fall 1977), 46-62.

A 183 Goldstein, Kenneth S., ed. Canadian Folklore Perspectives. St. John's: Memorial Univ., 1978. 68 pp.

A 184 Halpert, Herbert. 'Folklore and Newfoundland: An Informal Introduction to the Materials and Methods of Folklore.' Papers of the Bibliographical Society of Canada, 8(1969), 10-22.

A 185 -- 'One Approach to Canadian Regional Folklore.' Bulletin of the Folklore Studies Assoc. of Canada, 1(Dec. 1977), 2-9.

B 186 Halpert, Herbert, and Neil V. Rosenberg. 'Folklore Work at Memorial University.' Canadian Forum, 53 (1974), 31-32.

A 187 --, and -- Folklore Studies at Memorial University: Two Reports. St. John's: Memorial Univ., 1978. 16 pp. [Rpt. of items 186 and 188].

B 188 --, and -- 'MUNFLA: The Development of a Folklore and Language Archive at Memorial University.' Laurentian University Review, 8(Feb. 1976), 107-14.

C 189 Heidt, Elizabeth. 'Folklore in Saskatchewan.' Saskatchewan History, 7(1954), 18-21.

B 190 Henderson, M. Carole [Carole Henderson Carpenter]. 'The Ethnicity Factor in Anglo-Canadian Folkloristics.' Canadian Ethnic Studies, 7:2(1975), 7-18.

A 191 -- 'Folklore Scholarship and the Sociopolitical Milieu in Canada.' Journal of the Folklore Institute, 10(1973), 97-107.

C 192 Henderson, M. Carole [Carole Henderson Carpenter], and Neil V. Rosenberg. 'The MacEdward Leach Collection of Canadian Folklore.' CFMSN, 5(1970), 1-10.

C 193 Henry, James. 'Cultural Legacy in Canadian Folklore.' Canadian Children's Literature, 10(1977-78), 78-83.

B 194 'The Institute of Folklore of the University of Sudbury.' CFMSN, 4(1969), 20-38.

B 195 Klymasz, Robert B. 'The Case for Slavic Folklore in Canada.' Slavs in Canada, 1(1966), 110-20.

C 196 -- 'Field Work in the Canadian Prairie Provinces.' Ethnomusicology, 10(1966), 324-25.

C 197 -- 'Folklore Studies at the National Museum of Man, Ottawa, Canada.' Folklore Forum, 5(1972), 11-13.

B 198 -- 'From Immigrant to Ethnic Folklore: A Canadian View of Process and Transition.' Journal of the Folklore Institute, 10(1973), 131-39.

C 199 Klymasz, Robert B. 'An Introduction to the Folklore Division of the National Museum.' Folklore and Folk Music Archivist, 10(1967), 2-9.

G 200 Kossar, Leon. "Canada's Newest and Oldest Cultural Movement." Slavs in Canada, 2(1968), 222-28.

A 201 Lacourcière, Luc. Oral Tradition: New England and French Canada. Québec: Archives de Folklore, Université Laval, 1972. 20 pp. Mimeo.

A 202 -- 'The Present State of French-Canadian Folklore Studies.' JAF, 74(1961), 373-81. Rpt. in Folklore Research Around the World. Ed. Richard Dorson. Bloomington: Indiana Univ. Press, 1961. Pp. 86-95.

PY 203 Latham, Sheila. 'Canadian Relevance: Indian and Eskimo Books for Young People.' In Review, 9(Summer 1975), 5-8.

G 204 Leechman, Douglas. 'The National Museum of Canada.' CGJ, 32(Jan. 1946), 2-13.

B 205 MacLennan, Gordon, ed. Canadian Centre for Folk Culture Studies: Annual Review, 1974. Ottawa: National Museum, CCFCS Mercury Series 12, 1975. 58 pp.

C 206 Mealing, Mark. "Doukhobor Society and Folklore: Introduction." Journal of the Folklore Society of Greater Washington, 4 (Spring 1973), pp. 6-12.

B 207 Mercer, Paul, and Mac Swackhammer. '"The Singing of Old Newfoundland Ballads and a Cool Glass of Beer Go Hand in Hand": Folklore and "Tradition" in Newfoundland Advertising.' Culture & Tradition, 3(1978), 36-45.

P 208 Newell, William W. 'On the Collection of Folklore.' St. John's Evening Herald, 2 Dec. 1892.

G 209 Porter, R. 'Teaching Folklore.' Lighthouse, 3:2(Sept. 1976), 10-12.

C 210 Posen, Shelley. 'Explorations in Canadian Folklore.' Quill & Quire, July 1976, pp. 12-13, 40.

GC 211 Potvin, Gilles. 'The Canadian Broadcasting Corporation and Canadian Folk Cultures: The Preservation of Ethnic Identity.' Ethnomusicology, 16(1972), 512-15.

C 212 Rioux, Marcel. 'Anthropology and Folklore.' Ottawa: National Museum, Bulletin 132, 1954, pp. 72-76.

B 213 -- 'Folk and Folklore.' JAF, 63(1950), 192-98.

C 214 Rioux, Marcel. 'The Meaning and Function of Folklore in Ile Verte.' Ottawa: National Museum, Bulletin 118, 1950, pp. 60-62.

B 215 Rosenberg, Neil V. 'Folklore in Atlantic Canada: The Enigmatic Symbol.' In Atlantic Provinces Literature Colloquium Papers. Ed. Kenneth MacKinnon. Saint John, N.B.: Atlantic Canada Institute, 1977. Pp. 79-86.

Gb 216 Rosenberg, Neil V., ed. Folklore and Oral History. St. John's: Memorial University, 1978, 101 pp.

B 217 Roy, Carmen, ed. Canadian Centre for Folk Culture Studies Annual Review 1972. Ottawa: National Museum, CCFCS Mercury Series 6, 1973. 21 pp.

B 218 -- Canadian Centre for Folk Culture Studies Annual Review 1973. Ottawa: National Museum, CCFCS Mercury Series 9, 1974. 44 pp.

B 219 -- An Introduction to the Canadian Centre for Folk Culture Studies. Ottawa: National Museum, CCFCS Mercury Series 7, 1973. 88 pp.

B 220 Tallman, Richard S. 'Folklore in the Schools: Teaching, Collecting and Publishing.' New York Folklore Quarterly, 28(1972), 163-86.

Gc 221 Thomas, Gerald. 'The French Presence in Newfoundland Today--Port-au-Port Peninsula and St. George's Bay.' Terre-Neuve, 1(Feb. 1977), 6-10.

C 222 -- 'Recording French Newfoundland's Heritage.' M.U.N. Gazette, 19 Dec. 1975, p. 5.

C 223 Thomas, Gillian. 'Women and Folklore.' Atlantis, Spring 1977, pp. 140-43.

F 224 Walton, Ivan H. 'Marine Lore.' In Michigan, A Guide to the Wolverine State. New York: Oxford, 1941. Pp. 113-34.

B 225 Widdowson, J. D. A. 'Oral History in Canada: The Newfoundland Contribution.' Sound Heritage, 4:1(1975), 51-55.

B 226 -- 'A Survey of Current Folklore Research in Newfoundland with Special Reference to the English West Country." Trans. of the Devonshire Assoc. for the Advancement of Science, Literature, and Art, 101(1960), 183-96.

3B   Works Containing More Than One Genre

GP 227 Armstrong, Audrey. Harness in the Parlour, A Book of
Early Canadian Fact and Folklore. Toronto: Musson,
1974. 90 pp.

PY 228 Ashwell, Reg. Coast Salish: Their Art, Culture, and
Legends. Saanichton, B.C.: Hancock, 1978. 86 pp.

A   229 Barbeau, C. Marius. Indian Days on the Western
Prairies. Ottawa: National Museum, Bulletin 163, 1960;
pb. 1974. 234 pp.

B   230 -- The Kingdom of the Saguenay. Toronto: Macmillan,
1935. 167 pp.

A   231 -- Quebec, Where Ancient France Lingers. Toronto:
Macmillan, 1936. 173 pp.

B   232 Barbeau, Marius, and Grace Melvin. The Indian Speaks.
Toronto: Macmillan, 1943. 117 pp.

FB 233 Beauchamp, William. Iroquois Folklore. Port Washington, WI: Friedman, 1965. 247 pp.

B   234 Beaugrand, Honoré. New Studies in Canadian Folklore.
Montreal: Renouf, 1904. 130 pp.

C   235 Beck, Horace P. 'Algonquin Folklore from Maniwaki.'
JAF, 60(1947), 259-64.

F   236 -- Folklore and the Sea. Middletown, CN: Wesleyan
Univ. Press, 1973. 463 pp.

B   237 Bleakney, F. Eileen. 'Folk-Lore from Ottawa and Vicinity.' JAF, 31(1918), 158-69.

A   238 Boas, Franz. The Central Eskimo. 1888; rpt. Lincoln:
Univ. of Nebraska Press, 1964. 261 pp.

B   239 -- 'The Folklore of the Eskimo.' JAF, 17(1904), 1-13.

A   240 -- Kwakiutl Ethnography. Ed. Helen Codere. Chicago:
Univ. of Chicago Press, 1966, 1975. 439 pp.

B   241 Brednich, Rolf W. Mennonite Folklife and Folklore: A
Preliminary Report. Ottawa: National Museum, CCFCS
Mercury Series 22, 1977. 111 pp.

GP 242 Brown, Andrew H. 'Salty Nova Scotia: In a friendly
New Scotland Gaelic songs still answer the skirling
bagpipes.' National Geographic, 77(1940), 575-624.

B   243 Brunvand, Jan. Norwegian Settlers in Alberta. Ottawa:
National Museum, CCFCS Mercury Series 8, 1973. 71 pp.

General

B 244 Buehler, Allan M. The Pennsylvania German Dialect and
the Life of an Old Order Mennonite. Cambridge, Ont.:
Author, 1977. 227 pp.

C 245 Burchill, George S. 'Miramichi Folklore.' Dalhousie
Review, 30(1950), 237-44.

Gb 246 Caplan, Ronald, ed. Down North: The Book of Cape
Breton's Magazine. Toronto: Doubleday, 1979. 141 pp.

G 247 Carlisle, David B., ed. Contributions to Canadian
Ethnology, 1975. Ottawa: National Museum, Ethnology
Service Mercury Series 31, 1976. 359 pp.

C 248 Chamberlain, Alexander F. 'Some Items of Algonkian
Folk-Lore.' JAF, 13(1900), 271-77.

GPY 249 Coull, Adrienne, comp. Souvenirs. Edmonton: Alberta
Education, 1979. 96 pp.

Pa 250 Crawford, Venetia, co-ordinator. Treasures of the
Pontiac in Song and Story. Shawville, P.Q.: Dickson
Enterprises, 1979. 153 pp.

B 251 Creighton, Helen. 'Fiddles, Folksongs, and Fishermen's
Yarns.' CGJ, 51(Dec. 1955), 212-21.

A 252 -- Folklore of Lunenburg County, Nova Scotia. Ottawa:
National Museum, Bulletin 117, 1950; rpt. McGraw-Hill
Ryerson, 1976. 163 pp.

B 253 -- 'Folklore of Victoria Beach, Nova Scotia.' JAF, 63
(1950), 131-46.

B 254 Devine, P. K. 'Newfoundland Folklore.' In Book of Newfoundland. Vol. I. Ed. Joseph R. Smallwood. St. John's:
Nfld. Book Publishers, 1937. Pp. 230-33.

A 255 Dunn, Charles W. Highland Settler: A Portrait of the
Scottish Gael in Nova Scotia. Toronto: Univ. of Toronto Press, 1953; Pb., 1968. 179 pp.

GP 256 Edwards, Bob [Robert Chambers], ed. The Calgary Eye-
Opener. Calgary, 1901-1922.

C 257 Einarsson, Magnús. 'The Folklore of New Iceland.'
Timarit Thjódraeknifélags Islendinga, 50(1969), 67-73.

C 258 English, Leo E. F. 'Newfoundland Folk Lore.' Service-
grams, April 1954, pp. 12-13.

C 259 -- 'Folk Lore of Newfoundland.' Maritime Advocate and
Busy East, May, 1950.

Gb 260 -- Historic Newfoundland. St. John's: Nfld. Tourist
Development Division, 1955; rev. 1968. 63 pp.

B   261   Farrer, Edward. 'The Folklore of Lower Canada.'
          Atlantic Monthly, 49(1882), 542-49.

A   262   Fauset, Arthur Huff. Folklore from Nova Scotia. Phila-
          delphia: American Folklore Society, Memoir 24, 1931.
          204 pp.

A   263   -- 'Folklore from the Half-Breeds in Nova Scotia.'
          JAF, 38(1925), 300-15.

B   264   Field, Edward, trans. Eskimo Songs and Stories. Collec-
          ted by Knud Rasmussen on the Fifth Thule Expedition.
          New York: Delacorte Press/Seymour Lawrence, 1973.
          102 pp.

F   265   Fletcher, Alice C. Indian Story and Song from North
          America. Boston: Small, Maynard, 1900. 126 pp.

Pc 266   Folklore of Prince Edward Island. Charlottetown: His-
          torical Society of P.E.I., c. 1955.

A   267   Fowke, Edith. Folklore of Canada. Toronto: McClelland
          & Stewart, 1976. 349 pp.

A   268   Fraser, Mary L. [Mother St. Thomas of the Angels].
          Folklore of Nova Scotia. [Toronto: Catholic Truth
          Society], 1931; rpt. Antigonish, N.S.: Formac, 1975.
          115 pp.

Gb 269   Freedman, Jim, and Jerome H. Barkow, eds. 'Myth and
          Culture.' Vol. I, Session I, Proc. of the Second Con-
          gress, Canadian Ethnology Society. Ottawa: National
          Museum, Ethnology Service Mercury Series 28, 1975.
          Pp. 1-151.

B   270   'French-Canadian Folklore.' Manuscripts of the Federal
          Writers' Project of the Works Progress Administration
          for the State of Rhode Island. Moonsocket, RI.

A   271   Garfield, Viola E., Paul S. Wingert, and C. Marius
          Barbeau. The Tsimshian: Their Arts and Music. New
          York: Augustin, 1951. 290 pp. Rpt. as The Tsimshian
          Indians and Their Arts. Pb. Seattle: Univ. of Wash-
          ington Press, 1966. 98 pp.

B   272   Gold, Gerald L., and Marc A. Tremblay. Communities and
          Culture in French Canada. Toronto: Holt, Rinehart &
          Winston, 1973. 364 pp.

P   273   Graham, Clara. This Was the Kootenay. Vancouver: Ever-
          green, 1963. 269 pp.

A   274   Greenough, William P. Canadian Folk-Life and Folk-
          Lore. New York: Richmond, 1897; rpt. Toronto: Coles,
          [1971]. 186 pp.

22

C 275 Hale, Horatio. 'Huron Folklore.' JAF, 1(1888), 177-83.

FA 276 Halpert, Herbert, and Violetta M. Halpert. 'Neither
        Heaven nor Hell.' In Mélanges en l'honneur de Luc
        Lacourcière: Folklore française d'Amerique. Eds. Jean-
        Claude Dupont et al. Montréal: Leméac, 1978. Pp. 207-
        21. Rpt. St. John's: Memorial Univ., 1979. 15 pp.

P 277 Harrington, Michael F. 'The Rich Folklore of New-
        foundland.' Saturday Night, 20 Feb. 1954, pp. 7-8.

G 278 Harrison, Charles. Ancient Warriors of the North
        Pacific. London: Witherby, 1925. 222 pp. [Haida
        customs and legends.]

GP 279 Heritage Canada. Heritage of Canada. Montreal: Reader's
        Digest, 1978. 376 pp.

B 280 Hill-Tout, Charles. 'Some Features of the Language
        and Culture of the Salish.' Atlantic Advocate, 7(1905),
        674-87.

Pby 281 Hofmann, Charles. Drum Dance. Legends, Ceremonies,
        Dances and Songs of the Eskimos. Toronto: Gage, 1974.
        95 pp.

B 282 Houser, George. J. The Swedish Community at Eriksdale,
        Manitoba. Ottawa: National Museum, CCFCS Mercury
        Series 14, 1976. 109 pp.

PY 283 Kaiper, Dan, and Nan Kaiper. Tlingit: Their Art, Cul-
        ture and Legends. Saanichton: Hancock, 1978. 95 pp.

B 284 Keithahn, Edward L. Monuments in Cedar. The Authentic
        Story of the Totem Pole. Ketchikan, AL: Roy Anderson,
        1945; rpt. Seattle: Superior, 1963. 160 pp.

C 285 Klymasz, Robert B. 'Slavic Folklore at the National
        Museum of Man, Ottawa.' Slavs in Canada, 3(1971),
        327-31.

G 286 Kohl, Johann Georg. Kitchi-Gami: Wandering Round Lake
        Superior. 1860; rpt. New York: Ross & Haines, 1956.
        428 pp.

Gc 287 Lacey, Laurie, ed. Lunenburg County Folklore and Oral
        History: Project '77. Ottawa: National Museum, CCFCS
        Mercury Series 30, 1979. 142 pp.

P 288 Lee, Hector H., ed. Folklore Archive for Nova Scotia
        Teachers. Vol. 1. Halifax: N.S. Dept. of Education,
        1971. 335 pp.

Ga 289 Lysenko, Vera. Men in Sheepskin Coats. Toronto: Ryer-
        son, 1947. 312 pp. [Ukrainians.]

P   290   Macdonald, S. P. 'Gael in New Scotland.' Canadian
          Magazine, 47(May 1916), 37-46.

B   291   MacLeod, Calum I.N. 'The Gaelic Tradition in Nova
          Scotia.' Lochlann, A Review of Celtic Studies. Ed.
          Alf Sommerfelt. Vol. I, Oslo, 1958, pp. 235-40.

Pa 292   MacNeil, Neil. The Highland Heart in Nova Scotia.
          Toronto: Saunders, 1948. 199 pp.

C   293   Masta, Henry L. Abenaki Indian Legends, Grammar and
          Place Names. Victoriaville, P.Q.: La voix des bois-
          francs, c. 1932. 110 pp.

A   294   Maud, Ralph, ed. The Salish People: The Local Contri-
          bution of Charles Hill-Tout. 4 vols. Vancouver:
          Talonbooks, 1978.

C   295   Milnes, Humphrey. 'German Folklore in Ontario.' JAF,
          47(1954), 35-43.

P   296   Moore, Gerald. The Grab-Bag of Newfoundland Folklore.
          St. John's: Town Crier, 1976.

PY 297   Oracle. Series of leaflets. Ottawa: National Museum
          of Man, 1975--.

P   298   Pendergast, James, and Gertrude Pendergast. Folklore
          Prince Edward Island. N.p., [Authors, 1973]. 47 pp.

Pc 299   Ramsay, Sterling. Folklore Prince Edward Island. Char-
          lottetown: Square Deal, 1976. 124 pp.

P   300   Ranch, Glenn N. Legends and Traditions of Northwest
          History. Souvenir ed. Vancouver: American Printing
          & Stationery, 1914.

Gb 301   Rand, Silas T. A Short Statement of Facts Related to
          the History, Manners, Customs, Language and Literature
          of the Micmac Tribe of Indians in Nova Scotia and P.E.
          Island. Halifax: Bowes, 1850. 40 pp.

Ga 302   Rasmussen, Knud. Across Arctic America; Narrative of
          the Fifth Thule Expedition. New York: Putnam, 1927.
          388 pp.

GbY 303   -- Fifth Thule Expedition. 3 vols. Yellowknife: Dept.
          of Education, N.W.T., 1967. 27 pp.; 32 pp.; 19 pp.

A   304   -- Report of the Fifth Thule Expedition, 1921-1924.
          Vol. 7: Intellectual Culture of the Iglulik Eskimos;
          vol. 8: The Netsilik Eskimos; vol. 9: Intellectual
          Culture of the Copper Eskimos. Copenhagen: Gylden-
          dalski Boghandel, 1929-1932.

General

P 305 Ravenhill, Alice. Folklore of the Far West with Some
       Clues to Characteristics and Customs. Victoria: Indian
       Arts and Welfare Society, 1953. 87 pp.

Gb 306 Reid, Stanford, ed., The Scottish Tradition in Canada.
        Toronto: McClelland & Stewart, 1976. 324 pp.

GP 307 Richardson, Evelyn M., comp. The Wreckwood Chair. Hali-
        fax: Royal Print, 1957. 51 pp.

Gc 308 Robertson, Marion. History and Folklore of Shelburne
        County. Halifax: N.S. Archives, c. 1962. Mimeo.

G 309   Robins, John D., ed. A Pocketful of Canada. Toronto:
        Collins, 1946. 430 pp.

Gb 310 Rose, Clyde, ed. The Blasty Bough. St. John's: Break-
        water, 1976. 219 pp.

C 311   Rose, E. H., and Herbert J. Rose. 'Folklore Notes
        from the Province of Quebec.' Folk-lore, 23(1912),
        345-47, 462-63; 24(1913), 360-62; 25(1914), 251-52.

C 312   Rose, Herbert J. 'Canadian Folklore.' Folk-Lore, 32
        (1921), 124-31.

A 313   Rudnyc'kyj, Jaroslav B. Readings in Canadian Slavic
        Folklore. 2 vols. Winnipeg: Univ. of Manitoba Press,
        1958-1961.

B 314   -- Ukrainian-Canadian Folklore Texts in English
        Translation. Winnipeg: Ukrainian Free Academy of
        Sciences, 1960. 232 pp.

B 315   Salo, Matt T., and Sheila M. G. Salo. The Kalderas in
        Eastern Canada. Ottawa: National Museum, CCFCS Mercury
        Series 21, 1977. 268 pp.

B 316   Sapir, Edward, and Morris Swadesh. Native Account of
        Nootkan Ethnography. Bloomington: Indiana Univ., 1955.
        457 pp.

P 317   Shaw, Beatrice M. H. 'The Vanishing Folklore of Nova
        Scotia.' Dalhousie Review, 3(1923), 342-49.

B 318   Skinner, Alanson. Notes on the Eastern Cree and North-
        ern Saulteaux. New York: American Museum of Natural
        History, 1911. 177 pp.

GP 319 Smallwood, Joseph R., ed. The Book of Newfoundland.
        6 vols. St. John's: Nfld. Book Pub., 1937-1975.

Gb 320 Smith, Marian W., ed. Indians of the Urban Northwest.
        New York: Columbia Univ. Press, 1949. 370 pp.

B   321   Stone, Kay. _Prairie Folklore_. Winnipeg: Univ. of Win-
            nipeg, 1976. 284 pp. Mimeo.

BY   322   Tallman, Richard S., ed. _Belief and Legend from_
            Northern King's County. [Canning, N.S.: Author], 1969.
            Mimeo.

Fa   323   Tax, Sol, ed. _Indian Tribes of Aboriginal America_. New
            York: Cooper Square, 1967. 410 pp.

C   324   Thomas, Amby. _Songs & Stories from Deep Cove, Cape_
            Breton. Ed. Ron MacEachern. Sydney: College of Cape
            Breton Press, 1979. 49 pp.

B   325   Thomas, Gerald. 'The Wild and the Tame: Animals in
            the Folklore of French Newfoundlanders.' _Culture &_
            Tradition, 2(1977), 65-74.

G   326   Thwaites, Reuben, ed. _The Jesuit Relations and Allied_
            Documents, 1610-1673. 74 vols. 1896-1901; rpt. New
            York: Pageant, 1956.

P   327   Waghorne, A. C. 'The Folklore of Newfoundland and Lab-
            rador.' _St. John's Evening Herald_, 28 Dec. 1892, p. 4;
            29 Dec. 1892, p. 4.

A   328   Waugh, F. W. 'Canadian Folk-Lore from Ontario.' _JAF_,
            31(1918), 4-82.

P   329   Wickersham, James. _Old Yukon Tales, Trails and Trials_.
            Washington, D.C.: Washington Law Book Co., 1938.
            514 pp.

GP   330   Wightman, F. A. 'Maritime Provincialisms and Con-
            trasts.' _Canadian Magazine_, 39(1912), 3-7, 168-72,
            226-30.

B   331   Wintemberg, W. J. 'Folk-Lore Collected at Roebuck,
            Grenville County, Ontario.' _JAF_, 31(1918), 154-57.

A   332   --   'Folk-Lore Collected in the Counties of Oxford and
            Waterloo, Ontario.' _JAF_, 31(1918), 135-53.

B   333   --   'Folk-Lore Collected in Toronto and Vicinity.' _JAF_,
            31(1918), 125-34.

A   334   --   _Folk-Lore of Waterloo County, Ontario_. Ottawa: Na-
            tional Museum, Bulletin 116, 1950. 68 pp.

B   335   --   'German-Canadian Folk-Lore.' _Ontario History_, 3
            (1902), 86-96.

C   336   --   'Items of French Canadian Folk-Lore.' _JAF_, 21(1908),
            362-63.

26

General

A   337   Wintemberg, W. J., and Katherine H. Wintemberg.
          'Folk-Lore from Grey County, Ontario.' <u>JAF</u>, 31(1918),
          83-124.

GP 338   Women's Institutes of Nova Scotia, comps. <u>Crocks,
          Pots and What-Nots</u>. N.p., n.d., 1973. 92 pp.

G   339   Wood, William C. H. <u>In the Heart of Old Canada</u>. Toron-
          to: Briggs, 1913. 310 pp.

For 3A see also items 636, 3282, 3773, 3782, 3800,
3803, 3816, 3817, 3821, 3847, 3862.

4 Folktales

4A General

FB 340 Ainsworth, Catherine H., comp. <u>Legends of New York State</u>. Buffalo, NY: Compiler, 1978. 94 pp.

GY 341 Anderson, Lorrie, Irene Aubrey, and Louise McDiarmid. <u>Storytellers' Rendezvous: Canadian Stories to Tell Children</u>. Ottawa: Canadian Library Assoc., 1979. 110 pp.

PY 342 Bezanson, W. B. <u>Stories of Acadia</u>. Dartmouth, N.S.: Author, 1924. 46 pp.

PY 343 -- <u>Stories of Acadia</u>. Kentville, N.S.: Kentville Pub., 1931. 67 pp.

PY 344 -- <u>Stories of Acadia</u>. Kentville: Kentville Pub., 1933. 62 pp.

PY 345 -- <u>Stories of Acadia</u>. Halifax: Nova Print, 1933. 57 pp.

P 346 Bird, William R. 'The House of Mystery.' <u>Canadian Magazine</u>, 83:4(1935), 7, 18, 20.

B 347 Burmeister, Klaus. 'Folklore in the Intercultural Context: Legends of the Calling River.' In <u>Ethnic Canadians: Culture and Education</u>. Ed. Martin L. Kovacs. Regina: Canadian Plains Research Center, Univ. of Regina, 1978. Pp.43-52.

GP 348 Chase, Eliza B. <u>In Quest of the Quaint</u>. Philadelphia: Ferris & Leach, 1902. 253 pp.

P 349 Darios, Louise. <u>Strange Tales of Canada</u>. Toronto: Ryerson, 1965. 162 pp.

P 350 Dolch, Edward W. and Marguerite P. Dolch. <u>Stories from Canada</u>. Champaign, IL: Gaviard, 1964. 168 pp.

GPc 351 Finnigan, Joan. <u>The Great Canadian Giant Book</u>. Toronto: NC Press, 1978. 196 pp.

28

Folktales

P   352   Gard, Robert E. 'As We Were Saying.' Alberta Folklore
          Quarterly, 1(1945), 1-9; 29-37.

F   353   Hand, Wayland. 'Status of European and American Legend
          Study.' Current Anthropology, 6(1965), 439-46.

PY 354   Hooke, Hilda M. Thunder in the Mountains. Toronto: Ox-
          ford, 1947. 223 pp.

P   355   Judson, Katherine B. Myths and Legends of British North
          America. Chicago: McClurg, 1917. 211 pp.

FP 356   Leach, Maria. Whistle to the Graveyard: Folktales to
          Chill Your Bones. New York: Viking, 1974. 128 pp.

Pc 357   MacArthur, F. H. Legends of Prince Edward Island. Char-
          lottetown: Simpson, 1966. 195 pp.

GP 358   McKelvie, B. A. Tales of Conflict. Vancouver: Daily
          Province, 1949. 99 pp.

PY 359   Macmillan, Cyrus. Canadian Fairy Tales. Toronto: Gundy,
          1922. 203 pp.

PY 360   -- Canadian Wonder Tales. 1918; rpt. Toronto: Clarke,
          Irwin, 1974. 288 pp.

GP 361   Norcross, E. C., and D. F. Tonkin. Vancouver Island of
          Frontier Days. Courtney, B.C.: Island Books, 1969.
          128 pp.

P   362   Paterson, T. W. Outlaws of the Canadian Frontier. Van-
          couver: Stagecoach, 1974. 72 pp.

GP 363   Pearson, John. Fur and Gold. Stories, Tales and Legends
          of British Columbia. White Rock, B.C.: S. K. Press
          Holdings, n.d. 112 pp.

PY 364   Quinton, Leslie (pseud.). The Lucky Coin and Other
          Folk Tales Canadians Tell. Toronto: McClelland & Stew-
          art, 1972. 128 pp.

P   365   Riley, Dan, Tom Primrose, and Hugh Dempsey. The Lost
          Lemon Mine. Calgary: Frontiers Unlimited, n.d. 40 pp.

FP 366   Rogers, Frank D. Folk-Stories of the Northern Border.
          Clayton, NY: Thousand Islands, 1897. 273 pp.

GP 367   Rogers, Grace M. Stories of the Land of Evangeline.
          1891; rpt. Toronto: McClelland & Stewart, 1923. 119 pp.

GP 368   Sherwood, Roland H. Atlantic Harbours: People, Places
          and Events. Windsor, N.S.: Lancelot, 1972. 119 pp.

P 369   Sherwood, Roland H. Story Parade. Sackville, N.S.: Tribune, 1948. 245 pp.

P 370   Skinner, Charles M. Myths and Legends Beyond Our Borders. Philadelphia: Lippincott, 1899. 319 pp.

G 371   Williams, Amelia A., ed. Tales of Colville and Kootenay. Toronto: Univ. of Toronto Press, 1977. 244 pp.

      4B Anglophone and Celtic

GP 372   Allen, Robert Thomas. A Treasury of Canadian Humour. Toronto: McClelland & Stewart, 1967. 128 pp.

P 373   Balcom, E. Joan. Fundy Tales. Kentville, N.S.: Saunders, 1969. 27 pp.

P 374   Barker, H. T. 'The Pool of Mineolta: A Legend of Early P.E.I.' Atlantic Advocate, 55(June 1965), 42-44.

GP 375   Barrett, Harry B. Lore and Legends of Long Point. Toronto: Burns & MacEachern, 1977. 239 pp.

P 376   Beattie, Earle. 'The Man They Called "Sam Slick."' Imperial Oil Review, 24(Dec. 1955), 2-7.

C 377   Beck, Horace P. 'Tales of the Banks Fishermen.' American Neptune, 13(Apr. 1953), 125-30.

P 378   Bedore, Bernie V. 'Shanty Tales.' Beaver, Winter 1961, pp. 48-49.

PY 379   -- Tall Tales of Joe Mufferaw. Arnprior, Ont.: A Mufferaw Distribution, 1966. 32 pp.

PY 380   -- Tall Tales of Joe Mufferaw. Toronto: Consolidated Amethyst Communications, 1979. 64 pp.

P 381   Blakeley, Phyllis R. Nova Scotia's Two Remarkable Giants. Windsor: Lancelot, 1970. 48 pp.

GP 382   Borrett, William C. Down East: Another Cargo of Tales Told Under the Old Town Clock. Halifax: Imperial, 1945. 232 pp.

GP 383   -- Down to the Sea Again, with Tales Told Under the Old Town Clock. Halifax: Imperial, 1947. 221 pp.

GP 384   -- East Coast Port, and Other Tales Told Under the Old Town Clock. Halifax: Imperial, 1944. 237 pp.

GP 385   -- Historic Halifax. Tales Told Under the Old Town Clock. Toronto: Ryerson, 1948. 234 pp.

Folktales

GP 386 Borrett, William C. More Tales Told Under the Old Town Clock. Halifax: Imperial, 1943. 233 pp.

GP 387 -- Tales Retold Under the Old Town Clock. Toronto: Ryerson, 1957. 212 pp.

GP 388 -- Tales Told Under the Old Town Clock. Halifax: Imperial, 1942. 196 pp.

P 389 Bremmer, Benjamin. Tales of Abegweit (Prince Edward Island). Charlottetown: Irwin, 1936. 132 pp.

P 390 Bryan, George S. Mystery Ship, the Mary Celeste in Fancy and in Fact. Philadelphia & New York: Lippincott, 1942. 319 pp.

B 391 Calder, James G. 'Humor and Misunderstanding in Newfoundland Culture.' Culture & Tradition, 4(1979), 49-66.

GP 392 Callbeck, Larue C. 'Sagas of the Strait.' Atlantic Advocate, 49(Feb. 1959), 58-61.

GPc 393 Cameron, James M. Wreck of the Melmerby and Other Stories. New Glasgow, N.S.: Hector, 1963. 117 pp.

G 394 Chittick, V. L. O. 'The Pervasiveness of Sam Slick.' Dalhousie Review, 33(Summer 1953), 88-101.

GP 395 Chute, Arthur H. 'Bluenose Skippers.' Blackwoods Magazine, 211(1922), 439-45.

P 396 Clark, Gregory. 'Paul Bunyon [sic], Superman Hero of the Lumberjacks.' Toronto Star Weekly, 19 Jan. 1924.

C 397 Clark, R. J. 'A Classical Foundation Legend from Newfoundland.' Folklore, 81(1970), 182-84.

GP 398 Clouston, Al. 'Come 'ere till I Tells Ya.' A Collection of Newfoundland Humour. St. John's: Author, 1978. 102 pp.

GP 399 Colombo, John Robert, ed. Other Canadas: An Anthology of Science Fiction and Fantasy. Toronto: McGraw-Hill Ryerson, 1979.

C 400 Creighton, Helen. 'Rudyard Kipling and the Halifax Doctor.' Atlantic Advocate, 55(June 1965), 50-55.

A 401 Creighton, Helen, and Edward D. Ives. 'Eight Folktales from Miramichi as told by Wilmot MacDonald.' Northeast Folklore, 4(1962), 3-70.

GP 402 Dempsey, Hugh A. The Best of Bob Edwards. Edmonton: Hurtig, 1975. 271 pp.

FC 403 Doering, J. Frederick. 'Legends from Canada, Indiana and Florida.' Southern Folklore Quarterly, 2(1938), 213-20.

C 404 Dunn, Charles W. 'Four Anecdotes from Cape Breton.'
Teangadoir, 4:27, 54-55.

GP 405 England, George A. 'The Graveyard of the Atlantic.'
Saturday Evening Post, 13 Dec. 1924, pp. 20-21, 162,
165, 169.

C 406 English, Leo E. F. 'Pirate Legends.' Newfoundland
Quarterly, 55(Dec. 1956), 34-35.

GP 407 Evans, R. G. Murder on the Plains. Calgary: Frontier,
n.d. 64 pp.

B 408 Fanning, W. Wayne. 'Storytelling at a Nova Scotia
General Store.' Culture & Tradition, 3(1978), 57-67.

A 409 Fauset, Arthur Huff. Folklore from Nova Scotia. New
York: American Folklore Society, 1931. Pp. 1-108.

P 410 Fay, Charles E. Mary Celeste - the Odyssey of an Aban-
doned Ship. Salem, MA: Peabody Museum, 1942. 261 pp.

P 411 Fitzhenry, Jack. 'The Widow's Curse.' Newfoundland
Quarterly, 45(Dec. 1945), 9-14.

B 412 Fowke, Edith. 'In Defence of Paul Bunyan.' New York
Folklore, 5(Summer 1979), 43-52.

A 413 Fraser, C. A. 'Scottish Myths from Ontario.' JAF, 6
(1893), 185-98.

A 414 Fraser, Mary L. Folklore of Nova Scotia. 1931; rpt.
Antigonish: Formac, 1975. Pp. 69-77; 94-100.

GP 415 Gard, Robert E. 'Alberta Aspects of the Bender Mystery.' Canadian Cattlemen, 8(Jan. 1945), 5; 48.

P 416 -- 'Alberta's Wild Bill Hickock.' Alberta Folklore
Quarterly, 2(1946), 62-65.

C 417 -- 'Collecting Alberta's Stories.' Canadian Cattlemen,
7(June 1944), 7, 10, 11, 38.

Pa 418 -- Johnny Chinook, Tall Tales and True from the Canadian West. London: Longmans, Green, 1945; rpt. Edmonton: Hurtig, 1967. 360 pp.

GP 419 Gesner, Claribel. Cape Breton Anthology. Windsor: Lancelot, 1971. 44 pp.

GP 420 -- Cape Breton Vignettes. Windsor: Lancelot, 1974.
60 pp.

GP 421 Gillespie, Gerald J. 'The Island of Sea Wolves.' Atlantic Advocate, 47(Jan. 1957), 51-59.

Folktales

Pc 422 Gillis, James D. The Cape Breton Giant. A Truthful Memoir. 1926; rpt. Sydney, N.S.: MacLeod, 1970. 64 pp.

GP 423 Gray, Art. Tales of Bygone Days. Kelowna, B.C.: n.p., 1963. 142 pp.

G 424 Guy, Ray. That Far Greater Bay. Ed. Eric Norman. Portugal Cove, Nfld.: Breakwater, 1976. 147 pp.

G 425 -- You May Know Them As Sea Urchins, Ma'am. Ed. Eric Norman. Portugal Cove: Breakwater, 1975. 170 pp.

FA 426 Halpert, Herbert. '"The Cut-Off Head Frozen On": Some International Versions of a Tall Tale.' Canadian Folklore Canadien, 1(1979), 13-23.

FB 427 -- 'The Humorous Grace Cante-Fable.' Mid-South Folklore, 3:3(1975), 71-82.

A 428 -- 'Tall Tales and Other Yarns from Calgary, Alberta.' California Folklore Quarterly, 4(1945), 29-49. Rpt. in Folklore of Canada. Ed. Edith Fowke. Toronto: McClelland & Stewart, 1976. Pp. 171-89.

P 429 Harrington, Michael F. 'Ancient Island's Legends and Tales Going for the Asking.' Atlantic Advocate, 61 (June 1971), 57-59; 61.

GPc 430 -- Sea Stories from Newfoundland. Toronto: Ryerson, 1958. 172 pp.

GP 431 Hastings, Macdonald. Mary Celeste: A Centenary Record. London: Michael Joseph, 1939. 174 pp.

PY 432 Hennigar, 'Ted' R. Scotian Spooks, Mystery and Violence. Windsor: Lancelot, 1978. 191 pp.

C 433 Ives, Edward D. 'The Burning Ship of the Northumberland Strait: Some Notes on That Apparition.' Northeast Folklore, 2(1958), 64-65.

B 434 -- 'Larry Gorman and the Cante Fable.' New England Quarterly, 32(1959), 226-37.

FB 435 -- 'The Man Who Plucked the Gorbey.' JAF, 74(1961), 1-8.

C 436 -- 'More Notes on the Burning Ship of the Northumberland Strait.' Northeast Folklore, 2(1959), 53-55.

P 437 J. D. P. 'Legend of Piper's Creek.' Christmas Bells (St. John's), 10 (Dec. 1901), 6-7.

B 438 Jackson, Kenneth. 'More Tales from Port Hood, Nova Scotia.' Scottish Gaelic Studies, 6(1949), 176-88.

B 439 Jackson, Kenneth. 'Notes on the Gaelic of Port Hood, Nova Scotia.' Scottish Gaelic Studies, 6(1949), 89-109.

Pb 440 Janes, L. W. The Treasury of Newfoundland Stories. St. John's: Maple Leaf Mills, n.d. 158 pp.

GP 441 Kirkpatrick, Ernest S. Tales of the St. John River. Toronto: Briggs, 1904. 132 pp.

F 442 Kirtley, Bacil F., ed. 'Folklore from Aroostook Co., Maine, and Neighboring Canada.' Northeast Folklore, 1(1958), 33-47, 65-73; 2(1959), 12-17, 26-29, 46-50, 55-58.

GP 443 Lawson, J. Murray. Yarmouth Past and Present. Yarmouth, N.S.: Author, 1902. 647 pp.

A 444 Leach, MacEdward. 'Celtic Tales from Cape Breton.' In Studies in Honor of Stith Thompson. Ed. W. Edson Richmond. Bloomington: Indiana Univ. Press, 1957. Pp. 40-54.

P 445 LeMessurier, H. W. 'A Native Baron Munchhausen.' Christmas Bells, 2(Dec. 1893), 14-15.

GP 446 Levy, Herman D. A History of Sherwood in the County of Lunenburg, Truro, N.S.: Author, 1953. 89 pp.

P 447 Lindsay, F. W. Cariboo Yarns. N.p.: Author, 1962. 60 pp.

GP 448 -- Outlaws in British Columbia. Quesnel, B.C.: Author, 1963. 64 pp.

GP 449 Lounds, M. Russell. The Sea, Ships and Sailors: Stories of the Sea in and Around Nova Scotia. Halifax: Petheric, 1970. 85 pp.

P 450 MacArthur, F. H. 'The Phantom Ship of the Maritimes.' Maritime Advocate, 46:2(1955), 17.

Pc 451 McCawley, Stuart. Cape Breton Humor. Glace Bay, N.S.: Brodie, 1929. 66 pp.

GP 452 Macdonald, David. 'Sam Slick Slept Here.' Maclean's, 1 July 1954, pp. 22-23, 30, 35-36.

GP 453 Macdonald, Hugh. Down Memory Lane, With Gems of Antigonish to Remember. Antigonish, N.S.: Casket, 1972. 136 pp.

GP 454 -- The Isle Royal. Antigonish: Casket, 1970. 97 pp.

P 455 -- Our Storied Past. The Ceilidh and Other Tales of Nova Scotia. Antigonish: Casket, 1967. 109 pp.

PY 456 Macdonald, Zillah K. Mystery of the Piper's Ghost. New
        York: Scholastic, 1954. 156 pp.

GP 457 MacKenzie, Michael. It Happened Yesterday. Grand Falls,
        Nfld.: Robinson-Blackmore, 1973. 113 pp.

GP 458 MacLennan, Hugh. 'Cape Breton, the Legendary Island.'
        Saturday Night, 3 July 1951, pp. 12-13.

 A 459 MacLeod, Calum I. N. Stories from Nova Scotia. Anti-
        gonish: Formac, 1974. 129 pp.

GP 460 Macleod, Grace D. Stories of the Land of Evangeline.
        Boston: Lothrop, 1891; rev. ed., 1923. 336 pp.

GP 461 MacMechan, Archibald M. Old Province Tales. Toronto:
        McClelland & Stewart, 1924. 345 pp.

GP 462 -- Sagas of the Sea. London: Dent, 1924. 156 pp.

GP 463 -- Tales of the Sea. Toronto: McClelland & Stewart,
        1947. 230 pp.

GP 464 -- There Go the Ships. Toronto: McClelland & Stewart,
        1928. 293 pp.

 C 465 Manny, Louise. 'Miramichi Folklore.' Northeast Folk-
        lore, 2(1959), 61-63.

 P 466 Martin, John P. The Babes in the Wood with a Road Guide
        to the Graves of the Children at Woodlawn. (Stories of
        Dartmouth). Halifax: Author, 1944. 20 pp.

GP 467 Paterson, T. W., ed. Canadian Treasure Trails. Langley:
        Stagecoach, 1976, 119 pp.

GP 468 Patton, Janice, ed. The Sinking of the "I'm Alone."
        (Stories from the Pierre Berton Show). Toronto:
        McClelland & Stewart, 1973. 47 pp.

 A 469 Pocius, Gerald L. 'Frank Williams, Newfoundland Joke-
        Teller.' Lore and Language, 2(Jan. 1977), 16-29; 2(July
        1977), 11-21; 2(Jan. 1978), 11-19. 2(July 1978), 6-25.

GP 470 Raddall, Thomas H. Footsteps on Old Floors: True Tales
        of Mystery. Garden City, NY: Doubleday, 1968. 239 pp.

Pb 471 Reader, H. J. Newfoundland Wit, Humor and Folklore.
        Corner Brook, Nfld.: Author, [1967]. 72 pp.

GP 472 Riley, D. E. 'The Lost Lemon Mine.' Alberta Folklore
        Quarterly, 2(March 1946), 15-18.

GPb 473 Roberts, Charles G. D. Around the Camp Fire. New York:
        Crowell, 1896. 349 pp.

GP   474   Roberts, Leslie. 'Atlantic Graveyard.' Saturday Evening Post, 26 Oct. 1946, pp. 9-11, 147.

Pc   475   Robins, John D. Logging with Paul Bunyan. Ed. Edith Fowke. Toronto: Ryerson, 1957. 97 pp.

 P   476   -- 'Prodding Nature: A Paul Bunyan Episode.' Canadian Forum, 7(1927), 114-17.

 B   477   -- 'Paul Bunyan.' Canadian Forum, 6(1926), 146-50. Rpt. in Our Sense of Identity. Ed. M. M. Ross. Toronto: Ryerson, 1954, Pp. 129-36.

GP   478   Robinson, Cyril G. Men Against the Sea: High Drama in the Atlantic. Windsor: Lancelot, 1971, 140 pp.

GPb 479   Russell, Ted. The Chronicles of Uncle Mose. Portugal Cove: Breakwater, 1975. 112 pp.

GPc 480   -- Tales from Pigeon Inlet. Portugal Cove: Breakwater, 1977. 175 pp.

GP   481   Scott, Marshall O. 'Changing Aspects of Sable Island.' Canadian Magazine, 18(1901-1902), 341-49.

 P   482   Shaw, Beatrice M. Hay. 'Nova Scotia Ghost Stories or Ghosts of Nova Scotia.' Column starting 1 May 1921 in Sunday Leader, Halifax.

GP   483   Sheppard, Robert, and Edwin Noftle. Newfie Laffs. Lewisporte, Nfld.: Authors, 1979. 44 pp.

Pb   484   Sherwood, Roland H. Maritime Mysteries. Windsor: Lancelot, 1976. 112 pp.

Pb   485   -- The Phantom Ship of Northumberland Strait and Other Mysteries of the Sea. Windsor: Lancelot, 1975. 48 pp.

Pb   486   -- Tall Tales of the Maritimes. Windsor: Lancelot, 1972. 36 pp.

GP   487   Simpson, Ted. The Forgotten Man and Our Own Robin Hood: Tales of Disaster, Starvation and Heartwarming Stories of Rescue. [Hall's Harbour, N.S.]: Author, 1973. 21 pp.

GY   488   Smallwood, Joseph R., and Leo E. F. English. Stories of Newfoundland. St. John's: Nfld. Gazette, n.d. 100 pp.

 P   489   Smith, A. de H. 'His Baby Carriage a Logging Wagon and His Splash Started Fundy Tides.' Toronto Star Weekly, 28 March 1925, p. 25.

GP   490   Smith, Harry J. Cape Breton Tales. Boston: Atlantic Monthly, 1920. 140 pp.

B   491   Smith, Susan. 'Urban Tales.' In <u>Folklore of Canada</u>.
          Ed. Edith Fowke. Toronto: McClelland & Stewart, 1976.
          Pp. 262-68.

GP 492   Smyth, Fred J. <u>Tales of the Kootenays</u>. 1938; rpt. Van-
          couver: Douglas, 1977. 205 pp.

FP 493   Snow, Edward R. <u>Ghosts, Gales and Gold</u>. New York: Dodd,
          1972. 263 pp.

GP 494   -- 'Island of Lost Ships.' <u>Colliers</u>, 7 Jan. 1955, pp.
          66-69.

FP 495   -- <u>Strange Tales from Nova Scotia to Cape Hatteras</u>.
          New York: Dodd, Mead, 1949. 322 pp.

GPc 496   'Some Newfoundland Stories. From the Records of the
          Noddy Club and Other Sources.' <u>Christmas Review Number</u>
          (St. John's), 1901, pp. 6-17.

GP 497   Spinks, William W. <u>Tales of the British Columbia Fron-
          tier</u>. Toronto: Ryerson, 1933. 134 pp.

BY 498   Spray, Carole. <u>Will O'The Wisp: Folk Tales and Legends
          of New Brunswick</u>. Fredericton: Brunswick, 1979. 132 pp.

GP 499   Stephens, David E. <u>It Happened at Moose River</u>. Windsor:
          Lancelot, 1974. 99 pp.

C   500   'Stories from Inverness County.' <u>Cape Breton's Maga-
          zine</u>, No. 12(1975), pp. 1-8.

A   501   Tallman, Richard S. '"You Can Almost Picture It": The
          Aesthetic of a Nova Scotia Storyteller.' <u>Folklore
          Forum</u>, 7(1974), 121-30.

GP 502   Trueman, Stuart. <u>Tall Tales and True Tales from Down
          East</u>. Toronto: McClelland & Stewart, 1979. 166 pp.

P   503   Tulk, Bob. <u>Even Funnier Newfoundland Jokes</u>. Corner
          Brook: Newfie Jokes. 1974. 72 pp. [Cover: <u>Even Funnier
          . . . Newfie Jokes</u>, #4.]

P   504   -- <u>Newfoundland Jokes</u>. Mount Pearl, Nfld.: Author,
          1972. 82 pp. [#2] [Cover: <u>New Newfie Jokes</u>.]

P   505   -- <u>New Newfoundland Jokes</u>. Mount Pearl: Author, 1973.
          [#3] [Cover: <u>Bob Tulk's Newfoundland Jokes: Here They
          Are . . . 'The Ones We Didn't Dare Print.'</u>]

P   506   -- <u>Newfoundland Jokes</u>. N.p., 1971. 82 pp. [#1] [Rpt.
          of <u>150 Newfoundland Jokes</u>. Cover: <u>Newfie Jokes</u>.]

P   507   -- <u>Newfoundland Jokes</u>. [Grand Falls]: Author, 1979.
          64 pp. [Cover: <u>Newfie Jokes</u>, #5.]

FP 508 Underwood, P. _Hauntings_. London: J. M. Dent, 1977.

A 509 Wareham, Wilfred. 'The Monologue in Newfoundland.' In _The Blasty Bough_. Ed. Clyde Rose. St. John's: Breakwater, 1976. Pp. 196-216.

C 510 Waugh, F. W. 'Canadian Folklore from Ontario.' _JAF_, 31(1918), 78-82.

P 511 White, Jack. 'The Legend of Piper's Hole.' _Atlantic Guardian_, 9(July 1952), 21-22.

GP 512 Wilson, Helen D. _More Tales from Barrett's Landing_. Toronto: McClelland & Stewart, 1967. 155 pp.

GP 513 -- _Tales from Barrett's Landing_. Toronto: McClelland & Stewart, 1964. 127 pp.

P 514 Wright, Bruce. 'The Beast of Bear Cove: A Walrus in the Bay of Fundy.' _Atlantic Advocate_, 48:(Dec. 1957), 61-62.

GP 515 Young, George. _Bluenose Capers_. Bridgewater, N.S.: Author, 1971. 92 pp.

P 516 -- 'Ghosts in Nova Scotia.' _Tales of the Supernatural_. Lunenburg, N.S.: Lunenburg Print, 1977. 87 pp.

GP 517 -- _Tales Told Over Mulled Rum_. Queensland, N.S.: Author, 1972. 83 pp.

4C Francophone

PbY 518 Aubry, Claude. _The Magic Fiddler and Other Legends of French Canada_. Toronto: Peter Martin, 1968. 98 pp.

C 519 Barbeau, C. Marius. 'The Bell Tolled Midnight.' _CGJ_, 9 (Dec. 1934), 273-82.

C 520 -- 'Canadian Folklore: Folk Tales.' _French Folklore Bulletin_, 24(1946), 87-90.

C 521 -- 'Canadian Legends.' _Dalhousie Review_, 26(1946), 217-26.

C 522 -- 'John Big-Timbers.' _CLA Bulletin_, 16(1960), 296-300.

C 523 -- 'Legends and History in the Oldest Geographical Names of the St. Lawrence." _CGJ_, 61(July 1960), 2-9.

C 524 -- 'Legends of the St. Lawrence.' _Quebec_, 7(Jan. 1933), 264-68.

Folktales

A(r)Y 525 Barbeau, C. Marius. The Tree of Dreams. Toronto: Oxford, 1955. 112 pp.

   C   526 -- 'The Tree of Dreams, A Christmas Legend of Notre-Dame de Lorette.' CGJ, 7(Dec. 1933), 249-60.

   C   527 -- 'The Witch-Canoe--La Chasse-Galerie.' CGJ, 5 (Dec. 1932), 205-14.

A(1)Y 528 Barbeau, C. Marius, and Michael Hornyansky. The Golden Phoenix and Other French-Canadian Fairy Tales. Toronto: Oxford, 1958. 144 pp.

   B   529 Barter, Geraldine. 'The Folktale and Children in the Tradition of French Newfoundlanders.' Canadian Folklore Canadien, 1(1979), 5-11.

   B   530 -- '"Sabot-Bottes et P'tite Galoch": A Franco-Newfoundland Version of AT 545, The Cat as Helper.' Culture & Tradition, 1(1976), 5-17.

C(1) 531 Beaugrand, Honoré. 'La Chasse-Galerie.' Quebec, 8(Jan. 1934), 220-24.

A(1) 532 -- La Chasse-Galerie and Other Canadian Stories. Montréal: Pelletier, 1900. 101 pp.

   C   533 -- 'The Christmas Collection for the Infant Jesus.' Quebec, 8(Dec. 1933), 204-9.

   C   534 -- 'Lutins in the Province of Quebec.' JAF, 5(1892), 327-28.

   C   535 -- 'The Werewolves. A Legend of Old Quebec.' Quebec, 10(Jan. 1936), 197-200.

   B   536 Bemer, John W. 'Nineteenth Century French-Canadian Folk Tales.' Journal of Canadian Fiction, 2:3(1973), 69-74.

B(r)Y 537 Boswell, Hazel. Legends of Quebec. Toronto: McClelland & Stewart, 1966. 120 pp.

   B   538 Bydanavicius, Vytautas. 'The Canadian French Tale and Its Analysis.' Cultural Wellsprings of Folktales. Part I, Chap. 5. New York: Manyland Books, 1970.

   P   539 C.H.U. 'Five Legends of Old Quebec.' Quebec, 9(Dec. 1934), 169-72.

   P   540 Campbell, R. M. 'A Legend of French Canada.' Canada-West Indies Magazine, Jan. 1934, pp. 55-56.

B(r)Y 541 Carlson, Natalie S. The Talking Cat and Other Stories of French Canada. New York: Harper, 1952. 87 pp.

39

A(1) 542 De Gaspé, Philippe-Aubert, père. Canadians of Old.
Trans. C. G. D. Roberts. 1890; rpt. Toronto: McClelland
& Stewart, 1974. 364 pp.

A 543 Dorson, Richard M. 'Canadiens.' Bloodstoppers and
Bearwalkers. Cambridge: Harvard Univ. Press, 1959.
Pp. 69-102.

A 544 -- 'Canadiens in the Upper Peninsula of Michigan.'
Archives de Folklore, 4(1949), 17-27.

A 545 -- 'Dialect Stories of the Upper Peninsula.' JAF, 61
(1948), 117-50.

A 546 Dorson, Richard, ed. Folktales Told around the World.
Chicago: Univ. of Chicago Press, 1975. Pp. 429-67.

PbY 547 Downie, Mary A. The Witch of the North. Ottawa: Oberon,
1975. 64 pp.

PY 548 Einarsson, Magnús. Everyman: The Quest for Treasure
Mountain. Ottawa: National Museum, 1979. 23 pp.

A 549 Fowke, Edith. Folktales of French Canada. Toronto: NC
Press, 1979. 144 pp.

P 550 Fréchette, Louis. 'Xmas in French Canada.' Quebec, 5
(Dec. 1930), 242-47; 276-79.

B(r) 551 Greenough, William P. Canadian Folk-Life and Folk-Lore.
1897; rpt. Toronto: Coles, n.d. Pp. 45-64.

B 552 Jolicoeur, Catherine. 'Le Vaisseau fantôme: Légende
étiologique.' Archives de Folklore, 11(1970), passim.

B 553 Lacourcière, Luc. 'The Analytical Catalogue of French
Folktales in North America.' Laurentian Review, 8(Feb.
1976), 123-28.

C 554 Lacourcière, Luc, and Felix A. Savard. 'Canadian Folk
Tales Recorded during the Summer of 1948 in Charlevoix
and Beauce Counties.' Ottawa: National Museum, Bulletin
118, 1950, pp. 63-65.

C 555 Layton, Monique. 'The Ten Miracles of Josaphat G.'
Canadian Journal of Research in Semiotics, 3(Winter
1975), 19-40.

P 556 LeMoine, James M. The Legendary Lore of the Lower St.
Lawrence. Quebec: Mercury, 1862. 33 pp.

B(1) 557 -- The Legends of the St. Lawrence. Quebec: Holiwell,
1898. 203 pp.

Gc 558 -- Maple Leaves: A Budget of Legendary, Historical,
Critical and Sporting Intelligence. 7 vols. Quebec:
Hunter Rose, 1863-1906.

B 559 Low, Margaret. 'The Motif of the External Soul in French Canadian Folktales.' Laurentian University Review, 8(Feb. 1976), 61-68.

P 560 MacWhirter, Margaret G. Treasure Trove in Gaspé and the Baie des Chaleurs. Quebec: Telegraph, 1919. 217 pp.

C 561 Marie-Ursule, Soeur. 'Civilization traditionnelle des Lavalois.' Archives de Folklore, 5-6(1951). Legends 11, 12, 13, 14, 16, 20, 28, 29, 42, pp. 184-99 passim.

B 562 Monteiro, George. 'Histoire de Montferrand: L'Athlète Canadien and Joe Mufraw.' JAF, 73(1960), 24-34.

P 563 N.A.G. 'Legend of the St. Augustin Draught Horse,' and "Midnight Mass of the Phantom Priest.' Quebec, 2(Dec. 1927), 2-3.

P 564 Rogers, Marion G. 'The Virgin of the Saguenay.' CGJ, 60(June 1960), 226-27.

P 565 'Rose Latulippe. A Legend of the "Mardi Gras" (Shrove Tuesday) in French Canada.' Quebec, 2(1927), 5-7.

C 566 Skinner, Charles M. 'Three Wishes: A Quaint Legend of the Canadian Habitants.' JAF, 19(1906), 341-42.

GP 567 Smith, Philip H. Acadia. A Lost Chapter in American History. Pawling, NY: Author, 1884. 381 pp.

A 568 Thomas, Gerald. 'The Folktale and Folktale Style in the Tradition of French Newfoundlanders.' Canadian Folklore Canadien, 1(1979), 71-78.

A 569 -- 'A Tradition Under Pressure: Folk Narratives of the French Minority of the Port-au-Port Peninsula, Newfoundland (Canada).' Studia Fennica 20: Folk Narrative Research, Helsinki, 1976, pp. 192-201.

GPY 570 Tremblay, Jack. Louis Cyr: The Story of 'The Strongest Man Who Ever Lived.' Fredericton: Brunswick, 1967. [21 pp.]

Pc 571 -- Ten Canadian Legends. Fredericton: Brunswick, 1955. 32 pp.

B(r)Y 572 Wallace, Paul A. W. Baptiste Larocque: Legends of French Canada. Toronto: Musson, 1923. 129 pp.

Pc 573 Warnock, Amelia Beers [Katherine Hale]. Legends of the St. Lawrence. Montreal: CPR, 1926. 49 pp.

GP 574 Weider, Ben. The Strongest Man in History: Louis Cyr. Vancouver: Mitchell, 1976. 104 pp.

C 575 Wintemberg, W. J. 'French-Canadian Folk Tales.' JAF,
17(1904), 265-67.

PbY 576 Woodley, Edward C. Legends of French Canada. Toronto:
Nelson, 1931. 105 pp.

GPbY 577 -- Untold Tales of Old Quebec. Toronto: Dent, 1949.
216 pp.

4D Indian and Inuit

A 578 Adamson, Thelma, ed. Folk-Tales of the Coast Salish.
Philadelphia: American Folklore Society, Memoir 27,
1934. 430 pp.

B 579 Ahenakew, Beth, and Sam Hardlotte, comps. Cree Legends.
2 vols. Saskatoon: Sask. Indian Cultural College, 1973.

B(r) 580 Ahenakew, Edward. 'Cree Trickster Tales.' JAF, 42(1929),
309-53.

B 581 -- Voices of the Plains Cree. Ed. Ruth M. Buck.
Toronto: McClelland & Stewart, 1973; pb. 1977. 204 pp.

B(r) 582 Anderson, Anne. Legends of Wesakecha. Told by the El-
ders. Edmonton: Alta. Prov. Museum, 1976. 44 pp.

PbY 583 Ayre, Robert. Sketco the Raven. Toronto: Macmillan,
1961; rpt. Richmond Hill, Ont.: Scholastic-Tab, 1974.
183 pp.

C 584 Baptie, S. As told by J. P. Hughes. 'Legend of Big
River.' Beaver, June 1939, pp. 42-43.

C 585 Barbeau, C. Marius. 'Bear Mother.' JAF, 59(1946), 1-12.

A 586 -- Haida Myths Illustrated in Argillite Carvings.
Ottawa: National Museum, Bulletin 127, 1953. 417 pp.

C 587 -- 'How the Raven Stole the Sun.' TRSC, 38(1944),
sec. 2, pp. 59-69.

A 588 -- Huron and Wyandot Mythology. Ottawa: National Museum, Memoir 80, 1915. 437 pp.

A 589 -- Huron-Wyandot Traditional Narratives (in transla-
tions and native texts). Ottawa: National Museum,
Bulletin 165, 1960. 337 pp.

C 590 -- 'The Man with the Wooden Wife.' Imperial Oil
Review, Dec. 1959, pp. 11-14.

A 591 -- Tsimsyan Myths. Ottawa: National Museum, Bulletin
174, 1961. 97 pp.

B 592 Barbeau, C. Marius. 'Wyandot Tales Including Foreign Elements.' JAF, 28(1915), 83-95.

C 593 Barbeau, C. Marius, and Charles Camsell. 'Loucheux Myths.' JAF, 28(1915), 249-57.

P 594 Barclay, Isabel. Song of the Forest. Ottawa: Oberon, 1977. 48 pp.

A 595 Bauer, George W. 'Cree Tales and Beliefs.' Northeast Folklore, 12(1971), 1-70.

B 596 -- Tales from the Cree. Cobalt, Ont.: Highway Book Shop, 1973. 47 pp.

FP 597 Bayliss, Clara K. A Treasury of Eskimo Tales. New York: Crowell, 1922. 135 pp.

FB 598 Beck, Horace P. Gluskap the Liar and Other Indian Tales. Freeport, ME: Bond Wheelwright, 1966. 182 pp.

B 599 Bell, James M. 'Fireside Stories of the Chippewyans.' JAF, 16(1903), 73-84.

C 600 Bell, Robert. 'History of the Che-che-puy-ew-tis (Legend of the Northern Crees).' JAF, 10(1897), 1-8.

C 601 -- 'Legends of the Slavey Indians of the Mackenzie River.' JAF, 14(1901), 26-29.

C 602 -- 'Ojibway Legends and Traditions.' JAF, 6(1893), 153-54.

Pb 603 Bemister, Margaret. Thirty Indian Legends of Canada. 1912; rpt. Vancouver: Douglas, 1973, 182 pp.

A 604 Bloomfield, Leonard. Sacred Stories of the Sweet Grass Cree. Ottawa: National Museum, Bulletin 60, 1930. 346 pp.

A 605 Boas, Franz. Bella Bella Tales. New York: American Folklore Society, Memoir 25, 1932. 152 pp.

A 606 -- Bella Bella Texts. New York: Columbia Univ. Press, 1928. 291 pp.

FB 607 -- 'Dissemination of Tales Among the Natives of North America.' JAF, 4(1891), 13-20.

A 608 -- 'Eskimo Tales and Songs.' JAF, 7(1894), 45-50; 10(1897), 109-15.

A 609 -- Kwakiutl Culture as Reflected in Mythology. New York: American Folklore Society, Memoir 28, 1935. 190 pp.

A   610   Boas, Franz. Kwakiutl Tales. New York: Columbia Univ.
           Press, 1910. 495 pp.

A   611   -- Kwakiutl Tales. New series. 2 vols. New York:
           Columbia Univ. Press, 1935.

FA   612   -- 'Mythology and Folk Tales of the North American
           Indians.' JAF, 27(1914), 380-423.

A   613   -- The Mythology of the Bella Coola Indians. New York:
           American Museum of Natural History, Memoir 2, 1898.
           102 pp.

B   614   -- 'Myths and Legends of the Catloltq of Vancouver
           Island.' American Antiquarian, 10(1888), 201-11,
           366-73.

B   615   -- 'Relations Between Northwest America and Northeast
           Asia.' In American Aborigines. Ed. Diamond Jenness.
           Toronto: Univ. of Toronto Press, 1933. Pp. 355-70.

B   616   -- 'Salishan Texts.' Proc. American Philosophical
           Society, 34(1895), 31-48.

A   617   -- 'Tsimshian Mythology.' 31st Annual Report of the
           Bureau of American Ethnology, Washington, 1916, pp. 29-
           1037.

A   618   -- Tsimshian Texts. Washington: Bureau of American
           Ethnology, Bulletin 27, 1902. 244 pp.

A   619   Boas, Franz, ed. Folktales of the Salishan and Sahaptin
           Tribes. New York: American Folklore Society, Memoir 11,
           1917. 201 pp.

A   620   Boas, Franz, and Alexander F. Chamberlain. Kutenai
           Tales. Washington: Bureau of American Ethnology, Bul-
           letin 59, 1918. 387 pp.

A   621   Boas, Franz, and George Hunt. Kwakiutl Texts. New York:
           American Museum of Natural History, Memoir 14, pt. 1,
           1902, 1906. 270 pp.; 269 pp.

B   622   Boas, Franz, and Henry Rink. 'Eskimo Tales and Songs.'
           JAF, 2(1889), 123-31.

BY   623   Bouchard, Randy, and Dorothy I. D. Kennedy, eds.
           Lillooet Stories. Victoria: B.C. Indian Language
           Project, 1973.

A   624   -- and -- 'Lillooet Stories.' Sound Heritage, 6:1
           (1977), 1-78. (Also sound program cassette.)

AY   625   -- and -- Shuswap Stories. Victoria: B.C. Indian
           Language Project, 1977. 80 pp.

Folktales

AY 626 Bouchard, Randy, and Dorothy I. D. Kennedy. Shuswap Stories. Vancouver: CommCept, 1979: 152 pp.

B 627 Boyle, David. 'The Killing of the Wa-sak-apee-quay by Pe-se-wuan, and Others.' Annual Archeological Report, Ontario, 1908, pp. 91-121.

PY 628 Brass, Eleanor. Medicine Boy and Other Cree Tales. Calgary: Glenbow-Alberta Institute, 1979. [79 pp.]

P 629 Browne, G. 'Indian Legends of Acadia.' Acadiensis, 2 (1902), 54-64.

P 630 Burkholder, Mabel G. Before the White Man Came: Indian Legends and Stories. Toronto: McClelland & Stewart, 1923. 318 pp.

C 631 Burrows, Elizabeth. 'Eskimo Tales.' JAF, 39(1926), 79-81.

C 632 Cape Breton's Magazine. 'The Celestial Bear, A Micmac Legend,' No. 3(1973), pp. 10-11, 18; 'Gluskap's Journey,' No. 9(1974), pp. 31-32; 'How Gluskap Found Summer,' No. 5(1973), p. 24; 'The Micmac Legend of Taken-from-Guts,' No. 11(1976), pp. 19-21.

Gc 633 Campbell, John. 'The Ancient Literature of America.' TRSC, 2(1896-97), sec. 2, pp. 41-67.

C 634 Canfield, William W. 'Caughnawaga Legend.' JAF, 19 (1906), 127-29.

P 635 Carmichael, Alfred. Indian Legends of Vancouver Island. Toronto: Musson, 1922. 97 pp.

A 636 Carpenter, Carole Henderson. "Native Folklore for Canadian Children." Proc. of the 5th Annual Conference of the Children's Literature Assoc. Eds. M. P. Esmonde and P. A. Ord. Villanova, PA: Villanova Univ., 1979. Pp. 57-63.

C 637 Carson, William. 'Ojibwa Tales.' JAF, 30(1917), 491-93.

C(r) 638 Cass, Elizabeth, E. 'The Flood.' Beaver, Spring 1960, p. 58.

C(r) 639 -- 'Ojibwa Tales.' Beaver, Winter 1963, p. 58.

C(r) 640 -- 'The Story of Ey-ash-chis.' Beaver, Summer 1964, pp. 50-52.

C(r) 641 -- 'Why Dogs Hate Cats.' Beaver, Summer 1968, p. 51.

PcY 642 Caswell, Helen R. Shadows from the Singing House: Eskimo Folk Tales. Edmonton: Hurtig, 1968. 108 pp.

C   643   Chamberlain, Alexander F. 'A Kootenay Legend: the
          Coyote and the Mountain Spirit." JAF, 7(1894), 195-96.

C   644   -- 'Mythology and Folk-lore of the Kootenay Indians.'
          American Antiquarian, 17(1887), 68.

B   645   -- 'Mythology of Indian Stocks North of Mexico.' JAF,
          18(1905), 111-22.

B   646   -- 'Nanibozho Among the Algonkian Tribes.' JAF, 4
          (1891), 192-213.

C   647   Chapman, J. W. 'Athapascan Traditions of the Lower Yu-
          kon.' JAF, 16(1903), 180-5.

B(r) 648 Clark, Ella E. Indian Legends of Canada. Toronto:
          McClelland & Stewart, 1960; pb. 1977. 177 pp.

FB(r) 649 -- Indian Legends of the Pacific North West. Berkeley
          and Los Angeles: Univ. of California Press, 1958.
          225 pp.

C   650   Clay, Charles. Swampy Cree Legends. As Told to Charles
          Clay by Kuskatchees, the Smoky One. Toronto: Macmillan,
          1938; rpt. Bewdley, Ont.: Pine Ridge, 1978. 95 pp.

PcY 651 Cleaver, Nancy, and Rosemary Knight. Snowshoe Rabbit
          and Wild Rose Legends; or How the Snowshoe Rabbit Got
          Its White Winter Coat, and How the Wild Rose Got Its
          Thorns. Cobalt: Highway Book Shop, 1978. 29 pp.

C   652   Clipsham, Muriel. 'Nainabush Stories.' Saskatchewan
          History, 3(Winter 1960), 19-24.

AY   653 Clutesi, George. Son of Raven, Son of Deer: Fables of
          the Tse-shaht People. Sidney, B.C.: Gray's, 1967; pb.
          1975. 126 pp.

FB   654 Coffin, Tristram P. Indian Tales of North America.
          Philadelphia: American Folklore Society, 1961. 157 pp.

F   655   Coleman, Sister Bernard, et al. Ojibway Myths and
          Legends. Minneapolis: Ross & Haines, 1962. 135 pp.

P   656   Cree, Charles C. 'Legend of Creation.' Alberta Folk-
          lore Quarterly, 2(1946), 69-71.

C   657   Cresswell, J. R. 'Folk-tales of the Swampy Cree of
          Northern Manitoba.' JAF, 36(1923), 404-6.

C   658   Davidson, D. S. 'Tales from Grand Lake, Victoria, Que-
          bec.' JAF, 41(1928), 275-82.

C   659   Deans, James. 'A Creation Myth of the Tsimshians of
          Northwest British Columbia.' JAF, 4(1891), 34.

C 660 Deans, James, 'The Daughter of the Sun: A Legend of the Tsimshians of British Columbia.' JAF, 4(1891) 32-33.

C 661 -- 'Legend of the Fin-back Whale Crest of the Haidas, Queen Charlotte's Island, B.C.' JAF, 5(1892), 43-47.

C 662 -- 'The Story of the Bear and His Indian Wife.' JAF, 2(1889), 255-60.

B 663 Deans, James, comp. Tales from the Totems of the Hidery. Ed. O. J. Triggs. 1889; rpt. Norwood, PA.: Norwood, 1974. 96 pp. [Haida.]

A 664 Desbarats, Peter, ed. What They Used to Tell About: Indian Legends from Labrador. Toronto: McClelland & Stewart, 1969. 92 pp.

C 665 Dixon, Roland B. 'The Mythology of the Central and Eastern Algonkins (sic).' JAF, 22(1909), 1-9.

B 666 Dumont, James. 'Journey to Daylight-Land: Through Ojibway Eyes.' Laurentian University Review, 8(Feb. 1976), 31-43.

PY 667 Dunlop, G. M. Tales of the Indians of the Plains. Edmonton: Institute of Applied Art, 1934. 67 pp.

CY 668 Ekagatok, Bernard. Naraye, Anarktee and Other Stories. Yellowknife: Dept. of Education, N.W.T., 1974.

C 669 Elliott, W. C. 'Lake Lillooet Tales.' JAF, 44(1939), 166-82.

CY 670 Etook, Tivi. In the Days Long Past. Montreal: La Fédération des Coopératives du Nouveau Québec, 1976. 48 pp.

CY 671 -- Whispering in My Ears and Mingling with My Dreams. Montreal: La Fédération des Coopératives du Nouveau Québec, 1975. 44 pp.

C 672 Farrand, Livingston, coll. 'Myths of the Bellabella.' Appendix I in Franz Boas, 'Tsimshian Mythology.' 31st Annual Report of the Bureau of American Ethnology, Washington, 1916, pp. 883-88.

B 673 Farrand, Livingston, and Theresa Mayer. 'Quileute Tales.' JAF, 32(1919), 251-79.

B 674 Fisher, Margaret W. 'The Mythology of the Northern and Northeastern Algonkians.' Papers of the Robert S. Peabody Foundation for Archaeology, 3(1946), 226-62.

Pc 675 Flint and Steel, with the Cree Legend of the Origin of Fire. Winnipeg: Manitoba Free Press, 1905. 24 pp.

PcY 676 Fox, Mary Lou, ed. Ko-Ko-Ko The Owl: An Ojibwa-Odawa Legend. Manitoulin Island, Ont.: Ojibwa Cultural Foundation, 1977. Unpaged.

PcY 677 -- Why the Beaver Has a Broad Tail. Cobalt: Highway Book Shop, 1975. 22 pp.

PcY 678 Fraser, Frances. The Bear Who Stole the Chinook and Other Stories. Toronto: Macmillan, 1959. 72 pp.

C(r) 679 French, C. H. 'Legend of Round Stone Lake.' Beaver, Apr. 1923, p. 264.

C 680 Frost, Helen K. 'Two Abenaki Legends.' JAF, 25(1912), 188-90.

C 681 Gallerneault, Bob. Saulteaux Legends. Saskatoon: Univ. of Saskatchewan, 1972. 48 pp.

C(r) 682 Gilles, George. 'Three Indian Tales.' Alberta Historical Review, 15 (Winter 1967), 25-28.

C 683 Golder, F. A. 'Tlingit Myths.' JAF, 20(1907), 290-95.

GPbY 684 Gooderham, Kent, ed. I Am An Indian. Toronto: Dent, 1969. 196 pp.

C(r) 685 Gordon, Charles H. M. 'Cree Indian Legends.' Beaver, Sept. 1924, pp. 436-37; Mar. 1925, pp. 83-85.

C 686 Graham, Dorothy. 'Lands and Legends of the Nahonni.' CGJ, 84 (June 1972), 188-95.

G 687 Greene, Alma. Tales of the Mohawks. Toronto: Dent, 1975. 192 pp.

Pb 688 Griffin, George H. Legends of the Evergreen Coast. Vancouver: Clark & Stuart, 1935. 141 pp.

CY 689 Griffin, Rachael, adaptor. The Princess Captured by Spirit Bears. Portland, OR: Portland Art Museum, 1977. 14 pp. [Haida.]

P 690 Grisdale, Alex. Wild Drums: Tales and Legends of the Plains Indians. Winnipeg: Peguis, 1974. 78 pp.

C 691 Hagar, Stansbury. 'The Celestial Bear.' JAF, 13(1900), 92-103.

C 692 -- 'Two Micmac Tales: Of Water Fairies; Of the Culloo.' Cape Breton's Magazine, No. 12(1975), pp. 22-23.

C 693 Hallowell, A. Irving. As Told by Chief William Berens. 'The Giant Mosquitoes.' Beaver, Dec. 1933, p. 22.

Folktales

B   694   Hallowell, A. Irving. 'Some Folktales of the Berens River Salteaux.' <u>JAF</u>, 52(1939), 155-79.

C   695   Hamilton, James C. 'The Algonquin Manabozho and Hiawatha.' <u>JAF</u>, 16(1903), 229-33.

B   696   -- 'Famous Algonquins: Algic Legends.' <u>Trans. of the Canadian Institute</u>, 6(1898-99), 285-312.

C   697   -- 'Two Algonquin Legends.' <u>JAF</u>, 7(1894), 201.

C(r) 698   Hanna, Marion W. 'Kispiox Legend.' <u>Beaver</u>, Autumn 1963, pp. 40-41.

C(r) 699   -- 'Wee-Gat, the Spirit.' <u>Beaver</u>, Summer 1972, pp. 15-16.

A(r) 700   Harris, Kenneth B., and Francis M. P. Robinson. <u>Visitors Who Never Left: The Origin of the People of Damelahamid</u>. Vancouver: Univ. of B.C. Press, 1974. 171 pp.

P   701   Harris, Martha D. <u>History and Folklore of the Cowichan Indians</u>. Victoria: Colonist, 1901. 89 pp.

C   702   Helm, June, and Vital Thomas. 'Tales from the Dogribs.' <u>Beaver</u>, Autumn 1966, pp. 16-20; Winter 1966, 52-54.

PbY 703   Hill, Kay. <u>Glooscap and His Magic: Legends of the Wabanaki Indians</u>. Toronto: McClelland & Stewart, 1963. 181 pp.

PbY 704   -- <u>More Glooscap Stories</u>. Toronto: McClelland & Stewart, 1970. 178 pp.

B   705   Hill-Tout, Charles. 'Report on the Ethnology of the Southeastern Tribes of Vancouver Island, British Columbia.' <u>Journal of the Royal Anthropological Institute</u>, 37(1907), 306-74.

P   706   Hindley, John I. <u>Indian Legends: Nanabush, the Ojibeway Saviour; Moosh-kuh-ung, or the Flood</u>. Barrie, Ont.: Author, 1898. 22 pp.

B   707   Hines, Donald M., ed. <u>Tales of the Okanogans</u>. Coll. by Mourning Dove. Fairfield, WA: Le Galleon Press, 1976. 182 pp.

C(r) 708   Hines, J. 'Creation of Young Dogs Tribe.' <u>Beaver</u>, Dec. 1925, pp. 26-27.

B   709   Hoffman, Walter. 'Notes on Ojibwa Folk-lore.' <u>American Anthropologist</u>, 2(1889), 215-23.

B   710   Honigmann, John J. 'European and Other Tales from the Western Woods Cree.' <u>JAF</u>, 66(1953), 309-31.

PY 711 Houston, James A. Akavak: An Eskimo Journey. Don Mills, Ont.: Longmans, 1968. 80 pp.

PY 712 -- Eagle Mask: A West Coast Indian Tale. Don Mills: Longmans, 1966. 63 pp.

PY 713 -- Ghost Paddle: A Northwest Coast Indian Tale. Don Mills: Longman, 1972. 65 pp.

PY 714 -- Kiviok's Magic Journey: An Eskimo Legend. Don Mills: Longman, 1973. 40 pp.

PY 715 -- Tikta'liktak: An Eskimo Legend. Toronto: Longmans, 1965. 63 pp.

PY 716 -- The White Archer: An Eskimo Legend. Don Mills: Longmans, 1967. 95 pp.

G 717 Hungry Wolf, Adolf. Blackfoot People. A Tribal Hand-book. Fort Macleod, Alta.: Good Medicine Books, 1975. 60 pp.

B(r) 718 Hungry Wolf, Adolf, ed. Legends Told by the Old People. Fort Macleod: Good Medicine Books, 1972. 61 pp.

B 719 Hunt, George, coll. 'Myths of the Nootka.' Appendix I in Franz Boas, 'Tsimshian Mythology.' 31st Annual Report of the Bureau of American Ethnology, Washington, 1916, pp. 888-935.

C(r) 720 Hunter, Marten. 'The Legends of Ne-Na-Bo-Jo.' Beaver, June 1922, pp. 11-14; July 1922, pp. 12-13.

FA 721 Ives, Edward D., ed. 'Malecite and Passamaquoddy Tales.' Northeast Folklore, 6(1964), 1-81.

B 722 Jack, Edward. 'Maliseet Legends.' JAF, 8(1895), 193-208.

B(r)Y 723 Jenness, Diamond. The Corn Goddess. Ottawa: National Museum, Bulletin 141, 1956. 111 pp.

A 724 -- 'Myths and Traditions from Alaska, the Mackenzie Delta and Coronation Gulf.' Eskimo Folk-Lore. Report of the Canadian Arctic Expedition, 1913-1918. Vol. 13, part A. Ottawa: King's Printer, 1924. 90 pp.

A 725 -- 'Myths of the Carrier Indians of British Columbia.' JAF, 47(1934), 97-257.

B(1) 726 Johnson, E. Pauline. Legends of Vancouver. 1911; rpt. Toronto: McClelland & Stewart, 1961. 176 pp.

BY 727 Johnston, Basil. How the Birds Got Their Colours. Toronto: Kids Can Press, 1978. [28 pp.]

Ga 728 Johnston, Basil. Ojibway Heritage. Toronto: McClelland & Stewart, 1976. 171 pp.

BY 729 Johnston, Patronella. Tales Of Nokomis. Don Mills, Ont.: Musson, 1975. 65 pp.

C(r) 730 Johnston, W. P. 'Chief Kwah's Revenge.' Beaver, Sept. 1943, pp. 22-23.

F 731 Jones, Hettie. Longhouse Winter, Iroquois Transformation Tales. New York: Holt, Rinehart & Winston, 1972. 41 pp.

B 732 Jones, William. 'Ojibwa Tales from the North Shore of Lake Superior.' JAF, 29(1916), 368-91.

A 733 -- Ojibwa Texts. Ed. Truman Michelson. 2 vols. Leyden, Netherlands: Brill, 1917-19.

B(r)Y 734 Kalluak, Mark, ed. and illus. How Kabloonat Became and Other Innuit Legends. Yellowknife: Dept. of Education, N.W.T., 1974. 141 pp.

BY 735 Kappi, Leoni. Inuit Legends. Yellowknife: Dept. of Education, N.W.T., 1977. 113 pp.

B 736 Kehoe, Alice B. 'Ghost Dance Legends in Saskatchewan.' Plains Anthropologist, Nov. 1968, pp. 293-304.

C(r) 737 Koon, Leir. 'The Hunter and the Giant.' Beaver, Spring 1962, pp. 16-19.

C 738 Kroeber, Alfred L. 'Animal Tales of the Eskimo.' JAF, 12(1899), 17-23.

B 739 -- 'Tales of the Smith Sound Eskimo.' JAF, 12 (1899), 166-82.

A 740 Laidlaw, George E. Ojibwa Myths and Tales. Series of articles in the Annual Archaeological Reports, Ontario, Nos. 26-30, 1914-1918.

Gc 741 Land, Peter M. 'Lake Medad and Its Legends.' Wentworth Historical Society, Papers and Records, 11(1924), 37-39.

GP 742 Lane, M. E., M. G. Steer, and M. C. Wright. Land of Shining Mountains: British Columbia in Legend and Story. Toronto: Dent, 1957. 354 pp.

Gb 743 Leechman, Douglas. Indian Summer. Toronto: Ryerson, 1949. 182 pp.

C 744 -- 'Loucheux Tales.' JAF, 63(1950), 158-62.

B 745 Leeson, B. W. 'A Quatsino Legend.' CGJ, 7(July 1933), 23-40.

P 746 'Legend of the Great Lorette Serpent.' Quebec, 2(Dec. 1927), 3-4.

BY 747 Lerman, Norman, comp. Legends of the River People. Ed. Betty Keller. Vancouver: November House, 1976. 128 pp. [Chilliwack Indians.]

PY 748 Limbrick, H. M. ("Wendigo"). Tales of the Tom-Tom from the Land of the Sleeping Giant. Fort William, Ont.: n.p., n.d. 16 pp.

C 749 Lofthouse, J. 'Chipewyan Stories.' Trans. Royal Canadian Institute, 10(1913), 43-51.

B 750 Lowie, R. H. 'Chipewyan Tales.' Anthropological Papers American Museum of Natural History, 10(1912), 171-200.

B 751 McClellan, Catharine. The Girl Who Married the Bear. Ottawa: National Museum, Ethnology Paper 2, 1970. 58 pp.

P 752 McKelvie, B. A. Legends of Stanley Park: Vancouver's Magnificent Playground. Pamp., n.p., n.d.

C 753 McLean, John. 'Blackfoot Indian Legends.' JAF, 3(1890), 296-98.

C 754 -- 'Blackfoot Mythology.' JAF, 4(1891), 165-72.

PY 755 Macmillan, Cyrus. Glooskap's Country and Other Indian Tales. Toronto: Oxford, 1956. 273 pp.

B(r)Y 756 Mason, Patricia F. Indian Tales of the Northwest. Vancouver: CommCept, 1976. 102 pp.

C 757 Masta, Henry L. Abenaki Indian Legends, Grammar, and Place Names. Victoriaville, P.Q.: La Voix des Bois Francs, 1932. 110 pp.

A 758 Mechling, William H. Malecite Tales. Ottawa: National Museum, Memoir 49, 1914. 133 pp.

A 759 -- 'Maliseet Tales.' JAF, 26(1913), 219-58.

A(r) 760 Melançon, Claude. Indian Legends of Canada. Trans. David Ellis. Toronto: Gage, 1974. 163 pp.

PaY 761 Melzack, Ronald. The Day Tuk Became a Hunter. Toronto: McClelland & Stewart, 1967. 92 pp.

PaY 762 -- Raven, Creator of the World. Toronto: McClelland & Stewart, 1970. 91 pp.

PbY 763 -- Why the Man in the Moon Is Happy and Other Eskimo Creation Stories. Toronto: McClelland & Stewart, 1977. 61 pp.

Folktales

B(r)Y 764 Metayer, Maurice. <u>Tales from the Igloo</u>. Edmonton: Hurtig, 1972. 127 pp.

B 765 Michelson, Truman. 'Micmac Tales.' <u>JAF</u>, 38(1925), 33-54.

C 766 -- 'Ojibwa Tales.' <u>JAF</u>, 24(1911), 249-50.

F 767 Morgan, John S. <u>When the Morning Stars Sang Together</u>. Agincourt, Ont.: Book Society of Canada, 1974. 201 pp.

C 768 Morice, Adrien G. 'Are the Carrier Sociology and Mythology Indigenous or Exotic?' <u>TRSC</u>, 10(1892), sec. 2, 109-126.

B 769 -- 'Three Carrier Myths.' <u>Trans. Royal Canadian Institute</u>, 5(1895), 1-36.

B 770 Morriseau, Norval. <u>Legends of My People: The Great Ojibway</u>. Toronto: Ryerson, 1965; pb. McGraw-Hill Ryerson, 1977. 130 pp.

PY 771 Morrison, Dorothy. <u>Tales the Eskimos Tell</u>. Regina: School Aids, 1944. 60 pp.

FP 772 Munn, Henry T. <u>Tales of the Eskimos</u>. Philadelphia: Lippincott, 1925. 196 pp.

P 773 Netro, Joe. <u>A Book of Indian Legends and Storys</u> (sic) <u>from Old Crow, Yukon Territory</u>. Whitehorse, Y.T.: Whitehorse Star, 1973. 28 pp.

C 774 Nowlan, Alden. 'The Captive: An Authentic Micmac Legend.' <u>Atlantic Advocate</u>, 57 (Aug. 1967), 54-55.

C 775 -- 'The Chief Who Refused to Die: An Authentic Micmac Legend.' <u>Atlantic Advocate</u>, 59:(Jan. 1969), 36-37.

C 776 -- 'The Invisible Boy: An Authentic Micmac Legend.' <u>Atlantic Advocate</u>, 57(Apr. 1967), 56-57.

C 777 -- 'The Man Who Wanted to Live Forever.' <u>Atlantic Advocate</u>, 57(Jan. 1967), 46-47.

C 778 -- 'The Snow Vampire: An Authentic Micmac Legend.' <u>Atlantic Advocate</u>, 57(Feb. 1967), 52-53.

A 779 Nungak, Zebedee, and Eugene Arima. <u>Eskimo Stories-Unikkaatuat</u>. Ottawa: National Museum, Bulletin 235, 1969. 139 pp.

C(r) 780 Ogden, Peter S. 'The Tale of Red Feather.' <u>Beaver</u>, Dec. 1951, pp. 10-13.

A 781 Parsons, Elsie Clews. 'Micmac Folklore.' <u>JAF</u>, 38(1925), 55-133.

PY 782 Partridge, Emelyn N. Glooscap the Great Chief. New
York: Sturgis & Walton, 1913. 293 pp.

C(r) 783 Patience, J. R. 'Why the Loon Walks Crooked.' Beaver,
June 1937, p. 4.

Gb 784 Piggott, Glyne, and Jonathan Kaye, eds. Odawa Language
Project, Second Report. Toronto: Centre for Linguistic
Studies, Univ. of Toronto, 1973. 399 leaves.

A 785 Preston, Richard J. Cree Narrative: Expressing the
Personal Meaning of Events. Ottawa: National Museum,
Ethnology Service Mercury Series 30, 1976. 316 pp.

B 786 Prince, J. Dyneley, ed. 'A Micmac Manuscript.' Proc. of
the 15th International Congress of Americanists, 1907,
pp. 87-124.

C 787 Quill, Norman. The Moons of Winter and Other Stories.
Ed. Charles Fiero. Red Lake, Ont.: NLGM, 1965. 47 pp.

Pc 788 A Quill from a Canada Wild Goose, with the Cree Legend
of Nih-Ka. Winnipeg: Manitoba Free Press, 1904. 16 pp.

FA 789 Radin, Paul. Literary Aspects of North American Mythology. Ottawa: National Museum, Bulletin 16, 1915; rpt.
Norwood, PA: Norwood, 1974. 51 pp.

A 790 -- Some Myths and Tales of the Ojibwa of Southwestern
Ontario. Ottawa: National Museum, Memoir 48, 1914.
83 pp.

FA 791 -- The Trickster: A Study in American Indian Mythology. 1956; rpt. New York: Greenwood, 1969. 211 pp.

A 792 Radin, Paul, and Albert B. Reagan. 'Ojibwa Myths and
Tales.' JAF, 41(1928), 61-146.

A 793 Rand, Silas T. Legends of the Micmacs. 1894; rpt. New
York: Johnson, 1971. 452 pp.

C 794 -- 'The Legends of the Micmacs.' American Antiquity,
12(1890), 3-14.

A 795 Rasmussen, Knud, and W. W. Worster. Eskimo Folk-Tales.
London: Gyldendal, 1921. 156 pp.

B 796 Reagan, Albert B. 'Some Myths of the Hoh and Quillayute
Indians.' Trans. Kansas Academy of Science, 38(1935),
43-85.

B 797 Reagan, Albert B., and L. V. M. Walters. 'Tales from
the Hoh and Quileute,' JAF, 46(1933), 297-347.

B(r) 798 Redsky, James. Great Leader of the Ojibway: Mis-Quono-
Quab. Ed. James R. Stevens. Toronto: McClelland &
Stewart, 1972. 127 pp.

Folktales

PbY 799 Reid, Dorothy M. Tales of Nanabozho. Toronto: Oxford, 1963; pb., 1979. 128 pp.

B 800 Rink, Signe. 'A Comparative Study of the Indian and Eskimo Legends.' Proc. of the 13th International Congress of Americanists, 1902, pp. 279-305.

B 801 Robertson, Marion. Red Earth: Tales of the Micmacs. Halifax: N.S. Museum, 1969. 98 pp.

PcY 802 Robinson, Gail, and Douglas Hill. Coyote the Trickster: Legends of the North American Indians. Toronto: Clarke, Irwin, 1975, 124 pp.

B(r) 803 Robinson, Michael P. Sea Otter Chiefs. N.p.: Friendly Cove, c. 1978. 90 pp. [Northwest Coast.]

C(r) 804 Robinson, William G. Tales of Kitamaat. 3rd ed. Kitimat, B.C.: Northern Sentinel, 1956. 46 pp. [Haisla folktales.]

C(r) 805 Rordam, Vita. 'Woman Who Spoke to a Dog.' Beaver, Winter 1967, p. 54.

P 806 Ross, S. J. 'Stories of the Northwest Coast.' Vancouver Public Aquarium Newsletter, 19(Nov.-Dec. 1975). 10 pp.

C 807 Russell, Frank. 'Athapascan Myths.' JAF, 13(1900), 11-18.

Pb 808 Sanderson, James F. 'Indian Tales of the Canadian Prairies.' Alberta Historical Review, 13(Summer 1965), 7-21.

C 809 Sapir, Edward A. 'A Flood Legend of the Nootka Indians of Vancouver Island.' JAF, 32(1919), 351-55.

B 810 -- 'Indian Legends from Vancouver Island.' JAF, 72 (1959), 106-14.

B 811 -- 'The Rival Whalers, A Nitinat Story.' International Journal of American Linguistics, 3(1929), 76-102.

A 812 Sapir, Edward, and Morris Swadesh. Nootka Texts. Philadelphia: Univ. of Pennsylvania, 1939. 334 pp.

C 813 Schaeffer, Claude. 'The Bear Foster Parent Tale: A Kutenai Version.' JAF, 60(1947), 286-88.

FB(r) 814 Schoolcraft, Henry R. Algic Researches, Comprising Inquiries Respecting the Mental Characteristics of the North American Indians. 2 vols. New York: Harper, 1839.

FB(r) 815 -- Indian Legends. Ed. Mentor H. Williams. East Lansing: Michigan State Univ. Press, 1956. 322 pp.

FB(r) 816 Schoolcraft, Henry R. The Myth of Hiawatha and Other Oral Legends, Mythologic and Allegoric, of the North American Indians. Philadelphia: Lippincott, 1856. 343 pp. [Later edition of Algic Researches.]

B(r)Y 817 Schwartz, Herbert T. Elik and Other Stories of the Mackenzie Eskimos. Toronto: McClelland & Stewart, 1970. 79 pp.

B(r)Y 818 -- Windigo and Other Tales of the Ojibways. Toronto: McClelland & Stewart, 1969. 40 pp.

B(r) 819 -- Tales from the Smokehouse. Edmonton: Hurtig, 1974. 104 pp.

B 820 Scollon, Ronald. The Context of the Informant Narrative Performance: From Sociolinguistics to Ethnolinguistics at Fort Chipewyan, Alberta. Ottawa: National Museum, Ethnology Service Mercury Series 52, 1979. 80 pp.

B 821 Sidney, Angela, et al. As Told to Julie Cruikshank. My Stories Are My Wealth. Whitehorse: Council for Yukon Indians, 1977. 117 pp.

C 822 Simms, Stephen C. 'Myths of the Bungees or Swampy Indians of Lake Winnipeg.' JAF, 19(1906), 334-40.

C 823 Skinner, Alanson. 'European Tales from the Plains Ojibwa.' JAF, 29(1916), 330-40.

B 824 -- 'Plains Cree Tales.' JAF, 29(1916), 341-67.

B 825 -- 'Plains Ojibwa Tales.' JAF, 32(1919), 280-305.

BY 826 Small, Lillian, comp. Indian Stories from James Bay. Cobalt: Highway Book Shop, 1972. 22 pp.

F 827 Smith, Marion W. Algonquian and Abenaki Indian Myths and Legends. Lewiston, ME: Central Maine, 1962. 40 pp.

BY 828 Snake, Sam, et al. The Adventures of Nanabush. Toronto: Doubleday, 1979. 84 pp.

B 829 Spalding, Alex, transcriber and translator. Eight Inuit Myths/Inuit Unipkaaqtuat Pingasuniarvinilit. Ottawa: National Museum, Ethnology Service Mercury Series 59, 1979. 102 pp.

B 830 Speck, Frank G. The Celestial Bear Comes Down to Earth; The Bear Sacrifice Ceremony of the Munsee-Mahigan in Canada as related by Nekatcit. Reading, PA: Reading Public Museum & Art Gallery, 1945. 91 pp.

Folktales

C   831   Speck, Frank G. 'Malecite Tales.' JAF, 30(1917), 479-85.

C   832   -- 'Mammoth or "Stiff-Legged Bear."' American Anthropologist, 37(1935), 159-63.

A   833   -- Myths and Folk-Lore of the Timiskaming, Algonquin, and Timagami Ojibwa. Ottawa: National Museum, Memoir 71, 1915. 87 pp.

A   834   -- 'Montagnais and Naskapi Tales from the Labrador Penninsula.' JAF, 38(1925), 1-32.

B   835   -- 'Some Micmac Tales from Cape Breton Island.' JAF, 28(1915), 59-69.

C   836   -- 'Some Naskapi Myths from Little Whale River.' JAF, 28(1915), 70-77.

C   837   Stamp, Harley. 'Adventures of Bukschinskewesk: A Malecite Tale.' JAF, 28(1915), 243-48.

C   838   -- 'The Water-Fairies.' JAF, 28(1915), 310-16.

GP   839   Stephen, Pamela. Winged Canoes at Nootka and other Stories of the Evergreen Coast. Toronto: Dent, 1955. 227 pp.

A(r)   840   Stevens, James R. Sacred Legends of the Sandy Lake Cree. Toronto: McClelland & Stewart, 1971. 144 pp.

A   841   Stories from Pangnirtung. Edmonton: Hurtig, 1976. 100 pp.

C   842   Swadesh, Morris, and Mary H. Swadesh. 'Nitinat Texts.' International Journal of American Linguistics, 7(1933), 195-208.

A   843   Swanton, John R. Haida Texts and Myths, Skidegate Dialect. Washington: Bureau of American Ethnology, Bulletin 29, 1905. 448 pp.

A   844   -- Haida Texts--Masset Dialect. New York: American Museum of Natural History, Memoir 14, pt. 2, 1908. 812 pp.

FA   845   -- Tlingit Myths and Texts. Washington: Bureau of American Ethnology, Bulletin 39, 1909. 451 pp.

B   846   -- 'Tlingit Myths and Texts.' International Journal of Linguistics, 10(1944), 168-80.

B   847   -- 'Types of Haida and Tlingit Myths.' American Anthropologist, 7(1905), 94-103.

BY   848   Tales from the Longhouse. By Indian Children of British Columbia. Sidney: Gray's, 1973. 112 pp.

C(r) 849   Taylor, Phyllis. 'Tales from the Delta.' Beaver, June 1953, p. 22.

B 850   Teit, James A. 'European Tales from the Upper Thompson Indians.' JAF, 29(1916), 301-30.

B 851   -- 'Kaska Tales.' JAF, 30(1917), 427-73.

A 852   -- The Mythology of the Thompson Indians. New York: American Museum of Natural History, Memoir 12, 1912, pp. 199-416.

A 853   -- 'Tahltan Tales.' JAF, 32(1919), 198-250; 34(1921), 223-53, 335-56.

C 854   -- 'Two Plains Cree Tales.' JAF, 34(1921), 320-21.

B 855   Teit, James, and Lucy Kramer. 'More Thompson Indian Tales.' JAF, 50(1937), 173-91.

FA 856   Thompson, Stith. European Tales among the North American Indians. Colorado Springs: Colorado College, 1919. 152 pp.

FA 857   -- The Folktale. New York: Holt, Rinehart & Winston, 1946. Pp. 297-363.

FA 858   -- Tales of the North American Indians. Bloomington: Indiana Univ. Press, 1929: rpt. 1968. 386 pp.

CY 859   Tora. Haida Legends. Vancouver: Intermedia, 1976. [26 pp.]

C 860   Velten, H. V. 'Three Tlingit Stories.' International Journal of American Linguistics, 10(1944), 168-80.

C 861   -- 'Two Southern Tlingit Tales.' International Journal of American Linguistics, 10(1939), 65-74.

A 862   Voudrach, Paul. Good Hope Tales. Ottawa: National Museum, Bulletin 204, 1967, pp. 29-86.

A 863   Wallis, Wilson D. 'Beliefs and Tales of the Canadian Dakotas.' JAF, 36(1923), 36-101.

A 864   Wallis, Wilson D., and Ruth S. Wallis. 'Folktales and Traditions.' The Micmac Indians of Eastern Canada. Minneapolis: Univ. of Minnesota Press, 1955. Pp. 317-493.

FB 865   Wardle, H. Newell. 'The Sedna Cycle: A Study in Myth Evolution.' American Anthropologist, 2(1900), 568-80.

PY 866   Weatherby, Hugh W. Tales the Totems Tell. Toronto: Macmillan, 1944. 96 pp.

Folktales

P 867 Webster, Helen L., ed. Legends of the Micmacs. New
       York: Longmans, Green, 1894. 449 pp.

C 868 Wells, Oliver N. Myths and Legends of the Staw-loh
       Indians of South Western British Columbia. Sardis, B.C.:
       Author, 1970. 42 pp.

C 869 -- As told by Chief August Jack Khatsahlano and
       Domanic Charlie. Squamish Legends. N.p.: Author, 1966.
       32 pp.

BY 870 Wilson, Marie, ed. We-Gyet Wanders On: Fables of the
       Northwest. Saanichton: Hancock, 1977. 80 pp.

C 871 'The Woman Who Wouldn't Marry.' Inuit Today, 5(Apr.
       1976), 40-44.

P 872 Young, Egerton R. Algonquin Indian Tales. New York:
       Eaton & Mains, 1903. 258 pp.

       4E Other Cultural Groups

PcY 873 Bannerji, Himani. The Two Sisters. Toronto: Kids Can,
        1978. 24 pp. [Bengali-Canadian.]

PcY 874 Bertelli, Mariella. The Shirt of the Happy Man. Toronto:
        Kids Can, 1977. 32 pp. [Italian-Canadian.]

C 875 Brednich, Rolf W. 'Appendix: Jokes Recorded in the
       Saskatchewan Valley.' Mennonite Folklife and Folklore:
       A Preliminary Report. Ottawa: National Museum, CCFCS
       Mercury Series 22, 1977. Pp. 85-90.

C 876 Brock, Peter. 'Vasya Pozdnyakov's Dukhobor Narrative.'
       Slavic and East European Review, 43(Dec. 1964-Jan.
       1965), 156-74.

PcY 877 Chandon, Odarka. Kyrylo the Tanner. Toronto: Kids Can,
        1977. 26 pp. [Ukrainian-Canadian.]

PcY 878 Cox, Rita. How Trouble Made the Monkey Eat Pepper.
        Toronto: Kids Can, 1977. 28 pp. [West-Indian Canadian.]

A 879 Dorson, Richard, ed. Folktales Told around the World.
       Chicago: Univ. of Chicago Press, 1975. Pp. 468-77.
       [Jewish.]

B 880 Einarsson, Magnús. 'Oral Tradition and Cultural Bound-
       aries: West Icelandic Verses and Anecdotes.' Canadian
       Ethnic Studies, 7:2(1975), 19-32.

B 881 Fauset, Arthur Huff. 'Folklore from the Half-Breeds in Nova Scotia.' JAF, 38(1925), 300-15.

A 882 Hoe, Ban Seng. 'Folktales and Social Structure: The Case of the Chinese in Montreal.' Canadian Folklore Canadien, 1(1979), 25-37.

GP 883 Janzen, Jacob. Tales from the Mennonite History. Waterloo, Ont.: Author, 1945. 96 pp.

A 884 Kirshenblatt-Gimblett, Barbara. 'Culture Shock and Narrative Creativity.' In Folklore in the Modern World. Ed. Richard M. Dorson. The Hague: Mouton, 1976.

A 885 -- 'A Parable in Context: A Social Interactional Analysis of a Storytelling Performance.' In Folklore: Performance and Communication. Eds. Kenneth Goldstein and Dan Ben-Amos. The Hague: Mouton, 1975. Pp. 105-30.

B 886 Klymasz, Robert B. 'The Ethnic Joke in Canada Today.' Keystone Folklore Quarterly, 15(1970), 167-73.

A 887 -- Folk Narrative among Ukrainian-Canadians in Western Canada. Ottawa: National Museum, CCFCS Mercury Series 4, 1973. 133 pp.

PY 888 Kovalik, Tibor. From Tale to Tale: Fairy Tales of Canadian Ethnic Communities. Oakville, Ont.: Mosaic, 1979. 55 pp.

Gc 889 Lee, Ronald. 'The Gypsies in Canada, III.' Journal of the Gypsy Lore Society, 48 (1969), 92-107.

PcY 890 Ling, Frieda, and Mee-Shaun Lau. The Maiden of We Long and The Axe and The Sword. Toronto: Kids Can, 1978. 25 pp. [Chinese-Canadian.]

PcY 891 McDougall, Marina Mezey. The Little Rooster's Diamond Penny. Toronto: Kids Can, 1978. 38 pp. [Hungarian-Canadian.]

PcY 892 Mascayano, Ismael. The Daughter of the Sun. Toronto: Kids Can, 1978. 24 pp. [Peruvian-Canadian.]

GP 893 'Norwegians in Canada.' Citizen, 13 (Oct. 1967), 12-22. [Anecdotes.]

G 894 Pawliw, Orest. 'Studies in Ukrainian Literature in Canada.' Slavs in Canada, 2(1968), 235-46.

G 895 Popoff, Eli. Tanya. Grand Forks, B.C.: Mir, 1975. 276 pp. [Doukhobors.]

Folktales

C 896 Rubin, Ruth. 'Yiddish Tales for Children.' In Folklore of Canada. Ed. Edith Fowke. Toronto: McClelland & Stewart, 1976. Pp. 291-94.

B 897 Rudnyc'kyj, Jaroslav B. Readings in Canadian Slavic Folklore. 2 vols. Winnipeg: Univ. of Manitoba, 1961.

B 898 Salo, Matt T., and Sheila M. G. Salo. 'Memorates and belief stories.' Appendix, The Kalderas in Eastern Canada. Ottawa: National Museum, CCFCS Mercury Series 21, 1977. Pp. 223-53.

B 899 Stone, Kay. 'I Won't Tell These Stories to My Kids.' Canadian Ethnic Studies, 7:2(1975), 33-41.

C 900 Troup, W. Edwin. 'Tales of the Twenty.' Canadian-German Folklore, 1(1961), 105-9.

CY 901 Ukrainian Canadian Committee. Women's Council, comp. The Flying Ship and Other Ukrainian Folk Tales. Trans. Victoria Symchych and Olga Vesey. Toronto: Holt, Rinehart & Winston, 1975. 93 pp.

C 902 Wintemberg, W. J. 'Alsatian Witch Stories.' JAF, 20 (1907), 213-15.

C 903 -- 'German Folk-Tales Collected in Canada.' JAF, 19 (1906), 241-44.

For 4A see also items 1, 12, 91, 179, 182, 236, 250, 276, 299-301, 321, 329, 332, 1763, 1768, 1770, 1772-1776, 1778, 1779, 1781, 1785, 1787, 1789, 1790, 1794, 1795, 1800, 1801, 3787, and 3834.

For 4B, 143, 292, 307, 322, 324, 1810, 1836, 1839, 1840, 1855, 1859, 2182, 3762, 3846, 3849, and 3853.

For 4C, 27, 234, 325, 1871, 3855, and 3875.

For 4D, 37, 228, 233, 238, 240, 264, 269, 278, 281, 283, 286, 293, 294, 304, 305, 316, 323, 1890, 1911, 1930, 1933, 1937, 1938, 3161, 3265, 3755, 3759, 3760, 3769, 3774, 3776, 3785, 3790, 3801, 3802, 3805, 3807, 3820, 3822, 3824, 3828, 3833, 3836, 3844, 3851, 3865, 3873, and 3876.

For 4E, 27, 314, 334, and 3799.

5 Folk Music and Dance

5A   General

G   904   Amtmann, Willy. Music in Canada 1600-1800. Montreal: Habitex, 1975. 320 pp.

C   905   Archer, Violet. 'Alberta and Its Folksongs.' CFMSN, 2 (1967), 45-55.

FR 906   Baggelaar, Kristin, and Donald Milton. Folk Music: More Than a Song. New York: Crowell, 1976. 419 pp. [Accounts of traditional and contemporary folk singers arranged alphabetically.]

C   907   Barbeau, C. Marius. 'Canadian Folk Songs.' University of Toronto Quarterly, 16(1947), 183-87.

C   908   -- 'Canadian Folk Songs.' JIFMC, 13(1961), 28-31.

C   909   -- 'Canadian Folk Songs. A Message of Greeting from Marius Barbeau.' Journal of the English Folk Dance and Song Society, 8(1952), 125.

C   910   -- 'Canadian Folk Songs as a National Asset.' Canadian Nation, Feb. 1928, pp. 18-22; Quebec, 3(Oct. 1928), 2-4.

C   911   -- 'The Folk Dances of Canada.' JIFMC, 3(1951), 29.

C   912   -- 'Folk Music: Canadian.' In Grove's Dictionary of Music and Musicians. Vol. III. Ed. Eric Blom. London: Macmillan, 1954. Pp. 211-14.

B   913   -- 'Folk Song.' In Music in Canada. Ed. Ernest MacMillan. Toronto: Univ. of Toronto Press, 1955. Pp. 32-54.

C   914   -- 'French and Indian Motifs in Our Music.' In Yearbook of the Arts in Canada, 1928-1929. Toronto: Macmillan, 1929. Pp. 125-32.

B   915   -- 'How Folk-Songs Travelled.' Music and Letters, 15 (1934), 306-23.

C   916   Barbeau, C. Marius. 'Some Reflections on Authenticity in Folk Music.' JIFMC, 3(1951), 15.

C   917   -- 'Why I Publish Folk Songs.' Canadian Author and Bookman, 37(Spring 1962), 8.

Pb 918   Barbeau C. Marius, et al. Come A-Singing! Canadian Folk Songs. Ottawa: National Museum, Bulletin 107, 1947; rpt. 1973. 59 pp.

C   919   Barbeau, C. Marius, and Helen Creighton. 'The Rediscovery of Folk Music.' CGJ, 84(Mar. 1972), 82-91.

P   920   Barkham, Peter. 'An Introduction to Canadian Folk Song Collections.' Come All Ye, 3(Aug. 1974), 9-11; 3(Sept. 1974), 9-11.

G   921   Blakeley, Phyllis. 'Music in Nova Scotia, 1605-1867.' Dalhousie Review, 31(1951), 94-101, 223-30.

G   922   Boulton, Harold. 'Folk Songs and Patriotism.' Quebec, 3(Jan. 1929), 2-5. Lecture given to the Empire Club, 1928.

P   923   Brannon, J. C. 'Does the Nation Sing?' Sing and String (Toronto), 5(Winter 1962-3), 17-21.

P   924   Brébeuf, Jean de. Jesous Ahatonhia, Huron Indian Carol (c. 1641). English interpretation by J. E. Middleton. Toronto: Rous & Mann, 1927. 18 pp.

P   925   Brown, Eileen. 'Folk Singers and Their Collectors.' Come All Ye, 4(1975), 108-17.

P   926   'Canada's First Christmas Carol.' Forward with Canada, 1948, pp. 11-12.

B   927   Carlisle, Roxane C. 'The Current Ethnomusicology Curriculum in Canadian Universities.' Ethnomusicology, 16 (1972), 488-98.

C   928   -- 'Ethnomusicology in a Multicultural Society.' Western Canadian Journal of Anthropology, 4(1974), 97-109.

C   929   -- Folk Music in Canada, 1974. Ottawa: National Museum, 1974. 7 pp. Mimeo.

BY 930   Cass-Beggs, Barbara. Canadian Folk Songs for the Young. Vancouver: Douglas, 1975. 48 pp.

P   931   -- 'Canadian Songs in Canadian Class Rooms.' B.C. Music Educator, 19(Winter 1976), 12-14.

B   932   -- Eight Songs of Saskatchewan. Toronto: Canadian Music Sales, 1963. 15 pp.

P   933   Cass-Beggs, Barbara. 'Folksong Collecting in Saskatchewan.' Sing and String (Toronto), 3(Winter 1964), 8-10.

C   934   -- 'Saskatchewan and Its Folksongs.' CFMSN, 2(July
1967), 41-42.

C   935   Cass-Beggs, Barbara, and Michael Cass-Beggs. Folk
Lullabies. New York: Oak, 1969. Pp. 11-18.

P   936   Colley, Louise. 'Folk Dancing Is for Everyone.' Food
for Thought, 10(Dec. 1949), 3-11.

B   937   Creighton, Helen. 'Canada's Maritime Provinces--An
Ethnomusicological Survey (Personal Observations and
Recollections).' Ethnomusicology, 16(1972), 404-14.

C   938   -- 'Collecting Folk Songs.' Music Across Canada, Apr.
1963, pp. 8-10.

C   939   -- 'Looking back on a satisfying career.' Canadian
Composer, Apr. 1977, pp. 24-25, 29. [Interview.]

CY   940   Creighton, Helen, and Eunice Sircom. Eight Ethnic Folk
Songs for Young Children. Toronto: Gordon V. Thompson,
1977. 20 pp.

CY   941   -- and -- Nine Ethnic Folk Songs for S.S.A.B. Toronto:
Gordon V. Thompson, 1977. 50 pp.

G(s)P   942   Davis, Brian, ed. The Poetry of the Canadian People,
1720-1920: Two Hundred Years of Hard Work. Toronto: NC
Press, 1977. 288 pp.

P   943   Davis, E. N. 'Recordings Treasure of Prairie Province.'
Globe & Mail (Toronto), 7 Sept. 1957, p. 7.

P   944   De Jarlis, Andy. Canadian Fiddle Tunes from the Red
River Valley. 2 vols. Toronto: BMI Canada, 1958.

P   945   Dilschneider, Donna. 'Rich store of lore uncovered';
'Grass roots music unveils colorful tales.' Leader-
Post (Regina), 24, 26 Aug. 1957.

C   946   Duncan, Chester. 'Folk Song as History.' Canadian
Literature, No. 8 (Spring 1961), pp. 51-53.

FB   947   Fife, Austin E., and Francesca Redden. 'The Pseudo-
Indian Folk Songs of the Anglo-American and the French-
Canadian.' JAF, 67(1954), 239-53; 379-94.

P   948   'The Folk Binge.' Time (Can. ed.), 30 Aug. 1963, p. 10.

P   949   Folk Songs of Canada. Recital by Juliette Gaultier de
la Verendrye. Ottawa: 1927. 8 pp.

C 950 Fowke, Edith. 'Canadian Folk Song Records.' Food For
Thought, Nov. 1957, pp. 57-61.

C 951 -- 'Canadian Folk Songs.' Canadian Forum, 29(1949),
177-79; 201-2.

C 952 -- 'Canadian Folk Songs for Children.' In Review,
Winter 1970, pp. 5-11.

B 953 -- 'Folk Music in Canada.' Canada Music Book, Spring/
Summer 1975, pp. 53-57.

C 954 -- 'The Folksongs of Canada.' Sing Out! 7(Summer 1975)
19-27.

C 955 -- 'A Guide to Canadian Folksong Records.' Canadian
Forum, 37(1957), 131-33.

A 956 -- The Penguin Book of Canadian Folk Songs. Harmonds-
worth, U.K.: Penguin, 1973. 224 pp.

G(s)Y 957 Fowke, Edith, ed. Canadian Vibrations Canadiennes.
Toronto: Macmillan, 1972. 154 pp.

Pa 958 Fowke, Edith, and Richard Johnston. Folk Songs of
Canada. Waterloo, Ont.: Waterloo Music, 1954. 198 pp.

Pa 959 -- and -- More Folk Songs of Canada. Waterloo: Waterloo Music, 1967; rpt. as Folk Songs of Canada, II,
1978. 207 pp.

PaY 960 Fowke, Edith, and Alan Mills. Canada's Story in Song.
Toronto: Gage, [1960]. 230 pp.

B 961 Frye, Northrop. 'Turning New Leaves.' Canadian Forum,
13(1954), 89, 91. Rpt. The Bush Garden: Essays on the
Canadian Imagination. Toronto: Anansi, 1971. Pp. 157-62.

P 962 Fulford, Robert. 'And May Each Rebel Swing.' Toronto
Daily Star, 6 Sept. 1960, p. 20.

C 963 George, Graham. 'Folk-Singing or Just Folks.' Saturday
Night, 30 Sept. 1961, pp. 33-35.

C 964 -- 'Music Where the Wind Blows Free.' Canadian Music
Journal, 6(Spring 1962), 12-18.

C 965 -- 'Seven Canadian Folk-Music Records.' Canadian Music
Journal, 1(1957), 47-51.

P 966 Gesser, Sam. 'The Mariposa Folk Festival.' Sing Out! 11
(Dec.-Jan. 1961-62), 48-49.

C 967 Gibbon, John Murray. 'Folk-song and Feudalism.' TRSC,
42(1948), sec. 2, pp. 73-84.

C 968 Gibbon, John Murray. 'The Music of the People.' Empire Club of Canada, Addresses ... 1929, pp. 278-88.

C 969 -- 'Women as Folk-song Authors.' TRSC, 41(1947), sec. 2, pp. 47-53.

P 970 Godwin, Mabel W. 'The First Canadian Christmas Carol.' CGJ, 43(Dec. 1951), 252-53.

G 971 Halpern, Ida. 'Aural History and Ethnomusicology.' Sound Heritage, 4:1(1975), 64-71; rpt. CFMJ, 4(1976), 39-42.

P 972 Hogan, Dorothy. 'Canadian Folk Music: A Foundation for Cultural Identity.' Recorder, 8(Sept. 1975), 10-14.

B 973 Hogan, Dorothy, and Homer Hogan. 'Canadian Fiddle Culture.' Communiqué: Canadian Studies, 3(Aug. 1977), 72-100.

P 974 'In the Realm of the Folk-Song.' Canadian Home Journal, June 1928, pp. 28, 34.

P 975 Jarrett, Merrick. 'Singalong! A Folk Music Program for Children.' Ontario Library Review, 54(June 1970), 86-90.

C 976 Johnston, Richard. 'Towards a Definition of Folk Music in a Polyglot Society.' Canada Music Book, 9(Autumn/ Winter 1974), 95-98.

B 977 Kallmann, Helmut. A History of Music in Canada 1534-1914. Toronto: Univ. of Toronto Press, 1960. Pp. 8-26, 27-44, 275-88.

G 978 -- 'Music in Canada.' Musicanada, July 1967, pp. 5-6.

C 979 -- 'Toward a Bibliography of Canadian Folk Music.' Ethnomusicology, 16(1972), 499-503.

C 980 Landry, Renée. 'The Need for a Survey of Canadian Archives with Holdings of Ethnomusicological Interest.' Ethnomusicology, 16(1972), 504-11.

FR 981 Lawless, Ray M. Folksingers and Folksongs in America. New York: Duell, Sloan & Pearce, 1960; rev. ed., 1965. 750 pp.

P 982 Lee, Marjorie. Dance with me! Toronto: Ryerson, c. 1949. 250 pp.

C(s) 983 Lloyd, A. L., and Isabel Aretz de Ramon y Rivera. Folk Songs of the Americas. London: Novello, 1965; pb. New York: Oak, 1966. Pp. 1-43.

P 984 Luccock, Norma. 'Canadian Music for Canada's Children.' B.C. Music Educator, 19(Fall 1976), 27-31.

Folk Music and Dance

P   985   McCuin, L. 'Folk Songs or Folkus Pocus.' Saturday
          Night, Nov. 1962, p. 3.

C   986   MacLeod, Margaret Arnett. 'Songs of the Insurrection.'
          Beaver, Spring 1957, pp. 18-23.

G   987   MacMillan, Ernest C. 'Canadian Musical Life.' CGJ, 19
          (Dec. 1939), 330-39.

G   988   -- A Canadian Song Book. Toronto: Dent, 1938.

C   989   McTaggart, Margaret S. 'A Preliminary Survey of Folk-
          music in B.C.' CFMSN, 2(July 1967), 67-71.

G(s) 990   Mills, Alan. The Alan Mills Book of Folk Songs and
            Ballads. Montreal: Whitcombe & Gilmore, 1949. 93 pp.

C   991   Mills, Isabelle. 'The Heart of the Folk Song.' CFMJ, 2
          (1974), 29-34.

C   992   Moriarty, Norma, and Sirri Moriarty. 'The Fiddle in
          Folklore.' Anthropological Journal of Canada, 12:3
          (1974), 2-9.

P   993   Newlove, Harold J. Fiddlers of the Canadian West. Swift
          Current, Sask.: Author, 1976. 272 pp.

C   994   Peacock, Kenneth. 'Establishing Perimeters for
          Ethnomusicological Field Research in Canada: On-going
          Projects and Future Possibilities at the Canadian
          Centre for Folk Culture Studies." Ethnomusicology, 16
          (1972), 329-34.

B   995   -- 'Folk and Aboriginal Music.' In Aspects of Music in
          Canada. Ed. Arnold Walter. Toronto: Univ. of Toronto
          Press, 1969, pp. 62-89.

B   996   -- A Practical Guide for Folk Music Collectors.
          Ottawa: Canadian Folk Music Society, 1966. 92 pp.
          Mimeo.

G   997   Posen, Shelley. 'On Folk Festivals and Kitchens: Authen-
          ticity in the Folksong Revival.' Canada Folk Bulletin,
          2(May-June 1979), 3-11.

C   998   -- 'Stalking the Wild Folksong.' Newsletter (Mariposa
          Folk Festival), June 1976, pp. 3-5.

CR   999   Rahn, Jay. 'Canadian Folk Music Holdings at Columbia
           University.' CFMJ, 5(1977), 45-49.

C 1000   Rosenberg, Neil V. 'Introduction: Folk Music Panel.'
          CFMJ, 5(1977), 3-5.

P 1001   Ruebsaat, Rika. 'Canadian Music in the Schools.' B.C.
          Music Educator, 22(Winter 1979), 19-22.

FR 1002   Sandberg, Larry, and Dick Weissman. The Folk Music
          Sourcebook. New York: Knopf, 1976. 260 pp.

 C 1003   Sargent, Margaret [Margaret S. McTaggart]. 'Folk and
          Primitive Music in Canada.' Ottawa: National Museum,
          Bulletin 123, 1951, pp. 75-79; rpt. JIFMC, 4(1952),
          65-68.

 P 1004   Sarjeant, William A. S. 'Folk Music in the Canadian
          Prairies.' Folk Review (England), 5(May 1976), 4-7;
          rpt. and rev. in Canada Folk Bulletin, 1(Sept.-Oct.
          1978), 3-10.

 G 1005   Schafer, Murray. 'Limits of Nationalism in Canadian
          Music.' Tamarack Review, 18(Winter 1961), 71-78.

 P 1006   Scott, John A. 'Miramichi--The Sound of Tradition.'
          Sing Out!, 15(July 1965), 28-33.

 G 1007   Smith, Dorothy B. 'Music in the Furthest West a
          Hundred Years Ago.' Canadian Music Journal, 2(Summer
          1958), 3-14.

 P 1008   'The Sound of Folk Music.' Time (Can. ed.), 10 Oct.
          1960, pp. 21-22.

 G 1009   Stewart, George. 'Popular Songs of Old Canada.'
          Monthly Review, (London), 19(1905), 64-75; rpt.
          Living Age, 28(1905), 162-67.

 P 1010   'Success Follows a Folk Song Fling.' Star Weekly, 4
          Nov. 1961, pp. 20-27. [Mariposa Folk Festival.]

 P 1011   Tait, J. A. 'In the Realm of Folk-Song.' Musical
          Canada, 7(Nov. 1928), 15, 16, 27.

 P 1012   Teitel, Jay. 'Miracle at Shelburne.' Toronto Life.
          Dec. 1976, pp. 80-86.

 G 1013   'Tenth Conference of the Canadian Music Council--A
          Report.' Canada Music Book, 9(Autumn/Winter 1974),
          87-92.

CR 1014   'Theses and Dissertations Involving Canadian Folk
          Music.' CFMJ, 4(1976), 55-56.

Ga 1015   Thomas, Philip J. Songs of the Pacific Northwest.
          Saanichton: Hancock, 1979. 176 pp.

 G 1016   Usher, Bill, and Linda Page-Harpa, eds. 'For What Time
          I Am in this World': Stories from Mariposa. Toronto:
          Peter Martin, 1977. 240 pp.

 P 1017   Waller, Adrian. 'These Songs Are Our Songs.' Reader's
          Digest (Can. ed.), July 1978, pp. 48-52.

Folk Music and Dance

G 1018   Warnock, Amelia Beers [Katherine Hale]. 'Musical
         Development in Canada.' Canadian Magazine of Politics,
         Science, Art and Literature, 36(May 1910), 59-64.

P 1019   Winkelman, Donald M. 'Fiddleville.' Sing Out! 17(Feb.-
         Mar. 1967), 16-17. [Shelburne Old Time Fiddlers'
         Contest.]

   5B Anglophone and Celtic

P 1020   Allen, Robert Thomas. 'Honor Your Partner, Lickety
         Scoot.' Canadian, 9 Feb. 1974, pp. 8-11.

P 1021   Allen, Ward. Canadian Fiddle Tunes. 2 vols. Toronto:
         BMI Canada, 1956.

FC 1022 Anderson, David D. 'Songs and Sayings of the Lakes.'
         Midwest Folklore, 12(1962), 5-16.

GP 1023 Anderson, James. Sawney's Letters and Cariboo Rhymes.
         1891; rpt. Barkerville, B.C.: Barkerville Restoration
         Advisory Committee, 1962. 64 pp.

C 1024   Ashton, John. 'Truth in Folksong: Some Developments
         and Applications.' CFMJ, 5(1977), 12-17.

P 1025   Axford, P. 'Ballads of Newfoundland Give Clues to Its
         Life.' Saturday Night, 12 Apr. 1949, p. 22.

P 1026   -- 'Saga of Newfoundland.' Canadian Forum, 27(1947),
         205-6.

P 1027   Baker, Dora. 'Music and Folk Dance Rallies.' Journal of
         Education (N.S.), 4:5(1933), 86-91.

B 1028   Barbeau, C. Marius. 'Folk Songs.' JAF, 31(1918), 170-79.

C 1029   The Barrelman Song Sheets, Newfoundland Series 1-6. St.
         John's: n.p., n.d. [Broadsides.]

C 1030   Barry, Phillips. 'John of Haselgreen.' BFSSNE, 3(1931),
         9.

C 1031   -- 'The Lightning Flash.' BFSSNE, 3(1931), 14-15.

C 1032   -- 'The Northwestern Man.' BFSSNE, 4(1932), 13-14.

F 1033   -- 'Some Aspects of Folk Song.' JAF, 25(1905), 274-83.

B 1034   -- 'Songs and Traditions of the Miramichi.' BFSSNE, 10
         (1935), 15-17; 11(1936), 21-23; 12(1937), 23-24.

C 1035   -- 'The Sons of North Britain.' JAF, 26(1913), 183-84.

A Bibliography of Canadian Folklore in English

F 1036　Barry, Phillips. 'Traditional Ballads in New England 2.'
JAF, 18(1898), 191-224.

C 1037　-- 'Willie Leonard, or, The Lake of Cold Finn.'
BFSSNE, 8(1934), 9-12.

FB 1038　Barry, Phillips, Fannie H. Eckstorm, and Mary W. Smyth.
British Ballads from Maine. New Haven: Yale Univ.
Press, 1929. 535 pp.

CR 1039　Bartlett, Jon. 'The P. J. Thomas Collection of British
Columbia Folk Songs.' CFMJ, 4(1976), 29-30.

F 1040　Beck, Earl C. Lore of the Lumber Camps. Lansing: Univ.
of Michigan Press, 1948. 348 pp.

F 1041　-- They Knew Paul Bunyan. Lansing: Univ. of Michigan
Press, 1956. 255 pp.

F 1042　Beck, Horace P. 'Folksong Affiliations of Maine.'
Folklore in Action. Ed. Horace P. Beck. Philadelphia:
American Folklore Society, 1962. Pp. 30-36.

C 1043　Bleakney, F. Eileen. 'Folklore from Ottawa and Vicinity.' JAF, 31(1918), 158-69.

C 1044　Blondahl, Omar. Newfoundlanders, Sing! St. John's: Pub.
for Robin Hood Flour Mills by E. J. Bonnell, 1964.
120 pp.

C 1045　-- 'Songs of Newfoundland Ports.' Atlantic Advocate,
47(Aug. 1957), 78-79.

FAR 1046　Bronson, Bertrand H. The Traditional Tunes of the Child
Ballads. 4 vols. Princeton: Princeton Univ. Press,
1959-1972.

G 1047　Burke, John. Burke's Popular Songs. St. John's: Long
Bros., 1929.

B 1048　Campbell, John L. A Collection of Folk Songs and Music
Made in Nova Scotia. N.p., 1947. 59 pp.

G 1049　-- 'Highland Links with Nova Scotia.' Scots Magazine,
Oct. 1953, pp. 29-32.

C 1050　Campbell, John L., and Margaret F. Shaw. 'Letters to
the Editor: Canadian Folk Song Collections.' JIFMC, 14
(1962), 174.

A 1051　Casey, George J., Neil V. Rosenberg, and Wilfred W.
Wareham. 'Repertoire Categorization and Performer-
Audience Relationships: Some Newfoundland Folksong
Examples.' Ethnomusicology, 16(1972), 397-403.

Folk Music and Dance

C 1052   Cass-Beggs, Barbara. 'Barbara Allen' (2 versions). Come
All Ye, 4(1975), 205-7

F 1053   Cazden, Norman. 'Regional and Occupational Orientations
of American Traditional Song.' JAF, 72(1959), 310-44.

G 1054   Chicanot, E. L., ed. Rhymes of the Miner. An Anthology
of Canadian Mining Verse. Gardenvale, P.Q.:   Federal
Publications, 1937. 22 pp.

G 1055   Chittick, V. L. O. 'Books and Music in Haliburton.'
Dalhousie Review, 38(1958-59), 207-21.

P 1056   Ciwko, Valentine. 'Good Music for Anyone Not Used to
It.' Canada Folk Bulletin, 1(May-June 1978), 3-6.

FAR 1057   Coffin, Tristram P. The British Traditional Ballad in
North America. Rev. ed., with supplement by Roger deV.
Renwick.   Austin: Univ. of Texas Press, 1977. 297 pp.

FC 1058   Collinson, Francis. 'The Repertoire of a Traditional
Gaelic Singer in the Outer Hebrides: With Reference
to Versions of Her Songs Known in Canada.' JIFMC, 14
(1962), 87-90.

FC 1059   Cowell, Sidney R. 'The Connection Between the Present-
ing of Psalms on Cape Breton Island and in Colonial
New England Churches.' JIFMC, 14(1962), 155-56.

C 1060   Cox, Gordon. 'The Christmas Carolling Tradition of
Green's Harbour, Trinity Bay, Newfoundland.' CFMJ, 3
(1975), 3-10.

C 1061   -- 'A Newfoundland Carolling Tradition.' Folk Music
Journal (London), 3(1977), 242-60.

B 1062   -- 'Some Aspects of Musical Acculturation in the
Repertoire of a Newfoundland Singer.' Culture &
Tradition, 2(1977) 91-105.

C 1063   Coyne, James H. 'The Bold Canadian--A Ballad of the
War of 1812.' Ontario History, 23(1926), 237-42.

C 1064   Creighton, Helen. 'Ballads from Devil's Island.' Dalhousie Review, 12(1933), 503-10.

C 1065   -- 'Carols and Other Songs For Christmas.' Canadian
Composer, Dec. 1969, pp. 14-16.

C 1066   -- 'Folk-singers of Nova Scotia.' Canadian Forum, 32
(1952), 86-87.

A 1067   -- Folksongs from Southern New Brunswick. Ottawa:
National Museum, 1971. 238 pp.

A 1068 Creighton, Helen. Maritime Folk Songs. Toronto: Ryer-
        son, 1962; pb. 1972; rpt. St. John's: Breakwater,1979.
        210 pp.

C 1069 -- 'Nova Scotia Folk Songs.' Journal of Education
        (N.S.), 8:2(1937) 206-8.

C 1070 -- 'Song Singers.' Maclean's, 15 Dec. 1937, pp. 18-32.

A 1071 -- Songs and Ballads from Nova Scotia. Toronto: Dent,
        1932; rpt. New York: Dover, 1966. 333 pp.

C 1072 -- 'Songs for Christmas.' Atlantic Advocate, 50(Dec.
        1959), 62-63, 65-68.

C 1073 -- 'Songs from Nova Scotia.' JIFMC, 12(1960), 84-85.

A 1074 Creighton, Helen, and Calum MacLeod. Gaelic Songs in
        Nova Scotia. Ottawa: National Museum, Bulletin 198,
        1964; rpt. 1979. 302 pp.

A 1075 Creighton, Helen, and Doreen H. Senior. Traditional
        Songs from Nova Scotia. Toronto: Ryerson, 1950. 284 pp.

C 1076 -- and -- Twelve Folksongs from Nova Scotia. London:
        Novello, 1940. 41 pp.

P 1077 'Der Rugged Labrador.' The Christmas Echo (St. John's),
        No. 2 (Christmas 1917), 1.

P 1078 Devine, John H. 'The Bard of Prescott Street.' New-
        foundland Stories and Ballads, 1:1(1954) 15-24.

C 1079 -- 'Newfoundland Sea Shanteys.' Newfoundland Stories
        and Ballads, 11:2(1965), 38-41.

C 1080 Devine, P. K. 'Sea Songs and Shanties.' Christmas
        Messenger (St. John's), 1(1927), 27-30.

B 1081 Dibblee, Randall, and Dorothy Dibblee. Folksongs from
        Prince Edward Island. Summerside, P.E.I.: Williams &
        Crue, 1973. 124 pp.

B 1082 Doerflinger, William M. 'Cruising for Ballads in Nova
        Scotia.' CGJ, 16(Feb.1938), 91-100.

FA 1083 -- Shantymen and Shantyboys; Songs of Sailor and
        Lumberman. New York: Macmillan, 1951; rpt. as Songs of
        the Sailor and Lumberman, 1972. 374 pp.

C 1084 Doering, J. Frederick. '"Donald Monroe": A Canadian
        Version of a Scottish Folk Song.' JAF, 55(1942),
        170-74.

B 1085 Doucette, Laurel. 'The Gatineau Valley Singing Tradi-
        tion: A Contemporary View.' CFMJ, 7(1979), 18-22.

BR 1086　Doucette, Laurel. 'An Introduction to the Puckett Collection of Ontario Folklore.' _CFMJ_, 3(1975), 22-29.

B 1087　Doyle, Gerald S. _Old-Time Songs and Poetry of Newfoundland_. St. John's: Gerald S. Doyle Ltd., 1927, 1940, 1955, 1966, 1978. 72 pp.; 80 pp.; 88 pp.; 86 pp.; 64 pp.

C 1088　Dunn, Charles W. 'Glengarry's Gaelic Heritage.' _Dalhousie Review_, 42(1962), 193-201.

FB 1089　Eckstorm, Fannie H., and Mary W. Smyth. _Minstrelsy of Maine_. Boston and New York: Houghton Mifflin, 1927. 390 pp.

C 1090　Emerson, Frederick R. 'Newfoundland Folk Music.' In _The Book of Newfoundland_. Vol. I. Ed. J. R. Smallwood. St. John's: Nfld. Book Pub., 1937. Pp. 234-38.

C 1091　English, Leo E. F. 'Old Sea Songs.' _Newfoundland Stories and Ballads_, 5:2(1959), 3-7.

C 1092　'English Folk Dancing in Canada.' _English Dance & Song_, 36(1974), 57.

B 1093　Fahs, Lois S. _Swing Your Partner; Old Time Dances of New Brunswick and Nova Scotia_. Truro, N.S.: n.p., 1939. 104 pp. Mimeo.

B 1094　Fauset, Arthur Huff. 'Ballads and Songs.' _Folklore from Nova Scotia_. New York: American Folklore Society, 1931. Pp. 109-26.

F 1095　Fergusson, Donald A., ed. _Beyond the Hebrides, Including the Cape Breton Collection_. Vol. II. _Collections of Gaelic Songs and Melodies_. Halifax: Editor, 1977. 343 pp.

P 1096　Finnie, Richard. 'When the Ice-Worms Nest Again.' _Maclean's_, 1 Nov. 1945, pp. 20, 51.

B 1097　Fowke, Edith. 'American Civil War Songs in Canada.' _Midwest Folklore_, 13(1963), 33-42.

B 1098　-- 'American Cowboy and Western Pioneer Songs in Canada.' _Western Folklore_, 21(1962), 247-56.

B 1099　-- 'Anglo-Canadian Folksong: A Survey.' _Ethnomusicology_, 16(1972), 335-50.

B 1100　-- 'British Ballads in Ontario.' _Midwest Folklore_, 13 (1963), 133-62.

C 1101　-- 'Broadside Ballads in Canada.' _Hoot_ (Toronto), No. 3 (1963), pp. 8-15.

C 1102 Fowke, Edith. 'Canadian Variations of a Civil War
        Song.' Midwest Folklore, 13(1963), 101-4.

FC 1103 -- 'The Child Ballads.' Hoot, No. 2(1963), pp. 16-21.

FC 1104 -- 'A Few Notes on Bawdy Ballads in Print, Record, and
        Tradition.' Sing and String (Toronto), 2(Summer 1963),
        3-9.

C 1105 -- 'Flora and I,' and 'The Bunch of Water Cresses.'
        Hoot, 2(Sept. 1966), 33-34; 44-45.

B 1106 -- 'Folk Songs in Ontario.' Canadian Literature, No. 16
        (Spring 1963), pp. 28-42.

C 1107 -- 'Folk Songs of Ontario.' Sing and String, 1(July
        1960), 4-9.

C 1108 -- 'Folk Songs of the County.' In Peterborough: Land
        of Shining Waters, An Anthology. Toronto: Univ. of
        Toronto Press, 1967. Pp. 391-98.

C 1109 -- 'The King and the Tinker.' JAF, 79(1966), 469-71.

B 1110 -- 'Labor and Industrial Protest Songs in Canada.'
        JAF, 82(1968), 34-50.

A 1111 -- Lumbering Songs from the Northern Woods. Austin:
        Univ. of Texas Press, 1970. 232 pp.

C 1112 -- 'Ontario and Its Folksongs.' CFMSN, 2(July 1967),
        31-35.

C 1113 -- 'Ontario Songs.' Hoot, 3(Feb.-Mar. 1967), 9-10.

C 1114 -- 'Pat O'Brien,' and 'You Lovers of Old Ireland.'
        Canada Folk Bulletin, 1(Nov.-Dec. 1978), 14-15; 40-41.

B 1115 -- '"The Red River Valley" Re-Examined.' Western Folk-
        lore, 23(1964), 163-72; rpt. Alberta Historical Review,
        13(Winter 1965), 20-25.

AY 1116 -- Ring Around the Moon. Toronto: McClelland & Stew-
        art, 1977. 160 pp.

A 1117 -- 'A Sampling of Bawdy Ballads from Ontario.' In
        Folklore & Society. Ed. Bruce Jackson. Hatboro, PA:
        Folklore Associates, 1966. Pp. 45-61.

C 1118 -- 'Sault Ste. Mary's Jail' and 'Life in a Prairie
        Shack.' Sing and String, No. 3(1961), pp. 7, 23.

B 1119 -- 'Songs of a Manitoba Family.' CFMJ, 3(1975), 35-46.

C 1120 -- 'Songs of the Northern Shantyboys.' Forest History.
        (Santa Cruz, CA), 14(Jan. 1971), 22-28.

C 1121 Fowke, Edith. 'The Squire of Edinburgh.' Canada Folk Bulletin, 1(Sept.-Oct. 1978), 36-37.

A 1122 -- Traditional Singers and Songs from Ontario. Hatboro, PA: Folklore Associates, 1965. 210 pp.

B 1123 Fraser, Alexander. 'The Gaelic Folk-Songs of Canada.' TRSC, 9(1903), sec. 2, pp. 49-60.

P 1124 French, William. 'Humor, Hardship and History.' Globe Magazine, 21 Jan. 1961, pp. 10, 29. [Nfld. songs.]

P 1125 Ganam, King. Canadian Fiddle Tunes. Toronto: BMI Canada, 1957.

P 1126 Garber, Jim. 'The Glendale Festival of Scottish Fiddling.' Sing Out! 26(July-Aug. 1977), 32-33.

B 1127 Gledhill, Christopher. Folk Songs of Prince Edward Island. Charlottetown: Square Deal, 1973. 84 pp.

C 1128 'George Mackay's Ross Ferry Song.' Cape Breton's Magazine, No. 8, 1974, pp. 2-3.

P 1129 Goldston, Vera. 'They're Swingin' Western Down East.' Atlantic Advocate, 59:9(May 1969), 34-39.

F 1130 Gordon, Robert W. Folk-Songs of America. New York: National Service Bureau, 1938.

F 1131 -- 'Old Songs That Men Have Sung.' Series in Adventure Magazine (New York), 1923-1927.

P 1132 Gould, M. R. 'Toronto Folk Festival.' Canadian Forum, 27(1947), 86-87.

C 1133 Green, Ernest. 'The Song of the Battle of the Windmill.' Ontario Historical Society Papers and Records, 34(1942), 43-45.

A 1134 Greenleaf, Elisabeth B., and Grace Y. Mansfield. Ballads and Sea Songs of Newfoundland. Cambridge: Harvard Univ. Press, 1933; rpt. Hatboro, PA: Folklore Associates, 1968. 395 pp.

C 1135 Grierson, Al. 'Alberta Homesteader.' Canada Folk Bulletin, 1(May-June 1978), 8-9.

A 1136 Grover, Carrie. A Heritage of Songs. Bethel, ME: n.p., n.d.; rpt. Norwood, PA: Norwood, 1973. 216 pp.

G 1137 Heath, T. G. 'Protest Songs of Saskatchewan.' Saskatchewan History, 25(1972), 81-91.

P 1138 Himsl, R. M. 'The Story of a Saskatchewan Folk Song.' Western Producer, 30 Mar. 1967.

P 1139   Holden, Frank. 'Folk Song in Newfoundland.' <u>Come All</u>
<u>Ye</u>, 1(Jan. 1972), 4-5, 10.

GP 1140   Hopkins, Anthony. <u>Songs from the Front and Rear</u>.
<u>Canadian Servicemen's Songs of the Second World War</u>.
Edmonton: Hurtig, 1979. 192 pp.

P 1141   Horwood, Jean A. 'Newfoundland Folk Music.' <u>Canadian</u>
<u>Library Assoc. Bulletin</u>, 9(1952), 127-29; rpt. <u>Food</u>
<u>for Thought</u>, 13(May-June 1953), 13-16.

B 1142   Ives, Edward D. '"Ben Deane" and Joe Scott: A Ballad
and Its Probable Author.' <u>JAF</u>, 72(1959), 53-66.

C 1143   -- 'The First Miramichi Folksong Festival.' <u>Northeast</u>
<u>Folklore</u>, 1(1958), 62-64.

A 1144   -- <u>Joe Scott, the Woodsman-Songmaker</u>. Champaign: Univ.
of Illinois Press, 1979. 473 pp.

C 1145   -- 'Larry Gorman and "Old Henry."' <u>Northeast Folklore</u>,
2(1959), 40-46.

A 1146   -- <u>Larry Gorman: The Man Who Made the Songs</u>. Bloomington: Indiana Univ. Press, 1964. 259 pp.

A 1147   -- <u>Lawrence Doyle: The Farmer Poet of Prince Edward</u>
<u>Island</u>. Orono: Univ. of Maine Press, 1971. 269 pp.

C 1148   -- 'The Life and Work of Larry Gorman: A Preliminary
Report.' <u>Western Folklore</u>, 19(1960), 18.

B 1149   -- 'Lumbercamp Singing and the Two Traditions.' <u>CFMJ</u>,
5(1977), 17-23.

C 1150   -- 'The Lumberman in Town.' <u>Northeast Folklore</u>, 2
(1959), 58-59.

C 1151   -- 'The Maid of the Head.' <u>Northeast Folklore</u>, 3
(1960), 12-13.

B 1152   -- 'A Man and His Song: Joe Scott and "The Plain
Golden Band."' <u>Folksongs and Their Makers</u>, by H.
Glassie, E. D. Ives and J. F. Szwed. Bowling Green,
OH: Bowling Green Univ. Popular Press, 1970. Pp.
69-146.

C 1153   -- 'Satirical Songs in Maine and the Maritime Provinces of Canada.' <u>JIFMC</u>, 14(1962), 65-69.

A 1154   -- 'Twenty-one Folksongs from Prince Edward Island.'
<u>Northeast Folklore</u>, 5(1963), 1-87.

C 1155   -- 'Young Jimmy Foulger: A Hitherto Unrecorded Ballad
in the Northeast.' <u>Northeast Folklore</u>, 1(1958), 10-12.

C 1156 Johnson, Charles H. 'Songs and Sagas of Newfoundland.' The Book of Newfoundland. Vol. I. Ed. J. R. Smallwood. St. John's: Nfld. Book Pub., 1937. Pp. 219-73.

GP 1157 Johnson, Ray. The Newfoundland I Love. Kingston, N.S.: Fable Press, 1974. 24 pp.

B 1158 Karpeles, Maud. 'British Folk Songs from Canada.' Journal of the Folk Song Society, 34(1930), 218-30.

B 1159 -- Folk Songs from Newfoundland. 2 vols. London: Oxford, 1934. 144 pp.

A 1160 -- Folk Songs from Newfoundland. London: Faber & Faber, 1971. 340 pp.

B 1161 Kirwin, William. 'The Influence of Ireland on the Newfoundland Ballad.' In Literature and Folk Culture: Ireland and Newfoundland. Eds. Alison Feder and Bernice Schrank. St. John's: Memorial Univ., 1977. Pp. 131-46.

F 1162 Korson, George G. Coal Dust on the Fiddle; Songs and Stories of the Bituminous Industry. 1943; rpt. Hatboro, PA: Folklore Associates, 1965. 460 pp.

B 1163 Lamson, Cynthia. 'Bloody Decks and a Bumper Crop': The Rhetoric of Sealing Counter Protest. St. John's: ISER, Memorial Univ., 1979. 121 pp.

C 1164 -- '"Bloody Decks and a Bumper Crop": The Rhetoric of Sealing Counter-Protest.' Culture & Tradition, 4(1979), 116-25.

FAR 1165 Laws, G. Malcolm, Jr. American Balladry from British Broadsides. Philadelphia: American Folklore Society, 1957. 315 pp.

FAR 1166 -- Native American Balladry. Philadelphia: American Folklore Society, 1964. 298 pp.

A 1167 Leach, MacEdward. Folk Ballads and Songs of the Lower Labrador Coast. Ottawa: National Museum, Bulletin 201, 1965. 332 pp.

F(s) 1168 Lomax, Alan. The Folk Songs of North America. Garden City, NY: Doubleday, 1960. 623 pp.

B 1169 Lovelace, Martin. 'W. Roy Mackenzie as a Collector of Folksong.' CFMJ, 5(1977), 5-11.

Gc 1170 McCawley, Stuart. Cape Breton Come-All-Ye. Glace Bay: Brodie, 1929. 64 pp. [Texts only.]

Gc 1171 MacDonald, Alphonse. Cape Breton Songster. Sydney, N.S.: n.p., 1935. 71 pp. [Texts only.]

P 1172 Macdonald, S. P. 'The Gael and the Sea.' _Canadian Magazine_, 43(1914), 309-12.

C 1173 MacEachern, Ronald J. 'Collecting in Cape Breton Island.' _CFMSN_, 13(Fall 1978), 7-10.

B 1174 Mackenzie, W. Roy. 'Ballad Singing in Nova Scotia.' _JAF_, 22(1909), 327-31.

A 1175 -- _Ballads and Sea Songs from Nova Scotia_. Cambridge: Harvard Univ. Press, 1928; rpt. Hatboro, PA: Folklore Associates, 1963. 421 pp.

B 1176 -- 'Ballads from Nova Scotia.' _JAF_, 25(1912), 182-87.

A 1177 -- _The Quest of the Ballad_. Princeton: Princeton Univ. Press, 1919. 247 pp.

B 1178 -- 'Three Ballads from Nova Scotia.' _JAF_, 23(1910), 371-80.

BR 1179 Mackinnon, Richard. 'Cape Breton Scottish Folksong Collections.' _Culture & Tradition_, 4(1979), 23-29.

C 1180 MacLeod, Ada. 'Songs of Our Highland Forefathers.' _Dalhousie Review_, 6(1926-27), 478-87.

P 1181 MacMechan, Archibald. _Three Sea Songs_. Halifax: Marshall, 1919. 10 pp.

P 1182 McNab, Mary. 'Back to the Folk Songs of Nova Scotia.' _Canadian Courier_, 12 Oct. 1912, pp. 17-29.

B 1183 MacOdrum, Maxwell M. _Nova Scotia Ballads_. Halifax: Author, 1922, 229 pp.

GP 1184 MacQuarrie, Gordon F. _The Cape Breton Collection of Scottish Melodies_. Medford, MA: Beaton, 1975.

C 1185 Manny, Louise. 'The Ballad of Peter Amberley.' _Atlantic Advocate_, 53(July 1963), 67-74.

C 1186 -- 'Captain Hewison.' _North Shore Leader_ (Newcastle, N.B.), 13 March 1958.

C 1187 -- 'New Brunswick--Collecting Songs of the Canadian Lumber Woods and Ballads.' _International Musician_, 52 (Dec. 1953), 25.

C 1188 -- 'The Old Songs; Miramichi Folksongs and Singers.' _Fredericton Gleaner_, 28 Sept. 1951.

A 1189 Manny, Louise, and J. Reginald Wilson. _Songs of Miramichi_. Fredericton: Brunswick, 1968. 330 pp.

C 1190 Martin, Eva. 'Folksongs: A Living Tradition in Urban Canada.' _In Review_, 8(Spring 1974), 5-11.

GP 1191   Matthews, John. _Tradition in Exile_. Toronto: Univ. of Toronto Press, 1962. [Local songs.]

Gb 1192   Mercer, Paul, ed. _The Ballads of Johnny Burke: A Short Anthology_. St. John's: Nfld. Historical Society, 1974. [40 pp.]

GP 1193   Messer, Don. _Canadian Hoedowns_. Toronto: Gordon V. Thompson, 1957.

GP 1194   -- _Don Messer's Folio: 'Centennial Edition.'_ Toronto: Canadian Music Sales, 1967.

GP 1195   -- _Don Messer's Way Down East Fiddlin'_. Toronto: Gordon V. Thompson, 1948.

C(s) 1196   Mills, Alan. _Favourite Songs of Newfoundland_. Toronto: BMI Canada, 1968. 50 pp.

P 1197   Mindess, Mary. 'The True Story of the Ballad "The Red River Valley."' _Winnipeg Free Press_, 4 June 1966.

G 1198   Moir, John S. _Rhymes of Rebellion_. Toronto: Ryerson, 1965. 81 pp.

P 1199   Mulligan, Alex, comp. _Square Dance Calls with Instruction_. N.P.: Author, n.d. 66 pp. Mimeo.

P 1200   Murphy, Charles. 'A Canadian Boat Song.' _Quebec_, 3(July 1928), 16-17.

Gc 1201   Murphy, James. _Murphy's Sealers' Song Book_. St. John's: Author, 1905. 28 pp.

Gc 1202   -- _Old Songs of Newfoundland_. St. John's: Author, 1912. 16 pp.

Gb 1203   -- _Songs and Ballads of Newfoundland, Ancient and Modern_. St. John's: Author, 1902. 90 pp.

Gb 1204   -- _Songs Sung By Old-Time Sealers of Many Years Ago_. St. John's: Author, 1925. 20 pp.

Gb 1205   -- _Songs Their Fathers Sung. For Fishermen_. St. John's: Author, 1923. 17 pp.

C 1206   Narváez, Peter. 'Country and Western in Diffusion: Juxtaposition and Syncretism in the Popular Music of Newfoundland.' _Culture & Tradition_, 2(1977), 107-13.

C 1207   -- 'The Folk Parodist.' _CFMJ_, 5(1977), 32-37.

P 1208   Nolan, Dick, ed. _The Ninth Edition of Newfoundland Songs_. St. John's: Bennett Brewing Co., 1974. 40 pp.

C 1209   Nowlan, Alden A. 'The Creation of Folk Songs.' _Northeast Folklore_, 1(1958), 48-49.

GP 1210   O'Donnell, John C. <u>Men of the Deeps</u>. Waterloo: Waterloo Music, 1975. 63 pp.

GPa 1211   'Old Favourites.' Weekly department in <u>The Family Herald</u>, Montreal, 1895-1967.

GPb 1212   <u>Old Favourites: Reprinted from The Family Herald and Weekly Star, 1898</u>. Montreal: Family Herald, 1898. 154 pp.

C 1213   Parker, John P. <u>Cape Breton Ships and Men</u>. Buckinghamshire, U.K.: Hazell, Watson, & Viney, 1960. Pp. 14-16, 84-86, 130-32.

A 1214   Peacock, Kenneth. 'The Native Songs of Newfoundland.' Ottawa: National Museum, Bulletin 190, 1960, pp. 213-39.

C 1215   -- 'Newfoundland and Its Folksongs.' <u>CFMSN</u>, 2(July 1967), pp. 2-5.

B 1216   -- 'Nine Songs from Newfoundland.' <u>JAF</u>, 67(1954), 123-36.

A 1217   -- <u>Songs of the Newfoundland Outports</u>. 3 vols. Ottawa: National Museum, Bulletin No. 197, 1965. 1035 pp.

B 1218   Pocius, Gerald. '"The First Day That I Thought of It Since I got Wed": Role Expectations and Singer Status in a Newfoundland Outport." <u>Western Folklore</u>, 35(1976), 109-22.

B 1219   Pompey, Sherman L. <u>New Versions and Variations of the Ballad of Barbara Allen Discovered 1959-61</u>. Knob Noster, MO: Author, 1962. 23 pp. Mimeo.

C 1220   Posen, Sheldon, and Michael Taft. 'The Newfoundland Popular Music Project.' <u>CFMJ</u>, 1(1973), 17-23.

A 1221   Proctor, George A. 'Old-Time Fiddling in Ontario.' Ottawa: National Museum, Bulletin 190, 1960, pp. 173-208.

P 1222   '"The Red River Valley," Story of Only Folk Song of the West.' <u>Western Home Monthly</u>, June 1930, p. 32.

A 1223   Rhodes, Frank. 'Dancing in Cape Breton Island, Nova Scotia.' Appendix in J. R. Fleet and T. M. Fleet, <u>Traditional Dancing in Scotland</u>. London: Routledge & Kegan Paul, 1964. Pp. 265-85.

FB 1224   Rickaby, Franz. <u>Ballads and Songs of the Shanty-boy</u>. Cambridge: Harvard Univ. Press, 1926. 244 pp.

C 1225   Robins, John D. 'Square Dance Calls.' In Folklore of
         Canada. Ed. Edith Fowke. Toronto: McClelland & Stew-
         art, 1976. Pp. 213-16.

C 1226   Rogers, T. B. 'Is There an Alberta Folk Music?' CFMJ,
         6(1978), 23-29.

P 1227   Rooney, Jeannette. 'The Music of Newfoundland.' E.P.A.
         Horizons, 6(June/July 1975), pp. 40-43.

A 1228   Rosenberg, Neil V. Country Music in the Maritimes: Two
         Studies. St. John's: Memorial Univ., 1976. 20 pp.

B 1229   -- '"Folk" and "Country" Music in the Canadian Mari-
         times: A Regional Model.' Journal of Country Music,
         5(1974), 76-83; rpt. in 1228.

C 1230   -- 'Studying Country Music and Contemporary Folk Music
         Traditions in the Maritimes: Theory, Techniques, and
         the Archivist.' Phonographic Bulletin, No. 14(May
         1976), pp. 18-21; rpt. in 1228.

P 1231   Ross, Mary Lowrey. 'Our Ontario Folk Song.' Saturday
         Night, 27 Aug. 1932, p. 10.

P 1232   Ruebsaat, Ulrika. 'Folk Music in Alberta.' Canada Folk
         Bulletin, 1(Mar. 1978), 3-9.

C 1233   -- 'The Red River Valley.' Come All Ye, 6(1977),
         38-40; rpt. Canada Folk Bulletin, 1(Jan. 1978), 30-31.
         [Parody.]

P 1234   'The Rush to the Klondyke Goldfields.' Review of
         Reviews (London), 16 Aug. 1897, pp. 241-52.

Gc 1235 Ryan, M. P. Ryan's Favourites: Old Songs of Newfound-
         land. Colliers, Nfld.: Author, 1957. 34 pp.

Gb 1236 Ryan, Shannon, and Larry Small. Haulin' Rope and Gaff:
         Songs and Poetry in the History of the Newfoundland
         Seal Fishery. St. John's: Breakwater, 1978. 192 pp.

P 1237   Saunders, Robert. 'The Greenpond Saga in History, Song
         and Story.' Newfoundland Quarterly, 54:4(1958), 7-9,
         47-48; 59:2(1960), 15-16, 35, 40; 60:1(1961), 17-20.

P 1238   Scott, Robert S. Canadian Fiddle Tunes. Toronto: BMI
         Canada, 1955.

C 1239   Senior, Doreen H. 'Folk Dancing in Nova Scotia.' Jour-
         nal of Education (N.S.), 6:2(1935), 173-74.

B 1240   Senior, Doreen H., and Helen Creighton. 'Songs
         Collected in the Province of Nova Scotia, Canada.'
         Journal of the English Folk Dance and Song Society,
         6(1951), 83-91.

81

C 1241 Shoolbraid, Murray. 'The Night Visit.' Come All Ye,
        2(Oct. 1973), 3-4.

B 1242 -- 'Scottish Songs in B.C.' Come All Ye, 6(1977),
        45-54.

P 1243 Smallwood, Joseph R., ed. 'Poetry and Ballads of New-
        foundland.' The Book of Newfoundland. Vol. I. St.
        John's: Nfld. Book Pub., 1937. Pp. 456-86.

P 1244 Songs of Newfoundland. St. John's: Dominion Ale Brew-
        ing Co., n.d. 32 pp.

FA 1245 Spielman, Earl V. 'The Fiddling Traditions of Cape
        Breton and Texas: A Study in Parallels and Contrasts.'
        Yearbook for Inter-American Musical Research, 8(1972),
        29-48.

P 1246 'Squid Jiggin' Ground (Newfoundland Folksongs).' Time
        (Can. ed.), 9 Jan. 1950, p. 12. [Arthur Scammell.]

B 1247 Story, George M. 'The St. John's Balladeers.' English
        Quarterly, 4(Spring 1971), 49-58. Rpt. in The Blasty
        Bough. Ed. Clyde Rose. St. John's: Breakwater, 1976.
        Pp. 159-70.

C 1248 Swanson, Robert E. 'Engineering and Balladeering in
        the Western Woods.' Sound Heritage, 6:3(1977), 2-9.

A 1249 Szwed, John F. 'Paul E. Hall: A Newfoundland Song-Maker
        and His Community of Song.' Folksongs and Their Makers,
        by H. Glassie, E. D. Ives, and J. F. Szwed. Bowling
        Green, OH: Bowling Green Univ. Popular Press, 1970. Pp.
        147-69.

C 1250 Taft, Michael. 'Dig Songs: Parody, Caricature, and Re-
        portage on an Archeological Site.' CFMJ, 5(1977), 38-
        44.

GR 1251 -- A Regional Discography of Newfoundland and Labra-
        dor, 1904-1972. St. John's: Memorial Univ., 1975.
        102 pp.

B 1252 -- '"That's Two More Dollars": Jimmy Linegar's Suc-
        cess with Country Music in Newfoundland.' Folklore
        Forum, 7(1974), 99-121.

B 1253 Thomas, Amby. Songs & Stories from Deep Cove, Cape
        Breton. Ed. Ron MacEachern. Sydney: College of Cape
        Breton Press, 1979. 49 pp.

C 1254 Thomas, Gerald. 'McCaffery: A soldier's song of pro-
        test.' Lore and Language, 1(July 1972), 15-19.

G 1255 Thomas, Philip J. 'B.C. Songs.' B.C. Library Quarterly,
        26(July 1962), 15-29.

C 1256 Thomas, Philip J. 'British Canadian Folk Music in B.C.'
        B.C. Music Educator, 18(Spring 1975); rpt. Come All Ye,
        4(1975), 210-14.

G 1257 -- 'The Cariboo Wagon Road 1858-1868: The Opening of a
        Frontier. Documents in Song.' Booklet to accompany tape
        recording of songs as part of teaching unit on the
        Cariboo Gold Rush. N.p., 1964.

C 1258 -- 'Oh, Bury Me Not on the Lone Prairie,' and 'I'm
        Only a Broken Down Mucker.' Come All Ye, 6(1977), 26-
        27, 32-33.

C 1259 -- 'Where Grampa's Gone." Come All Ye, 3(Nov. 1974),
        11-12.

B 1260 -- 'Where the Rivers Flow.' CFMJ, 3(1975), 47-55.

F 1261 Walton, Ivan H. 'Songs of the Great Lake Sailors.'
        JIFMC, 3(1951), 93-96.

B 1262 -- 'Songs of the Great Lakes.' In Folklore of Canada.
        Ed. Edith Fowke. Toronto: McClelland & Stewart, 1976.
        Pp. 196-212.

C 1263 Waugh, F. W. 'Canadian Folk-Lore from Ontario.' JAF, 31
        (1918), 72-78.

C 1264 Webb, C. W. 'The Slave's Song.' Sing and String, 1(Feb.
        1962), 21.

C 1265 Webb, C. W., and Nellie Webb. Five songs collected
        in Prescott and Brockville. Sing and String, No. 5
        (Winter 1962-1963), passim.

B 1266 Weiss, Michael V. 'Songs from Western Canada.' CFMJ, 1
        (1973), 38-46.

C 1267 Wenker, Jerome. 'A Computer Aided Analysis of Canadian
        Folksongs.' In Computing in the Humanities. Ed. Serge
        Lusignan and John S. North. Waterloo, Ont.: Univ. of
        Waterloo Press, 1977. Pp. 222-32.

P 1268 Wente, Margaret. 'Sally Greer and All That Crowd.'
        Canadian, 29 Apr. 1978, pp. 6-7.

B 1269 West, Paul. 'The Unwitting Elegiac: Newfoundland Folk
        Song.' Canadian Literature, No. 7(1961), pp. 34-44.

GP 1270 Whelan, Michael. Poems and Songs. Newcastle, N.B.: Ans-
        low, 1895. 98 pp.

GP 1271 White, John, comp. Burke's Ballads. St. John's: n.p.,
        1960.

FA 1272 Wilgus, D. K. <u>Anglo-American Folksong Scholarship Since</u>
<u>1898</u>. New Brunswick, NJ: Rutgers Univ. Press, 1959.
466 pp.

C 1273 Wintemberg, W. J. '"Lord Lovel and Lady Nancy": A
Traditional Ballad.' <u>TRSC</u>, 13(1920), sec. 2, pp. 19-36.

C 1274 Wright, R. T. 'Lords of the Forest.' <u>Spin</u> (England),
3:9(1965), 8-13.

C 1275 Wyborn, Peter. 'Songs Past and Present.' <u>Hoot</u>, No. 3
(1963), pp. 18-20.

P 1276 Zinyk, Diane E., and William A. S. Sarjeant. 'A New
Voice in Canadian Folksong.' <u>Folk Review</u> (London),
7(Nov. 1977), 19-23. [Margaret Christl.]

5C Francophone

C 1277 Allaire, Gaston G. 'Musical Instruments in the Museum
of the Acadian Archives of the University of Moncton,
New Brunswick.' <u>CFMSN</u>, 4(1969), 38-40.

P 1278 'Allegorical Cars Typefying French Canadian Folk Songs
which took part in the Montreal St. Jean Baptiste Pro-
cession of 1928.' <u>Quebec</u>, 3(Jan. 1929) 1-5; 4(Feb. 29),
14-15; 4(Mar. 29), 36-37.

C 1279 Arsenault, Georges. '"Le chien à Paneau": An Acadian
Satirical Song.' <u>Island Magazine</u>, 2(Spring-Summer
1977), 37.

C 1280 Barbeau, C. Marius. 'Christmas Carols on the St. Lawrence.' <u>CGJ</u>, 61(Dec. 1960), 208-11.

A 1281 -- 'The Ermatinger Collection of Voyageur Songs
(ca. 1830).' <u>JAF</u>, 67(1954), 147-61.

C 1282 -- 'Folksong in Quebec.' <u>The Times</u> (London), 1 July
1927.

C 1283 -- 'Folksongs in Quebec. Echoes of the Old World.'
<u>Quebec</u>, 5(Dec. 1930), 249.

C 1284 -- 'Folk-Songs of French Canada.' In <u>Empire Club of</u>
<u>Canada, Addresses ... 1925</u>. Toronto: Macoomb, 1926.
Pp. 180-96.

C 1285 -- 'Folk-Songs of French Canada.' In <u>Empire Club of</u>
<u>Canada. Addresses ... 1929</u>. Toronto: Best, 1930. Pp.
101-10.

C 1286   Barbeau, C. Marius. 'Folk Songs of French Canada.'
         Music and Letters (London), 13(1932), 168-82.

C 1287   -- 'Folk-Songs of French Canada.' Educational Record
         of the Province of Quebec, 54(1943), 47-53.

A 1288   -- Folk Songs of Old Quebec. Ottawa: National Museum,
         Bulletin 75, 1935. 72 pp.

C 1289   -- 'French-Canadian Folk-Song.' Musical Youth Magazine
         (Montreal), 2(May 1957), 8, 13.

C 1290   -- 'French Canadian Folk-Songs.' Musical Quarterly, 29
         (1943), 122-37.

C 1291   -- 'How the Folk Songs of French Canada Were Discov-
         ered.' CGJ, 49(Aug. 1954), 58-65; rpt. as 'The Redis-
         covery of Folk Music.' CGJ, 84(Mar. 1972), 82-91.

C 1292   -- 'I Dressed Me All in Feathers.' JAF, 63(1950),
         181-84.

A 1293   -- Jongleur Songs of Old Quebec. Toronto: Ryerson,
         1962. 202 pp.

B 1294   -- 'Songs of Old.' Quebec, Where Ancient France
         Lingers. Québec: Librairie Garneau, 1936. Pp. 93-115.

C 1295   -- 'Songs of the Old World.' The Times, 15 May 1939.

C 1296   -- 'Summary of "Rondes" from French Canada.' JIFMC,
         8(1956), 40.

B 1297   -- 'Voyageur Songs.' Beaver, June 1942, pp. 15-19.

B 1298   -- 'Voyageur Songs of the Missouri.' Bulletin of the
         Missouri Historical Society, 10(1954), 336-50.

A 1299   Barbeau, C. Marius, and Edward Sapir. Folk Songs of
         French Canada. New Haven, CN: Yale Univ. Press, 1925.
         216 pp.

G 1300   Blegen, Theodore C. The Voyageurs and Their Songs. St.
         Paul: Minnesota Historical Society, 1966. 24 pp.

C 1301   Bouthillier, Robert. 'Mon pére m'avait fait promette.'
         Canada Folk Bulletin, 1(Sept.-Oct. 1978), 24-25.

A 1302   Brassard, François. 'French-Canadian Folk Music
         Studies: A Survey.' Ethnomusicology, 16(1972), 351-60.

B 1303   -- 'The Return of the Soldier Husband.' Ottawa:
         National Museum, Bulletin 118, 1950, pp. 66-71.

P 1304   Burpee, L. J. Songs of French Canada. Toronto: Musson,
         1909. 87 pp.

P 1305 C.H.V. 'French Canadian Folksongs.' Quebec, 1(Nov. 1926), 2-3.

P 1306 Call, Frank O. 'Folk Song.' The Spell of French Canada. Boston: Page, 1926. Pp. 276-307.

P 1307 Canadian Folk Song and Handicraft Festival. Chateau Frontenac, Quebec, 1927; 1928; 1930. [Annotated programs.]

C 1308 Cass-Beggs, Barbara. 'Métis Songs.' Come All Ye, 3(July 1974), 3-9.

B 1309 -- Seven Métis Songs of Saskatchewan. Toronto: BMI Canada, 1967. 31 pp.

B 1310 Coltman, Bob. 'Habitantbilly: French-Canadian Old Time Music.' Old Time Music, 11(Winter 1973/74), 9-13; 12 (Spring 1974), 9-14.

B 1311 Complin, Margaret. 'Pierre Falcon's "Chanson de la Grenouillère."' TRSC, 33(1939), sec. 2, pp. 49-58.

GP 1312 De Montigny, Louvigny Testard. The Order of Good Cheer: Canadian Historical Ballad Opera of the First Settlers in Canada. Trans. J. Murray Gibbon. Toronto: Dent, 1929. 30 pp.

B 1313 Doyon, Madeline. 'Folk Dances in Beauce County.' JAF, 63(1958), 171-74.

B 1314 Fowke, Edith, and Richard Johnston. Folk Songs of Quebec. Waterloo: Waterloo Music, 1957. 93 pp.

CR 1315 Fraser, Ian F. 'The French-Canadian Folk Song.' In Bibliography of French-Canadian Poetry. New York: Columbia Univ. Press, 1935. Pp. 102-5.

P 1316 'The French Canadian Folksong.' Art of Music (New York), 5(1915), 374-76.

C(s) 1317 Gascoigne, Margaret. Chansons of Old French Canada. Quebec: CPR, 1929. 31 pp.

C 1318 Gaudet, Laura C. Songs of Acadia (Chants d'Acadie). New York: BMI, 1945. 32 pp.

B(s) 1319 Gibbon, John Murray. Canadian Folk Songs (Old and New). Toronto: Dent, 1927. 177 pp.

C 1320 Grant-Schaefer, G. Alfred. French Canadian Songs. Boston: Schmidt, 1925. 21 pp.

C 1321 Greenough, William P. 'Chansons Canadiennes.' Canadian Folk-Life and Folk Lore. New York: Richmond, 1897. Pp. 129-48.

A 1322 Griggs, Mary Ann. The Folk-Song in the Traditional
Society of French Canada. Sudbury: La Société His-
torique du Nouvel-Ontario, 1969. 22 pp.

C 1323 Hopkins, Edward. 'The Hopkins Book of Canoe Songs.'
Beaver, Autumn 1971, pp. 54-56.

P 1324 Jasmin, Hélène. 'Breton-Cyr: Keeping Quebec traditional music alive and thriving.' Canadian Composer,
Apr. 1977, pp. 16, 18, 22.

C 1325 Jones, James E. French-Canadian Songs. London: Frederick Harris, 1920. 16 pp.

P 1326 Kempf, P. 'Treasure Trove of Melody in Canada's Folk
Songs.' Musician, 32(July 1927), 14-15.

C 1327 Knight, Edward. Canadian Airs, collected by Lieutenant
Back, R.N., during the late Arctic expedition under
Captain Franklin. London: Power, 1823.

C 1328 Krassen, Miles. 'An Analysis of a Jean Carignan
Record.' Folklore Forum, 7(1974), 161-67; rpt. CFMJ,
2(1974), 40-44.

C 1329 Lacourcière, Luc, and Felix A. Savard. 'Canadian Folk
Songs Collected at Baie-des-Rochers (Charlevoix) County.' Ottawa: National Museum, Bulletin 123, 1951, pp.
84-87.

P 1330 Lanigan, G. T. National Ballads of Canada. Montreal:
Lovell, 1865. 15 pp.

C 1331 Lewis, J. O. 'Twelve Habitant Songs.' Canadian Magazine,
58(1922), 182-99.

P 1332 Liebich, Mrs. Franz. 'Canadian Folk-Song.' Musical
Times, 67(1926), 886-87.

P 1333 McLennan, William. Songs of Old Canada. Montreal: Dawson, 1886. 83 pp.

C 1334 MacLeod, Margaret Arnett. 'Dickson the Liberator.'
Beaver, Summer 1956, pp. 4-7.

A 1335 -- Songs of Old Manitoba. Toronto: Ryerson, 1959.
93 pp.

P 1336 MacMillan, Ernest. 'The Folk Song Festival at Quebec--
Some Impressions.' Toronto Conservatory of Music
Quarterly Review, 9(Summer 1927), 130.

B 1337 MacMillan, Ernest, ed. Twenty-one Folk-Songs of French
Canada. Oakville, Ont.; Frederick Harris, 1928. 53 pp.

PY 1338   Mills, Alan. Chantons un peu ('Sing a Little'): Thirty
          French Folk Songs for Young Folk. Toronto: BMI Canada,
          1961. 52 pp.

F(s) 1339   -- Favorite French Folk Songs; Sixty-five Traditional
          Songs of France and Canada. New York: Oak, 1963. 98 pp.

P 1340   N.A.G. 'The Quebec Folk Song Festival.' Quebec, 3(May
          1928), 2-5.

CR 1341   'Primary Source Inventory of the Benoit Collection of
          Acadian Folk Songs.' CFMSN, 4(1969), 14-19.

B 1342   Proctor, George A. 'Musical Styles of Gaspé Songs.'
          Ottawa: National Museum, Bulletin 190, 1963, pp. 209-
          12.

P 1343   Prud'homme, Louis A. 'French Canadian Folk Songs.'
          Canadian Magazine, 56(1920), 53-59.

B 1344   Rahn, Jay. 'Text Underlay in Gagnon's Collection of
          French-Canadian Songs.' CFMJ, 4(1976), 3-14.

P 1345   Renault, Raoul. 'French Canadian Songs.' Le Courier
          du Livre (Québec), 4(1900), 281-90; 327-38.

P(s) 1346   Robertson, W. Graham. French Songs of Old Canada. Lon-
          don: Heinemann, 1904. 60 pp.

B 1347   Sapir, Edward. 'French-Canadian Folk Songs.' Poetry
          (Chicago), 16(1920), 175-85.

C 1348   -- 'Three Folk Songs of French Canada.' Queen's Quar-
          terly, 29(1922), 286-90.

C 1349   Somervell, Arthur, arr. Twelve Ancient French-Canadian
          Folk-Songs. Coll. Marius Barbeau, trans. Harold Boul-
          ton. London: Boosey, 1927. 39 pp.

P 1350   Spell, L. 'Music in New France in the Seventeenth
          Century.' Canadian Historical Review, 18(June 1927),
          119-31.

R 1351   Thomas, Gerald, comp. Songs Sung by French Newfound-
          landers: A Catalogue of the Holdings of the Memorial
          University of Newfoundland Folklore and Language
          Archive. St. John's: Memorial Univ., 1978. 94 pp.

FB 1352   Tiersot, Julien. Forty-four French Folk Songs and
          Variants from Canada, Normandy, and Brittany. New York:
          Schirmer, 1910. 118 pp.

C 1353   Weekes, Mary. 'Three Prairie Folk-Songs.' Beaver, Mar.
          1934, pp. 45-49.

Folk Music and Dance

C 1354   Willan, Healey, arr. Chansons Canadiennes (French Canadian Folk Songs). 2 vols. Oakville: Frederick Harris, 1929. 27 pp.; 39 pp.

B 1355   Wood, William C. H. 'Footnotes to Canadian Folksongs.' TRSC, 2(1896), sec. 2, pp. 77-125; rpt. Toronto: Canadiana, 1968. 48 pp.

B 1356   Wyman, Loraine. 'Songs from Percé.' JAF, 33(1920), 321-35.

5D   Indian and Inuit

A 1357   Amoss, Pamela. Coast Salish Spirit Dancing. Seattle: Univ. of Washington Press, 1978. 193 pp.

B 1358   Barbeau, C. Marius. 'Asiatic Survivals in Indian Songs.' Musical Quarterly, 20(1934), 107-16; rpt. Queen's Quarterly, 47(1940), 67-76.

C 1359   -- 'Buddhist Dirges of the North Pacific Coast.' JIFMC, 14(1962), 16-21.

C 1360   -- 'The Dragon Myths and Ritual Songs of the Iroquoians.' JIFMC, 3(1951), 81-85.

C 1361   -- 'Chanting Buddhist Dirges.' Alaska Beckons. Caldwell, ID: Caxton, 1947. Pp. 183-202.

B 1362   -- 'Indian Songs of the Northwest.' Canadian Music Journal, 2(Autumn 1957), 16-25.

B 1363   -- 'Songs of the Northwest.' Musical Quarterly (New York), 19(1933), 101-11.

C 1364   -- Three Songs of the West Coast. Oakville: Frederick Harris, 1929. 14 pp.

C 1365   -- 'Totems and Songs.' CGJ, 50(May 1955), 176-81.

A 1366   -- 'Tsimshian Songs.' The Tsimshian: Their Arts and Music. Ed. Viola E. Garfield, Paul S. Wingert, and C. Marius Barbeau. New York: Augustin, 1951. Pp. 95-280.

B 1367   Beckwith, Martha W. 'Dance Forms of the Moqui and Kwakiutl Indians.' Proc. of the 15th International Congress of the Americanists, Part 2, 1907, pp. 79-114.

FC 1368 Bierhorst, John. A Cry from the Earth: Music of the North American Indians. New York: Four Winds 1979. 131 pp.

89

F 1369   Blue, Arthur W. 'Music of the North American Indian.'
         Tawow, 2(Summer 1971), 4-9.

C 1370   Boas, Franz. 'Chinook Songs.' JAF, 1(1888), 220-26.

A 1371   -- 'Dance and Music in the Life of the Northwest Coast
         Indians.' In The Function of Dance in Human Society.
         Ed. Franziska Boas. New York: Boas School, 1944. 63 pp.

B 1372   -- 'Eskimo Tales and Songs.' JAF, 2(1894), 45-50; 10
         (1897), 109-15.

B 1373   -- 'On Certain Songs and Dances of the Kwakiutl.' JAF,
         1(1888), 49-64.

B 1374   -- 'Songs of the Kwakiutl Indians.' Internationales
         Archiv für Ethnographie (Leyden: Brill), 9(1896), 1-9.

B 1375   Boas, Franz, and Henry Rink. 'Eskimo Tales and Songs.'
         JAF, 2(1889), 123-31.

B 1376   Boyle, David. 'Iroquois Music.' Annual Archeological
         Report, Ontario, 1898, pp. 143-56.

C 1377   Burlin, Natalie C. 'The Kwakiutls.' In The Indians'
         Book. New York: Dover, 1968. Pp. 297-307.

F 1378   Burton, Frederick R. American Primitive Music; With
         Especial Attention to the Songs of the Ojibways. New
         York: Moffat, Yard, 1909. 284 pp.

C 1379   Carpenter, Edmund S., ed. Anerca. Toronto: Dent, 1959.
         45 pp.

C 1380   -- 'Eskimo Poetry: Word Magic.' Explorations, No. 4
         (Feb. 1955), pp. 101-11.

B 1381   Cavanagh, Beverley. 'Imagery and Structure in Eskimo
         Song Texts.' CFMJ, 1(1973), 3-15.

C 1382   -- 'Some Throat Games of Netsilik Eskimo Women.' CFMJ,
         4(1976), 43-47.

G 1333   Crawford, David E. 'The Jesuit Relations and Allied
         Documents; Early Sources for an Ethnography of Music
         among American Indians.' Ethnomusicology, 11(1967),
         199-206.

C 1384   Cringan, Alexander T. 'Indian Music.' Annual Archeo-
         logical Report, Ontario, 1906, pp. 158-61.

B 1385   -- 'Iroquois Folk Songs.' Annual Archeological Report,
         Ontario, 1903, pp. 137-52.

B 1386   -- 'Pagan Dance Songs of the Iroquois.' Annual Archeo-
         logical Report, Ontario, 1899, pp. 168-89.

C 1387 Cringan, Alexander T. 'Traditional Songs of the Iroquois Indians.' Musical Times, 41(1900), 114.

F(s) 1388 Cronyn, George W. ed. The Path of the Rainbow: An Anthology of Songs and Chants from the Indians of North America. New York: Liveright, 1934. 360 pp.

C 1389 Davidson, John F. 'Ojibwa Songs.' JAF, 58(1945), 303-5.

B 1390 De Laguna, Frederick. 'Indian Masks from the Lower Yukon.' American Anthropologist, 38(1936), 569-85. [Dances.]

C 1391 De Nevi, Don. 'Essays in Musical Retribalization: Hudson Bay.' Music Educators' Journal, 56(Sept. 1969), 66-68.

C 1392 Deans, James. 'A Weird Mourning Song of the Haidas.' American Antiquarian, 13(1891), 52-54.

C 1393 Dempsey, Hugh A. 'Social Dances of the Blood Indians of Alberta.' JAF, 69(1956), 47-52.

A 1394 Densmore, Frances. Music of the Indians of British Columbia. Washington: Bureau of American Ethnology, Bulletin 136, 1943, pp. 1-99; rpt. New York: Da Capo, 1972. 99 pp.

A 1395 -- Nootka and Quileute Music. Washington: Bureau of American Ethnology, Bulletin 124, 1939; rpt. New York: Da Capo, 1972. 358 pp.

C 1396 -- 'The Origin of a Siwash Song.' American Anthropologist, 47(1945), 173-75.

G 1397 -- 'Peculiarities in the Singing of the American Indians.' American Anthropologist, 32(1930), 651-60.

P 1398 Drew, Leslie A. 'Indian Concert Bands.' Beaver, Summer 1971, 26-29.

F 1399 Driver, Wilhelmine. 'Music.' In Indians of North America. Ed. Harold E. Driver. Chicago: Univ. of Chicago Press, 1961. Pp. 212-23.

B 1400 Drucker, Philip. 'Kwakiutl Dancing Societies.' Anthropological Records, 2(1940), 201-30.

F 1401 Eells, Myron. 'Indian Music.' American Antiquarian, 1 (1879), 249-53. [Klallam songs.]

B 1402 Estreicher, Zygmunt. 'The Music of the Caribou Eskimos.' Encyclopedia Arctica. Vol. 2. New York, 1931.

B 1403 Fenton, William N. 'The Feast of the Dead, or Ghost Dance at Six Nations Reserve, Canada.' In Symposium on

Local Diversity in Iroquois Culture. Ed. W. N. Fenton.
Washington: Bureau of American Ethnology, Bulletin 149,
1951, pp. 139-66.

A 1404 Fenton, William N., and Gertrude P. Kurath. The Iroquois Eagle Dance, An Off-shoot of the Calumet Dance.
Washington: Bureau of American Ethnology, Bulletin 156,
1953. 324 pp.

C 1405 Fillmore, John C. 'A Woman's Song of the Kwakiutl Indians.' JAF, 6(1893), 285-90.

F 1406 Fletcher, Alice C. Indian Games and Dances. Boston:
Birchard, 1915. 139 pp.

P 1407 Fraser, Hermia H. The Arrow-Maker's Daughter and Other
Haida Chants. Toronto: Ryerson, 1957. 16 pp.

P 1408 -- Songs of the Western Islands. Toronto: Ryerson,
1945. 10 pp. [Haida.]

B 1409 Galpin, Francis W. 'The Whistles and Reed Instruments
of the American Indians of the North-West Coast.'
Royal Museum Assoc. Proceedings (London), 29(Mar. 1903),
115-38.

C 1410 George, Graham. 'Songs of the Salish Indians of British
Columbia.' JIFMC, 14(1962), 22-29.

C 1411 Glynn-Ward, H. 'Dance of the Salish.' Beaver, Mar.
1940, pp. 50-52.

B 1412 Goddard, Pliny E. 'Dancing Societies of the Sarsi
Indians.' Anthropological Papers of the American Museum
of Natural History, 11(1914), 461-74.

B 1413 -- 'Notes on the Sun Dance of the Cree of Alberta.'
Anthropological Papers of the American Museum of
Natural History, 16(1919), 295-310.

B 1414 -- 'Notes on the Sun Dance of the Sarsi.' Anthropological Papers of the American Museum of Natural History,
16(1919), 271-82.

F 1415 Gordon, Charles H. M. 'Music of the North American
Indian.' Beaver, June 1933, p. 67.

C 1416 Hague, Eleanor. 'Eskimo Songs.' JAF, 28(1915), 96-98.

C 1417 Halpern, Ida. 'Kwa-kiutl Music.' JIFMC, 14(1962),
159-60.

B 1418 -- 'Music of the B.C. Northwest Coast Indians.' Proc.
of the Centennial Workshop on Ethnomusicology. Victoria:
Gov't. of B.C., 1968. Pp. 23-41.

B 1419   Halpern, Ida. 'On the Interpretation of Meaningless Nonsense-Syllables in the Music of the Pacific Northwest Indians.' Ethnomusicology, 20(1976), 253-71.

F 1420   Hauser, Michael. "Formal Structure in Polar Eskimo Drum Songs." Ethnomusicology, 21(Jan. 1977), 33-53.

B 1421   Herzog, George. 'Salish Music.' Contributions to Anthropology, 36(1949), 93-109.

C 1422   Honigmann, John J. 'Dance of the Ancient Ones.' Beaver, Autumn 1968, pp. 44-47.

FC 1423   Houston, James. Songs of the Dream People: Chants and Images from the Indians and Eskimos of North America. Don Mills: Longman, 1972. 83 pp.

B 1424   Hymes, Dell. 'Masset Mourning Songs.' Alcheringa; Ethnopoetics. 2(Summer 1971), 53-63.

FB 1425   Johnston, Thomas F. Eskimo Music by Region: A Comparative Circumpolar Study. Ottawa: National Museum, Ethnology Service Mercury Series 32, 1976. 222 pp.

B 1426   Kiefer, Thomas M. 'Continuous Geographical Distribution of Musical Patterns: A Test Case from the Northwest Coast.' American Anthropologist, 71(1969), 701-6.

C 1427   Kinsey, Mabel C. 'An Ojibwa Song.' JAF, 46(1933), 416-17.

B 1428   Kolinski, Mieczyslaw. 'An Apache Rabbit Dance Song Cycle as Sung by the Iroquois.' Ethnomusicology, 16 (1972), 415-64.

B 1429   -- 'An Iroquois War Dance Song Cycle.' CAUSM Journal, 1(Fall 1972), 51-64.

C 1430   -- 'Two Iroquois Rabbit Dance Song Cycles.' CFMSN, 5 (1970), 11-38; 6(1971), 26-45.

C 1431   Koller, James. 'Wolf Songs and Others of the Tlingit.' Alcheringa; Ethnopoetics, 2(Summer 1971), 31-34.

C 1432   Kurath, Gertrude P. 'Antiphonal Songs of Eastern Woodland Indians.' Musical Quarterly, 42(1956), 520-26.

FB 1433   -- 'A Comparison of Plains and Pueblo Songs.' Ethnomusicology, 13(1969), 512-17.

A 1434   -- Dance and Song Rituals of the Six Nations Reserve. Ottawa: National Museum, Bulletin 220, 1968. 205 pp.

B 1435   -- 'Dogrib Choreography and Music.' In The Dogrib Hand Game. Eds. June Helm and Nancy O. Lurie. Ottawa: National Museum, Bulletin 205, 1966, pp. 12-28.

C 1436   Kurath, Gertrude P. 'Iroquois Mid-Winter Medicine Rites.' JIFMC, 3(1951), 96-100.

A 1437   -- Iroquois Music and Dance: Ceremonial Arts of the Two Seneca Longhouses. Washington: Bureau of American Ethnology, Bulletin 187, 1964. 268 pp.

B 1438   -- 'Local Diversity in Iroquois Music and Dance.' In Symposium on Local Diversity in Iroquois Culture. Ed. William N. Fenton. Washington: Bureau of American Ethnology, Bulletin 149, 1951, pp. 109-38.

C 1439   Laidlaw, George E. 'The Sun Dance among the Blackfeet.' American Antiquity, 8(1886), 169-70.

C 1440   Lane, C. 'The Sun Dance of the Cree Indians.' Canadian Record of Science, 2(1887), 22-26.

C 1441   Large, Isabel G. 'Music Among the Coast Indians of Northern British Columbia.' Conservatory Monthly, 11 (1912), 211-14.

FA 1442   Laubin, Reginald, and Gladys Laubin. Indian Dances of North America. Norman: Univ. of Oklahoma Press, 1977. 538 pp.

C 1443   Leechman, Douglas. 'Eskimo Music.' American Mercury, Sept. 1929, pp. 67-69.

C 1444   Lerman, Norman H. 'An Okanagan Winter Dance.' Anthropology in British Columbia, 4(1953-54), 35-36.

FBY 1445   Lewis, Richard, ed. I Breathe a New Song: Poems of the Eskimo. New York: Simon & Shuster, 1971. 128 pp.

C 1446   Lowenstein, Tom. Eskimo Poems from Canada and Greenland. London: Anchor, 1973. 149 pp.

B 1447   Lutz, Maija M. The Effects of Acculturation on Eskimo Music of Cumberland Peninsula. Ottawa: National Museum, Ethnology Service Mercury Series 41, 1978. 167 pp.

B 1448   McIlwraith, Thomas F. Bella Coola Indians. 2 vols. Toronto: Univ. of Toronto Press, 1948. Pp. 267-337.

C 1449   McLean, John. 'The Blackfoot Sun-Dance.' Canadian Institute Proc., 6(1889), 231-37.

P 1450   McQuesten, C. 'The Sun Dance of the Blackfoot.' Rod and Gun in Canada, 13(1912), 169-77.

BY 1451   Mallon, Mick, ed. Inuit Artists, Vol. I, II, and III. Yellowknife: Dept. of Education, N.W.T., 1978. 191 pp. [Songs.]

C 1452 Marsh, D. B. 'Padlemiut Drum Dance.' Beaver, Mar. 1946,
        pp. 20-21.

C 1453 Morgan, Fred. 'Friday Night Drum.' Beaver, Autumn 1962,
        pp. 52-55.

F 1454 Nettl, Bruno. Music in Primitive Culture. Cambridge:
        Harvard Univ. Press, 1956. 182 pp.

FB 1455 -- North American Indian Musical Styles. JAF, 67
        (1954), 45-56, 297-307, 351-68; rpt. Philadelphia:
        American Folklore Society, Memoir 45, 1954. 51 pp.

FB 1456 -- 'Studies in Blackfoot Indian Musical Culture.'
        Ethnomusicology, 11(1967), 141-60, 293-309; 12(1968),
        11-48, 192-207.

FB 1457 Niblack, Albert P. 'Singing Drums, Rattles and
        Whistles.' In The Coast Indians of Southern Alaska
        and Northern British Columbia, Part 7. Report of the
        National Museum, Washington, 1888.

B 1458 Obomsawin, Alanis. 'Sounds and Voices of Our People.'
        artscanada, 30(Dec. 1973-Jan. 1974), 81-89.

B 1459 Pelinski, Rámon, et al. Inuit Songs from Eskimo Point.
        Ottawa: National Museum, Ethnology Service Mercury
        Series 60, 1979. 122 pp.

C 1460 Prest, J. O. 'Cree Sun Dance at Hobbema.' Beaver,
        (Nov. 1923), pp. 45-47.

BY 1461 Rasmussen, Knud, coll. and trans. Beyond the High
        Hills. Cleveland: World, 1961. 32 pp.

BY 1462 -- We Lived by Animals. Ottawa: Dept. of Indian Af-
        fairs, 1976. [17 pp.] [Songs.]

C 1463 Reade, John. 'Some Wabanaki Songs.' TRSC, 5(1897),
        sec. 2, pp. 1-8.

C 1464 A Resident Nurse. 'Medicine Dance.' Beaver, June 1944,
        pp. 34-35.

F 1465 Roberts, Helen H. Musical Areas in Aboriginal North
        America. New Haven, CO: Yale Univ. Press, 1936. 41 pp.

C 1466 -- 'Songs of the Nootka Indians of Western Vancouver
        Island.' Midwest Folklore, 7(1957), 134-36.

B 1467 Roberts, Helen H., and H. K. Haeberlin. 'Some Songs of
        the Puget Sound Salish.' JAF, 31(1918), 496-520.

A 1468 Roberts, Helen H., and Diamond Jenness. Songs of the
        Copper Eskimo. Report of the Canadian Arctic Expedi-
        tion, 1913-18. Vol. 14. Ottawa: King's Printer, 1925.
        506 pp.

A 1469 Roberts, Helen H., and Morris Swadesh. Songs of the
        Nootka Indians of Western Vancouver Island. Philadel-
        phia: American Philosophical Society, 1955. 128 pp.

C 1470 Rousselière, Guy Mary. 'Innusivut: Our Way of Living.'
        Beaver, Spring 1959, pp. 29-36. [Inuit songs.]

C 1480 Saindon, J. Emile. 'Two Cree Songs from James Bay.'
        Primitive Man, 7(Jan. 1934), 6-7.

C 1481 Sapir, Edward. 'Songs for a Comox Dancing Mask.' Ethnos,
        4(Apr.-June 1939), 49-55.

C 1482 'Sarcee Grub Dance.' Calgary Herald, 1 Oct. 1884; rpt.
        Alberta Historical Review, 17(Summer 1969), 9.

C 1483 Sargent, Margaret [Margaret S. McTaggart]. 'Seven Songs
        from Lorette.' JAF, 63(1950), 175-80.

C 1484 Shaw, A. C. 'A Sun Dance Among the Sarcees.' Canadian
        Magazine, 3(1894), 10-17.

B 1485 Skinner, Alanson B. 'The Sun Dance of the Plains Cree,'
        and 'The Sun Dance of the Plains Ojibway.' Anthropo-
        logical Papers of the American Museum of Natural His-
        tory, 16(1919), 283-93; 311-15.

C 1486 Smith, Nicholas N. 'Saint Francis Indian Dances--1960.'
        Ethnomusicology, 6(1962), 15-19.

C 1487 Steenhoven, Geert van den. 'Songs and Dances; Charac-
        teristic Life-Expression of the Eskimo.' Eskimo, 50
        (Mar. 1959), 3-6.

C 1488 Stuart, Wendy B. 'Coast Salish Gambling Music.' CFMJ, 2
        (1974), 3-12.

B 1489 -- Gambling Music of the Coast Salish Indians. Ottawa:
        National Museum, Ethnology Division Mercury Series 3,
        1973. 114 pp.

B 1490 Suttles, Wayne. 'The Plateau Prophet Dance Among the
        Coast Salish.' Southwestern Journal of Anthropology, 13
        (1957), 352-96.

A 1491 Swanton, John R. 'Haida Songs.' Publications of the
        American Ethnological Society, 3(1912), 1-63; rpt. Ley-
        den: Brill, 1912. 63 pp.

C 1492 Tegoodliak. 'Songs of the Eskimo.' Beaver, Spring 1954,
        p. 2.

Folk Music and Dance

B 1493   Vennum, Thomas, Jr., 'Ojibwa Origin-Migration Songs
          of the mitewiwin.' JAF, 91(1978), 753-91.

A 1494   Wallis, Wilson D. 'The Sun Dance of the Canadian
          Dakota.' Anthropological Papers of the American Museum
          of Natural History, 16(1921), 317-80.

A 1495   Wallis, Wilson D., and Ruth S. Wallis. 'Dances, Games
          and Songs.' The Micmac Indians of Eastern Canada. Min-
          neapolis: Univ. of Minnesota Press, 1955. Pp. 191-230.

C 1496   Wickwire, Wendy. 'Traditional Musical Culture at the
          Native Canadian Centre in Toronto.' CFMJ, 4(1976),
          48-55.

C(s) 1497 Wiebe, Rudy. 'Songs of the Canadian Eskimo.' Canadian
          Literature, No. 52 (Spring 1972), pp. 57-69.

B 1498   Witmer, Robert. 'Recent Change in the Musical Culture
          of the Blood Indians of Alberta.' Yearbook for Inter-
          American Musical Research, 9(1973), 64-94.

C 1499   -- '"White" Music Among the Blood Indians of Alberta.'
          CFMJ, 2(1974), 35-39.

C 1500   Wuttunee, William I. C. 'Thirst Dance of the Crees.'
          Beaver, Winter 1962, pp. 20-23.

     5E   Other Cultural Groups

C 1501   Clarfield, Geoffrey. 'Music in the Moroccan Jewish
          Community of Toronto.' CFMJ, 4(1976), 31-38.

C 1502   Creighton, Helen. 'Dances, Games, and Songs.' Folklore
          of Lunenburg County, Nova Scotia. Ottawa: National Mu-
          seum, Bulletin 117, 1950, pp. 78-84.

B 1503   Dz'obko, J. My Songs. A Selection of Ukrainian Folk-
          songs in English Translation. Winnipeg: Ukrainian
          Canadian Pioneer Library, 1958. 102 pp.

B 1504   -- Ukrainian Lemko and Other Folksongs. Winnipeg: Uk-
          rainian Canadian Pioneer Library, 1956. 126 pp.

G 1505   Ewach, Honoré. Ukrainian Songs and Lyrics. A Short
          Anthology of Ukrainian Poetry. Winnipeg: Ukrainian
          Publishing Co., 1933. 77 pp.

C 1506   Feintuch, Burt. 'Sointula, British Columbia: Aspects
          of a Folk Music Tradition.' CFMJ, 1(1973), 24-31.

G 1507   Gibbon, John Murray. 'Contributions of Austro-German
         Music to Canadian Culture.' TRSC, 43(1949) sec.2,
         pp. 57-71.

C 1508   Hawryluk-Charney, Halia. 'Ukrainian Christmas Carols
         (Koliadky and Schedriwky).' ZHinochyj svit (Winnipeg),
         13:1(1962), 17-19.

C 1509   Henry, Frances. 'Black Music in the Maritimes.' CFMJ, 3
         (1975), 11-21.

G 1510   Kirkconnell, Watson. 'Ukrainian-Canadian Poetry.' In
         Canadian Overtones. Winnipeg: Columbia Press, 1935. Pp.
         76-82.

C 1511   Kirshenblatt-Gimblett, Barbara. 'Yivo Folksong Project:
         New York, Montreal, Toronto.' CFMJ, 1(1973), 16-17.

C 1512   Klymash, Bohdan, comp. Ukrainian Folk Dance. A Sympo-
         sium, No. 1. Winnipeg: UNYF of Canada, 1961. 58 pp.
         Mimeo.

C 1513   Klymasz, Robert B. 'Social and Cultural Motifs in Cana-
         dian Ukrainian Lullabies.' Slavic and East European
         Journal, 12(1968), 176-84.

C 1514   -- '"Sounds You Never Heard Before": Ukrainian Country
         Music in Western Canada.' Ethnomusicology, 16(1972),
         372-80.

A 1516   -- The Ukrainian-Canadian Immigrant Folksong Cycle.
         Ottawa: National Museum, Bulletin 234, 1970. 106 pp.

C 1517   -- 'The Ukrainian Folksong in Canada.' Blue Yodel, 3
         (March 1965), 3-4.

C 1518   -- 'Ukrainian Incest Ballads from Western Canada.'
         CFMJ, 1(1973), 35-37.

A 1519   -- The Ukrainian Winter Folksong Cycle in Canada.
         Ottawa: National Museum, Bulletin 236, 1970. 156 pp.

A 1520   Klymasz, Robert B., and James Porter. 'Traditional
         Ukrainian Balladry in Canada.' Western Folklore, 33
         (1974), 89-132.

A 1521   Livesay, Florence R. Songs of Ukrainia. London: Dent,
         1916. 175 pp.

C 1522   McIntyre, Paul. Black Pentecostal Music in Windsor.
         Ottawa: National Museum, CCFCS Mercury Series 15, 1976.
         124 pp.

B 1523   Martens, Helen. 'The Music of Some Religious Minorities
         in Canada.' Ethnomusicology, 16(1972), 360-71.

C 1524 Mealing, F. Mark. 'Sons-of-Freedom Songs in English.' CFMJ, 4(1976), 15-24.

C 1525 Medwidsky, Bohdan. 'A Ukrainian Assassination Ballad in Canada.' CFMJ, 6(1978), 30-37.

P 1526 Paluk, William. 'Folk Dancing.' Canadian Cossacks, 1943, pp. 35-42.

A 1527 Peacock, Kenneth. A Garland of Rue: Lithuanian Folk-songs of Love and Betrothal. Ottawa: National Museum, 1971. 60 pp.

B 1528 -- 'The Music of the Doukhobors.' Alphabet, No. 11 (Dec. 1965), pp. 35-44.

A 1529 -- Songs of the Doukhobors. Ottawa: National Museum, Bulletin 231, 1970. 167 pp.

B 1530 -- A Survey of Ethnic Folk Music Across Western Canada. Ottawa: National Museum, Anthropology Paper 5, 1965. 13 pp.

A 1531 -- Twenty Ethnic Songs from Western Canada. Ottawa: National Museum, Bulletin 211, 1966. 91 pp.

B 1532 Pelinski, Ramón. 'The Music of Canada's Ethnic Minorities.' Canada Music Book, Spring/Summer 1975, pp. 59-86.

C 1533 Proracki, Anthony, and Alan Henderson. 'Ukrainian-Canadian Folk Music of the Waterford Area.' CFMJ, 2(1974), 19-28.

B 1534 Qureshi, Regula. 'Ethnomusicological Research Among Canadian Communities of Arab and East Indian Origin.' Ethnomusicology, 16(1972), 381-96.

F 1535 Rubin, Ruth. Jewish Folk Songs in Yiddish and English. New York: Oak, 1965. 96 pp.

F 1536 -- 'Slavic Influences in Yiddish Folk Song.' In Folk-lore & Society. Ed. Bruce Jackson. Hatboro, PA: Folk-lore Associates, 1966. Pp. 131-52.

F 1537 -- Voices of a People. New York: McGraw-Hill, 1963. 496 pp.

C 1538 -- 'Yiddish Folk Songs Current in French Canada.' JIFMC, 12(1960), 76-78.

B 1539 Song, Bang-song. The Korean-Canadian Folk Song: An Ethnomusicological Study. Ottawa: National Museum, CCFCS Mercury Series 10, 1974. 225 pp.

P 1540 Songs sung by the Famous Canadian Jubilee Singers, the
Royal Paragon Male Quartette and Imperial Orchestra.
Hamilton, Ont.: Duncan Lithograph, n.d. 51 pp.

G 1541 Staebler, H. L. 'Random Notes on Music of Nineteenth-
Century Berlin, Ontario.' Waterloo Historical Society,
37th Annual Report, 1949.

For 5A see also items 16, 25, 32, 33, 38, 42, 63, 65,
68, 71, 82, 107, 112, 113, 123, 127, 139, 147, 179,
1712, 3766, 3797, and 3809.

For 5B, 23, 69, 70, 106, 178, 207, 242, 250, 251, 3414,
3415, 3763, 3791, 3810, 3829, 3831, 3852, 3864, 3867,
and 3872.

For 5C, 27, 36, 3815, 3829, 3839, and 3863.

For 5D, 14, 22, 41, 264, 281, 1903, 1929, 1949, 1959,
1963, 2457, 2487, 3777, 3794, 3804, 3812, 3813, 3838,
3841, 3851, 3869, and 3874.

For 5E, 334, 3806, 3814, 3816, and 3831.

6 Folk Speech and Naming

C 1542 Ahrend, E. R. 'Ontario Speech.' American Speech, 9 (1934), 136-39.

C 1543 Akrigg, G. P. V. 'British Columbia Place Names.' Western Folklore, 12(1953), 44-49.

Gb 1544 Akrigg, G. P. V., and Helen Akrigg. 1001 British Columbia Place Names. Vancouver: Discovery, 1969. 195 pp.

A 1545 Alexander, Henry. The Story of Our Language. Toronto: Nelson, 1940. 242 pp.

A 1546 Armstrong, George H. The Origin and Meaning of Place Names in Canada. Toronto: Macmillan, 1930; rpt. 1972. 312 pp.

C 1547 Baker, Edna. Prairie Place Names. Toronto: Ryerson, 1928. 28 pp.

B 1548 Barbeau, C. Marius. 'The Language of Canada in the Voyages of Jacques Cartier (1534-38).' Ottawa: National Museum, Bulletin 173, 1959, pp. 108-229.

C 1549 -- 'Legends and History in the Oldest Geographical Names of the St. Lawrence.' CGJ, 61(July 1960), 208-11. [Articles with the same title in Inland Seas, 17 (Summer 1961), 105-13, and Quarterly Journal of the Great Lakes Historical Society (Cleveland), 17(1961), 105-14.]

Gc 1550 Bell, Charles N. Some Historical Names and Places of the Canadian Northwest. Winnipeg: Manitoba Free Press, 1885. 8 pp.

F 1551 Bergen, Fanny. 'Popular American Plant-Names.' JAF, 7 (1894), 89-104; 9(1896), 179-96; 11(1898), 273-83.

P 1552 Berton, Pierre. "A Glossary of Distinct Canadian Terms." Toronto Star, 31 Oct. 1962, p. 37.

B 1553 Boas, Franz. Geographical Names of the Kwakiutl Indians. New York: Columbia Univ. Press, 1934. 83 pp.

P 1554 Brown, Harrison. Admirals, Adventurers and Able Seamen. Vancouver: Keystone, 1954. 30 pp.

Gc 1555 Brown, Thomas J. Place Names of the Province of Nova Scotia. Halifax: Royal Print, 1922. 158 pp.

C 1556 Buyniak, V. O. 'Place Names of the Early Dukhobor [sic] Settlement in Saskatchewan.' Slavs in Canada, 3(1971), 143-49.

C 1557 Cameron, Alex R. 'Place Names.' Saskatchewan History. 1(May 1948), 23-24; 1(Oct. 1948), 21-22; 2(Jan. 1949), 28-29.

B 1558 Chamberlain, Alexander F. 'Dialect Research in Canada.' Dialect Notes, 1(1890), 43-56.

B 1559 -- 'The Vocabulary of Canadian French.' Proc. of the 15th Session of the International Congress of Americanists, 1(1906), 21-31.

Ga 1560 Chambers, J. K., ed. Canadian English: Origins and Structures. Toronto: Methuen, 1975. 144 pp.

B 1561 Chartier, Emile. 'The So-Called French-Canadian Patois.' Queen's Quarterly, 39(1932), 240-49.

P 1562 Coffman, Barbara. 'Nicknames and the Twenty.' Canadian-German Folklore, 7(1979), 83-85.

C 1563 Colbourne, W., and G. Reid. 'Newfoundland's Naked Man.' RLS, No. 8(1978), pp. 30-41.

B 1564 Corry, J. H. 'Some Canadian Cities (Meaning and Origin of Names).' CGJ, 26(June 1943), 297; 27(July 1943), 17; 27(Dec. 1943), 263; 27(Jan. 1944), 40.

C 1565 Cotter, H. M. S. 'A Fur Trade Glossary.' Beaver, Sept. 1941, pp. 36-39.

B 1566 Creighton, Helen. 'Cape Breton Nicknames and Tales.' In Folklore in Action. Ed. Horace Beck. Hatboro, PA: Folklore Associates, 1962. Pp. 71-76.

B 1567 Day, Gordon M. The "Mots Loups" of Father Mathevet. Ottawa: National Museum, 1975. 430 pp.

B 1568 Dempsey, Hugh A. Indian Names for Alberta Communities. Calgary: Glenbow, 1969. 19 pp.

A 1569 Devine, P. K. Devine's Folklore of Newfoundland in Old Words, Phrases and Expressions; Their Origin and Meaning. St. John's: Robinson, 1937. 80 pp.

Ga 1570   A Dictionary of Canadianisms on Historical Principles.
           Produced for W. J. Gage by the Lexicographical Centre
           for Canadian English, Univ. of Victoria, 1967. 927 pp.

 C 1571   Dictionary of Chinook Jargon or Indian Trade Language
           of the North Pacific Coast. 1899; rpt. Seattle: Shorey
           Book Store, 1973. 42 pp.

 C 1572   Dillard, Joseph L. 'The West African Day-Names in Nova
           Scotia.' Names, 19(1971), 257-61.

 C 1573   Douglas, Robert. Meaning of Canadian City Names. Otta-
           wa: Acland, 1922. 21 pp.

 C 1574   -- 'The Place Names of Canada.' Scottish Geographical
           Magazine (Edinburgh), 36(1920), 154-57.

Gc 1575   -- Place Names of Prince Edward Island. Ottawa: Ac-
           land, 1925. 55 pp.

 B 1576   Duff, Louis B. 'Names are Pegs to Hang History On.'
           Ontario History, 23(1926), 223-36.

 B 1577   -- The Romance of Our Place Names. Fort Erie, Ont.:
           Review Co., 1934. 22 pp.

 B 1578   Emeneau, Murray B. 'The Dialect of Lunenburg, Nova
           Scotia.' Language, 11(1935), 140-47; 16(1940), 214-15.

 A 1579   England, George A. 'Newfoundland Dialect Items.' Dia-
           lect Notes, 5(1925), 322-46.

 G 1580   Fergusson, C. Bruce. Place Names and Places of Nova
           Scotia. Halifax: Public Archives, 1967. 751 pp.

Gc 1581   Frame, Elizabeth, comp. A List of Micmac Names of
           Places, Rivers, etc. in Nova Scotia. 1892; rpt.
           Norwood, PA: Norwood, n.d. 12 pp.

GP 1582   Gardiner, Herbert F. Nothing But Names. Toronto: Mor-
           ang, 1899. 561 pp.

 B 1583   Geikie, A. Constable. 'Canadian English.' Canadian
           Journal, 2(1857), 344-55.

 C 1584   Greenleaf, Elisabeth B. 'Newfoundland Words.' American
           Speech, 6(1931), 306.

Ga 1585   Hamilton, William B. The Macmillan Book of Canadian
           Place Names. Toronto: Macmillan, 1978. 340 pp.

 C 1586   Harbron, John D. 'Spaniards on the Coast.' Beaver,
           Summer 1957, pp. 4-8.

 C 1587   Harrington, Lyn. 'Chinook Jargon.' Beaver, Winter 1958,
           pp. 26-29.

103

C 1588   Harrington, Michael F. 'Newfoundland Names.' Atlantic
         Advocate, 47(Oct. 1956), 71-77.

C 1589   Hibben, T. N. Dictionary of Chinook Jargon; Indian
         Trade Language of the Pacific Coast. Victoria: Author,
         1892. 33 pp.

A 1590   Higinbotham, John D. 'Western Vernacular.' Alberta His-
         torical Review, 10(Autumn 1962), 9-17. Rpt. in Folklore
         of Canada. Ed. Edith Fowke. Toronto: McClelland &
         Stewart, 1976. Pp. 243-51.

G 1591   Holmgren, Eric J., and Patricia M. Holmgren. Over 2000
         Place Names of Alberta. Saskatoon, Sask.: Western
         Producer, 1977. 326 pp.

B 1592   Howay, F. W. 'The Origin of the Chinook Jargon.' B.C.
         Historical Quarterly, 6(1942), 225-50.

C 1593   Howley, M. F. 'Newfoundland Name-Lore, Articles 1 and
         2.' Newfoundland Quarterly, 64(Fall, 1965), 14-18.
         [Rpt. from Newfoundland Quarterly, 19(1901).]

C 1594   Ipellie, Alootook. 'Inuit Names.' Inuit Today, 5(June
         1976), 44-47.

B 1595   Jackson, Kenneth. 'Notes on the Gaelic of Port Hood,
         Nova Scotia.' Scottish Gaelic Studies, 6(1949), 89-109.

Gc 1596 Johnson, George. 'Place Names of Canada.' Ottawa
         Literary and Scientific Society Trans., 1(1898), 24-62.

C 1597   Jones, C. Meredith. 'Indian, Pseudo-Indian Place
         Names in the Canadian West.' Onomastica, No. 12(1955),
         pp. 7-19.

C 1598   Jordan, J. 'Induction to Dialect.' New Newfoundland
         Quarterly, 65(Feb. 1967), 23-26.

B 1599   Keenleyside, Hugh L. 'Place Names of Newfoundland.'
         CGJ, 29(Dec. 1944), 255-67.

B 1600   Kerr, James. 'British Columbia Place Names.' CGJ, 2
         (Feb. 1931), 153-70.

C 1601   King, William C. Scottish Place Names in Canada.
         Winnipeg: Canadian Institute of Onomastic Sciences
         and Ukrainian Free Academy of Sciences, 1970. 32 pp.

C 1602   Kirwin, William J. 'A Collection of Popular Etymolo-
         gies in Newfoundland Vocabulary.' RLS, No. 3(1971),
         pp. 16-18.

C 1603   --   'A Glossary of c.1900 by J. P. Howley (1847-1918).'
         RLS, No. 8(1978), pp. 22-27.

B 1604 Kirwin, William J. 'Lines, Coves, and Squares in New-foundland Names.' American Speech, 40(1965), 163-70.

C 1605 -- 'Newfoundland Usage in the "Survey of Canadian English."' RLS, No. 5(1974), pp. 9-14.

B 1606 Klymasz, Robert B. 'The Canadianization of Slavic Sur-names. A Study in Language Contact.' Names, 11(1963), 81-105, 182-95, 229-53.

B 1607 Knight, Margaret Bennett. 'Scottish Gaelic, English and French: Some Aspects of the Macaronic Tradition of the Codroy Valley, Newfoundland.' RLS, No. 4(1972), pp. 25-30.

C 1608 Leechman, Douglas. 'The Chinook Jargon.' American Speech, 1(1926), 531-34.

B 1609 McAtee, W. L. Folk Names of Canadian Birds. Ottawa: National Museum, Bulletin No. 149, 1957. 74 pp.

Ga 1610 McConnell, R. E. Our Own Voice: Canadian English and How It Came To Be. Toronto: Gage, 1978. 288 pp.

C 1611 MacLeod, Calum I. N. 'Nova Scotia's "Operation Gael-ic."' Food for Thought, 16(Dec. 1955), 109-12.

Gb 1612 Middleton, Evelyn M. C. Place Names of the Pacific Northwest Coast. Victoria: Elldee, 1969. 226 pp.

B 1613 Moore, William F. Indian Place Names in Ontario. Tor-onto: Macmillan, 1930. 48 pp.

C 1614 Newell, William W. 'A Remarkable Oath.' JAF, 7(1894), 60.

P 1615 Orkin, Mark M. Canajan, Eh? Toronto: General, 1973. 128 pp.

P 1616 -- French Canajan, Hé? Toronto: Lester & Orpen, 1975. 126 pp.

B 1617 -- Speaking Canadian English. Toronto: General, 1970. 276 pp.

B 1618 -- Speaking Canadian French. Toronto: General, 1967; rev. 1971. 132 pp.

C 1619 Orrell, John. 'Canadianisms.' Beaver, Winter, 1971, pp. 20-22.

A 1620 Patterson, George. 'Notes on the Dialect of the People of Newfoundland.' JAF, 8(1895), 27-40; 9(1896), 19-37; 10(1897), 203-13.

A 1621 Patterson, George. 'Notes on the Dialect of the People of Newfoundland.' Trans. of the N.S. Institute of Natural Science, 9(1896), 44-78.

C 1622 Peel, Bruce. 'Place Names.' Saskatchewan History, 2(May 1949), 29.

C(s) 1623 Porter, Bernard H. 'A Newfoundland Vocabulary.' Northeast Folklore 3(1960), 35-38.

C 1624 Rand, Silas T. Micmac Place-names in the Maritime Provinces and the Gaspé Peninsula. Ed. W. P. Anderson. Ottawa: Geographic Board, 1919. 116 pp.

C 1625 Reed, T. A. 'The Historic Value of Street Names.' Ontario History, 25(1929), 385-87.

B 1626 Rouleau, E. 'Some Newfoundland Vernacular Plant Names.' Studies on the Vascular Flora of the Province of Newfoundland (Canada). Montreal: Institut Botanique de Université de Montréal, 1956. Pp. 25-40.

B 1627 Rudnyc'kyj, Jaroslav B. Canadian Place Names of Ukrainian Origin. Winnipeg: Ukrainian Free Academy of Sciences, 1957. 96 pp.

C 1628 -- Canadian Slavic Namelore. Winnipeg: Ukrainian Free Academy of Sciences, 1956. 32 pp.

A 1629 -- Manitoba Mosaic of Place Names. Winnipeg: Canadian Institute of Onomastic Sciences, 1970. 221 pp.

Gc 1630 Russell, E. T. What's in a Name? Saskatoon: Western Producer, 1973. 364 pp.

B 1631 Sandilands, John. Western Canadian Dictionary and Phrase-Book. 1913; rpt. Edmonton: Univ. of Alberta, 1977. 64 pp.

A 1632 Scargill, M. H. 'Canadianisms from Western Canada, with special reference to British Columbia.' TRSC, 6 (1968), Sec. 2, pp. 181-98.

Ga 1633 -- 'The Growth of Canadian English.' In Literary History of Canada. Ed. Carl F. Klinck. Toronto: Univ. of Toronto Press, 2nd ed. 1976. Pp. 265-73.

Ga 1634 -- Modern Canadian English Usage. Toronto: McClelland & Stewart, 1974. 143 pp.

Ga 1635 -- A Short History of Canadian English. Victoria: Sono Nis, 1976. 63 pp.

C 1636 Scott, S. Osborne, and D. A. Mulligan. 'The Red River Dialect.' Beaver, Dec. 1951, pp. 42-45.

B 1637 Seary, E. R. 'The Anatomy of Newfoundland Place Names.' *Names*, 6(1958), 193-207.

C 1638 -- 'The French Element in Newfoundland Place Names.' *Onomastica*, No. 16 (1958), p. 16.

B 1639 -- 'Linguistic Variety in the Place Names of Newfoundland.' *CGJ*, 65(Nov. 1962), 146-55.

G 1640 -- *Family Names of the Island of Newfoundland*. St. John's: Memorial Univ., 1976. 541 pp.

C 1641 -- 'The Place Names of Newfoundland.' In *The Book of Newfoundland*. Vol. III. Ed. J. R. Smallwood. St. John's: Nfld. Book Pub., 1967. Pp. 257-64.

A 1642 -- *Place Names of the Avalon Peninsula of the Island of Newfoundland*. Toronto: Published for Memorial Univ. by Univ. of Toronto Press, 1971. 383 pp.

A 1643 Seary, E. R., G. M. Story, and W. J. Kirwin. *The Avalon Peninsula of Newfoundland: An Ethnolinguistic Study*. Ottawa: National Museum, Bulletin 219, 1968. 115 pp.

B 1644 Sinclair, D. Maclean. 'Gaelic in Nova Scotia.' *Dalhousie Review*, 30(1950), 252-60.

C 1645 Small, Lawrence G. 'Traditional Expressions in a Newfoundland Community: Genre Change and Functional Variability.' *Lore and Language*, 2(July 1975), 15-18.

B 1646 Stoker, John T. 'Spoken French in Newfoundland.' *Culture*, 25(1964), 349-59.

C 1647 Story, George M. 'A Critical History of Dialect Collecting in Newfoundland.' *RLS*, No. 6(1975), pp. 1-4.

B 1648 -- 'The Dialects of Newfoundland.' In *The Book of Newfoundland*. Vol. III. Ed. J. R. Smallwood. St. John's: Nfld. Book Pub., 1967. Pp. 559-63.

C 1649 -- 'Newfoundland Dialect.' In *The Story of Newfoundland*. Ed. A. B. Perlin. St. John's: Guardian, 1959. Pp. 68-70.

B 1650 -- 'Newfoundland Dialect: An Historical View.' *CGJ*, 70(Apr. 1965), 126-32.

C 1651 -- *A Newfoundland Dialect Dictionary--A Survey of the Problems*. St. John's: Memorial Univ., 1956. 14 pp.

C 1652 -- 'Newfoundland English Usage.' *Encyclopaedia Canadiana*, Vol. 7, 1958, pp. 321-22.

B 1653 -- 'Research in the Language and Place Names of Newfoundland.' *Journal of the Can. Linguistic Assoc.*, 3 (1957), 47-55.

C 1654   Story, George M., and William Kirwin. 'The Dictionary of Newfoundland English: Progress and Promise.' <u>RLS</u>, No. 5(1974), pp. 15-17.

C 1655   Story, G. M., W. Kirwin, and J. D. A. Widdowson. 'Collecting for <u>The Dictionary of Newfoundland English</u>.' <u>Annals of the N.Y. Academy of Science</u>, 211(June 1973), 104-8.

C 1656   Strong, W. D. 'More Labrador Survivals.' <u>American Speech</u>, 6(1931), 290-91.

P 1657   Swanson, Robert E. 'A Logger's Dictionary.' In <u>Rhymes of a Western Logger</u>. Vancouver: Lumberman Printing, 1943. Pp. 49-56.

B 1658   Taft, Michael. 'The Case of 'Up She Comes' in Newfoundland Culture.' <u>Lore and Language</u>, 2(Jan. 1979), 10-24.

B 1659   Thomas, Edward H. <u>Chinook: A History and Dictionary</u>. Portland, OR: Metropolitan, 1925. 179 pp.

C 1660   -- 'The Chinook Jargon.' <u>American Speech</u>, 2(1927), 374-84.

B 1661   Thomas, Gerald. 'Some Examples of <u>Blason Populaire</u> from the French Tradition of Western Newfoundland.' <u>RLS</u>, No. 7(1976), pp. 29-33.

B 1662   Tompkinson, Grace. 'Shakespeare in Newfoundland.' <u>Dalhousie Review</u>, 20(1940), pp. 60-70.

B 1663   Turner, Allen R. 'Saskatchewan Place Names: A Mirror Held Up to History.' <u>Saskatchewan History</u>, 18:3(1965), 81-88.

C 1664   Tweedie, W. M. 'British Maritime Provinces Word-List.' <u>Dialect Notes</u>, 1(1890), 377-81.

B 1665   Tyrrell, J. B. 'Algonquian Indian Names.' <u>Trans. Royal Canadian Institute</u>, 10(1915), 213-31.

C 1666   -- <u>Algonquian Indian Names of Places in Northern Canada</u>. Toronto: University Press, 1915. 231 pp.

Gb 1667   Walbran, John T. <u>British Columbia Coast Names, 1592-1906</u>. 1909; rpt. Vancouver: Douglas, 1971. 546 pp.

C 1668   Wells, Oliver N. <u>A Vocabulary of Native Words in the Halkomelem Language as used by the Native People of the Lower Fraser Valley, B.C.</u> Trans. C. Casey Wells. Sardis, B.C.: Author, 1965. 47 pp.

C 1669   Wheeler, E. P. <u>List of Labrador Eskimo Place Names</u>. Ottawa: National Museum, Bulletin 131, 1953. 105 pp.

Gc 1670 White, James. <u>Place Names in Quebec, the Thousand Islands, and Northern Canada</u>. Ottawa: Geographic Board, 1910. 302 pp.

C 1671 Widdowson, J. D. A. 'A Checklist of Newfoundland Expressions.' <u>Lore and Language</u>, 2(Jan. 1979), 33-40.

C 1672 -- 'Settlement Patterns and Newfoundland Folklore.' In <u>The Graduate Society 1967</u>. Eds. D. H. Barnes and R. J. Wiseman. [St. John's], 1967. Pp. 14-15.

B 1673 -- 'Some Items of a Central Newfoundland Dialect.' <u>Canadian Journal of Linguistics</u>, 10(Fall 1964), 37-46.

P 1674 Wilkinson, Ron. 'Labelling the Land: Canada Needs 2,000,000 More Place Names.' <u>CGJ</u>, 87(July 1973), 12-19.

FC 1675 Wintemberg, W. J. 'Algonkian Words in American English.' <u>JAF</u>, 16(1903), 128-29; 21(1908), 82.

B 1676 -- <u>Folk-Lore of Waterloo County, Ontario</u>. Ottawa: National Museum, Bulletin 116, 1950, pp. 29-46.

C 1677 -- '"Squaw Winter," "Indian Winter," "Dogwood Winter."' <u>JAF</u>, 20(1907), 235-36.

G 1678 Wood, William C. H. <u>Place-names of Quebec</u>. Montreal: Gazette, 1922. 20 pp.

See also items 10, 79, 85, 150, 244, 260, 292-294, 301, 3765, 3767, 3787, 3822, 3826, 3827, 3857, 3871.

7 Minor Genres: Proverbs, riddles, games, practical jokes, children's lore

FR 1679 Abrahams, Roger. Jump-Rope Rhymes: A Dictionary. Austin: Univ. of Texas Press, 1969. 228 pp.

FR 1680 Abrahams, Roger, and Lois Rankin. Counting-Out Rhymes: A Dictionary. Austin: Univ. of Texas Press, 1979. 252 pp.

P 1681 Allen, Robert Thomas. 'The Tribal Customs of Space-Age Children.' Maclean's, 6 July, 1963, pp. 18-19, 42-45.

P 1682 Alspector, J. C. 'Fun in the Ladies Room.' Canadian, 29 Apr. 1978, p. 8. [Graffiti.]

AY 1683 Barbeau, C. Marius. Roundelays--Dansons à la ronde. Ottawa: National Museum, Bulletin 151, 1958. 104 pp.

B 1684 Beauchamp, William M. 'Iroquois Games.' JAF, 9(1896), 269-77.

A 1685 Bleakney, F. Eileen. 'Folk-Lore from Ottawa and Vicinity.' JAF, 31(1918), 158-69.

C 1686 Boas, Franz. 'Two Eskimo Riddles from Labrador.' JAF, 39(1926), 486.

F 1687 Bolton, Henry C. The Counting-Out Rhymes of Children. 1888; rpt. Detroit: Gale, 1969. 123 pp.

B 1688 Boyle, David. 'Canadian Folklore.' Articles in the Globe (Toronto), 13 Nov. 1897--8 Jan. 1898.

C 1689 Brown, Mrs. W. Wallace. 'Some Indoor and Outdoor Games of the Wabanaki Indians.' TRSC, 6(1888), sec. 2, pp. 41-46.

GP 1690 Bull, W. Perkins. From Rattlesnake Hunt to Hockey. Toronto: Perkins Bull Foundation, 1934. 564 pp.

C 1691 Chamberlain, Alexander F. 'Folk-lore of Canadian Children.' JAF, 8(1895), 252-55.

C 1692 -- 'Folklore of Canadian Children.' Canadian Magazine, 61(1923), 197-202.

C 1693   'Children Play for Keeps.' Canada Today/Aujourd'hui (Washington, D.C.), 9:5(1978), 7.

P 1694   Chittick, V. L. O. 'Haliburton's Wise Sayings and Homey Imagery.' Dalhousie Review, 38(1958-1959), 348-63.

P 1695   Chojnacki, Lillian. 'Cinderella's Curious Yella.' Weekend Magazine, 30 May 1970, pp. 8-10.

GP 1696   Colombo, John Robert. Colombo's Little Book of Canadian Proverbs, Graffiti, Limericks and Other Vital Matters. Edmonton: Hurtig, 1975. 143 pp.

C 1697   Cosbey, Robert C. '"Down the Okanagan": Skipping Songs from Regina.' CFMJ, 1(1973), 31-32.

A 1698   Creighton, Helen. Folklore of Lunenburg County, Nova Scotia. Ottawa: National Museum, Bulletin 117, 1950, pp. 73-78; 105-122.

F 1699   Culin, Stewart. Games of the North American Indians. 24th Annual Report of the Bureau of American Ethnology, Washington, 1902-3, pp. 1-846; rpt. New York: Dover, 1975. 846 pp.

C 1700   Doering, J. Frederick. 'More Folk Customs from Western Ontario.' JAF, 58(1945), 153-55. [Games.]

B 1701   Dorsey, George A. 'Games of the Makah Indians of Neah Bay.' American Antiquity, 23(1901), 69-73.

B 1702   Dunn, Charles W. 'Gaelic Proverbs in Nova Scotia.' JAF, 72(1959), 30-35.

B 1703   Durand, L. 'Play Rhymes of the Dominion.' Globe, 13 Nov.- 18 Dec. 1909.

C 1704   Eager, Evelyn. 'Our Pioneers Say.' Saskatchewan History, 6(Winter 1953), 1-12.

C 1705   Einarsson, Magnús. 'Icelandic Pular.' In Folklore of Canada. Ed. Edith Fowke. Toronto: McClelland & Stewart, 1976. Pp. 287-90.

C 1706   Ewers, John C. 'Some Winter Sports of Blackfoot Indian Children.' Masterkey, 18(1944), 180-87.

A 1707   Fauset, Arthur Huff. 'Game Songs and Counting-Out Rhymes,' 'Nursery Rhymes and Other Verses,' and 'Riddle Tales and Riddles.' Folklore from Nova Scotia. New York: American Folklore Society, 1931. Pp. 127-76.

C 1708   Fidler, Vera. 'String Figures,' Beaver, Winter 1963, pp. 18-21.

C 1709   Fowke, Edith. 'Autograph Verses from Saskatchewan.'
         Folklore of Canada. Toronto: McClelland & Stewart,
         1976. Pp. 236-43.

C 1710   -- 'Canadian Folk Songs for Children.' In Review, 4
         (Winter 1970), 5-11.

Gc 1711 -- 'Children's Rhymes, Past and Present.' Hoot, 2
         (Sept. 1966), 40-43, 49.

AY 1712 -- Sally Go Round the Sun: 100 Songs, Rhymes, and
         Games of Canadian Children. Toronto: McClelland &
         Stewart, 1969. 160 pp.

C 1713   Gatschet, Albert S. 'Micmac Fans and Games.' Bulletin
         of the Free Museum of Science and Arts, Univ. of Penn-
         sylvania, 2(1900), 190-94.

P 1714   Gibbs, Lesley. 'Where Are the Old Games?' Globe Maga-
         zine, 14 June, 1969, p. 14.

B 1715   Glassford, R. Gerald. 'Organization of Games and Adap-
         tive Strategies of the Canadian Eskimo.' In The Cross-
         Cultural Analysis of Sport and Games. Ed. Gunther Lus-
         chen. Champaign, IL: Stipes, 1970. Pp. 70-85.

A 1716   Greenleaf, Elisabeth B. 'Riddles of Newfoundland.'
         Marshall Review, 1(Mar. 1938), 5-20. Rpt. in Folklore
         of Canada. Ed. Edith Fowke. Toronto: McClelland &
         Stewart, 1976. Pp. 130-42.

C 1717   Halpert, Herbert. 'Skipping Rhymes from Calgary, Alber-
         ta.' California Folklore Quarterly, 3(1944), 154-55.

A 1718   Helm, June, and Nancy O. Lurie. The Dogrib Hand Game.
         Ottawa: National Museum, Bulletin 205, 1966. 101 pp.

C 1719   Howard, James H. 'The Micmac Bowl Game.' American
         Indian Tradition, 8(1962), 206-9.

G 1720   Howell, Nancy, and Maxwell L. Howell. Sports and Games
         in Canadian Life: 1700 to the Present. Toronto: Macmil-
         lan, 1975. 378 pp.

A 1721   Jenness, Diamond. 'Eskimo String Figures.' JAF, 36
         (1923), 281-94.

A 1722   -- 'String Figures of the Eskimos.' Report of the
         Canadian Arctic Expedition, 1913-1918. Vol. 13, Part B.
         Ottawa: King's Printer, 1924. 192 pp.

C 1723   Kitpou, Shaman Chief, comp. and trans. The Tribal Laws
         of the Children of Light. Wawa, Ont.: Wawa Print, 1974.
         16 pp.

C 1724 Laidlaw, George E. 'Gambling among the Cree with Small Sticks.' American Antiquity, 23(1901), 275-76.

C 1725 Leon, Alice. 'Variants of Counting-Out Rhymes.' JAF, 8(1895), 255-56.

P 1726 Lingard, Bill. 'Lacrosse--The Fastest Game on Two Feet.' Beaver, Autumn 1969, pp. 12-16.

C 1727 Lunardini, Rosemary. '"Tuque Bleue."' Beaver, Winter 1976, pp. 40-45. [Snowshoeing.]

C 1728 Lund, Rolf T. 'Skiing in Canada: The Early Years.' Beaver, Winter 1977, pp. 48-53.

C 1729 McLean, John. 'Blackfoot Amusements.' American Antiquity, 23(1901), 163-69.

P 1730 McRae, Earl. 'Days of Sun and Laughter.' Canadian, 13 Aug. 1977, pp. 6-9. [Children's games.]

F 1731 Matthews, Washington. 'Counting-Out Rhymes among Indian Children.' American Anthropologist, 2(1889), 320.

C 1732 Morison, Mrs. O. 'Tsimshian Proverbs.' JAF, 2(1889), 285-86.

B 1733 Morrison, Monica. 'Wedding Night Pranks in Western New Brunswick.' Southern Folklore, 38(1974), 285-97.

C 1734 Murphy, James. 'Newfoundland Proverbs.' Christmas Review, (St. John's), 1895, p. 12.

C 1735 Newell, William W. 'A Wabanaki Counting-Out Rhyme.' JAF, 3(1890), 71-73.

P 1736 Newfoundland Cook Book. St. John's: Macy's, 1973. [Proverbs: p. 26 and passim.]

P 1737 Nichols, Mark. 'Pint-Sized Pirates of Blue Rocks.' Coronet, Aug. 1957, pp. 44-51.

P 1738 Pearson, Ian. 'Love Conkers All.' City, Toronto Star, 22 Oct. 1978, pp. 10-12. [Games.]

P 1739 Philpott, Elmore. 'Canadian Sidewalk Songs.' Canadian Home Journal. May 1938, pp. 65-66.

F 1740 Porter, Grace C. Negro Folk Singing Games and Folk Games of the Habitants. London: Currier, 1914. 35 pp.

B 1741 Posen, I. Sheldon. 'Pranks and Practical Jokes at Children's Summer Camps.' Southern Folklore Quarterly, 38(1974), 299-309.

BY 1742 Roberts, Miriam. Poems, Riddles, and Stories by Newfoundland Children. N.p., 1977. Pp. 133-58. [Riddles.]

B 1743   Robertson, Mrs. Donald (Marion). 'Counting Out Rhymes
         from Shelburne County, Nova Scotia.' Northeast Folk-
         lore, 3(1960), 27-32.

P 1744   Ross, Valerie. 'Child's Play.' City, Toronto Star,
         13 Nov. 1977, pp. 27-29.

B 1745   Scott, John R. 'Play at the Newfoundland Seal Fishery.'
         Culture & Tradition, 1(1976), 63-71.

B 1746   -- 'Practical Jokes of the Newfoundland Seal Fishery.'
         Southern Folklore Quarterly, 38(1974), 275-83.

G 1747   Sellar, Thomas. 'Choice Fragments': Being a Collection
         of Wise and Witty Sayings. Montreal: John Wilson, 1866.
         98 pp.

P 1748   Shea, A. 'Newfoundland Sled Ride.' Beaver, Fall 1957,
         pp. 26-29.

F 1749   Taylor, Archer. 'American Indian Riddles.' JAF, 57
         (1944), 1-15.

A 1750   Tremblay, Maurice. 'Nous irons jouer dans l'Isle' JAF,
         63(1950), 163-70. Rpt. in Folklore of Canada. Ed. Edith
         Fowke. Toronto: McClelland & Stewart, 1976. Pp. 53-91.

C 1751   'Waltes, an Ancient Micmac Game.' Cape Breton's Maga-
         zine. No. 6(Dec. 1973), pp. 9-12.

A 1752   Waugh, F. W. 'Canadian Folk-Lore from Ontario.' JAF,
         31(1918), 41-72.

C 1753   Wintemberg, W. J. Folk-Lore of Waterloo County, Ontario.
         Ottawa: National Museum, Bulletin 116, 1950, pp. 51-58.

C 1754   -- 'Folk-Lore Collected at Roebuck, Grenville County,
         Ontario.' JAF, 31(1918), 156-57.

A 1755   -- 'Folk-Lore Collected in the Counties of Oxford and
         Waterloo, Ontario.' JAF, 31(1918), 141-53.

C 1756   -- 'Folk-Lore Collected in Toronto and Vicinity.' JAF,
         31(1918), 130-133.

A 1757   Wintemberg, W. J., and Katherine H. Wintemberg. 'Folk-
         lore from Grey County, Ontario.' JAF, 31(1918), 103-24.

         See also items 90, 254, 258-260, 292, 321, 1116, 1190,
         3812, 3862, 3866.

8 Superstitions and Popular Beliefs: Including folk medicine, folk religion, and the supernatural

8A General

P 1758 'The Beaver: A Cure for All Ills.' Beaver, Sept. 1931, pp. 283-84.

C 1759 'Beavers. (Divination [1758] through Beavers: Cape Breton, Nova Scotia).' Folk-Lore, 2(1891), 248.

P 1760 Beers, W. George. 'The Canadian Mecca.' Century Magazine, 24(May 1882), 1-16.

P 1761 Braddock, John. 'Monsters of the Maritimes.' Atlantic Advocate, 58(Jan. 1968), 12-17.

B 1762 Childs, Ralph De S. 'Phantom Ships of the North-East Coast of North America.' New York Folklore Quarterly, 5(1949), 146-65.

P 1763 Clark, Daniel. Ghosts and their Relations. Toronto: Warwick, 1874. 306 pp.

R 1764 Clark, Samuel D. Church and Sect in Canada. Toronto: Univ. of Toronto Press, 1948. 458 pp.

P 1765 Cocking, Clive. 'Is it morally right to kill a Sasquatch?' Saturday Night, Oct. 1978, pp. 30-43.

GP 1766 Colombo, John Robert. Colombo's Book of Marvels. Toronto: NC Press, 1979. 215 pp.

GP 1767 -- Mostly Monsters. Toronto: Hounslow, 1977. 126 pp.

A 1768 Creighton, Helen. Bluenose Magic. Toronto: Ryerson, 1968. 297 pp.

P 1769 Dunbabin, Thomas. 'Canada's Horn of the Unicorn.' Beaver, Spring 1956, pp. 8-11.

Pc 1770 Gaal, Arlene B. Beneath the Depths. N.p.: Valley Review, 1976. 122 pp. [Ogopogo.]

PY 1771 Garner, Betty S. Canada's Monsters. Hamilton: Potlatch, 1977. 95 pp.

GP 1772 Gellatly, Dorothy H. A Bit of Okanagan History. West-
         bank, B.C.: Kelowna Printing, rev. ed., 1958. 133 pp.
         [Ogopogo.]

Pc 1773 Green, John. On the Track of the Sasquatch. Agassiz,
         B.C.: Cheam, 1969. 78 pp.

Pc 1774 -- The Sasquatch File. Agassiz: Cheam, 1970. 80 pp.

GPb 1775 -- Sasquatch, The Apes Among Us. Saanichton: Hancock,
         1978. 492 pp.

Pc 1776 -- Year of the Sasquatch. Agassiz: Cheam, 1970. 80 pp.

F 1777   Guenette, Robert, and Frances Guenette. The Mysterious
         Monsters. Los Angeles: Sun Classics Pictures, 1975.
         162 pp.

A 1778   Henderson, M. Carole (Carole Henderson Carpenter).
         'Monsters of the West: The Sasquatch and the Ogopogo.'
         In Folklore of Canada. Ed. Edith Fowke. Toronto:
         McClelland & Stewart, 1976. Pp. 251-62.

P 1779   Hervey, Sheila. Some Canadian Ghosts. Richmond Hill,
         Ont.: Simon & Schuster, 1973. 208 pp.

P 1780   Hunter, Don, and René Dahinden. Sasquatch. Toronto:
         McClelland & Stewart, 1973. 192 pp.

A 1781   Lambert, R. S. Exploring the Supernatural: The Weird in
         Canadian Folklore. London: Barker, 1955; rpt. Toronto:
         McClelland & Stewart, 1966. 198 pp.

P 1782   Lennox, Gary. 'The Diviners.' Weekend Magazine, 17
         Sept. 1977, p. 3.

P 1783   McCowan, Dan. 'Animal Mythology.' Beaver, Dec. 1950,
         16-18.

Ga 1784 McKechnie, Robert E, II. Strong Medicine. Vancouver:
         Douglas, 1972. 193 pp. [B.C.]

P 1785   MacLean, R. P. Ogopogo: His Story. Kelowna, B.C.:
         Kelowna Courier, 1952. Pamphlet.

P 1786   Maine, Dal. 'Ghost Stories of Old Canada.' Winnipeg
         Free Press (Magazine Section), 18 June 1938.

PY 1787 Marks, William. 'I Saw Ogopogo.' N.p.: Polka Dot
         Series, Vol. 1, No. 1, 1971. 48 pp.

B 1788   Martin, Peggy. 'Drop Dead: Witchcraft Images and Ambi-
         guities in Newfoundland Society.' Culture & Tradition,
         2(1977), 35-50.

Pb 1789 Moon, Mary. Ogopogo, the Okanagan Mystery. Vancouver:
         Douglas, 1977. 195 pp.

FB 1790   Napier, John R. Bigfoot; The Yeti and Sasquatch in Myth and Reality. London: Cape, 1972; New York: Dutton, 1973; pb. New York: Berkley Medallion, 1974. 240 pp.

GP 1791   O'Connor, D'Arcy. The Story of Oak Island and the World's Greatest Treasure Hunt. Toronto: Longman, 1978. 256 pp.

G 1792   Owen, A. R. G. Psychic Mysteries of Canada. Toronto: Fitzhenry & Whiteside, 1975. 243 pp.

FP 1793   Patterson, Roger. Do Abominable Snowmen of America Really Exist? Yakima, WA: Franklin, 1966.

FP 1794   Sanderson, Ivan T. Abominable Snowman: Legend Come to Life. Philadelphia & New York: Chilton, 1961. 505 pp.

P 1795   Sonin, Eileen. Especially Ghosts. Toronto: Clarke, Irwin, 1970. 185 pp.

F 1796   Sprague, Roderick, and Grover S. Krantz, eds. The Scientist Looks at the Sasquatch. Moscow: Univ. Press of Idaho, 1977. 156 pp.

F 1797   Sweeney, James B. A Pictorial History of Sea Monsters and Other Dangerous Marine Life. New York: Bonanza, 1972. 314 pp.

P 1798   Thorstein, Eric. 'Close Encounters of a Monstrous Kind.' Weekend, 6 May 1978, pp. 16-17.

P 1799   Wilhelm, Ross. 'The Spanish in Nova Scotia in the Sixteenth Century--A Hint in the Oak Island Treasure Mystery.' Dalhousie Review, 50(1970-71), 451-69.

P 1800   Wright, Bruce S. 'The Specimen of Heron Island: "There Were Giants on Earth."' Atlantic Advocate, 65(Oct. 1974), 42-44.

F 1801   Wyman, Walker D. Mythical Creatures of the U.S.A. and Canada. River Falls, WI: Univ. of Wisconsin--River Falls Press, 1978. 105 pp.

8B   Anglophone and Celtic

GC 1802   Aldrich, Frederick A., and Elizabeth Brown. 'The Giant Squid in Newfoundland.' Newfoundland Quarterly, 65(Feb. 1967), 4-8.

GP 1803   Armstrong, Audrey. Sulphur and Molasses. Toronto: Musson, 1977. 96 pp.

F 1804   Beauchamp, W. M., F. D. Bergen, and W. W. Newell.
         'Current Superstitions Among the English-Speaking
         Population of U.S. and Canada.' JAF, 2(1889), 12-22;
         105-12.

F 1805   Bergen, Fanny D. Animal and Plant Lore Collected from
         the Oral Tradition of English Speaking Folk. Boston &
         New York: American Folklore Society, 1899; rpt. 1969.

C 1806   Boyle, David. 'Canadian Folk-Lore.' Series in the
         Globe, 13 Nov.-18 Dec., 1897; partially reprinted
         in JAF, 11(1898), 159-61.

GP 1807 Campbell, Lyall. Sable Island, Fatal and Fertile Cres-
         cent. Windsor: Lancelot, 1974. 104 pp.

C 1808   Chamberlain, Alexander F. 'Superstitions Concerning
         the Deaf.' JAF, 4(1891), 79.

Gb 1809 Coyne, James H. 'David Ramsay and Long Point in Legend
         and History.' TRSC, 13(1919), sec. 2, pp. 11-26.

A 1810   Creighton, Helen. Bluenose Ghosts. Toronto: Ryerson,
         1957; rpt. Toronto: McGraw-Hill Ryerson, 1976. 280 pp.

GP 1811 Crooker, William S. The Oak Island Quest. Windsor:
         Lancelot, 1978. 194 pp.

GP 1812 Dale, Bonnycastle, Jr. 'Sea Monsters of Nova Scotia.'
         CGJ, 10(Apr. 1935), 167-75.

A 1813   Devine, P. K. Devine's Folk Lore of Newfoundland in Old
         Words, Phrases and Expressions. St. John's: Robinson,
         1937. Pp. 59-61; 66-77.

P 1814   Edmonds, Alan. 'They Laughed When He Started Dowsing.'
         Weekend Magazine, 13 May 1972, p. 20.

P 1815   Evans, J. A. S. 'The Amherst Ghost.' Atlantic Advocate,
         48(Oct. 1957), 75-77.

A 1816   Fauset, Arthur Huff. "Folk Notions." Folklore from
         Nova Scotia. New York: American Folklore Society, 1931.
         Pp. 177-204.

A 1817   Fraser, Mary L. Folklore of Nova Scotia. 1931; rpt. An-
         tigonish: Formac, 1975. Pp. 24-51.

GP 1818 Furneaux, Rupert. Money Pit: The Mystery of Oak Island.
         1972; rpt. Toronto: Collins, 1976. 160 pp.

A 1819   Halpert, Herbert. 'Ireland, Sheila and Newfoundland.'
         In Literature and Folk Culture: Ireland and Newfound-
         land. Eds. Alison Feder and Bernice Schrank. St.
         John's: Memorial Univ., 1977. Pp. 147-71.

P 1820 Harris, R. F. 'The Ghost Ship of Mahone Bay.' Atlantic
        Advocate, 57(Nov. 1966), 41-44.

GP 1821 Harris, Reginald V. The Oak Island Mystery. Toronto:
         Ryerson, 1958. 211 pp.

C 1822 Haslam, H. L. 'Twentieth Century Witchcraft.' Dalhousie
        Review, 19(1939), 227-33.

P 1823 Hennigar, 'Ted' R. Scotian Spooks. Windsor: Lancelot,
        1978. 191 pp.

P 1824 Holland, Clive. 'Some Superstitions of Seafaring
        Folks.' Nautical Magazine (London), 143(1940), 12-15.

A 1825 Hufford, David J. 'A New Approach to the 'Old Hag': The
        Nightmare Tradition Re-examined.' In American Folk
        Medicine. Ed. Wayland D. Hand. Berkeley: Univ. of Cali-
        fornia Press, 1976. Pp. 73-85.

C 1826 Jamieson, Charles. 'Are There Such Things as "Tokens"?
        Do "Spirits" Walk Abroad?' Newfoundland Quarterly, 28
        (Dec. 1928), 15-16.

C 1827 -- 'The Ghostly Light Off Come-By-Chance.' Newfound-
        land Quarterly, 28(Autumn, 1928), 28.

C 1828 Jamison, Mrs. C. V. 'Signs and Omens from Nova Scotia.'
        JAF, 6(1893), 38.

A 1829 Jones, Michael O. Why Faith Healing? Ottawa: National
        Museum, CCFCS Mercury Series 3, 1972. 52 pp.

C 1830 Kiesel, T. A. 'Superstitions Concerning the Deaf in
        Cape Breton Island.' American Annals of the Deaf, 35:4
        (1890), 255-57.

B 1831 Kinsella, J. Payson. Some Superstitions and Traditions
        of Newfoundland. St. John's: Union, 1919.

C 1832 Leeson, Alice M. 'Certain Canadian Superstitions.' JAF,
        10(1897), 76-78.

C 1833 LeMessurier, H. W. 'A Restless Ghost.' Holly Leaves
        (St. John's), Christmas 1971, [pp. 25-26].

P 1834 Lintot, G. A. M. 'Some Observations on Water Divining.'
        B.C. Provincial Engineer, June 1953.

GP 1835 MacDonald, David. 'Oak Island's Mysterious Money Pit.'
         Reader's Digest, Jan. 1965, pp. 136-40; Can. ed., pp.
         22-26.

A 1836 McDonald, Neil T. The Baldoon Mysteries: A Weird Tale
        of the Early Scotch Settlers of Baldoon. Wallaceburg,
        Ont.: Colwell, 1871; 3rd ed. 1910. 62 pp.

C 1837 MacKenzie, A. E. D. 'Baldoon.' Beaver, Autumn 1972, pp. 48-51.

P 1838 Merry, E. D. 'Oak Island Hoards Her Gold.' American Mercury, 84(May 1957), 65-70.

P 1839 Moon, Mary. 'I saw it this time as a great writhing eel-like mass.' B.C. Motorist, Nov.-Dec. 1973, pp. 12, 14-16, 52-53, 59-60, 62. [Ogopogo.]

P 1840 Mosher, Edith. The Sea and the Supernatural. Windsor: Lancelot, 1974. 52 pp.

GP 1841 O'Hanlon, Betty. 'The Treasure of Oak Island: Is It A Myth or a $30 Million Fact?" Atlantic Advocate, 56 (Feb. 1965), 34-39.

P 1842 Otten, R. O. 'The Ghost is Foiled in Lac Seul's Haunted Room.' Beaver, Jan. 1921, p. 21.

C 1843 Patterson, George. 'Notes on the Folk-Lore of Newfoundland.' JAF, 8(1895), 285-90; 10(1897), 214-15.

P 1844 Phillips, R. A. J. 'The Klondike Legend.' CGJ, 64(Mar. 1962), 76-85.

C 1845 Poushinsky, J. M., and N. W. Poushinsky. 'Superstition and Technological Change: An Illustration.' JAF, 86 (1973), 289-93.

G 1846 Rich, E. E. 'The Fur Traders: Their Diet and Drugs.' Beaver, Summer 1976, pp. 41-53.

B 1847 Riddell, William R. 'Popular Medicine in Upper Canada a Century Ago.' Ontario History, 25(1929), 398-404.

GP 1848 Robertson, Marion, comp. Old Settlers' Remedies. Barrington: n.p., 1960; rpt. Windsor: Lancelot, 1975. 34 pp.

C 1849 Rose, Herbert J. 'Couvade in Ontario.' Folk-Lore, 29 (1918), 87.

B 1850 -- 'Ontario Beliefs.' Folk-Lore, 24(1913), 219-27.

GP 1851 Rosenbaum, Ron. 'The Mystery of Oak Island.' Esquire, Feb. 1973, pp. 77-85, 154-56, 160.

P 1852 Sclanders, Ian. 'The Lively Ghosts of Chignecto.' Maclean's, 15 Oct. 1953, pp. 18-19, 108-10.

P 1853 Shaw, H. B. 'What's Happened to Ghosts?' Atlantic Advocate, 57(Dec. 1966), 52-57.

P 1854 Silver, Marietta. 'Was There Never a Garden.' N.S. Historical Quarterly, 4(1974), 147-54.

Superstitions and Popular Beliefs

P 1855   Steele, Harwood E. R. <u>Ghosts Returning</u>. Toronto: Ryerson, c. 1950. 272 pp.

C 1856   'Superstitions in Newfoundland.' <u>JAF</u>, 9(1896), 222-23.

A 1857   Teit, James A. 'Water-Beings in Shetlandic Folk-Lore, as Remembered by Shetlanders in British Columbia.' <u>JAF</u>, 31(1918), 180-201.

C 1858   Thomas, Amby. 'Folk Cures.' <u>Canada Folk Bulletin</u>, 2 (July-Aug. 1979), 8.

PbY 1859   Trueman, Stuart. <u>Ghosts, Pirates and Treasure Trove</u>. Toronto: McClelland & Stewart, 1975. 155 pp.

C 1860   W. P. 'Superstitions in Newfoundland.' <u>Christmas Echo</u>, (St. John's), No. 2(Christmas 1917), pp. 19-20.

C 1861   Waghorne, A. C. 'Death Signs and Weather Signs from Newfoundland and Labrador.' <u>JAF</u>, 13(1900), 297-99.

A 1862   Waugh, F. W. 'Canadian Folk-Lore from Ontario.' <u>JAF</u>, 31 (1918), 4-41.

A 1863   Widdowson, J. D. A. 'The Bogeyman: Some Preliminary Observations on Frightening Figures.' <u>Folklore</u>, 82 (1971), 99-115.

B 1864   Widdowson, J. D. A., and J. H. Moss. 'Figures Used for Threatening Children, 1: A Newfoundland Example.' <u>Lore and Language</u>, 1:7(1972), 20-24.

P 1865   Widerman, Jane. 'The Haunting of Toronto.' <u>City</u>, <u>Toronto Star</u>, 29 Oct. 1978, pp. 15-19.

C 1866   Wintemberg, W. J. 'Folk-Lore Collected at Roebuck, Grenville County, Ontario.' <u>JAF</u>, 31(1918), 143-144.

C 1867   -- 'Folk-Lore Collected in the Counties of Oxford and Waterloo, Ontario.' <u>JAF</u>, 31(1918), 135-40.

A 1868   Wintemberg, W. J., and Katherine H. Wintemberg. 'Folk-Lore from Grey County, Ontario.' <u>JAF</u>, 31(1918), 83-102.

Gb 1869   Wix, Edward. <u>Six Months of a Newfoundland Missionary's Journal from February to August 1835</u>. 1836; rpt. Toronto: Canadiana House, 1969. 264 pp. [Superstitions.]

    8C Francophone

C 1870   Beaugrand, Honoré. 'Lutins in the Province of Quebec.' <u>JAF</u>, 5(1892), 327-28.

C(1) 1871 Beaugrand, Honoré. 'The Werewolves: A Legend of Old
           Quebec.' Quebec, 10(Jan. 1936), 197-200.

P 1872 Dewey, A. Gordon. 'Famous Canadian Trials. Sorcery and
        Sacrilege in Old Montreal.' Canadian Magazine, 46(1915),
        52-54.

G 1873 Giovanni, M. 'The Role of the Religious in Pharmacy
        under Canada's "Ancien Regine."' Culture, 24:1, 2(1963),
        13-32; 138-51.

C 1874 Jolicoeur, Catherine. 'Folk Medicine in the Gaspé
        Peninsula.' Revue d'Histoire de la Gaspésie, 10(1972),
        248-50.

C 1875 -- 'The Ghost Ship.' Western Folklore, 22(1963),
        194-95.

C 1876 -- 'A Pound of Flesh.' Revue d'Histoire de la Gaspé-
        sie, 11(1973), 94-95.

A 1877 Lacourcière, Luc. 'A Survey of Folk Medicine in French
        Canada from Early Times to the Present.' In American
        Folk Medicine. Ed. Wayland D. Hand. Berkeley: Univ. of
        California Press, 1976. Pp. 203-14.

B 1878 Layton, Monique. 'Magico-Religious Elements in the
        Traditional Beliefs of Maillardville, B.C.' BC Studies,
        No. 27 (Autumn 1975), pp. 50-61.

P 1879 Macdonald, David. 'The Cursed Stones of Louisbourg.'
        Maclean's, 15 May 1953, pp. 24-25, 33, 35-37.

P 1880 St. Germaine, Venant. 'A Merman in Lake Superior.'
        Beaver, Sept. 1942, pp. 29-30.

      8D Indian and Inuit

P 1881 Anderson, George. 'Pagan Eskimos.' Beaver, June 1943,
        pp. 38-40.

C 1882 Barbeau, C. Marius. 'The Hydra Reborn in the New
        World.' Art Quarterly, 12(Spring 1949), 156-64.

C 1883 -- 'The Old-World Dragon in America.' Proc. of the
        29th International Congress of Americanists, 1952,
        pp. 115-22.

C 1884 -- 'Sirens of the Seas.' Beaver, Dec. 1944, pp. 20-23.

A 1885 -- 'Supernatural Beings of the Huron and Wyandot.'
        American Anthropologist, 16(1914), 288-313.

B 1886 Barnett, Homer G. Indian Shakers: A Messianic Cult of the Pacific Northwest. Carbondale: Southern Illinois Univ. Press, 1957. 378 pp.

B 1887 Bell, Robert. 'The "Medicine-Man"; or Indian and Eskimo Notions of Medicine.' Canadian Medical and Surgical Journal, Mar.-Apr. 1886, pp. 1-13.

P 1888 Black, A. K. 'Shaking the Wigwam.' Beaver, Dec. 1934, pp. 13, 39.

B 1889 Boas, Franz. 'Current Beliefs of the Kwakiutl Indians.' JAF, 45(1932), 177-260.

A 1890 -- The Religion of the Kwakiutl Indians. 2 vols. New York: Columbia Univ. Press, 1930. 284 pp.; 288 pp.

C 1891 -- 'Religious Beliefs of the Central Eskimo.' Popular Science Monthly, 57(1900), 624-31.

B 1892 Boyle, David. 'The Paganism of the Civilized Iroquois of Ontario.' Journal of the Anthropological Institute (London), 30(1900), 263-74.

C 1893 Brant-Sero, J. O. 'O-no-dah, Canadian Iroquois Herb.' JAF, 24(1911), 251.

P 1894 Burgesse, J. A. 'Windigo.' Beaver, Mar. 1947, pp. 4-5.

C 1895 Carpenter, Edmund S. 'The Timeless Present in the Mythology of the Aivilik Eskimos.' Anthropologica, 3(1956), 1-4. Rpt. in Eskimo of the Canadian Artic. Ed. Victor F. Valentine and Frank G. Vallee. Toronto: McClelland & Stewart, 1968. Pp. 39-42.

C 1896 -- 'Witch-fear among the Aivilik Eskimos.' American Journal of Psychiatry, 110 (Sept. 1953), 194-99. Rpt. in Eskimo of the Canadian Arctic. Eds. Victor F. Valentine and Frank G. Vallee. Toronto: McClelland & Stewart, 1968. Pp. 55-66.

C 1897 Chamberlain, Alexander F. 'Kootenay Medicine Men.' JAF, 14(1901), 95-99.

C 1898 -- 'The Thunder Bird Amongst the Algonkians.' American Anthropologist, 3(1890), 51-54.

C 1899 Cooper, John M. 'Field Notes on Northern Algonkian Magic.' Proc. of the 23rd International Congress of Americanists, 1928. pp. 513-19.

C 1900 -- 'The Northern Algonquian Supreme Being.' Anthropological Series, Catholic Univ. of America (Washington), 2(1934), 1-78.

123

C 1901 Dailey, Robert C. 'The Midewiwin, Ontario's First
Medical Society." Ontario History, 50(Summer 1958),
133-37.

C 1902 Darby, George E. 'Indian Medicine in British Columbia.'
Canadian Medical Assoc. Journal, 28(1933), 433-38.

B 1903 Dempsey, Hugh A. Blackfoot Ghost Dance. Calgary: Glenbow, 1968. 19 pp.

C 1904 Denny, Cecil. 'Blackfoot Magic.' Beaver, Sept. 1944,
pp. 14-15.

C 1905 Douglas, Frederick H., and Regina Flannery. 'The
Shaking-Tent Rite Among the Montagnais of James Bay.'
Primitive Man, 12(1939), 11-16.

B 1906 Douglas, Gilian. 'Revenge at Guayasclums.' Beaver,
Sept. 1952, pp. 6-9.

C 1907 Ewers, John C. 'Love Medicine.' Beaver, Autumn 1958,
pp. 40-41.

P 1908 Felstead, Edwin. 'Eskimo Sorcerers.' Occult Review
(London), 55(1932), 98-101.

B 1909 Fenton, William H. 'Masked Medicine Societies of the
Iroquois.' Washington: Smithsonian Report for 1940,
1941, pp. 397-430.

C 1910 Fieber, Frank. 'Natural Medicines of the Cree Indians.'
Beaver, Spring 1979, pp. 57-59.

A 1911 Foster, Michael K. From the Earth to Beyond the Sky.
An Ethnographic Approach to Four Longhouse Iroquois
Speech Events. Ottawa: National Museum, Ethnology
Service Mercury Series 20, 1974. 448 pp.

C 1912 Frederiksen, Svend. 'Some Preliminaries on the Soul
Complex in Eskimo Shamanistic Belief.' Journal of the
Washington Academy of Sciences, 54(Apr. 1964), 109-12.
Rpt. in Eskimo of the Canadian Artic. Ed. Victor F.
Valentine and Frank G. Vallee. Toronto: McClelland &
Stewart, 1968. Pp. 49-54.

C 1913 Godsell, Philip H. 'Overcoming Competition. The Story
of the Home Made Weetigo.' Beaver, Aug.-Sept. 1921,
pp. 5-7.

C 1914 Gordon, C. H. M. 'The Fraternity of Medicine Men.'
Beaver, Dec. 1930, pp. 107-8.

B 1915 Hagar, Stansbury. 'Micmac Magic and Medicine.' JAF,
9(1896), 170-77.

C 1916 Hagar, Stansbury. 'Weather and the Seasons in Micmac Mythology.' _JAF_, 10(1897), 101-5.

B 1917 Haliburton, Robert G. 'On the Festival of the Dead.' _Proc. and Trans. of the N.S. Institute of Science_, 1(1863), 61-85.

B 1918 Harris, William R. 'Practice of Medicine and Surgery by the Canadian Tribes in Champlain's Time. _Annual Archeological Report_, Ontario, 1915, pp. 35-54.

Pb 1919 Hawkes, E. W. 'Eskimo Magic.' _Wide World Magazine_ (London), 61(1928), 141-45.

A 1920 Hellson, John C. _Ethnobotany of the Blackfoot Indians_. Ottawa: National Museum, Ethnology Service Mercury Series 19, 1974. 138 pp.

C 1921 Hind, Henry Y. 'Of Some of the Superstitions and Customs Common Among the Indians in the Valley of the Assiniboine and Saskatchewan.' _Canadian Journal_ [N.S.], 22(1859), 253-62.

B 1922 Hoffman, Walter J. 'The Midewiwin or 'Grand Medicine Society' of the Ojibwa.' _7th Annual Report of the Bureau of American Ethnology_, Washington, 1891, pp. 149-299.

B 1923 Honigmann, John J. 'Witch-fear in post-contact Kaska society.' _American Anthropologist_, 49(1947), 222-43.

B 1924 Jenness, Diamond. 'Canadian Indian Religion.' _Anthropologica_, 1(1955), 1-17.

A 1925 -- _The Faith of a Coast Salish Indian_. Victoria: B.C. Provincial Museum, Anthropology in British Columbia, Memoir 3, 1955. 92 pp.

C 1926 -- 'An Indian Method of Treating Hysteria.' _Primitive Man_, 6(1933), 13-19.

B 1927 Johnson, Frederick. 'Notes on Micmac Shamanism.' _Primitive Man_, 16(July & Oct. 1943), 53-80.

C 1928 Jones, William. 'Algonkin Manitou.' _JAF_, 18(1905), 183-90.

C 1929 Kehoe, Alice B. 'The Ghost Dance Religion in Saskatchewan, Canada.' _Plains Anthropologist_, 13(1968), 296-304.

F 1930 Kirtley, Bacil F. 'Unknown Hominids and New World Legends.' _Western Folklore_, 23(1964), 77-90.

B 1931 Lacey, Laurie. _Micmac Indian Medicine: A Traditional Way of Health_. Antigonish: Formac, 1977. 74 pp.

125

C 1932   Lacey, Laurie. 'Npisum (My Medicine): The Micmac Indian Approach to Health and the Maintenance of Well-Being.' Culture & Tradition, 2(1977), 13-19.

FA 1933   Landes, Ruth. Ojibwa Religion and the Midewiwin. Madison: Univ of Wisconsin Press, 1968. 250 pp.

G 1934   Lane, Barbara. A Comparative and Analytical Study of Some Aspects of Northwest Coast Religion. Ann Arbor, MI: University Microfilms, 1953.

G 1935   Large, R. Geddes. Drums and Scalpel: From Native Healers to Physicians on the North Pacific Coast. Vancouver: Mitchell, 1968. 145 pp.

P 1936   Learmouth, L. A. 'The Curse of Neovitcheak.' Beaver, Sept. 1946, pp. 3-5.

B 1937   Locher, G. W. The Serpent in Kwakiutl Religion. Leyden: Brill, 1932. 118 pp.

P 1938   McDonald, John. 'Supernatural Stories of the Northwest.' Beaver, Dec. 1932, pp. 245-46.

B 1939   McIlwraith, T. F. 'Certain Beliefs of the Bella Coola Indians Concerning Animals.' Annual Archeological Report, Ontario, 1924-25, pp. 17-27.

C 1940   Maclean, John. 'Blackfoot Medical Priesthood.' Alberta Historical Review, 9(Spring 1961), 1-7.

C 1941   -- 'The Medicine Stone.' Beaver, Dec. 1927, pp. 116-17.

B 1942   MacNeish, June H. 'Contemporary Folk Beliefs of a Slave Indian Band.' JAF, 67(1954), 185-98.

C 1943   Morgan, M. V. 'Indian Medicine.' Beaver, Sept. 1933, p. 38.

B 1944   Morice, Adrien G. 'Déné Surgery.' Trans. Royal Canadian Institute, 7(1901), 15-27.

C 1945   Parker, A. C. 'Indian Medicine and Medicine Men.' Annual Archeological Report, Ontario, 1928, pp. 9-17.

C 1946   Podolinsky, Alika. 'Divination Rites.' Beaver, Summer 1964, pp. 40-41.

C 1947   Raynor, Wilma. 'Windigo Summer.' Beaver, Summer 1957, pp. 32-33.

C 1948   Reid, A. P. 'Religious Beliefs of the Ojibois or Sauteux Indians.' Journal of the Royal Anthropological Institute of Great Britain, 3(1873), 106-13.

A 1949   Ridington, Robin. Swan People: A Study of the Dunneza
          Prophet Dance. Ottawa. National Museum, Ethnology Ser-
          vice Mercury Series 38, 1978. 132 pp.

B 1950   Ridington, Robin, and Tonia Ridington. 'The Inner Eye
          of Shamanism and Totemism.' History of Religions, 9
          (May 1970), 49-61.

B 1951   Rogers, Edward S. The False Face Society of the
          Iroquois. Toronto: Univ. of Toronto Press, 1966. 16 pp.

B 1952   Shaeffer, Claude E. Blackfoot Shaking Tent. Calgary:
          Glenbow, 1969. 20 pp.

B 1953   Smith, David M. Inkonze: Magico-Religious Beliefs to
          Contact-Traditional Chipewan Trading at Fort Resolution,
          NWT, Canada. Ottawa: National Museum, Ethnology
          Service Mercury Series 6, 1973. 21 pp.

B 1954   Smith, Harlan I. 'Materia Medica of the Bella Coola
          and Neighboring Tribes of British Columbia.' Ottawa:
          National Museum, Bulletin 56, 1929, pp. 47-69.

C 1955   -- 'Sympathetic Magic and Witchcraft among the Bella
          Coola.' American Anthropologist, 27(1925), 116-21.

C 1956   Speck, F. Staniford. 'Niagara Falls and Cayuga
          Medicine.' New York Folklore Quarterly, 1(1945), 205-8.

B 1957   Speck, Frank G. 'Medicine Practices of the Northeastern
          Algonquians.' Proc. of the 19th International Congress
          of Americanists, 1917, pp. 303-31.

B 1958   -- 'Spiritual Beliefs Among the Labrador Indians.'
          Proc. of the 21st International Congress of American-
          ists, 1925, pp. 266-75.

B 1959   Spier, Leslie. The Prophet Dance of the Northwest and
          Its Derivatives. Menasha, WI: Banta, 1935. 74 pp.

C 1960   Stefansson, Vilhjalmur. 'Notes on the Theory and Treat-
          ment of Diseases among the Mackenzie River Eskimo.'
          JAF, 21(1908), 43-45.

Pa 1961   -- 'Religious Beliefs of the Eskimo.' Harper's, 127
          (1913), 869-78.

FB 1962   Suttles, Wayne. 'On the Cultural Track of the Sas-
          quatch.' Northwest Anthropological Research Notes, 6
          (1972), 65-90.

FB 1963   -- 'The Plateau Prophet Dance Among the Coast Salish.'
          Southwest Journal of Anthropology, 13(1957), 352-96.

A 1964   Teicher, Morton I. Windigo Psychosis: A study of a
relationship between belief and behavior among the
Indians of Northeastern Canada. American Ethnological
Society, 1960 (Distrib. by Univ. of Washington Press,
Seattle & London). 129 pp.

C 1965   Turquetil, Arsène. 'The Religion of the Central Eskimo.'
Primitive Man, 2(July/Oct. 1929), 57-64. Rpt. in Eskimo
of the Canadian Arctic. Ed. Victor F. Valentine and
Frank G. Vallee. Toronto: McClelland & Stewart, 1968.
Pp. 43-48.

B 1966   Van Wart, Arthur F. 'The Indians of the Maritime
Provinces: Their Diseases and Native Cures.' Canadian
Medical Assoc. Journal, 59(1948), 573-77.

B 1967   Wallis, W. D. 'Medicines Used by the Micmac Indians.'
American Anthropologist, 24(1922), 24-30.

C 1968   Watt, Ellen. 'Transferral of a Bundle.' Beaver, Summer
1967, pp. 22-25.

B 1969   Weaver, Sally. Medicine and Politics among the Grand
River Iroquois. Ottawa: National Museum, 1972. 182 pp.

G 1970   Wilkerson, Frank. 'The Haunted Tribe.' Alberta Historical Review, 20(Spring 1972), 3-12.

C 1971   Wilson, R. N. 'The Sacrificial Rite of the Blackfoot.'
TRSC, 3(1909), sec. 2, pp. 3-21.

C 1972   Wuttunnee, William I. C. 'Peyote Ceremony.' Beaver,
Summer 1968, pp. 22-25.

        8E   Other Cultural Groups

A 1973   Creighton, Helen. Folklore of Lunenburg County, Nova
Scotia. Ottawa: National Museum, Bulletin 117, pp. 15-
57; 85-104.

C 1974   Doering, J. Frederick. 'Pennsylvanian German Folk
Medicine in Waterloo County, Ontario.' JAF, 49(1936),
194-98.

B 1975   Doering, J. Frederick, and Eileen E. Doering. 'Some
Western Ontario Folk Beliefs and Practices.' JAF, 51
(1938), 60-68; 54(1941), 197.

F 1976   Hostetler, John A. 'Folk and Scientific Medicine in
Amish Society.' Human Organization (Ithaca, NY), 22
(Winter 1963), 269-75.

F 1977   Kirshenblatt-Gimblett, Barbara, and Harris Lenowitz. 'The Evil Eye (The Good Eye) Eyn-hore.' Alcheringa Poetics, 5(Spring-Summer 1973), 71-77.

B 1978   Perkowski, Jan. Vampires, Dwarves, and Witches among the Ontario Kashubs. Ottawa: National Museum, CCFCS Mercury Series 1, 1972. 85 pp.

C 1979   Popoff, Eli. Historical Exposition on Doukhobor Beliefs. Grand Forks, B.C.: n.p., 1966.

B 1980   Salo, Matt T. Roles of Magic and Healing: The Tietäjä in the Memorates and Legends of Canadian Finns. Ottawa: National Museum, 1973. 21 pp.

B 1981   Stephenson, Peter H. 'Hutterite Belief in the Evil Eye.' Culture, Medicine and Psychiatry, 3(1979), 247-65.

A 1982   Wintemberg, W. J. Folk-Lore of Waterloo County, Ontario. Ottawa: National Museum, Bulletin 116, 1950, pp. 2-28.

B 1983   -- 'German-Canadian Folk-Lore.' Ontario History, 3 (1901), 86-96.

C 1984   -- 'Items of German-Canadian Folk-Lore.' JAF, 12 (1899), 45-49.

C 1985   -- 'Some Items of Negro-Canadian Folk-Lore.' JAF, 38 (1925), 621.

For 8A see also items 236, 299, 321, 356, and 357.

For 8B, 276, 292, 322, 331-333, 337, 338, 411, 432, 433, 436, 456, 482, 484, 485, 493-495, 498, 508, 514, 516, 2182, and 3762.

For 8C, 325, 336, 555, 2376, and 2381.

For 8D, 240, 294, 304, 323, 326, 814, 1436, 2411, 2508, 2520, 2531, 2543, 2570, 2595, 2603, 3065, 3764, 3794, 3795, and 3824.

For 8E, 332, 898, and 902.

9 Folklife and Customs

9A General

Gb 1986 Abrahamson, Una. God Bless Our Home: Domestic Life in Nineteenth Century Canada. Toronto: Burns & MacEachern, 1966. 238 pp.

GP 1987 Allen, G. P. Days to Remember: Observances of Significance in Our Multicultural Society. Toronto: Ont. Ministry of Culture & Recreation, 1977. 78 pp.

Gb 1988 Anderson, Allan. Remembering the Farm. Toronto: Macmillan, 1977. 256 pp. (Extracts: 'Rural Roots,' Canadian, 29 Oct. 1977, pp. 2-7.)

FGP 1989 Andrews, R. W. Glory Days of Logging--Action in the Big Woods--British Columbia to California. Seattle: Superior, 1956. 176 pp.

Ga 1990 Anspach, Lewis A. A History of the Island of Newfoundland. London: Author, 1819. 512 pp.

G 1991 Ballantyne, R. M. Hudson's Bay, or, Everyday Life in the Wilds of North America. 1848; rpt. Edmonton: Hurtig, 1972. 328 pp.

G 1992 Banfill, B. J. Labrador Nurse. Philadelphia: Macrae Smith, 1953. 256 pp.

B 1993 Barbeau, C. Marius. 'Maple Sugar.' CGJ, 38(Apr. 1949), 176-89.

C 1994 -- 'The Poor Man's Trail.' CGJ, 9(July 1934), 3-14.

Gb 1995 Barber, Mary, and Flora MacPherson. Christmas in Canada. Toronto: Dent, 1959. 134 pp.

GP 1996 Barlee, N. L. Gold Creeks and Ghost Towns. Summerland, B.C.: n.p., n.d. 183 pp.

GP 1997 Basque, Garnet. Canadian Treasure Trove. Vancouver: Author, 1973. 102 pp.

130

Folklife and Customs

A 1998   Bauman, Richard. 'Belsnickling in a Nova Scotia Island Community.' <u>Western Folklore</u>, 31(1972), 229-43.

A 1999   -- 'The LaHave Island General Store: Sociability and Verbal Arts in a Nova Scotia Community.' <u>JAF</u>, 85(1972), 330-341.

G 2000   Berglud, Berndt, and Clare E. Bosby. <u>The Edible Wild: A Complete Cookbook and Guide to Edible Wild Plants in Canada and North America</u>. Toronto: Pagurian, 1971. 188 pp.

G 2001   Bigsby, John J. <u>The Shoe and Canoe: or, Pictures of Travel in the Canadas</u>. 2 vols. London: Chapman & Hall, 1850.

Gb 2002   Bird, Isabella L. <u>The English Woman in America</u>. 1856; rpt. Toronto: Univ. of Toronto Press, 1966. 497 pp.

C 2003   <u>Black Creek Pioneer Village Recipes</u>. Toronto: Metropolitan Toronto & Region Conservation Authority, n.d. 24 pp.

C 2004   Bourneuf, Agnes. 'Nova Scotian Childhood: The French Walk.' <u>New Yorker</u>, 27 Nov. 1948, pp. 77-81.

Gc 2005   Bradwin, Edmund W. <u>The Bunkhouse Man: A Study of Work and Pay in the Camps of Canada 1903-14</u>. Toronto: Univ. of Toronto Press, 1972. 336 pp.

Gb 2006   Breckenridge, Muriel. <u>Every Day a Feast</u>. Toronto: McGraw-Hill Ryerson, 1978. 244 pp.

G 2007   Brehaut, Mary C., ed. <u>Historic Highlights of Prince Edward Island</u>. Charlottetown: Historical Society of P.E.I., 1955. 130 pp.

G 2008   -- <u>Historic Sidelights</u>. Charlottetown: Historical Society of P.E.I., 1956. 98 pp.

Gc 2009   Broadfoot, Barry. <u>The Pioneer Years: 1895-1914. Memories of Settlers Who Opened the West</u>. Toronto: Doubleday Canada, 1976. 403 pp. (Extracts: 'The Homesteaders,' <u>Canadian</u>, 16 Oct. 1976, pp. 5-13.)

Gb 2010   Browne, Patrick W. <u>Where the Fishers Go</u>. Toronto: Musson, 1909. 370 pp. [Labrador.]

G 2011   Bruce, Jean. <u>The Last Best West</u>. Toronto: Fitzhenry & Whiteside, 1976. 177 pp.

G 2012   Burpee, Lawrence J., and C. Marius Barbeau. 'The People of Canada.' <u>CGJ</u>, 18(May 1939), 227-47.

B 2013   Calvin, D. D. 'Rafting on the St. Lawrence.' <u>CGJ</u>, 3 (Oct. 1931), 270-86.

131

G 2014 Campbell, Henry C. _Early Days on the Great Lakes. Art of William Armstrong_. Toronto: McClelland & Stewart, 1971. 122 pp.

G 2015 _The Canadian Home Cookbook_. 1877; rpt. Toronto: Coles, n.d. 168 pp.

B 2016 Careless, J. M. S. _The Pioneers. An Illustrated History of Early Settlement in Canada_. Toronto: McClelland & Stewart, rev. ed., 1973. 127 pp.

G 2017 Carroll, Joy. _Pioneer Days 1840-1860_. Toronto: Natural Science of Canada, 1978. 128 pp.

Gc 2018 Carver, Caroline. _The Canadian Christmas Book_. Montreal: Tundra, 1975. 96 pp.

Gc 2019 Clark, Andrew H. _Three Centuries and the Island: A Historical Geography of Settlements and Agriculture in Prince Edward Island, Canada_. Toronto: Univ. of Toronto Press, 1959. 287 pp.

GP 2020 Comeau, Napoleon A. _Life and Sport on the North Shore of the Lower St. Lawrence and Gulf_. Quebec: Daily Telegraph, 1909. 440 pp.

C 2021 Davies, Blodwen. 'The Folklore of Pioneering.' _Bulletin of the Canadian Museums Assoc_. Dec. 1957, pp. 7-12.

GP 2022 Dempsey, Hugh. 'The "Thin Red Line" in the Canadian West.' _American West_, 7(1970), 24-30. [The R.C.M.P.]

C 2023 Devore, Roy W. 'The River Drivers.' _Alberta Historical Review_, 8(Winter 1960), 21-23.

G 2024 Doerflinger, William. 'Down North in a Cargo Schooner.' _CGJ_, 9(July 1934), 58-72.

B 2025 Doucette, Laurel. 'Folk Festival: The Gatineau Valley Church Picnic.' _Culture & Tradition_, 1(1976), 55-62.

B 2026 -- _Skill and Status: Traditional Expertise within a Rural Canadian Family_. Ottawa: National Museum, CCFCS Mercury Series 28, 1979. 177 pp.

GP 2027 Downs, Art, ed. _Pioneer Days in British Columbia_. Vol. 1. Surrey: Foremost, 1973. 160 pp. Vol. 2. Surrey: Heritage, 1975. 160 pp.

G 2028 Dunbar, Nancy J., comp. _Images of Sport in Early Canada_. Montreal: McGill-Queen's Univ. Press, 1976. 95 pp.

C 2029 Duncan, Dorothy. _Black Creek Pioneer Village_. Toronto: Metropolitan Toronto & Region Conservation Authority, n.d. 34 pp.

Ga 2030   Duncan, Norman. <u>Dr. Grenfell's Parish: The Deep Sea Fishermen</u>. New York: Revell, 1905. 155 pp.

Pc 2031   Einarsson, Magnús. <u>Everyman's Heritage: An Album of Canadian Folk Life</u>. Ottawa: National Museum, 1978. 177 pp.

G 2032   Elliott, Jean L., ed. <u>Two Nations, Many Cultures: Ethnic Groups in Canada</u>. Scarborough, Ont.: Prentice-Hall, 1979. 395 pp.

GP 2033   Ellis, Eleanor A. <u>Northern Cookbook</u>. Edmonton: Hurtig, 1979. 368 pp.

Gb 2034   Farrow, Moira. <u>Nobody Here But Us: Pioneers of the North</u>. Vancouver: Douglas, 1972. 219 pp.

P 2035   Florin, Lambert. <u>Alaska, the Yukon and British Columbia Ghost Towns</u>. Seattle: Superior, 1971. 72 pp.

P 2036   -- <u>Ghost Town Treasures</u>. Seattle: Superior, c. 1963. 192 pp.

Gb 2037   Foster, Annie H., and Anne Grierson. <u>High Days and Holidays in Canada</u>. Toronto: Ryerson, 1938; rev. 1956. 95 pp.

G 2038   Fraser, Joshua. <u>Shanty, Forest, and River Life in the Backwoods of Canada</u>. Montreal: Lovell, 1883. 361 pp.

C 2039   Garratt, Blanche P. <u>Canadian Country Preserves and Wines</u>. Toronto: Lorimer, 1975. 133 pp.

C 2040   -- <u>A Taste of the Wild</u>. Toronto: Lorimer, 1975. 144 pp.

G 2041   Gillham, Charles E. <u>Raw North</u>. New York: Barnes, 1947. 275 pp.

Ga 2042   Glazebrook, G. P. de T. <u>Life in Ontario: A Social History</u>. Toronto: Univ. of Toronto Press, 1968. 316 pp.

P 2043   Gotlieb, Sondra. <u>Cross Canada Cooking. Favorite Recipes of Canadians from Many Lands</u>. Saanichton: Hancock, 1976. 160 pp.

Gb 2044   Gould, Ed. <u>Logging: British Columbia's Logging History</u>. Saanichton: Hancock, 1975. 224 pp.

Gb 2045   -- <u>Ranching: The History of Ranching in Canada</u>. Saanichton: Hancock, 1977. 196 pp.

Gb 2046   Grant, Ted, and Andy Russell. <u>Men of the Saddle: Working Cowboys of Canada</u>. Scarborough: Van Nostrand Reinhold, 1978. 192 pp.

G 2047   Gray, James H. Red Lights on the Prairie. Toronto: Mac-
         millan, 1971. 207 pp.

Gb 2048 Grenfell, Wilfred T. Tales of Labrador. London: Nisbet,
         1916. 240 pp.

Gb 2049 Griesback, W. A. I Remember. Western Canada 1870-1940.
         Toronto: Ryerson, 1946. 353 pp.

Ga 2050 Guillet, Edwin C., ed. The Valley of the Trent. Tor-
         onto: Champlain Society, 1957. 474 pp.

G 2051   Haight, Canniff. Country Life in Canada Fifty Years
         Ago. 1885; rpt. Belleville, Ont.: Mika, 1971. 303 pp.

Ga 2052 Hall, E., comp. Early Canada: a collection of histor-
         ical photographs by officers of the Geological Survey
         of Canada. Ottawa: Queen's Printer, 1967. 136 pp.

Gc 2053 Hamilton, William B. Local History in Atlantic Canada.
         Toronto: Macmillan, 1974. 241 pp.

Ga 2054 Hansen, Ben, photographer. Newfoundland Portfolio. St.
         John's: Breakwater, 1977. 112 pp.

Gc 2055 Harris, Lorraine. Halfway to the Goldfields. Vancouver:
         Douglas, 1977. 144 pp.

Gb 2056 Healy, William J. Women of Red River. 1923; rpt. Winn-
         ipeg: Peguis, 1977. 274 pp.

Ga 2057 Jameson, Anna. Winter Studies and Summer Rambles in
         Canada. 1838; rpt. Toronto: McClelland & Stewart, 1965.
         173 pp.

G 2058   Jeffreys, Charles W. 'Christmas with Samuel Hearne.'
         CGJ, 11(Dec. 1935), 267-72.

Gc 2059 Johnston, Jean. Wilderness Women. Toronto: Peter Mar-
         tin, 1973. 242 pp.

Gc 2060 Karras, A. L. Face the North Wind. Toronto: Burns &
         MacEachern, 1977. 191 pp. [Folklife of trappers.]

G 2061   Kelly, Leroy V. The Range Men. Toronto: Briggs, 1913.
         468 pp. [Southern Alta.]

BY 2062 Kurelek, William. Lumberjack. Montreal: Tundra, 1974.
         41 pp.

B 2063   Langdon, Eustella. Pioneer Gardens at Black Creek Pio-
         neer Village. Toronto: Rinehart & Winston, 1972. 64 pp.

GP 2064 Lazeo, Lawrence A. Lost Treasure in British Columbia.
         N.p.: Author, 1973. 48 pp.

GP 2065   Lazeo, Lawrence. <u>Treasure Trails of British Columbia</u>. New Westminster: Author, 1970. 36 pp.

GP 2066   -- <u>Treasure Trails of Western Canada</u>. New Westminster: Author, 1972. 47 pp.

B 2067   Leechman, Douglas. <u>Vegetable Dyes from North American Plants</u>. Toronto: Southern Ont. Unit of the Herb Society of America, 1969. 59 pp.

PG 2068   LeMoine, James M. <u>The Chronicles of the St. Lawrence</u>. Montreal: Dawson, 1878. 380 pp.

G 2069   Lind, Carol J. <u>Big Timber, Big Men: A History of Loggers in a New Land</u>. Saanichton: Hancock, 1978. 160 pp.

G 2070   Lower, Arthur R. M. 'Canada at the Turn of the Century, 1900.' <u>CGJ</u>, 71(July 1965), 2-13.

P 2071   'Lunenburg: Its Future Is in Its Past; Old-Fashioned Flavors; Hooked Rugs.' <u>Chatelaine</u>, Sept. 1977, pp. 82-91.

C 2072   MacDougall, Diane N. 'Sourdough Thermometer.' <u>Beaver</u>, Summer 1973, pp. 48-49.

Gc 2073   McDougall, John. <u>Forest, Lake and Prairie. Twenty Years of Frontier Life in Western Canada 1842-62</u>. Toronto: Briggs, 1895. 267 pp.

Ga 2074   -- <u>Rural Life in Canada</u>. 1913; rpt. Toronto: Univ. of Toronto Press, 1972. 248 pp.

B 2075   MacEwan, J. W. Grant. <u>Blazing the Old Cattle Trail</u>. Saskatoon: Western Producer, 1962. 248 pp.

B 2076   -- <u>Hoofprints and Hitching Posts</u>. Saskatoon: Modern, 1964. 249 pp.

B 2077   -- <u>The Sodbusters</u>. Toronto: Nelson, 1948. 240 pp.

Gb 2078   McGowan, Don C. <u>Grassland Settlers: The Swift Current Region during the Era of the Ranching Frontier</u>. Regina: Canadian Plains Research Center, Univ. of Regina, 1975.

G 2079   McGrath, Judy W. <u>Dyes from Lichens and Plants: A Canadian Dyer's Guide</u>. Toronto: Van Nostrand, 1977. 160 pp.

G 2080   MacGregor, James G. <u>Blankets and Beads. A History of the Saskatchewan River</u>. Edmonton: Institute of Applied Arts, 1949. 278 pp.

G 2081   -- <u>Senator Hardisty's Prairies 1840-1889</u>. Saskatoon: Western Producer, 1978. 273 pp.

Ga 2082   MacKay, Donald. <u>The Lumberjacks</u>. Toronto: McGraw-Hill Ryerson, 1978. 319 pp.

G 2083 McLean, John. Notes of a Twenty-five Years' Service in the Hudson's Bay Territory. 1849; rpt. Toronto: Champlain Society, 1932. 402 pp.

G 2084 MacLeod, Heather, et al. Edible Wild Plants of Nova Scotia. Halifax: N.S. Museum, 1977. 135 pp.

C 2085 MacLeod, Margaret Arnett. 'Red River New Year.' Beaver, Dec. 1953, pp. 43-48.

Gb 2086 McNeil, Bill. Voice of the Pioneer. Toronto: Macmillan, 1978. 258 pp.

G 2087 MacNutt, W. Stewart. New Brunswick and Its People. Fredericton: N.B. Travel Bureau, n.d. 48 pp.

G 2088 Main, J. R. K. 'Early Transportation in Canada.' CGJ, 77(July 1968), 14-21.

Gb 2089 Millais, John G. Newfoundland and Its Untrodden Ways. London: Longmans, Green, 1907. 340 pp.

Gb 2090 Montero, Gloria. The Immigrants. Toronto: Lorimer, 1977. 222 pp.

B 2091 Morgan, E. C. 'Pioneer Recreation and Social Life.' Saskatchewan History, 18(Spring 1965), 41-54.

G 2092 Morris, Audrey G. Gentle Pioneers. Toronto: Hodder & Stoughton, 1968. 253 pp.

G 2093 Morse, William I. Gravestones of Acadie and other essays concerning Annapolis Country. London: A. Smith, 1929. 110 pp.

Ga 2094 Mowat, Farley, and John De Visser. This Rock Within the Sea: A Heritage Lost. Boston/Toronto: Little, Brown, 1968. [160 pp.]

GPY 2095 Newman, Fran, and Claudette Boulanger. Hooray for Today. Richmond Hill, Ont.: North Winds Press, 1979. 56 pp.

Gc 2096 Ormsby, Margaret A., ed. A Pioneer Gentlewoman in British Columbia: The Recollections of Susan Allison. Vancouver: Univ. of B.C. Press, 1976, 261 pp.; pb. 1977, 196 pp.

Gb 2097 Palmer, Howard. Land of the Second Chance: A History of Ethnic Groups in Southern Alberta. Lethbridge: Lethbridge Herald, 1974. 260 pp.

GP 2098 Paterson, Thomas. W. British Columbia: The Pioneer Years. Langley: Stagecoach, 1977. 192 pp.

P 2099 Paterson, Thomas W. Outlaws of the Canadian Frontier. Vancouver: Stagecoach, 1974. 72 pp.

Gc 2100 Rasmussen, Linda, et al. A Harvest Yet to Reap: A History of Prairie Women. Toronto: Women's Press, 1976. 240 pp.

G 2101 Richeson, D. R. Western Canadian History Museum Interpretations. Ottawa: National Museum, History Division Mercury Series 27, 1979. 158 pp.

Gb 2102 Robertson, Heather. Salt of the Earth. Toronto: Lorimer, 1974. 228 pp.

Gc 2103 Ross, Alexander. The Red River Settlement. London: Smith Elder, 1856. 416 pp.

C 2104 Ross, W. Gillies. 'Whaling in Hudson Bay.' Beaver, Spring 1973, pp. 4-11.

B 2105 Rowles, Edith. 'Bannock, Beans and Bacon: An Investigation of Pioneer Diet.' Saskatchewan History, 5(Winter 1952), 1-15.

Gb 2106 Shakespeare, Mary, and Rodney H. Pain. West Coast Logging 1840-1910. Ottawa: National Museum, History Division Mercury Series 22, 1977. 84 pp.

G 2107 Smith, Margot, and Carol Pasternak. Pioneer Women of Western Canada. Toronto: Ont. Institute for Studies in Education, 1978. 134 pp.

Ga 2108 Sprecht, Allen, ed. 'Skeena Country.' Sound Heritage, 5:1(1976). [Audio-Supplement, 'Skeena: River of the Clouds,' produced by I. Orchard.]

GP 2109 Starbird, Ethel A. 'The People Who Made Saskatchewan.' National Geographic, 155(1979), 651-79.

G 2110 Stearns, Winfrid A. Labrador: A Sketch of its Peoples, its Industries and its Natural History. New York: C. T. Dillingham, 1884. 295 pp.

G(1)a 2111 Stegner, Wallace. Wolf Willow. New York: Viking, 1966. 306 pp.

G 2112 Stein, Thelma. Food and Culture in the Canadian Mosaic. Toronto: McClelland & Stewart, 1979.

C 2113 Stout, C. H. 'Saddle Notches, Candles and Oil.' Alberta Historical Review, 6(Autumn 1958), 16-24.

Gb 2114 Symons, R. D. Where the Wagon Led. Toronto: Doubleday, 1973. 343 pp.

G 2115 Taylor, Geoffrey W. Timber. History of the Forest Industry in B.C. Vancouver: Douglas, 1975. 209 pp.

CY 2116 Tilney, Philip. A Baker's Dozen. Ottawa: National Museum, 1973. 4 pp.

C 2117 -- Eight Unusual Recipes. Ottawa: National Museum, 1973. 9 pp.

Gb 2118 Townsend, Charles W., ed. Captain Cartwright and His Labrador Journal. Boston: Dona Estes, 1911. 385 pp.

B 2119 Turner, Allan R. 'Pioneer Farming Experiences.' Saskatchewan History, 8(1955), 41-55.

B 2120 Turner, John P. 'Men of the Long Portage.' CGJ, 6 (Jan. 1933), 5-16.

Gc 2121 Turner, Nancy J., and Adam F. Szczawinski. Edible Garden Weeds of Canada. Ottawa: National Museum, 1978. 184 pp.

Gc 2122 -- and -- Edible Wild Fruits and Nuts of Canada. Ottawa: National Museum, 1979. 224 pp.

Gc 2123 -- and -- Wild Coffee and Tea Substitutes of Canada. Ottawa: National Museum, 1978. 111 pp.

Pb 2124 'Upper Canada Village.' Canadian Homes, June 1961, special issue.

G 2125 Wallace, Frederick W. Wooden Ships and Iron Men. Toronto: Hodder & Stoughton, 1924. 337 pp.

Gc 2126 Weinhard, Philip. 'Early High River and the Whiskey Traders.' Alberta Historical Review, 4(Summer 1956), 12-16.

GP 2127 White, Howard, ed. Raincoast Chronicles First Five: Stories and History of the B.C. Coast. Madeira Park, B.C.: Harbour Pub., 1976. 270 pp.

Gb 2128 Whitton, Charlotte. A Hundred Years A-Fellin'. Some Passages from the Timber Saga of the Ottawa in the Century 1842-1942. Ottawa: Runge, 1943. 172 pp.

G 2129 Woodcock, George. The Canadians: A Cultural History. Toronto: Fitzhenry & Whiteside, 1979. 320 pp.

Pa 2130 Zimmerman, Lynn. 'People of the Margaree.' Harrowsmith, 3:3(1979), 74-82.

9B   Anglophone and Celtic

G 2131   Allan, Iris. 'The McDougalls - Pioneers of the Plains.'
Beaver, Summer 1973, pp. 14-19.

Gb 2132   Archibald, Mrs. Charles. 'Early Scottish Settlers in
Cape Breton.' _Collections of the N.S. Historical Soci-
ety_, 17(1914), 69-100.

Pb 2133   Armstrong, Audrey. _The Blacksmith of Fallbrook; the
story of William Cameron, blacksmith, woodcarver,
raconteur_. Toronto: Musson, 1979. 96 pp.

G 2134   Austin, Leona M. _Wooler--100 Years through the Lens
of a Camera_. Belleville: Mika, 1975. 132 pp.

G 2135   Baird, Andrew. _Sixty Years on the Klondike_. Vancouver:
Black, 1965. 111 pp.

Gb 2136   Barbour, Florence G. _Memories of Life on the Labrador
and in Newfoundland_. New York: Carlton, 1973. 113 pp.

G 2137   Barratt, Glynn R. 'Whalers and Weavers.' _Beaver_, Winter
1977, 54-59.

Pa 2138   Barrett, Wayne, photographer. _King's Landing. Country
Life in Early Canada_. Intro., George MacBeath. Toronto:
Oxford, 1979. 98 pp.

B 2139   Bartlett, Robert H. 'The Sealing Saga of Newfoundland.'
National Geographic, 56(July 1929), 91-130.

Gb 2140   Bates, Christina. _Out of Old Ontario Kitchens_. Toronto:
Pagurian, 1978. 190 pp.

C 2141   Beavan, Mrs. F. _Sketches and Tales Illustrative of Life
in the Backwoods of New Brunswick, North America_. London: Routledge, 1845. 142 pp.

C 2142   Bedore, Bernie. _The Shanty_. Arnprior: Mufferaw Enterprises, 1963, 1975. 84 pp.

G 2143   Bergen, Myrtle. _Tough Timber: The Loggers of British
Columbia: Their Story_. Toronto: Progress, 1966. 250 pp.

G 2144   Berry, Gerald L. 'Fort Whoop-Up and the Whiskey
Traders.' _Alberta Historical Review_, 1(July 1953),
6-11.

G 2145   Binnie-Clark, Georgina. _Wheat and Women_. Toronto: Univ.
of Toronto Press, 1979. 313 pp.

B 2146   Blake, Verschoyle B., and Ralph Greenhill. _Rural Ont-
ario_. Toronto: Univ. of Toronto Press, 1969. 173 pp.

C 2147   Blakeley, Phyllis R. 'Early Christmas Customs in Nova Scotia.' Atlantic Advocate, 56(Dec. 1965), 25-29.

C 2148   -- 'Easter Custom of Egg Tipping.' Atlantic Advocate, 56(Mar. 1964), 16.

Gc 2149   -- Glimpses of Halifax 1867-1900. Halifax: Public Archives of N.S., 1949, rpt. 1973. 213 pp.

C 2150   -- 'New Years in Nova Scotia: The Customs of the Past.' Atlantic Advocate, 62(Jan. 1972), 20, 22-3.

C 2151   Bond, G. J. 'Old Christmas Customs.' In The Book of Newfoundland. Vol. II. Ed. J. R. Smallwood. St. John's: Nfld. Book Pub., 1937. P. 259.

G 2152   Boyle, David, ed. The Township of Scarborough, 1796-1896. Toronto: Briggs, 1896. 302 pp.

Pc 2153   Brown, Ron. Ghost Towns of Ontario. Vol. 1 Southern Ontario. Langley: Stagecoach, 1978. 200 pp.

Fb 2154   Brown, Theo. 'The Mummer's Play in Devon and Newfoundland,' Folk-Lore, 63(1952), 30-34.

C 2155   Bruemmer, Fred. 'The Mummers.' Beaver, Winter 1966, pp. 24-25.

C 2156   -- 'Whalers of the North.' Beaver, Winter 1971, pp. 44-51.

GP 2157   Buckler, Ernest. Ox Bells and Fireflies. Toronto: McClelland & Stewart, 1968. 302 pp.

Pc 2158   -- 'We Never Heard of Dorothy Dix.' Atlantic Advocate, 48(Jan. 1958), 65-67.

C 2159   Burns, Jane. '"Every One Has Good": A Study of the Occupational Folklife of a St. John's Cab Driver.' Culture & Tradition, 4(1979), 79-87.

A 2160   Butler, Victor. The Little Nord Easter: Reminiscences of a Placentia Bayman. Ed. Wilfred W. Wareham. St. John's: Memorial Univ. 1975. Rpt. Portugal Cove: Breakwater, 1977. 262 pp.

B 2161   -- Sposin' I Dies in D'Dory. St. John's: Jesperson, 1977. 89 pp.

Gc 2162   Byrnes, John M. The Paths to Yesterday, Memories of Old St. John's, Newfoundland. Boston: Meador, 1931. 235 pp.

Gb 2163   Calkin, John B. Old Time Customs, Memories and Traditions and Other Essays. Halifax: MacKinley, 1918. 188 pp.

Folklife and Customs

Gb 2164   Cameron, James M. The Pictonian Colliers. Halifax: N.S.
          Museum, 1974. 356 pp.

Gb 2165   Chiaramonte, Louis J. Craftsmen-Client Contracts: Inter-
          personal Relations in a Newfoundland Fishing Community.
          St. John's: ISER, Memorial Univ., 1970. 64 pp.

Gb 2166   Conant, Thomas. Upper Canada Sketches. Toronto: Briggs,
          1898. 243 pp.

 C 2167   Creighton, Helen. 'Easter on Cape Sable Island.' Atlan-
          tic Advocate, 54(Mar. 1946), 16.

Gc 2168   -- 'Fishing for Albacore.' CGJ, 3(July 1931), 65-76.

 B 2169   -- 'Old Christmas Customs in Nova Scotia.' CGJ, 63
          (Dec. 1961), 218-21.

Gc 2170   Criddle, Alma. 'The Criddles of Aweme.' Beaver, Spring
          1978, pp. 15-19.

Gb 2171   Cross, Michael S. 'The Lumber Community of Upper Can-
          ada, 1815-1867.' Ontario History, 52(1960), 213-34.

 G 2172   Crout, A. J. Tall Tales from the Tall Timbers. N.P.:
          Author, n.d. 198 pp.

 B 2173   De Boilieu, Lambert. Recollections of Labrador Life.
          1861; rpt. Toronto: Ryerson, 1969. 134 pp.

Gc 2174   Deming, Clarence. By-Ways of Nature and Life. New York:
          G. P. Putnam's Sons, 1884. 383 pp.

Gc 2175   Dempsey, Hugh A. 'Calgary's First Stampede.' Alberta
          Historical Review, 3(Summer 1955), 3-13.

GP 2176   Dennis, Clara. Cape Breton Over. Toronto: Ryerson,
          1942. 342 pp.

GP 2177   -- Down in Nova Scotia, My Own, My Native Land. Toronto:
          Ryerson, 1934. 410 pp.

 C 2178   [Devine, P. K.] 'The London Tavern.' Christmas Annual
          (St John's), 1909, p. 15.

 C 2179   Devine, P. K. 'Musing Among the Mounds.' Christmas Echo
          (St. John's), No. 2 (Christmas 1917), pp. 18-19.

 C 2180   -- 'Quaint Christmas Customs.' Christmas Bells (St.
          John's), No. 10(Dec. 1901), p. 4.

 B 2181   Dickie, Gordon. 'Cultural Origins in Colonial Life.'
          Dalhousie Review, 37(1957), 41-51, 165-74.

 B 2182   Dimock, Celia C. Children of the Sheiling. Sydney:
          Lynk, n.d. 98 pp.

Gb 2183   Dodd, Jack. The Wind in the Rigging. Torbay, Nfld.:
          Author, 1972. 159 pp.

B 2184   Dodge, Helen C. My Childhood in the Canadian Wilderness. New York: Vantage, 1961. 74 pp.

Gc 2185   Duncan, Dorothy. Bluenose: A Portrait of Nova Scotia. Toronto: Collins, 1946. 273 pp.

A 2186   Dunn, C. W. Highland Settler: A Portrait of the Scottish Gael in Nova Scotia. Toronto: Univ. of Toronto Press, 1953. 179 pp.

A 2187   England, George Allan. Vikings of the Ice: Being the Log of a Tenderfoot on the Great Newfoundland Seal Hunt. 1924; rpt. as The Greatest Hunt in the World. Montreal: Tundra, 1969. 323 pp.

Ga 2188   Faris, James C. Cat Harbour: A Newfoundland Fishing Settlement. St. John's: ISER, Memorial Univ., 1972. 185 pp.

B 2189   -- 'The Dynamics of Verbal Exchange: A Newfoundland Example.' Anthropologica, 8(1966), 235-48.

GP 2190   Farnham, C. H. Cape Breton Folk. Cape Breton: Normaway Handcrafts, n.d. 19 pp.

Gb 2191   Fergusson, C. Bruce, ed. Uniacke's Sketches of Cape Breton and other papers relating to Cape Breton Island. Halifax: Public Archives of N.S., 1958. 198 pp.

C 2192   Finnigan, Joan. Canadian Colonial Cooking. Toronto: NC Press, 1976. 48 pp.

G 2193   -- I Come from the Valley. Toronto: NC Press, 1976. 160 pp.

Ga 2194   Firestone, Melvin. Brothers and Rivals: Patrilocality in Savage Cove. St. John's: ISER, Memorial Univ., 1967. 143 pp.

Gc 2195   Forsyth, Robert. 'Homesteading on the Carrot River.' Beaver, Summer 1971, pp. 53-57.

G 2196   Francis, Daniel. 'Whaling on the Eastmain.' Beaver, Summer 1977, pp. 4-13.

Gc 2197   Franks, Patricia. Grandma was a Pioneer. Cobalt: Highway Book Shop, 1977. 105 pp.

GP(1) 2198   Freeman, Bill. Shantymen of Cache Creek. Toronto: Lorimer, 1975. 166 pp.

Gc 2199   Fudge, John M. The Late Capt. J. M. Fudge: His Life Story as a Fisherman and Businessman. [Moncton: Atlas Press, n.d.] 60 pp. [Nfld.]

A 2200 Galbraith, John Kenneth. The Scotch. Toronto: Macmillan, 1964. 145 pp.

G 2201 Gard, Anson A. Pioneers of the Upper Ottawa and the Humours of the Valley. Ottawa: Emerson, 1906.

Gb 2202 Garland, M. A. 'Some Phases of Pioneer Religious Life in Upper Canada.' Ontario History, 25(1929), 231-47.

Ga 2203 Geikie, John C. George Stanley; or, Life in the Woods. London: Routledge, 1864. Rpt. as Life in the Woods, London: Strahan, 1873; and Adventures in Canada, Philadelphia: Porter, 1872. 408 pp.

C 2204 George, Ernest S. 'Ranching in Southern Alberta.' Alberta Historical Review, 3(Spring 1955), 33-39.

Gc 2205 Gibson, David. 'Conditions in York County a Century Ago.' Ontario History, 24(1927), 356-65.

Gb 2206 Gill, Janice M. Nova Scotia Down-Home Cooking. Toronto: McGraw-Hill Ryerson, 1978. 208 pp.

G 2207 Godsell, Philip H. 'Stage Steamer and Pack Train.' Alberta Folklore Quarterly, 2(1946), 72-77.

C 2208 Gordon, Charles H. M. 'Christmas Forty Years Ago.' Beaver, Dec. 1923, pp. 84-86.

Gc 2209 Goudie, Elisabeth. Woman of Labrador. Ed. David W. Zimmerly. Toronto: Peter Martin, 1973. 166 pp.

Gb 2210 Greene, William H. The Wooden Walls Among the Ice Floes. Telling the Romance of the Newfoundland Seal Fishery. London: Hutchinson, 1933. 298 pp.

C 2211 Greenhill, Pauline. 'Ritual and Status: Working in an Office.' Culture & Tradition, 4(1979), 103-15.

A 2212 Guillet, Edwin C. Early Life in Upper Canada. 1933; rpt. Toronto: Univ. of Toronto Press, 1963. 782 pp.

B 2213 -- Pioneer Days in Upper Canada. 1933; rpt. Toronto: Univ. of Toronto Press, 1964. 216 pp.

B 2214 -- The Pioneer Farmer and Backwoodsman. 2 vols. Toronto: Univ. of Toronto Press, 1963. 372 pp.; 404 pp.

B 2215 -- Pioneer Settlements in Upper Canada. 1933; rpt. Toronto: Univ. of Toronto Press, 1970. 152 pp.

B 2216 -- Pioneer Travel in Upper Canada. 1933; rpt. Toronto: Univ. of Toronto Press, 1966. 241 pp.

A 2217 Halpert, Herbert, and George M. Story, eds. Christmas Mumming in Newfoundland. Toronto: Pub. for Memorial Univ. by Univ. of Toronto Press, 1969. 246 pp.

C 2218   Harrington, Michael F. 'Newfoundland Old-Time Christmas.' Atlantic Advocate, 48(Dec. 1957), 22-23.

C 2219   -- 'Old English Mummers' Christmas Play in Newfoundland.' Atlantic Advocate, 51(Dec. 1960), 54-55.

G 2220   Harrison, Phyllis, ed. The Home Children. Winnipeg: Watson & Dwyer, 1979. 271 pp. [Letters.]

G 2221   Harvey, Mary M. 'Gardens of Shelburne, Nova Scotia, 1785-1820.' Bulletin of the Assoc. for Preservation Technology, 7:2(1975), 32-73.

B 2222   Henry, Lorne J., and Gilbert Paterson. Pioneer Days in Ontario. Toronto: Ryerson, 1938. 234 pp.

Ga 2223   High River Pioneers' and Old Timers' Association. Leaves from the Medicine Tree. Lethbridge, Alta.: Herald, 1960. 529 pp.

Gb 2224   Higinbotham, John D. When the West Was Young. Historical Reminiscences of the Early Canadian West. Toronto: Ryerson, 1933. 328 pp.

GP 2225   Hill, Douglas. The Scots to Canada. London: Gentry, 1972. 136 pp.

G 2226   Hill, G. Domestic Life in Early Halifax. Halifax: N.S. Museum, 1976. 12 pp.

C 2227   Hillis, James M. 'Life in the Lumber Camp.' Ontario History, 59(1967), 157-62.

B 2228   Hovinen, Elizabeth. 'Quakers of Yonge Street.' CGJ, 92 (Jan. 1976), 52-57.

Gb 2229   Howes, E. A. With a Glance Backward. Toronto: Oxford, 1939. 197 pp.

Gb 2230   Howison, John. Sketches of Upper Canada, Domestic, Local and Characteristic. 1821; rpt. Toronto: Coles, 1970. 339 pp.

B 2231   Hughson, John W., and Courtney C. J. Bond. Hurling Down the Pine. Old Chelsea, P.Q.: Historical Society of the Gatineau, rev. ed. 1965. 119 pp.

G 2232   Innis, Mary Q., ed. Mrs. Simcoe's Diary. Toronto: Macmillan, 1965. 223 pp.

C 2233   Ippolito, Pat. 'Children of Peace Temple.' CanAntC, 3 (Aug. 1968), 17-19.

FA 2234   Ives, Edward D. 'Fleetwood Pride, 1864-1960.' Northeast Folklore, 9(1967), 1-60.

2235 James, C. J. 'Some Reminiscences.' Christmas Bells, No. 25(1917), pp. 15-16.

C 2236 Jameson, Sheilagh S. 'Era of the Big Ranches.' Alberta Historical Review, 18(Winter 1970), 1-9.

B 2237 Jesperson, Ivan. Fat-Back & Molasses: A Collection of Favourite Old Recipes from Newfoundland and Labrador. St. John's: Jesperson, 1974. 180 pp.

Gc 2238 Jukes, Joseph B. Excursions in and about Newfoundland during the Years 1839 and 1840. 1842; rpt. Toronto: Canadiana House, 1969.

Gb 2239 Keegan, Norah. Footprints in the Sand. St. John's: Jesperson, 1979. 65 pp.

Gc 2240 Kendrick, Mary F. Down the Road to Yesterday: A History of Springfield, Annapolis County, Nova Scotia. Bridgewater, N.S.: F. J. Macpherson, 1941. 141 pp.

C 2241 Kennedy, Alan. 'Reminiscences of a Lumberjack.' Saskatchewan History, 19(1966), 24-34.

G 2242 Knight, Rolf. Stump Ranch Chronicles and Other Narratives. Vancouver: New Star, 1977. 144 pp.

C 2243 Laba, Martin. '"The Bayman Food Market is in the Townie Dump": Identity and the Townie Newfoundlander.' Culture & Tradition, 3(1978), 7-16.

C 2244 Langdon, Eustella. Pioneer Gardens at Black Creek Pioneer Village. Toronto/Montreal: Holt, Rinehart & Winston, 1972. 62 pp.

Gc 2245 Langton, H. H., ed. A Gentlewoman in Upper Canada: The Journals of Anne Langton. 1950; rpt. Toronto: Clarke, Irwin, 1964. 207 pp.

Gc 2246 Langton, John. Early Days in Upper Canada. Toronto: Macmillan, 1926. 310 pp.

A 2247 Lawton, J. T., and P. K. Devine. Ye Old King's Cove. St. John's: n.p., 1944. 106 pp.

Gb 2248 Leopold, Caroline B. The History of New Ross, in the County of Lunenburg, Nova Scotia. New Ross: Committee in Charge, 150th Anniversary of New Ross, 1966. 61 pp.

G 2249 Lett, William P. Recollections of Bytown and its Old Inhabitants. Ottawa: Citizen Printing, 1874. 95 pp.

Gc 2250 Lotz, Jim, and Pat Lotz. Cape Breton Island. Vancouver: Douglas, David, and Charles, 1974. 208 pp.

C 2251 Lynch, Mary J. 'Christmas in an Out Harbor.' The Colonist for Christmas No. of 1887, 2:2(1887), 2.

B 2252   McCarl, Robert S., Jr. 'The Communication of Work Technique.' Culture & Tradition, 3(1978), 108-16.

G 2253   McClung, Nellie R. Clearing the West, My Own Story. Toronto: Allen, 1935; rpt. 1964. 378 pp.

Gc 2254   Macdonald, Christine. 'Pioneer Church Life in Saskatchewan.' Saskatchewan History, 13(1960), 1-18.

G 2255   MacDonald, H. H. Down Memory Lane: Gems of Antigonish to Remember. N.p.: Author, 1972. 136 pp.

Gc 2256   Macdonnell, John A. Sketches Illustrating the Early Settlement and History of Glengarry in Canada. Montreal: Foster Brown, 1893. 337 pp.

B 2257   MacEwan, J. W. Grant. John Ware's Cow Country. Edmonton: Institute of Applied Art, 1960. 261 pp.

C 2258   McGrath, Patrick T. 'The Fisherfolk of Newfoundland.' Outing, 44(June 1904), 306-21.

Pc 2259   MacGregor, Francis. Days That I Remember. Stories with a Scottish Accent. Windsor: Lancelot, 1976. 44 pp.

Gb 2260   MacGregor, J. G. North West of 16. Toronto: McClelland & Stewart, 1958; rpt. Saskatoon: Western Producer, 1977. 224 pp.

GP 2261   MacLean, Angus H. God and the Devil at Seal Cove. Halifax: Petheric, 1976. 126 pp. [Cape Breton.]

B 2262   MacLennan, Gordon. 'A Contribution to the Ethnohistory of Saskatchewan's Patagonian Welsh Settlement.' Canadian Ethnic Studies, 7:2(1975), 57-72.

G 2263   McLeod, Evelyn S. 'Restless Pioneers.' Beaver, Summer 1976, pp. 34-41.

C 2264   McNamara, Charles. 'The Camboose Shanty.' Ontario History, 51(1959), 73-78.

GP(1) 2265   MacPhail, Margaret. Loch Bras D'Or. Windsor: Lancelot, 1970. 164 pp.

PY 2266   Major, Kevin, ed. Doryloads. Newfoundland Writings and Art Selected and Edited for Young People. Portugal Cove: Breakwater, 1974. 203 pp.

A 2267   Mannion, John J. Irish Settlements in Eastern Canada: A Study of Cultural Transfer and Adaptation. Toronto: Univ. of Toronto Press, 1974. 219 pp.

Gc 2268   Margaret, Len. St. Leonard's Cook Book. Portugal Cove: Breakwater, 1977.

146

C 2269   Martin, J. Lynton. <u>I. Lumbering. A History of Everyday</u>
          <u>Things in Nova Scotia.</u> Halifax: N.S. Museum, n.d.
          11 pp.

CY 2270   Mason, Joe. <u>My Sixteenth Winter: Logging on the French</u>
          <u>River.</u> Cobalt: Highway Book Shop, 1974. 50 pp.

Gb 2271   Matthews, J. S. <u>Early Vancouver. Narratives of Pioneers</u>
          <u>of Vancouver, B.C. Collected during 1931-1932.</u> 2 vols.
          Vancouver: Brock Webber, 1959. 168 pp.; 316 pp.

Ga 2272   Matthews, Ralph. <u>'There's No Better Place Than Here':</u>
          <u>Social Change in Three Newfoundland Communities.</u> Tor-
          onto: Peter Martin, 1976. 164 pp.

Gb 2273   Maxwell, Percy A. <u>Letters Home During His Years as a</u>
          <u>Homesteader in the Developing Period of Canada's West.</u>
          Toronto: Elizabeth Maxwell, 1967.

C 2274   May, John. 'Bush Life in the Ottawa Valley.' <u>Ontario</u>
          <u>History,</u> 12(1914), 153-64.

C 2275   Melchen, Elizabeth V. 'Christmas Lore: Janneying in
          Newfoundland.' <u>New York Folklore Quarterly,</u> 7(1951),
          272-74.

Gb 2276   Minhinnick, Jeanne. <u>At Home in Upper Canada.</u> Toronto:
          Clarke, Irwin, 1970. 227 pp.

G 2277   -- 'Some Personal Observations on the Use of Paint in
          Early Ontario.' <u>Bulletin of the Assoc. for Preservation</u>
          <u>Technology,</u> 7:2(1975), 13-31.

GbY 2278 Minifie, James. <u>Homesteader: A Prairie Boyhood Recalled.</u>
          Toronto: Macmillan, 1972. 222 pp.

C 2279   Moodie, D. W. 'Gardening on Hudson Bay: The First Cent-
          ury.' <u>Beaver,</u> Summer 1978, pp. 54-59.

Gb 2280   Moodie, Susanna. <u>Life in the Clearings.</u> 1853; rpt. Tor-
          onto: Macmillan, 1959. 384 pp.

Ga 2281   -- <u>Roughing It in the Bush.</u> 1852; rpt. Toronto: McClel-
          land & Stewart, 1962. 238 pp.

Gb 2282   Moreton, Julian. <u>Life and Work in Newfoundland.</u> London:
          Rivingtons, 1863. 106 pp.

C 2283   Morris, I. C. 'The Old Fisher Folk.' <u>Newfoundland Quar-</u>
          <u>terly,</u> 20(1901); rpt. 64(Fall 1965), 4-5.

Pc 2284   Mowat, Farley. 'Will Ye Let the Mummers In?' <u>Weekend</u>
          <u>Magazine,</u> 24 Dec. 1966, pp. 6-9.

Gb 2285   Mowat, Farley, and David Blackwood. The Wake of the
          Great Sealers. Toronto: McClelland & Stewart, 1973.
          157 pp.

 G 2286   Moyles, R. G. 'Complaints is many and various, but the
          odd Divil likes it.' Nineteenth Century Views of New-
          foundland. Toronto: Peter Martin, 1975. 187 pp.

Gc 2287   Murphy, Michael P. Pathways Through Yesterday. St.
          John's: Town Crier, 1976. 189 pp.

 A 2288   Murray, Hilda C. More than 50%: Women's Life in a New-
          foundland Outport 1900-1950. St. John's: Breakwater,
          1979. 160 pp.

 C 2289   Neddrie, John G. 'Pioneering in the Eagle Valley.'
          Alberta Historical Review, 9(Spring 1961), 8-11.

 G 2290   Need, Thomas. Six Years in the Bush; or, Extracts from
          the Journal of a Settler in Upper Canada, 1832-1838.
          London: Simpkin Marshall, 1838. 126 pp.

Gc 2291   Newcomb, Maud. Nova Scotia in Grandfather's Day. N.p.:
          Author, 1978. 40 pp.

 C 2292   Newfoundland Cook Book. St. John's: Macy's, 1973.
          73 pp.

 P 2293   'Newfoundlandiana.' Newfoundland Quarterly, 56(Dec.
          1957), 3.

 P 2294   Nightingale, Marie. Out of Old Nova Scotia Kitchens.
          1970; rpt. Halifax: Pagurian, 1976. 214 pp.

 P 2295   'Ontario's homage to the past.' Special issue of Globe
          Magazine, 17 June, 1961. 24 pp. [Upper Canada Village.]

 G 2296   Ossenberg, Richard J. 'Social Class and Bar Behavior
          during an Urban Festival.' Human Organization, 28
          (1969), 29-34. [Calgary Stampede.]

Gb 2297   Owen, E. A. Pioneer Sketches of Long Point Settlement.
          Toronto: Briggs, 1898. 578 pp.

Gc 2298   Parker, John P. Cape Breton Ships and Men. London:
          Hazell Watson & Viney, 1967. 197 pp.

 B 2299   Parsons, A. A. 'Memoirs of Christmas - How the Great
          Festival Used to be Celebrated.' Holly Leaves, (St.
          John's), 1917, pp. 19-20.

 P 2300   Patterson, Edith. Tales of Early Manitoba from the
          Winnipeg Free Press. Pamp. N.p., 1970.

Ga 2301   Philbrook, Tom. Fisherman, Logger, Merchant, Miner:
          Social Change and Industrialism in Three Newfoundland

<u>Communities</u>. St. John's: ISER, Memorial Univ., 1966. 212 pp.

G 2302 Pictou Heritage Society. <u>Country Roads: Rural Pictou County, Nova Scotia</u>. Halifax: Petheric, 1974. 76 pp.

C 2303 Poldon, Amelia. 'Women in Pioneer Life.' <u>Ontario History</u>, 17(1919), 25-29.

G 2304 Pollard, William C. <u>Life on the Frontier: A Sketch of the Parry Sound Colonists</u>. London: Stockwell, n.d.

A 2305 Porter, Helen. <u>Below the Bridge</u>. St. John's: Breakwater, 1979. 126 pp.

Gb 2306 Powell, Benjamin W., Sr. <u>Labrador By Choice</u>. Ed. Joan M. Cartledge. N.p.: Author, 1979. 179 pp.

Gc 2307 Preston, Richard A. <u>For Friends at Home: A Scottish Emigrant's Letters from Canada, California, and the Cariboo, 1844-1864</u>. Montreal: McGill-Queen's Univ. Press, 1975. 352 pp.

P 2308 Ramsey, Bruce. <u>Barkerville. A Guide in Word and Picture to the Fabulous Gold Camp of the Cariboo</u>. 2nd ed. Vancouver: Mitchell, 1961. 92 pp.

G 2309 -- <u>Ghost Towns of British Columbia</u>. Vancouver: Mitchell, 1963. 226 pp.

C 2310 Ritchie, T. 'Joseph Van Norman, Ironmaster of Upper Canada.' <u>CGJ</u>, 77(Aug. 1968), 52-57.

G 2311 Rose, Hilda. <u>The Stump Farm--A Chronicle of Pioneering</u>. Boston: Little Brown, 1928. 178 pp.

G 2312 Rosser, Frederick T. <u>The Welsh Settlement in Upper Canada</u>. London, Ont.: Univ. of Western Ontario, 1954. 150 pp.

B 2313 Russell, Loris S. <u>Everyday Life in Colonial Canada</u>. Toronto: Copp Clark, 1973. 206 pp.

C 2314 Rutstrum, Calvin. 'Sourdough.' <u>Beaver</u>, Autumn 1973, pp. 40-43.

G 2315 Scargall, Jeanne. <u>Pioneer Potpourri: Recipes, Remedies, Memories</u>. Toronto: Methuen, 1974. 151 pp.

B 2316 Scherk, Michael G. [A Canuck]. <u>Pen Pictures of Early Pioneer Life in Upper Canada</u>. Toronto: Briggs, 1905; rpt. Toronto: Coles, 1972. 280 pp.

B 2317 Sider, Gerald M. <u>Mumming in Outport Newfoundland</u>. Toronto: New Hogtown Press, c. 1977. 31 pp.

B 2318 Skelton, Isabel. The Backwoodsman: A Chronicle of Pioneer Home Life in Upper and Lower Canada. Toronto:
Ryerson, 1924. 261 pp.

Gb 2319 Smith, William L. The Pioneers of Old Ontario. Toronto:
Morang, 1923. 343 pp.

B 2320 Spencer, Audrey. Spinning and Weaving at Upper Canada
Village. Toronto: Ryerson, 1964. 40 pp.

Gc 2321 Squire, Harold. A Newfoundland Outport in the Making.
The Early History of Eastport. Together with an Eye-
Witness Account of the Greenland Disaster. Eastport:
Author, 1974. 95 pp.

B 2322 Stead, Robert J. C. 'The Old Prairie Homestead.' CGJ,
7(July 1933), 13-22.

Gb 2323 Stewart, Frances. Our Forest Home. Ed. E. S. Dunlop.
Toronto: Presbyterian Printing, 1889. 210 pp.

C 2324 Story, George M. 'Buried Treasure.' Springdale News
(Nfld.), 15 Feb. 1966, p. 7; 3 Mar. 1966, p. 10;
17 Mar. 1966, p. 9.

C 2325 -- 'The Flat Islands Newfoundlander.' Canadian Forum,
53(March 1974), 24-25.

Gb 2326 Strickland, Samuel. Twenty-Seven Years in Canada West.
1853; rpt. Edmonton: Hurtig, 1970. 344 pp.

B 2327 Szwed, John F. 'Gossip, Drinking and Social Control:
Consensus and Communication in a Newfoundland Parish.'
Ethnology, 5(1966), 434-41.

Ga 2328 -- Private Cultures and Public Imagery. Interpersonal
Relations in a Newfoundland Peasant Society. St.
John's: ISER, Memorial Univ. 1966. 188 pp.

B 2329 Taft, Michael. 'The Itinerant Movie-Man and His Impact
on the Folk Culture of the Outports of Newfoundland.'
Culture & Tradition, 1(1976), 107-119.

C 2330 Talbot, Percy R. 'Pioneering on Strawberry Plain. Early
Days at Lacombe.' Alberta Historical Review, 3(Summer
1955), 14-33.

Gc 2331 Thomas, Jean M. 'Recollections and Reminiscences; Homesteading at Indian Head.' Saskatchewan History, 4(Spring
1951), 68-72.

Ga 2332 Thompson, George S. Up to Date; or, The Life of a Lumberman. Peterborough, Ont.: Times Print., 1895. 126 pp.

C 2333 Tilly, Ernest. 'Ye Old Times in Catalina.' Newfoundland
        Quarterly, 56(1957), Mar., pp. 7, 31-34; June, pp. 7-9;
        Sept., pp. 43-45; Dec., p. 8.

A 2334 Tizzard, Aubrey M. On Sloping Ground: Reminiscences of
        Outport Life in Notre Dame Bay, Newfoundland. Ed. J. D.
        A. Widdowson. St. John's: Memorial Univ., 1979. 390 pp.

Gb 2335 Traill, Catharine Parr. The Backwoods of Canada. 1836;
        rpt. Toronto: McClelland & Stewart, 1966. 125 pp.

B 2336 -- The Canadian Settler's Guide. 1855; rpt. Toronto:
        McClelland & Stewart, 1969. 251 pp.

G 2337 Trimble, David. When I Was a Boy. Don Mills: Dent,
        1976. 106 pp.

C 2338 Waghorne, Arthur C. 'Christmas Customs in Newfoundland.'
        JAF, 6(1893), 63-65.

C 2339 -- 'Hunting the Wren.' JAF, 6(1893), 143-44.

P 2340 Wallace, Frederick W. 'Life on the Grand Banks.' National-
        al Geographic, 40(July 1921), 1-28.

B 2341 Way, Beryl W. 'Upper Canada Village.' CGJ, 62(1961),
        218-33.

C 2342 Whittle, William. 'Christmas "Fools" and "Mummers" in
        Newfoundland.' JAF, 6(1893), 63-65.

A 2343 Widdowson, John D. A. If You Don't Be Good: Verbal
        Social Control in Newfoundland. St. John's: ISER,
        Memorial Univ., 1977. 345 pp.

B 2344 Williams, Helen E. Spinning Wheels and Homespun. Tor-
        onto: McClelland & Stewart, 1923. 314 pp.

G 2345 Zimmerly, David. Cain's Land Revisited: Culture Change
        in Central Labrador. St. John's: Memorial Univ., 1975.
        346 pp.

9C Francophone

P 2346 A. C. 'The Habitant.' Quebec, 1(Dec. 1926), 11-12.

A 2347 Anderson, Jay A. 'The Early Development of French-
        Canadian Foodways.' In Folklore of Canada. Ed. Edith
        Fowke. Toronto: McClelland & Stewart, 1976. Pp. 91-99.

P 2348 Asselin, E. Donald. A French-Canadian Cookbook. Edmon-
        ton: Hurtig, 1968. 149 pp.

Gc 2349　Barbeau, C. Marius. 'Gaspé Peninsula.' CGJ, 3(Aug.
　　　　　1931), 79-92.

Gc 2350　-- 'In the Heart of the Laurentians.' CGJ, 7(July
　　　　　1933), 3-12.

Gc 2351　-- 'Rocher-Malin-Temiscouta.' CGJ, 7(Oct. 1933),
　　　　　177-87.

Gc 2352　-- 'Saguenay.' CGJ, 16(June 1938), 285-92.

Pb 2353　Beaulieu, Mirelle. The Cooking of Provincial Quebec.
　　　　　Trans. David Ellis. Toronto: Gage, 1975. 156 pp.

Pb 2354　Boswell, Hazel. French Canada. Toronto: McClelland &
　　　　　Stewart, 1938; rev. 1967. 76 pp.

P 2355　Bouchard, Georges. '"Habitants" in the Sugar Bush.'
　　　　　Quebec, 4(Apr. 1929), 54-57.

Pb 2356　-- Other Days Other Ways. Silhouettes of the Past in
　　　　　French Canada. Montreal: Carrier, 1928. 189 pp.

P 2357　-- 'The Work of Women on the Farm.' Quebec, 8(July
　　　　　1933), 130-36.

C 2358　Brann, Esther. 'A Quebec Sketch Book.' CGJ, 1(June
　　　　　1930), 104-31.

C 2359　C. H. V. 'Twelfth-Day (Le Jour des Rois).' Quebec,
　　　　　1(Jan. 1927), 9.

Ga 2360　Call, Frank O. The Spell of Acadia. Boston: Page, 1930.
　　　　　427 pp.

GP 2361　Davies, Blodwen. Gaspé, Land of History and Romance.
　　　　　Toronto: Ambassador, 1949. 233 pp.

G 2362　Dechene, A. M. 'French Participation in Early Alberta.'
　　　　　Alberta Historical Review, 2(Oct. 1954), 11-27.

A(1) 2363　De Gaspé, Phillipe-Aubert, père. Canadians of Old.
　　　　　Trans. C. G. D. Roberts. 1890; rpt. Toronto: McClelland
　　　　　& Stewart, 1974. 364 pp.

B 2364　Douville, Raymond, and Jacques Casanova. Daily Life in
　　　　　Early Canada. Trans. Carole Congreve. New York: Macmil-
　　　　　lan, 1964. 268 pp.

GP 2365　Eaton, E. F. 'Ted.' Waste Not Want Not. Saint John:
　　　　　N.B. Museum, 1978. 95 pp. [Acadian recipes.]

Gc 2366　Ells, S. C. 'Canadian Voyageurs.' CGJ, 42(Feb. 1951),
　　　　　80-89.

G 2367　Fennie, Richard. 'Filming Rural French Canada.' CGJ,
　　　　　14(Apr. 1937), 183-98.

A 2368   Fréchette, Louis Honoré. Christmas in French Canada.
          Toronto: Morang, 1899. 262 pp.

G 2369   Godbout, J. Adelard. 'Agriculture in Quebec--Past-
          Present-Future.' CGJ, 28(Apr. 1944), 157-81.

G 2370   Grant, George M., ed. French-Canadian Life and Charac-
          ter. Chicago: Belfond, 1899. 249 pp.

G 2371   Grant, William L., ed. The History of New France by
          Marc Lescarbot. 3 vols. Toronto: Champlain Society,
          1907-1914.

A 2372   Greenough, William P. Canadian Folk-Life and Folk-Lore.
          New York: Richmond, 1897; rpt. Toronto: Coles, n.d.
          199 pp.

Gc 2373   Harrington, Lyn, and Richard Harrington. 'Ile-Aux-
          Coudres.' CGJ, 43(Aug. 1951), 50-57.

Ga 2374   Harris, Richard Colebrook [R. Cole Harris]. The Seig-
          neurial System in Early Canada: A Geographical Study.
          Madison: Univ. of Wisconsin Press, 1966. 274 pp.

G 2375   Harvey, Jean-Charles. The Many Faces of Quebec. Trans.
          Alta L. Cook. Toronto: Macmillan, 1966. 207 pp.

C 2376   Jolicoeur, Catherine. 'Traditional Use of Herbs in Que-
          bec.' Potomac Herb Journal, 7:4(1971), 3-5.

G 2377   King, Joseph E. 'The Glorious Kingdom of Saguenay.'
          Canadian Historical Review, 31(1950), 380-400.

G 2378   McLennan, John S. Louisbourg from its Foundation to its
          Fall 1713-1758. Sydney, N.S.: Fortress, 1957. 330 pp.

P 2379   Martin, Pol. 'A Réveillon Québécois.' Toronto Calendar
          Magazine, Dec. 1976, pp. 4-8.

C 2380   Meredith, Brian. 'A Seignory on the Ottawa.' CGJ, 7
          (Nov. 1933), 221-34.

A 2381   Miner, Horace. St. Denis: A French-Canadian Parish.
          Chicago: Univ. of Chicago Press, 1939. 283 pp.

A 2382   Nute, Grace L. The Voyageur. New York: Appleton-Century,
          1931. 289 pp.

F 2383   -- The Voyageur's Highway. St. Paul: Minnesota Histor-
          ical Society, 1941. 113 pp.

Pb 2384   Regan, John W. First Things in Acadia. Halifax: First
          Things, 1936. 304 pp.

Gb 2385   Rioux, Marcel. Quebec in Question. Trans. James Boake.
          Toronto: James, Lewis & Samuel, 1971. 191 pp.

C 2386   Roberts, Charles G. D. 'An Acadian "Bûche de Nöel."'
         Maritime Advocate, 36(May 1945), 5, 29-30.

GP 2387 Smith, Edwin. 'The Magdalen Islands.' CGJ, 4(June
         1932), 331-48.

Gc 2388 Woodley, Edward C. Canada's Romantic Heritage. Toron-
         to: Dent, 1940. 288 pp.

Gb 2389 -- Old Quebec: Trails and Homes. Toronto: Ryerson,
         1946. 137 pp.

Gc 2390 -- The Province of Quebec through Four Centuries.
         Toronto: Gage, 1944. 230 pp.

      9D Indian and Inuit

B 2391   Abler, T. S. 'Longhouse and Palisade: Northeastern
         Iroquoian Villages of the Seventeenth Century.' Ontario
         History, 62(1970), 17-40.

A 2392   Adams, John W. The Gitksan Potlatch. Toronto: Holt,
         Rinehart & Winston, 1973. 132 pp.

FPY 2393 Andrews, Ralph W. Indian Primitive. New York: Bonanza,
         1960. 174 pp. [Northwest Coast Indians.]

C 2394   Assiniwi, Bernard. Indian Recipes. Toronto: Copp Clark,
         1972. 161 pp.

C 2395   Baird, Irene. 'The Eskimo Woman.' Beaver, Spring 1959,
         pp. 48-55.

Gc 2396 Balikci, Asen. The Netsilik Eskimo. Toronto: Doubleday,
         1970. 264 pp.

A(1) 2397 Barbeau, C. Marius. The Downfall of Temlaham. Toronto:
         Macmillan, 1928; rpt. Edmonton: Hurtig, 1973. 253 pp.

BY 2398 -- Indian Days in the Canadian Rockies. Toronto: Mac-
         millan, 1923. 208 pp.

C 2399   -- 'An Indian Paradise Lost.' CGJ, 1(June 1930),
         132-48.

A 2400   -- Medicine Men on the North Pacific Coast. Ottawa:
         National Museum, Bulletin 152, 1958; rpt. 1973. 95 pp.

B(1) 2401 -- Mountain Cloud. Toronto: Macmillan, 1944, 300 pp.

C 2402   -- 'Tobacco, A Peace-Maker.' CGJ, 47(Sept. 1953),
         106-15.

C 2403 Barbeau, C. Marius. 'Tobacco for the Fur Trade.'
Beaver, Dec. 1942, pp. 36-39.

C 2404 -- 'Totemic Atmosphere on the North Pacific Coast.'
JAF, 67(1954), 103-22.

Ga 2405 Barnett, Homer G. The Coast Salish of British Columbia.
Eugene: Univ. of Oregon Press, 1955. 320 pp.

B 2406 -- The Nature and Function of the Potlatch. Eugene:
Univ. of Oregon Press, 1968. 132 pp.

C 2407 Bauer, Mrs. George, ed. Traditional Indian Recipes.
Cobalt: Highway Book Shop, 1975. 55 pp.

Gb 2408 Beaglehole, J. C., ed. The Journals of Captain James
Cook on His Voyages of Discovery. III The Voyage of the
'Resolution' and 'Discovery', 1776-1780. 2 vols. Pub.
for the Hakluyt Society. Cambridge, U.K.: University
Press, 1967.

Gb 2409 Bishop, C. Northern Ojibwa: An Ethnohistorical Study.
Toronto: Holt, Rinehart & Winston, 1973. 379 pp.

B 2410 Blau, Harold. 'Function and the False Faces: A Classification of Onondaga Masked Rituals and Themes.' JAF,
79(1966), 564-80.

Ga 2411 Boas, Franz. The Kwakiutl of Vancouver Island. New York:
American Museum of National History, Memoir 8, pt. 2,
1909, pp. 301-522.

Ga 2412 -- Report of the north-western tribes of Canada, nos.
1-12. London: British Assoc. for the Advancement of
Science, 1889-1898.

A 2413 -- The Social Organization and Secret Societies of the
Kwakiutl. Report of the U.S. National Museum, Washington, 1895, pp. 311-738.

G 2414 Bock, Philip K. The Micmac Indians of Restigouche.
Ottawa: National Museum, Bulletin 213, 1966. 95 pp.

G 2415 Briggs, Jean L. Aspects of Inuit Value Socialization.
Ottawa: National Museum, Ethnology Service Mercury
Series 56, 1979. 63 pp.

GY 2416 British Columbia Heritage Series: Our Native People.
10 vols. Victoria: Dept. of Education, 1951-53.

C 2417 Brown, Jennifer. '"A Colony of Very Useful Hands."'
Beaver, Spring 1977, pp. 39-45.

GPc 2418 Bruemmer, Fred. Seasons of the Eskimo. A Vanishing Way
of Life. Toronto: McClelland & Stewart, 1971. 160 pp.

Gb 2419 Bruton, F. A., ed. Narrative of a Journey Across the Island of Newfoundland in 1822 by W. E. Cormack. London: Longmans, Green, 1928. 138 pp.

Gc 2420 Bryce, George. 'The Pre-Selkirk Settlers of Old Assiniboia.' TRSC, 12(1918), sec.2, pp. 155-63.

B 2421 Calf Robe, Benjamin A. Siksika, A Blackfoot Legacy. Fort Macleod: Good Medicine Books, 1979. 107 pp.

C 2422 Callihoo, Victoria. 'Our Buffalo Hunts.' Alberta Historical Review, 8(Winter 1960), 24-25.

PY 2423 Campbell, Maria. People of the Buffalo: How the Plains Indians Lived. Vancouver: Douglas, 1976. 32 pp.

PY 2424 -- Riel's People: How the Métis Lived. Vancouver: Douglas & McIntyre, 1978. 48 pp.

G 2425 Carlson, Roy L. 'Culture of the B.C. Coast Indians.' In Proc. of the Centennial Workshop in Ethnomusicology. Vancouver: Univ. of British Columbia, 1967. Pp. 16-22.

G 2426 Carpenter, Edmund. Eskimo Realities. New York: Holt, Rinehart & Winston, 1973. 212 pp.

C 2427 -- 'Serpent on the Hill--The Story of a Sacred Grove.' CGJ, 56(July 1958), 215.

Gc 2428 Carpenter, Jock. Fifty Dollar Bride, Marie Rose Smith: A Chronicle of Métis Life in the 19th Century. Sidney: Gray's, 1977. 196 pp.

G 2429 Carruthers, Janet. 'Land of the Ojibway.' Beaver, Mar. 1952, pp. 42-45.

G 2430 Carter, Anthony. This is Haida. Saanichton: Hancock, 1966. 144 pp.

G 2431 Catlin, George. Illustrations of the Manners, Customs, and Condition of the North American Indians. 2 vols. 7th ed., London: H. G. Bohn, 1848.

G 2432 Chadwick, Edward M. The People of the Longhouse. Toronto: Church of England Pub., 1897. 166 pp.

G 2433 Clay, Charles. 'Indians as I Have Known Them.' CGJ, 8 (Jan. 1934), 43-50.

BY 2434 Clutesi, George. Potlatch. Sidney: Gray's, 1971; pb. 1973. 189 pp.

C 2435 Codere, Helen. 'The amiable side of Kwakiutl life: the potlatch and the play potlatch.' American Anthropologist, 58(1956), 334-51.

B 2436   Codere, Helen. Fighting with property; a study of
          Kwakiutl potlatching and warfare, 1792-1930. New
          York: Augustin, 1950. 136 pp.

Gb 2437   -- 'Kwakiutl.' In Perspectives in American Indian
          Culture Change. Ed. Edward H. Spicer. Chicago: Univ.
          of Chicago Press, 1961. Pp. 431-516.

G 2438   Colden, Cadwallader. History of the Five Indian Nations
          of Canada. 2 vols. New York: Barnes, 1904; rpt. Toronto:
          Coles, c. 1972. 204 pp.; 283 pp.

Gb 2439   Collison, W. H. In the Wake of the War Canoe. Toronto:
          Musson, 1915. 352 pp.

G 2440   Copway, George. The Traditional History and Character-
          istic Sketches of the Ojibway Nation. 1850; rpt. Toron-
          to: Coles, c. 1972. 298 pp.

PY 2441   Corbett, Edward A. Blackfoot Trails. Toronto: Macmil-
          lan, 1934. 139 pp.

BY 2442   Cowan, Susan, ed. We Don't Live in Snow Houses Now.
          Ottawa: Canadian Arctic Producers, 1976. 194 pp.

G 2443   Crosby, Thomas. Up and Down the North Pacific Coast by
          Canoe and Mission Ship. Toronto: Frederick Clarke
          Stephenson, 1914. 403 pp.

G 2444   Crowe, Keith J. A Cultural Geography of Northern Foxe
          Basin, N.W.T. Ottawa: Dept. of Indian Affairs, 1969.
          130 pp.

G 2445   Cruikshank, Julie. Athapaskan Women: Lives and Legends.
          Ottawa: National Museum, Ethnology Service Mercury
          Series 57, 1979. 202 pp.

G 2446   Cruikshank, Julie, and Jim Robb. Their Own Yukon. A
          Photographic History of the Yukon Indian People.
          Whitehorse: Yukon Indian Cultural Education Society
          and Yukon Indian Brotherhood, 1975. 180 pp.

P 2447   Curtis, Edward, S. In the Land of the Head-Hunters.
          Yonkers-on-Hudson, NY: World, 1915. 112 pp.

FA 2448   -- The North American Indian; being a series of vol-
          umes picturing and describing the Indians of the United
          States and Alaska. 20 vols. Ed. Frederick W. Hodge.
          Seattle: Curtis, 1907-1930.

FA 2449   -- Portraits of North American Indian Life. New York:
          American Museum of Natural History, 1972. 176 pp.

Ga 2450   Dawson, George M. Report on the Queen Charlotte
          Islands, 1878. Montreal: Dawson, 1880. 239 pp.

G 2451   Dempsey, Hugh A. 'The Story of the Blood Reserve.'
        Alberta Historical Review, 1(Nov. 1953), 27-36.

G 2452   Denny, Cecil. 'Indians of the Early West.' Alberta
        Historical Review, 4(Fall 1956), 22-26; 5(Spring 1957),
        26-28.

Gc 2453   Dewdney, Selwyn, and Franklin Arbuckle. They Shared to
        Survive: The Native Peoples of Canada. Toronto: Mac-
        millan, 1975. 220 pp.

C 2454   Dodwell, C. H. 'The Copper Eskimos of Coronation Gulf.'
        CGJ, 13(June 1936), 61-81.

G 2455   Driver, Harold. 'Girls' Puberty Rites in Western North
        America.' Univ. of California Anthropological Records,
        6:2(1941), 21-90.

Ga 2456   Drucker, Philip. The Indians of the Northwest Coast.
        1955; rpt. Garden City, NY: Natural History Press,
        1963. 224 pp.

B 2457   -- 'Kwakiutl Dancing Societies.' Berkeley: Univ. of
        California, Anthropological Records, 2:6(1940), 201-30.

G 2458   -- The Northern and Central Nootkan Tribes. Washing-
        ton: Bureau of American Ethnology, Bulletin 144, 1951.
        480 pp.

A 2459   Drucker, Philip, and Robert F. Heizer. To Make My Name
        Good: A Re-examination of the Southern Kwakiutl Pot-
        latch. Berkeley: Univ. of California Press, 1967.
        160 pp.

C 2460   Edwards, Grant T. 'Oolachen Time in Bella Coola.'
        Beaver, Autumn 1978, pp. 32-37.

Ga 2461   Efrat, Barbara, and W. J. Langlois, eds. 'nut·ka·
        Captain Cook and the Spanish Explorers on the Coast.'
        Sound Heritage, 7:1(1978), 1-101.

Ga 2462   -- and -- 'nu·tka· The History and Survival of Nootkan
        Culture.' Sound Heritage, 7:2(1978), 1-65.

B 2463   Ernst, Alice H. The Wolf Ritual of the Northwest Coast.
        Eugene: Univ. of Oregon, 1952. 107 pp.

C 2464   Eskimo Life of Yesterday. 1922; rpt. Saanichton: Han-
        cock, 1977. 48 pp.

G 2465   The Eskimos. A People that Refuses to Disappear.
        Special issue, Unesco Courier, January 1975. 34 pp.

B 2466   Farrand, Livingston. Traditions of the Chilcotin
        Indians. New York: American Museum of Natural History,
        Memoir 4, 1900, pp. 1-54.

Ga 2467   Fisher, Robin. Contact and Conflict: Indian-European Relations in British Columbia, 1774-1890. Vancouver: Univ. of B.C. Press, 1977. 268 pp.

G 2468   Fleming, Archibald L. Archibald the Arctic. New York: Appleton-Century-Crofts, 1956. 399 pp.

G 2469   Ford, Clellan S. Smoke from their fires; the life of a Kwakiutl chief. 1941; rpt. Hamden, CN: Archon, 1968. 248 pp. [Charles Nowell.]

B 2470   Foster, Michael K. From the Earth to Beyond the Sky: An Ethnographic Approach to Four Longhouse Iroquois Speech Events. Ottawa: National Museum, Ethnology Service Mercury Series 16, 1974. 448 pp.

FA 2471   Fowler, Don D. In a Sacred Manner We Live: Photographs of the North American Indian by Edward S. Curtis. Don Mills: Longmans, 1972. 152 pp.

Gc 2472   Franklin, John. Narrative of a Journey to the shores of the Polar Sea, in the years 1819, 1820, 1821 and 1822. London: Murray, 1823. 768 pp.

Gc 2473   -- Narrative of a second expedition to the shores of the Polar Sea in years 1825, 1826 and 1827. London: Murray, 1828. 320 pp.

G 2474   Freeman, Minnie A. Life Among the Qallunaat. Edmonton: Hurtig, 1978. 217 pp.

C 2475   French, C. H. 'Indian Ice Cream.' Beaver, Dec. 1923, pp. 104-5.

G 2476   Frison-Roche, Roger. Hunters of the Arctic. 1966; rpt. Don Mills: Dent, 1974. 260 pp.

C 2477   Gavin, Angus. 'Breathing Hole Sealing.' Beaver, Mar. 1940, pp. 26-31.

C 2478   Gilhooly, Ursula. 'Oranges and Eskimos.' CGJ, 65(Dec. 1962), 210-15.

G 2479   Goddard, Pliny E. Indians of the Northwest Coast. 1924; rpt. New York: Cooper Square, 1972. 175 pp.

G 2480   Graburn, Nelson H. H. Eskimos Without Igloos: social and economic development in Sugluk. Boston: Little, Brown, 1969. 244 pp.

Gb 2481   Graburn, Nelson H. H., and B. Stephen Brown. Circumpolar Peoples. Pacific Palisades, CA: Goodyear, [c 1973]. 236 pp.

A 2482 Guédon, Marie-Françoise. People of the Tetlin, Why Are You Singing? Ottawa: National Museum, Ethnology Service Mercury Series 9, 1974. 241 pp.

Ga 2483 Gunther, Erna. Indian Life on the Northwest Coast of North America. As Seen by the Earliest Explorers and Fur Traders During the Last Decades of the Eighteenth Century. Chicago: Univ. of Chicago Press, 1972. 277 pp.

B 2484 Hagar, Stansbury. 'Micmac Customs and Traditions.' American Anthropologist, 8(1895), 31-42.

B 2485 Hale, Horatio. The Iroquois Book of Rites. 1883; rpt. Toronto: Univ. of Toronto Press, 1963. 222 pp.

P 2486 Halliday, William M. Potlatch and Totem. Toronto: Dent, 1935. 240 pp.

C 2487 Hardisty, Richard. 'The Last Sun Dance.' Alberta Folklore Quarterly, 2(1946), 57-61. Rpt. in Folklore of Canada. Ed. Edith Fowke. Toronto: McClelland & Stewart, 1976. Pp. 18-22.

C 2488 Harrington, Robert F. 'Eulachan and the Grease Trails of British Columbia.' CGJ, 74(Jan. 1967), 28-31.

G 2489 Hawkes, E. W. The Labrador Eskimo. Ottawa: National Museum, Memoir 91, 1916. 165 pp.

P 2490 Hayes, H. R. Children of the Raven. The Seven Indian Nations of the Northwest Coast. Toronto: McGraw-Hill Ryerson, 1975. 314 pp.

Ga 2491 Heidenreich, Conrad. Huronia. Toronto: McClelland & Stewart, 1971. 337 pp.

Ga 2492 Henriksen, Georg. Hunters in the Barrens: The Naskapi on the Edge of the White Man's World. St. John's: ISER, Memorial Univ., 1973. 131 pp.

G 2493 Hodge, Frederick W. Handbook of the Indians of Canada. Ottawa: Geographic Board of Canada, 1913. 631 pp.

G 2494 Hood, Robert. 'Some Account of the Cree and Other Indians, 1819.' Alberta Historical Review, 15(Winter 1967), 6-17.

C 2495 Howard, James H. 'The St. Anne's Day Celebration of the Micmac Indians, 1962.' South Dakota Museum News, 26:3-4(1965), 5-13.

Ga 2496 Howard, Joseph K. Strange Empire: A Narrative of the Northwest. New York: Morrow, 1952; rpt. Toronto: Swan, 1965. 480 pp.

Folklife and Customs

G 2497 Hungry Wolf, Adolf. <u>The Blood People</u>. Toronto: Fitzhenry & Whiteside, 1977. 960 pp.

G 2498 -- <u>Indian Summer</u>. Invermere, B.C.: Good Medicine Books,
1975. 120 pp.

G 2499 -- <u>Life in Harmony with Nature</u>. Invermere: Good Medicine Books, 1970. 32 pp.

C 2500 -- <u>The Spirit at Hidden Valley</u>. Fort Macleod: Good
Medicine Books, 1972. 90 pp.

G 2501 -- <u>Teachings of Nature</u>. Invermere: Good Medicine Books,
1975. 60 pp.

B 2502 Hungry Wolf, Beverly. <u>The Ways of My Grandmother</u>. Invermere: Good Medicine Books, 1978. 80 pp.

Gb 2503 Iglauer, Edith. <u>The New People: The Eskimo's Journey
into Our Time</u>. 1966; rpt. as <u>Inuit Journey</u>. Vancouver:
Douglas & McIntyre, 1979. 240 pp.

G 2504 <u>The Inuit World</u>. Cape Dorset: Kingait Press, 1977.
26 pp.

C 2505 Iserhoff, Juliette, et al. <u>Traditional Indian Recipes
from Fort George, Quebec</u>. Cobalt: Highway Book Shop,
1971. 56 pp.

C 2506 Iserhoff, Sam. 'Bear Customs Among the Indians.'
<u>Beaver</u>, Sept. 1925, pp. 174-75.

Gc 2507 Jenness, Diamond. 'Canada's Debt to the Indians.' <u>CGJ</u>,
18(May 1939), 269-76; rpt. 65(Oct. 1962), 112-17.

B 2508 -- 'The Carrier Indians of the Bulkley River; Their
Social-Religious Life.' <u>U.S. Bureau of American Ethnology Papers</u>, No. 133, 1943, pp. 469-586.

C 2509 -- 'Indian Vikings of the Northwest Coast.' <u>CGJ</u>, 8
(May 1934), 235-46.

Ga 2510 -- <u>The Indians of Canada</u>. Ottawa: National Museum,
Bulletin 65, 1932; rpt. Toronto: Univ. of Toronto
Press, 1977. 460 pp.

A 2511 -- 'The Life of the Copper Eskimo.' <u>Report of the
Canadian Arctic Expedition: 1913-1918</u>. Vol. 12. Part A.
Ottawa: King's Printer, 1922; rpt. New York: Johnson,
1970. 277 pp.

A 2512 -- <u>The Ojibwa Indians of Parry Island, Their Social
and Religious Life</u>. Ottawa: National Museum, Bulletin
78, 1935. 115 pp.

GP 2513   Jenness, Diamond. The People of the Twilight. 1928;
          rpt. Chicago: Univ. of Chicago Press, 1959. 250 pp.

Gb 2514   -- The Sarcee Indians of Alberta. Ottawa: National
          Museum, Bulletin 90, 1938. 98 pp.

Gb 2515   -- The Sekani Indians of British Columbia. Ottawa:
          National Museum, Bulletin 84, 1937. 82 pp.

 C 2516   -- 'Wild Rice.' CGJ, 2(June 1931), 477-82.

Ga 2517   Jewitt, John R. The Adventures & Sufferings of John R.
          Jewitt, captive among the Nootka, 1803-1805. Ed. Derek
          G. Smith. Toronto: McClelland & Stewart, c. 1974.
          195 pp.

 C 2518   Johnston, Alexander. 'Uses of Native Plants by the
          Blackfoot Indians.' Alberta Historical Review, 8(Autumn
          1960), 8-13.

Ga 2519   Kane, Paul. Wanderings of an Artist among the Indians
          of North America. 1859; rpt. Toronto: Radisson Society,
          1925. 329 pp.

Gb 2520   Kelsey, Henry. The Kelsey Papers. Ottawa: Public
          Archives of Canada and Public Record Office of North
          Ireland, 1929. 128 pp.

 G 2521   Krause, Aurel. The Tlingit Indians. Trans. Erna Gunther.
          Seattle: Univ. of Washington, 1956, 1970. 320 pp.

GY 2522   Kurelek, William. The Last of the Arctic. Toronto:
          Pagurian, 1977. 92 pp.

 B 2523   LeClercq, Cretien. New Relations of Gaspesia with the
          Customs and Religion of the Gaspesian Indians. Trans.
          W. F. Ganong. Toronto: Champlain Society, 1910.

 C 2524   Leechman, Douglas. 'Aboriginal Tree-Felling.' Ottawa:
          National Museum, Bulletin 118, 1950, pp. 44-49.

 C 2525   -- 'Cannas--A Sumptuous Feast.' Beaver, Summer 1972,
          pp. 4-6.

Gb 2526   -- Native Tribes of Canada. Toronto: Gage, 1955.
          357 pp.

Gc 2527   -- 'Old Crow's Village.' CGJ, 37(July 1948), 2-16.

 G 2528   -- 'The Savages of James Bay.' Beaver, June 1945,
          pp. 14-17.

Gb 2529   -- Vanta Kutchin. Ottawa: National Museum, Bulletin
          130, 1954. 32 pp.

 C 2530   Light, D. W. Tattooing Practices of the Cree Indians.
          Calgary: Glenbow, 1972. 23 pp.

B 2531   Lopatin, Ivan A. Social Life and Religion of the Indians in Kitimat, British Columbia. Los Angeles: Univ. of Southern California Press, 1945. 118 pp.

Gc 2532   Lyon, G. F. The Private Journal of Captain G. F. Lyon of H.M.S. Hecla. London: Murray, 1824. 468 pp. [Description of Inuit life.]

Gb 2533   McClellan, Catharine. My Old People Say: An Ethnographic Survey of Southern Yukon Territory. 2 vols. Ottawa: National Museum, 1975. 637 pp.

PY 2534   McConkey, Lois. Sea and Cedar: How the Northwest Coast Indians Lived. Vancouver: Douglas, 1973. 32 pp.

B 2535   MacDonald, George S. 'Haida Burial Practices: Three Archaeological Examples.' Ottawa: National Museum, Archaeological Survey Mercury Series 9, 1973. Pp. 1-59.

Ga 2536   McFeat, Tom, ed. Indians of the North Pacific Coast. Toronto: McClelland & Stewart, 1966. 270 pp.

Ga 2537   McIlwraith, Thomas F. The Bella Coola Indians. 2 vols. Toronto: Univ. of Toronto Press, 1948. 763 pp.; 672 pp.

G 2538   Mackenzie, Alexander. The Journals and Letters of Sir Alexander Mackenzie. Ed. W. Kaye Lamb. Toronto: Macmillan, 1970. 551 pp.

G 2539   McKervill, H. W. The Salmon People: The Story of Canada's West Coast Salmon Fishing Industry. Sidney: Gray's, 1967. 198 pp.

B 2540   MacLean, John. 'The Blackfoot Sun Dance.' Proc. Royal Canadian Institute, 6(1889), 231-37.

G 2541   -- Canadian Savage Folk: The Native Tribes of Canada. 1896; rpt. Toronto: Coles, 1971. 641 pp.

G 2542   -- The Indians, Their Manners and Customs. Toronto: Briggs, 1889; rpt. Toronto: Coles, 1970. 351 pp.

B 2543   MacLeod, William C. 'Certain Mortuary Aspects of Northwest Coast Culture.' American Anthropologist, 27(1925), 122-48.

GP 2544   McLuhan, T. C., comp. Touch the Earth: A Self-Portrait of Indian Existence. London: Sphere, 1973. 185 pp.

Gb 2545   Maillard, A. S. An Account of the Customs and Manners of the Micmakis and Maricheets Savage Nations &c... London: Hooper & Morley, 1758. 138 pp.

Ga 2546   Mandelbaum, David G. The Plains Cree: An Ethnographic, Historical and Comparative Study. Regina: Canadian Plains Research Center, Univ. of Regina, 1979. 400 pp.

GY 2547   Marsh, Winifred P. People of the Willow: The Padlimiut
          Tribe of the Caribou Eskimo. Toronto: Oxford, 1976.
          63 pp.

PY 2548   Marshall, Ingeborg. The Red Ochre People: How Newfound-
          land's Beothuck Indians Lived. Vancouver: Douglas, 1977.
          48 pp.

 C 2549   Mason, Leonard. The Swampy Cree; A Study in Accultura-
          tion. Ottawa: Queen's Printer, 1967. 75 pp.

 G 2550   Mead, Margaret. 'The Eskimos.' Beaver, Autumn 1959, pp.
          32-41.

Gc 2551   Morice, Adrien G. 'The Western Dénés.' Proc. Royal
          Canadian Institute, 7(1889), 109-74.

 G 2552   Muise, D. A. ed. Approaches to Native History in
          Canada: Papers of a Conference held at the National
          Museum of Man, October 1975. Ottawa: National Museum,
          History Division Mercury Series 25, 1978. 135 pp.

 G 2553   Myers, Marybelle. 'People who know how to dream.'
          North, March/April 1974, pp. 32-35.

 G 2554   Neatby, Leslie H., trans. and ed. My Life Among the
          Eskimos: The Baffinland Journals of Bernhard Adolph
          Hantzsch, 1909-1911. Saskatoon: Univ. of Saskatchewan,
          1977. 396 pp.

Gb 2555   Nuligak. I, Nuligak. Ed. and trans., Maurice Metayer.
          Toronto: Peter Martin, 1975. 208 pp.

 C 2556   O-Ge-Mas-Es. 'Passing the Spring Out.' Beaver, Aug.
          1922, pp. 11-13; Sept. 1922, pp. 6-8.

Gc 2557   Oswalt, Wendell H. 'The Eskimo People: The Earliest
          Accounts.' Beaver, Autumn 1977, pp. 21-27.

Gb 2558   Overold, Joanne, ed. Our Métis Heritage... A Portrayal.
          Yellowknife: Métis Assoc. of N.W.T., 1977.

Gc 2559   Parry, William E. Journal of a Second Voyage for the
          Discovery of a North West Passage. New York: Duycnik,
          1824. 464 pp. [Inuit life.]

 B 2560   Parsons, Elsie C. 'Micmac Notes.' JAF, 39(1926), 460-
          485.

Ga 2561   Pastore, Ralph T. Newfoundland Micmacs: A History of
          Their Traditional Life. St. John's: Nfld. Historical
          Society, 1978. 36 pp.

 G 2562   Patterson, E. Palmer. The Canadian Indian: A History
          Since 1500. Don Mills: Collier-Macmillan, 1972. 210 pp.

GY 2563   Pitseolak. _Pictures Out of My Life_. Ed. Dorothy Eber.
           Toronto: Oxford, 1971. 96 pp.

GY 2564   Pitseolak, Peter. _People from Our Side_. Ed. Dorothy
           Eber. Edmonton: Hurtig, 1975. 159 pp.

 G 2565   Pocaterra, George W. 'Among the Nomadic Stoneys.'
           Alberta Historical Review, 11(Summer 1963), 12-19.

 C 2566   Pohorecky, Z. S. 'The Great Cree Stone.' _CGJ_, 73(Sept.
           1966), 88-91.

Gb 2567   Pryde, Duncan. _Nunaga: My Land, My Country_. Edmonton:
           Hurtig, 1971. 285 pp. [Inuit culture.]

 C 2568   Radin, Paul. 'Some Aspects of Puberty Fasting Among the
           Ojibwa.' Ottawa: National Museum, Bulletin 2, 1914,
           pp. 69-78.

FGa 2569   -- _The Winnebago Tribe_. 1923; rpt. New York: Johnson,
           1970. 560 pp.

FC 2570   Reagan, Albert B. 'Various Uses of Plants by West Coast
           Indians.' _Washington Historical Quarterly_, 25(1934),
           133-37.

PY 2571   Ridington, Robin, and Jillian Ridington. _People of the
           Trail: How the Northern Forest Indians Lived_. Vancou-
           ver: Douglas & McIntyre, 1978. 48 pp.

Ga 2572   Rohner, Ronald P., and Evelyn C. Rohner. _The Kwakiutl
           Indians of British Columbia_. New York: Holt, Rinehart
           & Winston, 1970. 111 pp.

 G 2573   Rosman, A., and P. G. Rabel. _Feasting with Mine Enemy:
           Rank and Exchange Among Northwest Coast Societies_. New
           York: Columbia Univ. Press, 1971.

 C 2574   Rousseau, Jacques. 'Mistassini Calendar.' _Beaver_, Sept.
           1949, pp. 33-37.

GP 2575   Rousselière, Guy-Mary. 'I Live with the Eskimos.' _Na-
           tional Geographic_, Feb. 1971, pp. 188-217.

 C 2576   Saskatchewan Indian Arts & Crafts Committee. _Smoke
           Tanning: Traditional Indian Method of Preparing Animal
           Hides_. Ottawa: National Museum of Man, n.d. 17 pp.

 B 2577   Sapir, Edward. 'A Girl's Puberty Ceremony among the
           Nootka Indians.' _TRSC_, 7(1913), sec. 2, pp. 67-80.

 B 2578   -- 'The Life of a Nootka Indian.' _Queen's Quarterly_,
           28(1921), 232-43; 351-67.

 B 2579   Sapp, Alan. _A Cree Life: The Art of Allen Sapp_. Van-
           couver: Douglas, 1977. 127 pp.

P 2580 Schmitter, Ferdinand. Upper Yukon Native Customs and Folk-Lore. Pamp. N.p., n.d.

G 2581 Scott, Duncan C. 'Traditional History of the Confederacy of the Six Nations.' TRSC, 5(1911), sec. 2, pp. 195-245.

G 2582 Sealey, D. Bruce, and Antoine S. Lussier. The Métis: Canada's Forgotten People. Winnipeg: Manitoba Métis Federation, 1975. 200 pp.

G 2583 Sendley, John, comp. The Nootkan Indian, A Pictorial. Port Alberni, B.C.: Alberni Valley Museum, 1977. 72 pp.

Ga 2584 Sewid, James. Guests Never Leave Hungry; the Autobiography of James Sewid, a Kwakiutl Indian. New Haven, CN: Yale Univ., 1969. 310 pp.

G 2585 Sismey, Eric D. 'H'Kusan, a Kwakiutl Village.' Beaver, Winter 1961, pp. 24-27.

C 2586 -- 'Quil'sten: Okanagan Steam Bath.' Beaver, Summer 1966, pp. 41-43.

C 2587 Skinner, Alanson. 'Bear Customs of the Crees and Other Indians.' Ontario History, 12(1914), 203-9.

Gb 2588 Snow, John. These Mountains Are Our Sacred Places: The Story of the Stoney Indians. Toronto: Samuel Stevens, 1977. 185 pp.

GY 2589 Speare, Jean E. The Days of Augusta. Vancouver: Douglas, 1973; pb. 1977. 80 pp.

Ga 2590 Speck, Frank G. Beothuk and Micmac. New York: Heye Foundation, 1922. 187 pp.

Ga 2591 -- Family Hunting Territories and Social Life of the Various Algonkian Bands of the Ottawa Valley. Ottawa: National Museum, Memoir 70, 1916. 87 pp.

Ga 2592 -- Naskapi. The Savage Hunters of the Labrador Peninsula. Norman: Univ. of Okla. Press, 1935. 248 pp.

C 2593 Speck, F. G., and R. W. Dexter. 'Utilization of Animals and Plants by the Malecite Indians of New Brunswick.' Journal of the Washington Academy of Sciences, 42 (1952), 1-7.

C 2594 -- and --. 'Utilization of Animals and Plants by the Micmac Indians of New Brunswick.' Journal of the Washington Academy of Sciences, 41(1951), 250-59.

A 2595   Steedman, Elsie V. 'Ethnobotany of the Thompson Indians of British Columbia, based on field notes by James A. Teit.' 45th Annual Report of the Bureau of American Ethnology, Washington, 1930, pp. 441-522.

C 2596   Steenhoven, Geert van den. 'Ennadai Lake People.' Beaver, Spring 1968, pp. 12-18.

B 2597   Stewart, Hilary. Indian Fishing. Early Methods on the Northwest Coast. Vancouver: Douglas, 1977. 181 pp.

P 2598   Stoddard, Natalie B. 'Micmac Foods.' Journal of Education, (N.S.), 15(Feb. 1962), 30-38.

GP 2599   -- The Micmac Indians of Nova Scotia. Halifax: N.S. Museum, 1972. 22 pp.

C 2600   Surtees, Ursula. Interior Salish Food Preparation. LAK-LA HAI-EE, Vol. 1. Kelowna, B.C.: Lamont-Surtees, 1974. 16 pp.

Ga 2601   Swanton, John R. Contributions to the Ethnology of the Haida. New York: American Museum of Natural History, Memoir 8, pt. 1, 1909, pp. 1-300.

FG 2602   -- The Indian Tribes of North America. Washington: Bureau of American Ethnology, Bulletin 145, 1952. 726 pp.

B 2603   -- 'Social conditions, beliefs and linguistic relationship of the Tlingit Indians.' 26th Annual Report of the Bureau of American Ethnology, Washington, 1908, pp. 391-485.

Gb 2604   Symington, Fraser. The Canadian Indian: The Illustrated History of the Great Tribes of Canada. Toronto: McClelland & Stewart, 1969. 271 pp.

C 2605   Tate, Albert. 'A Winter Buffalo Hunt.' Alberta Historical Review, 6(Autumn 1958), 25-26.

B 2606   Teit, James A. The Salishan Tribes of the Western Prairies. Ed. Franz Boas. 45th Annual Report of the Bureau of American Ethnology, Washington, 1930, pp. 23-396.

Ga 2607   -- The Thompson Indians of British Columbia. Ed. Franz Boas. New York: American Museum of Natural History, Memoir 2, 1900, pp. 167-392.

A 2608   -- 'Traditions of the Lillooet Indians of British Columbia." JAF, 25(1912), 287-371.

A 2609   Teit, James A. Traditions of the Thompson River Indians of British Columbia. American Folklore Society, Memoir 6, 1898. 137 pp.

G 2610   Tetso, John. Trapping is My Life. Toronto: Peter Martin, 1970. 116 pp.

G 2611   Thompson, David. David Thompson's Narrative, 1784-1812. Ed. Richard Glover. Toronto: Champlain Society, 1962. 410 pp.

F 2612   Tooker, Elizabeth. The Iroquois Ceremonies of Mid-Winter. Syracuse, NY: Syracuse Univ. Press, 1970. 189 pp.

G 2613   Trigger, Bruce. The Huron: Farmers of the North. New York: Holt, Rinehart & Winston, 1969. 130 pp.

Gb 2614   Turner, John P. 'Buffalo Days on Red River.' CGJ, 8 (Feb. 1934), 63-72.

B 2615   Turney-High, Harry H. Ethnography of the Kutenai. Menasha, WI: American Anthropological Association, 1941. 202 pp.

FG 2616   Underhill, Ruth. Indians of the Pacific Northwest. Washington: U.S. Dept. of the Interior, 1945. 232 pp.

G 2617   Updike, Lee R., and R. D. Symons. The First People: An Artist's Reconstruction of Five Native Canadian Cultures. Saskatoon: Western Producer, 1978. 147 pp.

G 2618   Upton, L. F. S. Micmacs and Colonists: Indian-White Relations in the Maritime Provinces, 1713-1867. Vancouver: Univ. of B. C. Press. 1979. 271 pp.

Ga 2619   Vancouver, George. A Voyage of Discovery to the North Pacific and Round the World. Ed. John Vancouver. 3 vols. 1798; rpt. New York: Da Capo, 1968.

Gb 2620   Van den Brink, J. H. The Haida Indians: Culture Change Mainly Between 1876 and 1970. Leyden: Brill, 1974. 276 pp.

G 2621   Van Kirk, Sylvia. 'Women and the Fur Trade.' Beaver, Winter 1972, pp. 4-21.

GP 2622   Van Steensel, Maja, ed. People of Light and Dark. Ottawa: Information Canada, 1966. 156 pp.

G 2623   Van Stone, James W. Athapaskan Adaptations: Hunters and Fishermen of the Sub-Arctic Forests. Chicago: Aldine, 1974. 145 pp.

Gb 2624   Van Stone, James W. The Changing Culture of the Snow-drift Chipewyan. Ottawa: National Museum, Bulletin 209, 1965. 133 pp.

Gb 2625   Wallis, Wilson D., and Ruth S. Wallis. The Malecite Indians of New Brunswick. Ottawa: National Museum, Bulletin 148, 1957. 54 pp.

Ga 2626   -- and -- The Micmac Indians of Eastern Canada. Minneapolis: Univ. of Minnesota Press, 1955. 515 pp.

PY 2627   Watetch, Abel. Payepot and His People. Regina: Saskatchewan History and Folklore Society, 1959. 66 pp.

B 2628   Waugh, F. W. Iroquois Foods and Food Preparation. Ottawa: National Museum, 1916; rpt. 1973. 235 pp.

PY 2629   Weekes, Mary. Great Chiefs and Mighty Hunters of the Western Plains. Regina: School Aids, n.d. 135 pp.

C 2630   -- 'An Indian's Description of the Making of a Buffalo Pound.' Saskatchewan History, 1(Oct. 1948), 14-17.

FG 2631   Weyer, Edward M., Jr. The Eskimos: Their Environment and Folkways. New Haven: Yale Univ. Press, 1932. 491 pp.

G 2632   Wherry, Joseph H. The Totem Pole Indians. New York: Funk, 1964. 152 pp.

FR 2633   White, Leslie A. The Ethnography and Ethnology of Franz Boas. Austin: Texas Memorial Museum, Univ. of Texas, 1963. 76 pp.

Gc 2634   Wilkinson, Douglas. Land of the Long Day. Toronto: Clarke, Irwin, 1966. 271 pp.

B 2635   Witthoft, John. 'Cayuga Midwinter Festival.' New York Folklore Quarterly, 2(Feb. 1946), 24-39.

Gb 2636   Woodcock, George. Peoples of the Coast: The Indians of the Pacific Northwest. Edmonton: Hurtig, 1977. 224 pp.

Gc 2637   Wright, J. V. The Ontario Iroquois Tradition. Ottawa: National Museum, Bulletin 210, 1966, rpt. 1973. 195 pp.

C 2638   Wuttunee, William I. E. 'Peyote Ceremony.' Beaver, Summer 1968, pp. 22-25.

A 2639   Yarrow, H. C. 'A Further Contribution to the Study of Mortuary Customs of the North American Indians.' 1st Annual Report of the Bureau of American Ethnology, Washington, 1881, pp. 87-203.

P 2640   Young, Egerton R. Stories from Indian Wigwams and
Northern Campfires. 1893; rpt. Toronto: Coles, 1970.
296 pp.

9E   Other Cultural Groups

Ga 2641   Adachi, Ken. The Enemy That Never Was. A History of the
Japanese Canadians. Toronto: McClelland & Stewart,
1976. 456 pp.

G 2642   Anderson, Grace M., and A. D. Higgs. A Future to In-
herit: The Portuguese Communities of Canada. Toronto:
McClelland & Stewart, 1976. 202 pp.

G 2643   Apramian, J. The Georgetown Boys. Hamilton: Printing
House, 1976. Unpaged. [Armenians.]

G 2644   Arnold, A. J. 'Jewish Pioneer Settlements.' Beaver,
Autumn 1975, pp. 20-26.

G 2645   Awan, Sadiq. The People of Pakistani Origin in Canada.
Ottawa: Canadian-Pakistan Assoc. of Ottawa-Hull, 1976.
48 pp.

G 2646   Bargen, Peter F. 'Mennonite Settlements in Alberta.'
Alberta Historical Review, 2(Jan. 1954), 13-22.

GY 2647   Barnett, D., and L. Knight. Hutterite People. Saskatoon: Western Extension College, 1977. 70 pp.

G 2648   Barss, Peter. Images of Lunenburg County. Toronto:
McClelland & Stewart, 1978. 161 pp.

C 2649   Bennhardt, Clara. 'Pennsylvania German Folklore to the
Fore.' Ontario History, 45(1953), 45-46.

A 2650   Blumstock, Robert. Békévar: Working Papers on a Canadian Prairie Community. Ottawa: National Museum, CCFCS
Mercury Series 31, 1979. 314 pp.

C 2651   Breithaupt, W. H. 'The Saangerfest of 1875.' Waterloo
Historical Society, 22nd Annual Report, Kitchener,
1934.

Gc 2652   Buchanan, Duncan W. 'The Mormons in Canada.' CGJ, 2
(Apr. 1931), 255-70.

PY 2653   Burke, Marguerite V. The Ukrainian Canadians. Toronto:
Van Nostrand Reinhold, 1976. 64 pp.

G 2654   Canada's Cultural Heritage: Ukrainian Contribution.
Winnipeg: Ukrainian Free Academy of Sciences, 1964.
16 pp.

G 2655 Clarke, E. W. 'The Pennsylvania Dutch in New Brunswick.' Pennsylvanian Dutchman, 2(Jan. 1950), 5.

GY 2656 Cooper, C. Mennonite People. Saskatoon: Western Extension College, 1978. 66 pp.

Gb 2657 Davies, Blodwen. A String of Amber: The Story of the
Mennonites. Vancouver: Mitchell, 1974. 228 pp.

G 2658 Davin, Nicholas F. The Irishman in Canada. 1877; rpt.
Shannon: Irish Univ. Press, 1969. 692 pp.

Ga 2659 De Gelder, Willem. The Dutch Homesteader on the
Prairies. Toronto: Univ. of Toronto Press, 1973. 92 pp.

A 2660 Dégh, Linda. People in the Tobacco Belt: Four Lives.
Ottawa: National Museum, CCFCS Mercury Series 13, 1975.
277 pp.

G 2661 Dempsey, Hugh A. Hutterites/Spiteri: The Hutterite
Diamond Jubilee. Calgary: Glenbow-Alberta Institute,
1978. 64 pp.

G 2662 Des Brisay, Mather B. History of the County of Lunenburg. 1895; rpt. Belleville: Mika, 1972. 585 pp.

G 2663 Drew, Benjamin. The Narratives of Fugitive Slaves in
Canada. 1856; rpt. Toronto: Coles, c. 1972. 387 pp.

P 2664 Enns, F. F. Elder Enns. 'Ohm Franz'. Trans. Margaret
Enns. Winnipeg: Author, 1979. 112 pp.

Gb 2665 Epp, Frank H. Mennonites In Canada, 1786-1920. Toronto:
Macmillan, 1974. 480 pp.

P 2666 Ethnic Cuisine for Everyday Cooking. Regina: Catholic
Women's League, 1975. 212 pp.

Gb 2667 Ewanchuk, Michael. Spruce, Swamp and Stone. A History
of the Pioneer Ukrainian Settlements in the Gimli Area.
Winnipeg: Author, 1977. 320 pp.

Gc 2668 Fieguth, Joyce. Flour Sacks and Binder Twine. North
Battleford, Sask.: McIntosh, 1973. 104 pp. [Mennon-
ites.]

G 2669 Francis, E. K. In Search of Utopia: The Mennonites in
Manitoba. Altona, Man.: Friesen, 1955. 294 pp.

G 2670 Fretz, J. Winfield. The Mennonites in Ontario. Mennonite Historical Society of Ontario, 1967. 42 pp.

G 2671 Gaida, Pranas, ed. The Lithuanians in Canada. Canada
Ethnica 5. Toronto: Lights Printing & Time Press, 1967.

G 2672　Gibbon, John Murray. Canadian Mosaic. Toronto: McClelland, 1938. 455 pp.

Gb 2673　Gingerich, Orland. The Amish of Canada. Waterloo: Conrad, 1972. 244 pp.

B 2674　Giuliano, Bruce B. Sacro O Profano? A Consideration of Four Italian-Canadian Religious Festivals. Ottawa: National Museum, CCFCS Mercury Series 17, 1976. 55 pp.

P 2675　Greig, Hugh, and Terry McLean. The Hope and the Promise: The Tender, Tragic, and Often Brutal Story of the Doukhobours. Langley: Stagecoach, 1977. 176 pp.

G 2676　Gutkin, Harry. Journey into Our Heritage--The Story of a People. Toronto: Lester & Orpen Dennys, 1979. 364 pp. [Jews.]

G 2677　Hardwick, Francis C. Return of the Vikings: Scandinavians in Canada. Vancouver: Tantalus, 1978. 86 pp.

Gb 2678　Harney, Robert, and Harold Troper. Immigrants: A Portrait of the Urban Experience, 1890-1930. Toronto: Van Nostrand Reinhold, 1975. 212 pp.

C 2679　Hawryluk, Maria. 'Easter Recipes.' ZHinochyj Svit (Winnipeg), 8:4(1957), 14-15.

C 2680　-- 'Tested Recipes for Ukrainian Christmas Eve Supper.' ZHinochyj Svit, 8:1(1957), 14-16.

C 2681　Hawryluk-Charney, Halia. 'Let Us Preserve Our Ukrainian Traditional Christmas.' ZHinochyj Svit, 16:1(1963), 14-15.

C 2682　-- 'Ukrainian Easter at Our Home.' ZHinochyj Svit, 6:4 (1955), 14-15.

C 2683　-- 'Ukrainian Easter Bakings.' ZHinochyj Svit, 12:4 (1961), 12-13.

Gb 2684　Hawthorn, Harry B., ed. The Doukhobors of British Columbia. Vancouver: Univ. of B.C. Press, 1955. 288 pp.

G 2685　Herrfort, A. K., and P. E. Snyder. Mennonite Country: Waterloo County Drawings. St. Jacob's, Ont.: Sand Hills, 1978. 84 pp.

Ga 2686　Heydenkorn, Benedykt. Memoirs of Polish Immigrants in Canada. Toronto: Canadian-Polish Research Institute, 1979. 323 pp.

Gc 2687　Hildebrand, Menno. 'The Sommerfeld Mennonites of Manitoba.' Mennonite Life, 25(July 1970), 99-107.

Ga 2688 Hoe, Ban Seng. <u>Structural Changes of Two Chinese Com-</u><u>munities in Alberta, Canada</u>. Ottawa: National Museum, CCFCS Mercury Series 19, 1976. 385 pp.

P 2689 Hoffer, Clara, and F. H. Kahan. <u>Land of Hope</u>. Saskatoon: Prairie Books, 1960. 157 pp.

G 2690 Horowitz, Aron. <u>Striking Roots. Reflections on Five</u> <u>Decades of Jewish Life</u>. Oakville: Mosaic, 1979. 401 pp.

BY(1) 2691 Horst, Isaac R. <u>Separate and Peculiar</u>. N.P.: Author, 1979. 76 pp. [Mennonites.]

B 2692 Horst, Mary Ann. <u>My Old Order Mennonite Heritage</u>. Kitchener, Ont.: Pennsylvania Craft Shop, 1970. 35 pp.

P 2693 -- <u>Pennsylvania Dutch Fun, Folklore and Cooking</u>. Kitchener: Pennsylvania Craft Shop, 1974. 63 pp.

FGa 2694 Hostetler, John A. <u>Amish Society</u>. Baltimore: Johns Hopkins, 1963. 369 pp.

FGa 2695 -- <u>Hutterite Society</u>. Baltimore: Johns Hopkins, 1975. 403 pp.

FGa 2696 Hostetler, John A., and Gertrude E. Huntingdon. <u>The</u> <u>Hutterites in North America</u>. New York: Holt, Rinehart & Winston, 1967. 118 pp.

Gb 2697 Houser, George J. <u>The Swedish Community at Eriksdale,</u> <u>Manitoba</u>. Ottawa: National Museum, CCFCS Mercury Series 14, 1976. 112 pp.

G 2698 Humeniuk, Peter. <u>Hardships and Progress of Ukrainian</u> <u>Pioneers</u>. Steinbach: Derksen, 1976. 236 pp.

PY(1) 2699 Hunsberger, A. I. <u>Nineteen Nineteen</u>. Kitchener, Ont.: Ainsworth, n.d. 244 pp. [German Canadians.]

Gb 2700 Hunsberger, David L., James Hertel, and Koni Lattner. <u>People Apart: Portrait of a Mennonite World in Waterloo</u> <u>County, Ontario</u>. St. Jacob's: Sand Hills, 1977. 111 pp.

PY 2701 Ito, Roy. <u>The Japanese Canadians</u>. Toronto: Van Nostrand Reinhold, 1978. 64 pp.

G 2702 Johnson, Gilbert. 'The Roumanians in Western Canada.' <u>Saskatchewan History</u>, 14(1965), 64-70.

C 2703 -- 'Swabian Folk Ways.' <u>Saskatchewan History</u>, 13(1964), 73-75.

Gb 2704 Kaye, Vladimir J. <u>Early Ukrainian Settlements in Can-</u><u>ada, 1895-1900</u>. Toronto: Univ. of Toronto Press, 1964.

173

Gb 2705   Keywan, Zonia, and Martin Coles. <u>Greater than Kings:</u>
                <u>Ukrainian Pioneer Settlement in Canada</u>. Montreal: Har-
                vest House, 1977. 168 pp.

 G 2706   Klippenstein, L., and J. G. Towes, eds. <u>Mennonite</u>
                <u>Memories; Settling in Western Canada</u>. Lincoln, NE:
                Centennial, 1977. 340 pp.

 B 2707   Klymasz, Robert B. 'The Letter in Canadian Ukrainian
                Folklore.' <u>Journal of the Folklore Institute</u>, 6(1969),
                39-49.

 B 2708   -- 'Speaking at/about/with the Dead: Funerary Rhetoric
                among Ukrainians in Western Canada.' <u>Canadian Ethnic</u>
                <u>Studies</u>, 7:2(1975), 50-56.

 B 2709   -- 'Ukrainian Harvest Customs.' <u>Beacon Ukrainian Rite</u>
                <u>Quarterly</u>, 6(Oct.-Dec. 1972), 22-25, 28.

 C 2710   Kmetyk, Marian. 'Ukrainian Harvest Rituals.' <u>ZHinochyj</u>
                <u>Svit</u>, 13:10(1962), 14-15.

 C 2711   Knill, William D. 'The Hutterites: Cultural Transmis-
                sion in a Closed Society.' <u>Alberta Historical Review</u>,
                16(Summer 1968), 1-10.

Gb 2712   Kosa, John. <u>Land of Choice, the Hungarians in Canada</u>.
                Toronto: Univ. of Toronto Press, 1956. 104 pp.

 G 2713   Kostash, Myrna. <u>All of Baba's Children</u>. Edmonton: Hur-
                tig, 1977. 280 pp. [Ukrainians.]

Gb 2714   Kovacs, Martin L., ed. <u>Ethnic Canadians. Culture and</u>
                <u>Education</u>. Regina: Canadian Plains Research Center,
                1978. 495 pp.

BY 2715   Kurelek, William, and Abraham Arnold. <u>Jewish Life in</u>
                <u>Canada</u>. Edmonton: Hurtig, 1976. 96 pp.

 G 2716   Lohrenz, Gerhard. <u>The Mennonites of Western Canada</u>.
                Steinbach: Derksen, 1974. 52 pp.

 C 2717   Lunenburg Hospital Society, Ladies Auxiliary. <u>Dutch</u>
                <u>Oven: A Cook Book of Coveted Traditional Recipes from</u>
                <u>the Kitchens of Lunenburg</u>. Lunenburg, N.S.: Lunenburg
                Progress Enterprise, 1953. 348 pp.

 G 2718   Lupul, Mandy R., ed. <u>Ukrainian Canadians, Multicul-</u>
                <u>turalism and Separatism</u>. Edmonton: Univ. of Alberta,
                1978. 177 pp.

 G 2719   Mage, Julius, and Robert Murdie. 'The Mennonites of
                Waterloo County.' <u>CGJ</u>, 80(Jan. 1970), 10-19.

Gb 2720 Malloff, Marjorie, and Peter Ogloff. 'Toil and Peaceful Life: Portraits of Doukhobors.' Sound Heritage, 6:4(1977), 1-78.

Ga 2721 Marlatt, Daphne. Steveston Recollected. A Japanese-Canadian History. Victoria: Aural History, Provincial Archives, 1975. 104 pp.

G 2722 Martin, Virgil E. The Early History of Jakobstettel. St. Jacob's, Ont.: Author, 1979. 102 pp. [German Canadians.]

Gb 2723 Matejko, Joanna, et al. Polish Settlers in Alberta. Toronto: Polish Alliance, n.d. 487 pp.

A 2724 Mealing, F. Mark. Doukhobor Life: A Survey of Doukhobor Religion, History, and Folklife. Castelgar, B.C.: Cotinneh, 1975. 67 pp.

C 2725 The Mennonite Treasury of Recipes. Steinbach: Derksen, 1962. 229 pp.

Gb 2726 Morton, James W. In the Sea of Sterile Mountains: The Chinese in British Columbia. Vancouver: Douglas, 1974. 280 pp.

G 2727 Nakano, Takeo, and Leatrice Nakano. Internment in Canada: A Japanese Man's Account. Toronto: Authors, 1978. 141 pp. Mimeo.

G 2728 'Norwegians in Canada.' Citizen, 13(Oct. 1967), 12-22.

PG 2729 Ontario Educational Communications Authority. Identity: The Black Experience in Canada. Toronto: Gage, 1979. 163 pp.

G 2730 Paluk, William. Canadian Cossacks: Essays, Articles, and Stories on Ukrainian Canadian Life. Winnipeg: Canadian Ukrainian Review, 1943. 130 pp.

G 2731 Paskievich, John. A Place Not Our Own: North End Winnipeg. Winnipeg. Queenston House, c. 1978. 80 pp.

Gb 2732 Patterson, G. James. The Greeks of Vancouver: A Study in the Preservation of Ethnicity. Ottawa: National Museum, CCFCS Mercury Series 18, 1976. 169 pp.

Gb 2733 -- The Romanians of Saskatchewan: Four Generations of Adaptation. Ottawa: National Museum, CCFCS Mercury Series 23, 1977. 85 pp.

Gb 2734 Paulsen, Frank M. Danish Settlements on the Canadian Prairies: Folk Traditions, Immigrant Experiences, and Local History. Ottawa: National Museum, CCFCS Mercury Series 11, 1974. 114 pp.

C 2735 Perkowski, Jan. 'Folkways of the Canadian Kashubs.'
        Slavs in Canada, 3(1971), 333-40.

Gc 2736 Piniuta, Harry, ed. and trans. Land of Pain, Land of
         Promise: First Person Accounts by Ukrainian Pioneers
         1891-1914. Saskatoon: Western Producer, 1979. 225 pp.

G 2737 Potrebenko, Helen. No Streets of Gold: A Social History
        of Ukrainians in Alberta. Vancouver: New Star, 1977.
        311 pp.

G 2738 Quiring, Walter. Mennonites in Canada: A Pictorial
        Review. Altona: Friesen, 1961. 208 pp.

G 2739 Radecki, Henry, and Benedykt Heydenkorn. A Member of a
        Distinguished Family. The Polish Group in Canada. Tor-
        onto: McClelland & Stewart, 1976. 240 pp.

Ga 2740 Reaman, G. Elmore. The Trail of the Black Walnut. Tor-
         onto: McClelland & Stewart, 1957; pb. 1975. 256 pp.

P 2741 Russell, Franklin. 'The Art of Lunenburg Cooking--and
        Eating.' Maclean's, 28 Mar. 1959, pp. 26-27, 51-54.

G 2742 Sack, Benjamin G. History of the Jews in Canada. Mont-
        real: Harvest, 1965. 300 pp.

G 2743 Santha, Paul. Three Generations, 1901-1957; The Hun-
        garian Colony at Stockholm, Saskatchewan, Canada.
        Stockholm: n.p., 1959. 94 pp.

G 2744 Sauder, Dorothy, ed. Sesquicentennial of the Amish
        Mennonites of Ontario. N.p.: Mennonite Historical
        Society of Ont. and the Western Ont. Mennonite Con-
        ference, 1972. 50 pp.

C 2745 Sawka, Patricia. 'The Hutterian Way of Life.' CGJ, 77
        (Oct. 1968), 126-31.

G 2746 Sheffe, Norman, ed. Many Cultures, Many Heritages. Tor-
        onto: McGraw-Hill, 1975. 544 pp.

C 2747 Shewchuk, Maria. 'Ancient Ukrainian Christmas Customs.'
        ZHinochyj Svit, 14:1(1963), 15-16.

G 2748 Sommerville, S. J. 'Icelanders in Canada.' CGJ, 21(Oct.
        1940), 193-202.

G 2749 Spada, A. V. The Italians in Canada. Canada Ethnica 6.
        Ottawa: Italo-Canadian Ethnic and Historical Research
        Centre, 1969.

Pa 2750 Staebler, Edna. Food That Really Schmecks. Toronto:
         McClelland & Stewart, 1968. 297 pp.

Pa 2751 Staebler, Edna. More Food That Really Schmecks. Toronto: McClelland & Stewart, 1979. 318 pp.

 B 2752 -- Sauerkraut and Enterprise. Toronto: McClelland & Stewart, rev. 1969. 96 pp.

 B 2753 Stechishin, Savella. Traditional Ukrainian Cookery. Winnipeg: Trident, 1957. 498 pp.

 C 2754 Steele, C. Frank. 'Canada's Hutterite Settlement.' CGJ, 22(June 1941), 308-14.

Gb 2755 Stoochnoff, John P. Doukhobors as They Are. Toronto: Ryerson, 1961. 102 pp.

 G 2756 Story, Merle. 'Hungarians in Canada.' CGJ, 55(Aug. 1957), 46-53.

Ga 2757 Tarasoff, Koozma J. In Search of Brotherhood. Vancouver: n.p., 1963. 1006 pp. Mimeo.

Ga 2758 -- A Pictorial History of the Doukhobors. Saskatoon: Modern Press, 1969. 280 pp.

 A 2759 -- Traditional Doukobor Folkways: An Ethnographic and Biographic Record of Prescribed Behaviour. Ottawa: National Museum, CCFCS Mercury Series 20, 1977. 307 pp.

 C 2760 Tilney, Philip. 'The Martenitsa: An Old World Custom with New World Significance.' Canadian Ethnic Studies, 7:2(1975), 42-49.

Gc 2761 Towes, Julius G., and Lawrence Klippenstein, eds. Manitoba Mennonite Memories. Altona: Friesen, 1974. 354 pp.

 G 2762 Tulloch, Headley. Black Canadians: A Long Line of Fighters. Toronto: NC Press, 1975. 188 pp.

 C 2763 Ukrainian Women's Association of Canada, Vancouver Branch. The Art of Cooking Ukrainian Style. A Book of Recipes. Vancouver: Lesia Ukrainia Branch, UWAC, 1965. 106 pp.

 G 2764 Warkentin, John H. 'Mennonite Agricultural Settlements of Southern Manitoba.' Geographical Review (London), 49(1959), 342-68.

 G 2765 Wilson, Keith, and James B. Wyndels. The Belgians in Manitoba. Winnipeg: Peguis, 1976. 100 pp.

Gc 2766 Woycenko, O. The Ukrainians in Canada. Winnipeg: Trident, 1967. 271 pp.

Gc 2767 Woywitka, Anne B. 'A Roumanian Pioneer.' Alberta Historical Review, 21(Autumn 1973), 20-27.

Gc 2768   Wright, James F. S. Slava Bohu: The Story of the Douk-
           hobors. New York: Farrar & Rinehart, 1940. 438 pp.

Gc 2769   Wright, James F. S. 'Ukrainian-Canadians.' CGJ, 25(Aug.
           1942), 74-87.

Gb 2770   Yuzyk, Paul. Ukrainian-Canadians: Their Place and Role
           in Canadian Life. Toronto: Univ. of Toronto Press,
           1967. 104 pp.

Gb 2771   -- The Ukrainians in Manitoba: A Social History. Tor-
           onto: Univ. of Toronto Press, 1953. 220 pp.

           For 9A see also items 4, 8, 9, 66, 103, 108, 115, 126,
           154, 227, 246, 297, 321, 361, 363, 368, 371, 2788, 2826,
           and 3787.

           For 9B, 29, 122, 255, 273, 298, 306, 319, 338, 408, 420,
           443, 446, 453, 457, 479, 480, 497, 512, 513, 1803, 2894,
           2904, 3758, 3779, 3830, 3837, 3843, 3856, 3857, and 3845.

           For 9C, 11, 230, 231, and 272.

           For 9D, 45, 153, 228, 229, 232, 238-240, 278, 280, 281,
           283, 294, 301-304, 316, 320, 323, 326, 581, 670, 671,
           684, 717, 728, 820, 1462, 3126, 3180, 3225, 3781, 3789,
           3794, 3795, 3842, and 3848.

           For 9E, 241, 243, 244, 282, 289, 315, 334, 882, 885,
           3816, and 3832.

10 Folk Art and Material Culture

10A General

GPb 2772   Abrahamson, Una. Crafts Canada. The Useful Arts. Toronto: Clarke Irwin, 1974. 191 pp.

G 2773   Acton, James. Canadian Book of Furniture. Toronto: Acton, 1923. 111 pp.

G 2774   Antonelli, Marylu, and Jack Forbes. Pottery in Alberta: The Long Tradition. Edmonton: Univ. of Alta. Press, 1978. 376 pp.

Ga 2775   Arthur, Eric, and Dudley Witney. The Barn, A Vanishing Landmark in North America. Toronto: McClelland & Stewart, 1972. 256 pp.

B 2776   Barbeau, C. Marius. 'All Hands Aboard Scrimshawing.' American Neptune, 12(Apr. 1952), 99-122.

Pc 2777   -- 'Are the Real Folk Arts and Crafts Dying Out?' Canadian Art, 5(Winter 1948), 128-33.

C 2778   -- 'The Beaver in Canadian Art.' Beaver, Sept. 1941, pp. 14-18.

C 2779   -- 'Country-Made Trade Goods.' Beaver, Sept. 1944, pp. 16-19.

C 2780   -- 'Early Americana.' CGJ, 53(July 1956), 2-11.

C 2781   -- 'The Hooked Rug--Its Origin.' TRSC, 36(1942), sec. 2, pp. 25-32.

C 2782   -- 'The House That Mac Built.' Beaver, Dec. 1945, pp. 10-13.

C 2783   -- 'Old Canadian Silver.' CGJ, 22(Mar. 1941), 150-62.

C 2784   -- "The Origin of the Hooked Rug." Antiques (New York), 52(Aug. 1947), 110-13.

C 2785   -- 'Our Beaver Emblem.' CGJ, 55(Dec. 1957), 244-50.

179

C 2786 -- 'Sashes for the Fur Trade.' Beaver, June 1941, pp. 24-27.

C 2787 Barbeau, C. Marius. 'Seafaring Folk Art.' Antiques, 66 (July 1954), 47-49.

Gb 2788 Barer-Stein, Thelma. You Eat What You Are: A Study of Canadian Ethnic Food Traditions. Toronto: McClelland & Stewart, 1979. 624 pp.

C 2789 Belcourt, G. A. 'Buffalo Hunt.' Beaver, Dec. 1944, pp. 13-17.

C 2790 Bériau, Oscar A. 'Home Weaving in Canada.' CGJ, 27 (July 1943), 18-29.

Gc 2791 Bonner, Mary G. Made in Canada. New York: Knopf, 1943. 110 pp.

Ga 2792 Brasser, Ted J. 'Bou'jou, Neejee': Profiles of Canadian Indian Art. Ottawa: National Museum of Man, 1976. 204 pp.

G 2793 Brett, Katherine B. Modesty to Mod. Toronto: Royal Ontario Museum, Univ. of Toronto, 1967. [Exhibition catalogue.]

C 2794 -- Ontario Handwoven Textiles. Toronto: Royal Ontario Museum, 1956. 18 pp.

Gb 2795 -- Women's Costume in Early Ontario, 1867-1907. Toronto: Royal Ontario Museum, 1965. 18 pp.

C 2796 Burjesse, J. A. 'Snowshoes.' Beaver, Mar. 1941, pp. 24-28.

C 2797 Burnham, Dorothy K. Cut My Cote. Toronto: Royal Ontario Museum, 1973. 36 pp.

B 2798 -- Pieced Quilts of Ontario. Toronto: Royal Ontario Museum, 1975. 64 pp.

Gb 2799 Burnham, Harold B. Canadian Textiles, 1750-1900. Toronto: Royal Ontario Museum, 1965. 30 pp.

Gc 2800 -- 'Ontario Textile Arts.' CanAntC, 6(May 1971), 65-67.

A 2801 Burnham, Harold B., and Dorothy K. Burnham. 'Keep Me Warm One Night.' Early Handweaving in Eastern Canada. Toronto: Univ. of Toronto Press, 1975. 416 pp.

P 2802 Cadure, William. 'A Trapper's Tilt.' Beaver, Summer 1966, pp. 16-17.

P 2803 Cameron, William. 'Great Barns.' Maclean's, Dec. 1972, pp. 40-43.

G 2804 The Canadian Handicrafts Guild. Montreal: The Guild,
        1912. 16 pp.

B 2805 Clemson, Donovan. Living with Logs. British Columbia's
        Log Buildings and Rail Fences. Saanichton: Hancock,
        1974. 94 pp.

B 2806 Collard, Eileen. Early Clothing in Southern Ontario.
        Burlington, Ont.: Collard, 1969. 27 pp.

G 2807 Collard, Elizabeth. Nineteenth-Century Pottery and Por-
        celain in Canada. Montreal: McGill Univ. Press, 1967.
        441 pp.

B 2808 Conroy, Mary. 300 Years of Canada's Quilts. Toronto:
        Griffin, 1976. 133 pp.

C 2809 Cooper, Russell. 'Weaver's Shop.' CanAntC, 8(May/June
        1973), 37-39.

C 2810 Cotter, H. M. S. 'The Birchbark Canoe: An Important
        Factor in H.B.C. Transport from Earliest Times.'
        Beaver, June 1922, pp. 5-8; July 1922, pp. 10-12.

FB 2811 Davidson, Daniel S. Snowshoes. Philadelphia: American
        Philosophical Society, Memoir 6, 1937. 207 pp.

P 2812 "Early Canadian Iron." CanAntC, 2(July 1967), 14-15.

Gb 2813 Ennals, Peter M. 'Nineteenth-Century Barns in Southern
        Ontario.' Canadian Geographer, 16(Fall 1972), 256-70.

Gc 2814 Fairweather, C. Lillian. 'Interiors of Pioneer Houses
        in New Brunswick.' CGJ, 28(May 1944), 238-43.

G 2815 Finley, Gregg. Heritage Furniture. Saint John: N.B.
        Museum, 1976. 63 pp.

B 2816 Folk Art of Nova Scotia, A Travelling Exhibition of
        20th Century Folk Art of Nova Scotia. Halifax: Art
        Gallery of N.S., 1976. 59 pp. [Exhibition Catalogue.]

C 2817 Folk Painters of the Canadian West. Ottawa: National
        Gallery, 1959. 32 pp. [Exhibition Catalogue.]

Gb 2818 Fox, William, et al. The Mill. Toronto: McClelland &
        Stewart, 1976. 224 pp.

C 2819 Gibbon, John Murray. 'Canada's Million and More Needle-
        craft Workers.' CGJ, 26(Mar. 1943), 44-55.

Gc 2820 -- 'Canadian Handicrafts Old and New.' CGJ, 26(Mar.
        1943), 130-43.

Gc 2821 -- Romance of the Canadian Canoe. Toronto: Ryerson,
        1951. 145 pp.

C 2822 Glover, R. 'York Boats.' Beaver, Mar. 1949, pp. 19-23.

Ga 2823 Gowans, Alan. Building Canada: An Architectural History of Canadian Life. Toronto: Oxford, 1966. 412 pp.

C 2824 Grass Roots Art. artscanada, Nos. 138/139(Dec. 1969), pp. 1-80.

B 2825 Green, H. Gordon, ed. A Heritage of Canadian Handicrafts. Toronto: McClelland & Stewart, 1967. 222 pp.

C 2826 Grimshaw, John. 'Edgeley--a Pioneer Village Reconstructed.' CGJ, 61(Nov. 1960), 170-73. [Black Creek Pioneer Village.]

Ga 2827 Harper, J. Russell. A People's Art. Primitive, Naïve, Provincial and Folk Painting in Canada. Toronto: Univ. of Toronto Press, 1974. 176 pp.

B 2829 Harrington, Lyn, and Richard Harrington. Covered Bridges of Central and Eastern Canada. Toronto: McGraw-Hill Ryerson, 1977. 100 pp.

C 2830 A History of Early Domestic Lighting in Canada. Ottawa: National Museum, 1971. 10 pp. [Exhibition pamphlet.]

G 2831 Hochbaum, H. Albert. 'Arctic Steeples.' Beaver, Winter 1977, pp. 28-35.

G 2832 Hubbard, R. H., and J. R. Hubbard. Three Hundred Years of Canadian Art. Ottawa: National Gallery, 1967. 254 pp.

P 2833 Jameson, L. M. 'Vancouver Folk Art Festival.' Canadian Forum, 14(1933), 104.

Gb 2834 Jury, W. Wilfred. The Grist Mill. London, Ont.: Univ. of Western Ontario, 1946. 10 leaves.

R 2835 Kallmann, Helmut. Canadian-built 19th Century Musical Instruments: A Check List. Edmonton: Edmonton Public Library, 1966.

B 2836 Koltun, Lilly A. The Cabinetmaker's Art in Ontario, c. 1850-1900. Ottawa: National Museum, History Division Mercury Series 26, 1979. 193 pp.

C 2837 Kossar, Leon. 'Folk Arts in Canada.' Illustrated Performing Arts, 5:3-4(1968), 16-20.

Pc 2838 Lee-Whiting, Brenda. 'Logging Tools.' Canadian Collector, July/Aug. 1979, 44-48.

B 2839 Leechman, Douglas. 'Good Fences Make Good Neighbours.' CGJ, 47(Dec. 1953), 218-35.

P 2840   Leitch, Adelaide. 'Handicrafts Under the Midday Moon.'
CGJ, 52(Mar. 1956), 114-17.

P 2841   -- 'Legends from New Brunswick Looms.' CGJ, 65(Oct.
1962), 118-21.

G 2842   Loosley, E. W. 'Early Canadian Costumes.' Canadian
Historical Review, 23(1942), 349-62.

G 2843   MacAnn, Aida. 'Busy Hands in New Brunswick.' CGJ, 20
(Mar. 1940), 127-42.

C 2844   McCook, James. 'Some Notes on Musical Instruments Among
the Pioneers of the Canadian West.' Canadian Music
Journal, 2(Winter 1958), 21-24.

Ga 2845   McKendry, Ruth. Quilts & Other Bed Coverings in the
Canadian Tradition. Scarborough: Van Nostrand Reinhold,
1979. 240 pp.

B 2846   -- 'Quilts in Canada.' Canadian Antiques & Art Review,
1:3(1979), 20-25.

C 2847   Mattie, Wesley C. 'The McKendry Quilt Collection.'
Canadian Collector, July/Aug. 1979, pp. 35-39.

B 2848   -- 'Museum of Man Folk Art Collection.' Canadian Antiques & Art Review, 1:3(1979), 26-31.

G 2849   Mayrand, Pierre, and John Bland. Three Centuries of
Architecture in Canada. Montreal: Federal Publications
Service, 1971. 123 pp.

G 2850   Morgan, Carl. Early Woodenware in Canada. Cheltenham,
Ont.: Boston Mills, 1977. 96 pp.

P 2851   Newton-White, Muriel E. Backhouses of the North.
Cobalt: Highway Book Shop, 1972. 38 pp.

G 2852   Nobbs, Percy E. 'Metal Crafts in Canada.' CGJ, 28
(May 1944), 212-25.

GP 2853   Peck, M. A. 'Handicrafts from Coast to Coast.' CGJ, 9
(Oct. 1934), 201-16.

G 2854   -- Sketch of the Activities of the Canadian Handicrafts Guild and of the Dawn of the Handicraft Movement in the Dominion. N.p., 1929. 22 pp.

GP 2855   Phillips, Robert A. J., and Alan Gowans. Up the Streets
of British Columbia. Ottawa: Heritage Canada, 1978.

B 2856   'Prairie Folk Art.' artscanada, Nos. 230/231(Oct.-Nov.
1979), pp. 1-19.

GP 2857   Priamo, Carol. Mills of Canada. Toronto: McGraw-Hill
          Ryerson, 1976. 196 pp.

 A 2858   Price, Ralph. 'Twas Ever Thus: A Selection of Eastern
          Canadian Folk Art. Toronto: Feheley, 1979. 87 pp.

 G 2859   Richardson, A. J. H. 'A Comparative Historical Study of
          Timber Building in Canada.' Bulletin of the Assoc. for
          Preservation Technology, 5:3(1973), 77-102.

 G 2860   Ritchie, Thomas. Canada Builds, 1867-1967. Toronto:
          Univ. of Toronto Press, 1967. 406 pp.

 C 2861   --   'A History of Windmills and their Place in Cana-
          dian Life.' CGJ, 79(Mar. 1969), 106-9.

 P 2862   Robinson, Cyril. 'Homecrafted for the Altar.' Weekend
          Magazine, 17 Aug. 1965, p. 18.

 C 2863   Roe, Frank G. 'The Old Log House in Western Canada.'
          Alberta Historical Review, 6(Spring 1958), 1-9.

 C 2864   --   'The Sod House.' Alberta Historical Review, 18
          (Summer 1970), 1-7.

Gb 2865   Russell, Carl P. Firearms, Traps and Tools of the Moun-
          tain Men. New York: Russell, 1967. 474 pp.

 C 2866   Shackleton, Philip. 'Canada's Covered Bridges.' CGJ, 44
          (Mar. 1952), 128-37.

 G 2867   Sherwood, Angus. 'Building in the North.' Bulletin of
          the Assoc. for Preservation Technology, 6:3(1974),
          1-25. [B.C.]

 G 2868   Simpson, Valerie. Women's Attire. Saint John: N.B. Mu-
          seum, 1977. 63 pp.

GP 2869   Smith, Jean, and Elizabeth Smith. Collecting Canada's
          Past. Toronto: Prentice-Hall, 1974. 223 pp.

GP 2870   Spence, Hilda, and Kevin Spence. A Guide to Early Cana-
          dian Glass. Don Mills: Longmans, 1966. 112 pp.

Gb 2871   Stevens, Gerald. Early Canadian Glass. Toronto: Ryerson,
          1967. 184 pp.

GPc 2872 --   In a Canadian Attic. Toronto: Ryerson, 1955, 1963.
          135 pp.

 B 2873   Symons, Harry. Fences. Illus. by C. W. Jeffreys. Toron-
          to: Ryerson, 1958. 155 pp.

 B 2874   --   Playthings of Yesterday; The Percy Band Collection.
          Toronto: Ryerson, 1963. 96 pp.

GPb 2875 Symons, Scott. Heritage. A Romantic Look at Early Canadian Furniture. Photographs by John de Visser. Toronto: McClelland & Stewart, 1971. 220 pp.

B 2876 Taggert, Kathleen M. 'The First Shelter of Early Pioneers.' Saskatchewan History, 11(1958), 81-93.

G 2877 'Three Documents on Ironworks in Canada and the Northeastern United States at the Beginning of the Nineteenth Century.' Bulletin of the Assoc. for Preservation Technology, 5:3(1973), 5-33.

B 2878 Tilney, Philip V. R. Artifacts from the CCFCS Collection: Sampling #1. Ottawa: National Museum, CCFCS Mercury Series 5, 1973. 61 pp.

C 2879 -- Play's the Thing. Ottawa: National Museum, 1976. 28 pp. [Catalogue of toy exhibition.]

C 2880 Traquair, Ramsay. 'Hooked Rugs in Canada.' CGJ, 26 (May 1943), 240-54.

Ga 2881 Trask, Deborah. Life how short, Eternity how long: Gravestone Carving and Carvers in Nova Scotia. Halifax: N.S. Museum, 1978. 100 pp.

G 2882 Watt, Robb, and Barbara Riley. Material History Bulletin. Ottawa: National Museum, History Division Mercury Series 21, 1977. 78 pp.

GP 2883 Warnock, Amelia Beers [Katherine Hale]. Canadian Houses of Romance. Toronto: Macmillan, 1926. 213 pp.

Gc 2884 Webster, Donald B., ed. The Book of Canadian Antiques. Toronto: McGraw-Hill Ryerson, 1974. 352 pp.

G 2885 -- Early Canadian Pottery. Toronto: McClelland & Stewart, 1971. 256 pp.

G 2886 Woodall, Ronald. Magnificent Derelicts: A Celebration of Older Buildings. Vancouver: Douglas, 1975. 147 pp.

Gb 2887 Woodall, Ronald, and T. H. Watkins. Taken by the Wind: Vanishing Architecture of the West. Toronto: General, 1977. 256 pp.

A 2889 Zimmerly, David, ed. Contextual Studies of Material Culture. Ottawa: National Museum, Ethnology Service Mercury Series 43, 1978. 58 pp.

10B Anglophone and Celtic

B 2890 Adamson, Anthony, and John F. Willard. The Gaiety of
Gables. Ontario's Architectural Folk Art. Toronto:
McClelland & Stewart, 1974. 128 pp.

C 2891 Agnes Etherington Art Centre. Tradition Plus One.
Patchwork Quilts from South Eastern Ontario. Kingston:
Queen's University, 1974. [Exhibition catalogue.]

G 2892 Angus, Margaret. The Old Stones of Kingston: Its
Buildings before 1867. Toronto: Univ. of Toronto Press,
1966. 120 pp.

G 2893 Arthur, Eric. Early Buildings of Ontario. Toronto:
Univ. of Toronto Press, 1938. 24 pp.

Pa 2894 Barrett, W. L., photographer. 'Time Warp at King's
Landing.' Harrowsmith, 3:8(1979), 62-69.

GP 2895 Brooksbank, Jack. Old Relics and Charming Retainers of
Rural Ontario. Cheltenham: Boston Mills, 1978. 42 pp.

Gb 2896 Byers, Mary, Jan Kennedy, and Margaret McBurney. Rural
Roots: Pre-Confederation Buildings of the York Region
of Ontario. Toronto: Univ. of Toronto Press, 1976.
272 pp.

P 2897 Clemson, Donovan. 'Ghost Towns of Lardeau.' B.C. Out-
doors, 23:6(1967), 44-48.

C 2898 Crowell, Ivan C. 'The Little Old Mills of New Brunswick.' Collections of the N.B. Historical Society, 19
(1966), 79-87.

Ga 2899 Cunningham, Robert, and John B. Prince. Tamped Clay
and Saltmarsh Hay. Artifacts of New Brunswick. Fredericton: Brunswick, 1976. 280 pp.

C 2900 Cutts, Anson B. 'The Old Scottish Architecture of Ontario.' CGJ, 39(Nov. 1949), 202-17.

C 2901 Davis, Marlene, et al. Nova Scotia Work Basket. Halifax:
N.S. Museum, 1976. 114 pp. [Traditional needlework.]

C 2902 Devine, P. K. 'The Old Sealing Gun.' Christmas Annual,
(St. John's), 1909, pp. 12, 15.

G 2903 Dobson, Henry, and Barbara Dobson. The Early Furniture
of Ontario and the Atlantic Provinces. Toronto: Feheley, 1977. 209 pp.

C 2904 Elliott, Shirley B. Domestic Life in Early Halifax.
Halifax: N.S. Museum, 1972. [12 pp.]

C 2905   Finley, Gregg. The Loyalists. Saint John: N.B. Museum, 1977. 64 pp. [Articles used by early settlers.]

G 2906   Foss, Charles, and Richard Vroom. Cabinetmakers of the Eastern Seaboard--A Study of Early Canadian Furniture. Toronto: Feheley, 1977. 168 pp.

C 2907   Fowke, Shirley H. 'The Chime of Ox-Bells.' Atlantic Advocate, 49(Apr. 1959), 77-79.

C 2908   Going, A. M. 'Old Mills of the Loyalists.' CGJ, 10 (Jan. 1935), 43-50.

G 2909   Greenhill, Ralph, Ken Macpherson, and Douglas Richardson. Ontario Towns. Ottawa: Oberon, 1974. 196 pp.

A 2910   Guillet, Edwin C. Pioneer Arts and Crafts. 1940; rpt. Toronto: Univ. of Toronto Press, 1968. 97 pp.

G 2911   Halloran, Joan. 'Wooden Forts of the Early Northwest: Fort William.' Bulletin of the Assoc. for Preservation Technology, 6:2(1974), 38-81.

Gb 2912   Hanks, Carole. Early Ontario Gravestones. Toronto: McGraw-Hill Ryerson, 1974. 94 pp.

G 2913   Humphreys, Barbara A. 'The Architectural Heritage of the Rideau Corridor.' Ottawa: Parks Canada, Occasional Papers in Archeology and History No. 10, 1974, pp. 11-71.

Gb 2914   Ingolsfrud, Elizabeth. All About Ontario Beds. Toronto: House of Grant, 1975. 63 pp.

Gb 2915   -- All About Ontario Chairs. Toronto: House of Grant, 1974. 63 pp.

Gb 2916   -- All About Ontario Chests. Toronto: House of Grant, 1973. 48 pp.

Gb 2917   -- All About Ontario Cupboards. Toronto: House of Grant, 1978. 96 pp.

Gb 2918   -- All About Ontario Desks. Toronto: House of Grant, 1979. 79 pp.

Gb 2919   -- All About Ontario Tables. Toronto: House of Grant, 1976. 63 pp.

P 2920   Law, Margaret L. 'The Hooked Rugs of Nova Scotia.' House Beautiful, July 1928, pp. 58-59, 86-88.

G 2921   Leechman, Douglas. 'The First Farm on the Fraser.' CGJ, 64(May 1962), 168-73.

C 2922 Leitch, Adelaide. 'The Sign of the Fish.' CGJ, 52(Feb. 1956), 86-88.

C 2923 -- 'Tartan Weavers of Cape Breton.' CGJ, 56(May 1958), 176-77.

C 2924 -- 'Where Handicrafts Build Homes.' CGJ, 42(May 1951), 234-36.

C 2925 MacKennon, S. 'Bagpipe in Canada.' CGJ, 4(Apr. 1932), 233-41.

G 2926 Mackenzie, Lois, and Kim Ondaatje. Old Houses of Ontario. Toronto: Gage, 1977. 192 pp.

GR 2927 Mackinnon, Joan. A Checklist of Toronto Cabinet and Chair Makers, 1800-1865. Ottawa: National Museum, History Division Mercury Series 11, 1975. 203 pp.

G 2928 -- Kingston Cabinetmakers 1800-1867. Ottawa: National Museum, History Division Mercury Series 14, 1976. 190 pp.

B 2929 Mackley, Florence. Handweaving in Cape Breton. Sydney: Author, 1967. 96 pp.

C 2930 -- 'Folk Art in Cape Breton.' CanAntC, 7(Jan./Feb. 1972), 57-59.

Ga 2931 MacLaren, George. Antique Furniture by Nova Scotia Craftsmen. Toronto: McGraw-Hill Ryerson, 1975. 146 pp.

Gb 2932 -- Antique Potteries of Nova Scotia. Halifax: Petheric, 1972. 28 pp.

Gc 2933 -- The Chairmakers of Nova Scotia. Halifax: N.S. Museum, 1966. 7 pp.

Gb 2934 -- Nova Scotia Furniture. Halifax: Petheric, 1969. 44 pp.

Gb 2935 -- Nova Scotia Glass. Halifax: N.S. Museum, 1968. 42 pp.

G 2936 -- The Romance of the Heating Stove in Nova Scotia. Halifax: N.S. Museum, 1972. 24 pp.

Gc 2937 -- The Woodcarvers of Nova Scotia. Halifax: N.S. Museum, 1971. 28 pp.

C 2938 McLeod, Evelyn S. 'Our Sod House.' Beaver, Autumn 1977, pp. 12-15.

Ga 2939 MacRae, Marion, and Antony Adamson. The Ancestral Roof: Domestic Architecture of Upper Canada. Toronto: Musson, 1963. 258 pp.

B 2940   Martin, J. Lynton. The Ross Farm Story. Halifax: N.S.
Museum, 1972. 41 pp. [Implements, tools, & vehicles.]

G 2941   Mills, David B. 'The Evolution of Folk Architecture in
Trinity Bay.' Newfoundland Quarterly, 5:2(1972), 17-23.

Ga 2942 Minhinnick, Jeanne. Early Furniture in Upper Canada
Village 1800-1837. Toronto: Ryerson, 1967. 43 pp.

P 2943   New Brunswick Pieced Quilt Patterns. Fredericton: N.B.
Women's Institute, 1977. 94 pp.

G 2944   O'Dea, Shane. The Domestic Architecture of Old St.
John's. St. John's: Nfld. Historical Society, 1973.
22 pp.

G 2945   Osborne, Brian S. 'The Cemeteries of the Midland Dist-
rict of Upper Canada: A Note on Mortality in a Frontier
Society.' Pioneer America, 6:1(1974) 46-55.

Ga 2946 Pain, Howard. The Heritage of Upper Canadian Furniture.
Toronto: Van Nostrand Reinhold, 1978. 548 pp.

GP 2947 Phillips, Robert A. J. Up the Streets of Ontario. Ottawa: Heritage Canada, 1976. 36 pp.

G 2948   Pictou Heritage Society. Wood and Stone. Halifax: Petheric, 1972. 79 pp.

A 2949   Pocius, Gerald L. 'Hooked Rugs in Newfoundland. The
Representation of Social Structure in Design.' JAF,
92(1979), 273-84.

A 2950   -- Textile Traditions of Eastern Newfoundland. Ottawa: National Museum, CCFCS Mercury Series 29, 1979.
89 pp.

Gb 2951 Rempel, J. I. Building with Wood, and Other Aspects of
the Nineteenth Century Building in Ontario. Toronto:
Univ. of Toronto Press, 1967. 287 pp.

G 2952   Roberts, William, and Mary Anne Roberts. Houses of Old
Toronto. Toronto: Pagurian, 1977. 96 pp.

C 2953   Rogers, Irene, and Ruth Mackenzie. "Furniture Making
on Prince Edward Island." CanAntC, 8(Mar./Apr. 1973),
44-49.

Gb 2954 Russell, Loris S. Lighting in the Pioneer Ontario Home.
Toronto: Royal Ontario Museum, 1966. 16 pp.

G 2955   Ryder, Huia G. Antique Furniture by New Brunswick
Craftsmen. Toronto: Ryerson, 1965; pb., 1973. 180 pp.

Ga 2956 Shackleton, Philip. The Furniture of Old Ontario.
Toronto: Macmillan, 1973. 399 pp.

Gc 2957　Shackleton, Philip. 'The Woodenware of Ontario Pio-
　　　　　neers.' CGJ, 46(May 1953), 174-81.

 B 2958　Shaw, Barbara B., and Ronald E. Merrick. The Village
　　　　　Blacksmith. Halifax: N.S. Museum, 1972. 16 pp.

GPc 2959　Stevens, Gerald. Early Ontario Furniture. Toronto: Roy-
　　　　　al Ontario Museum, 1966. 16 pp.

GPc 2960　-- Early Ontario Glass. Toronto: Royal Ontario Museum,
　　　　　1965. 16 pp.

 G 2961　Stewart, Don R. A Guide to Pre-Confederation Furniture
　　　　　of English Canada. Toronto: Longman, 1967. 150 pp.

 C 2962　Tibbets, D. C. 'The Newfoundland Tilt.' Habitat, 11:5
　　　　　(1968), 14-17.

Pb 2963　Trueman, Stuart. 'The Last of the Collar Men.' Weekend
　　　　　Magazine, 10 Nov. 1973, pp. 2-9.

Gc 2964　Vienneau, Azor. The Bottle Collector. Halifax: Pether-
　　　　　ic, 1969. 42 pp.

 G 2965　Webster, Donald B. English-Canadian Furniture of the
　　　　　Georgian Period. Toronto: McGraw-Hill Ryerson, 1979.
　　　　　232 pp.

Pc 2966　Wilson, Jane E. 'Portrait of a Country Artist.' Har-
　　　　　rowsmith, 3:1(1979), 58-63, 83.

 P 2967　Wooding, F. H. "Artistry in Pine Roots." CGJ, 53(Dec.
　　　　　1956), 232-35.

10C　Francophone

 B 2968　Barbeau, C. Marius. 'The Arts of French Canada.' In
　　　　　The Arts of French Canada, 1616-1870. Detroit: Detroit
　　　　　Institute of Arts, 1946. 52 pp. [Exhibition catalogue.]

 C 2969　-- 'The Arts of French Canada.' Art Quarterly, Autumn
　　　　　1946, pp. 329-42.

 B 2970　-- Assomption Sash. Ottawa: National Museum, Bulletin
　　　　　93, 1939; rpt. 1972. 51 pp.

 C 2971　-- 'Crafts in Early French Canada.' Canadian Railway
　　　　　Employees' Monthly, 37(1951), 230-32.

 C 2972　-- 'Folk Arts in French Canada.' Educational Record
　　　　　of the Province of Quebec, 18(1942), 40-45.

Ga 2973 Barbeau, C. Marius. I Have Seen Quebec. Toronto: Mac-
         millan, 1957. Unpaged.

C 2974   -- 'Isle aux Coudres.' CGJ, 12(Apr. 1936), 201-12.

C 2975   -- 'Laurentian Wood Carvers.' CGJ, 11(Oct. 1935), 181-
         90.

C 2976   -- 'Native Quebec Art.' Saturday Night, 12 Jan. 1935.

C 2977   -- 'Old Canadian Pottery.' Educational Record of the
         Province of Quebec, 64(1948), 112-15.

C 2978   -- 'Quebec Wood Carvers.' Quebec, 7(Sept. 1932), 170-
         74.

C 2979   -- 'Traditional Arts of Quebec.' Canadian Review of
         Music and Art, 3(Oct.-Nov. 1944), 23-25.

C 2980   -- 'Traditional Arts of Quebec.' Saturday Night, 5
         Jan. 1935.

C 2981   -- 'Traditional Arts of Quebec.' Technique (Montreal),
         18(1943), 304-10.

C 2982   -- 'Two Centuries of French-Canadian Wood Carving.'
         Canadian Forum, 17(1936) 24, 25.

P 2983   Bériau, Oscar A. 'Domestic Crafts in Québec.' Quebec,
         9(March 1934), 36-38.

C 2984   -- 'The Handicraft Renaissance in Quebec.' CGJ, 7
         (Sept. 1933), 143-49.

A 2985   Boily, Lise. The Bread Ovens of Quebec. Ottawa: Nation-
         al Museum, 1979. 135 pp.

C 2986   Bruemmer, Fred. 'Historic Mills of Quebec.' CGJ, 74
         (Apr. 1967), 118-23.

GP 2987 Carless, William. 'Homespun. A Tale of Yesterday and
         Today.' Quebec, 4(Sept. 1929), 195-98.

   2988 Cartwright, Jean B. 'Canada's Oldest House.' CGJ, 52
         (Jan. 1956), 24-29.

P 2989   Cox, Carolyn. 'The Rugs of Chéticamp.' Canadian Homes
         and Gardens, Apr. 1938, pp. 66-69.

C 2990   Dunn, Josephine H. 'The Wood Carvers of St. Jean-Port-
         Joli.' CGJ, 45(Dec. 1952), 234-41.

C 2991   'Edmond Chatigny, patenteux.' artscanada, Nos. 230/231
         (Oct.-Nov. 1979), pp. 23-24.

GP 2992 Fortier, John. 'Louisbourg Lives Again.' Conservation
         Canada, 2:3(1976), 3-7.

G 2993   'The Fortress of Louisbourg.' <u>Bulletin of the Assoc.</u>
<u>for Preservation Technology</u>, 4:1-2(1972), 3-40; 110
figures.

C 2994   Gillies, D. A. 'Canot du Maître or Montreal Canoe.'
<u>CGJ</u>, 56(Mar. 1958), 114-19.

G 2995   Gowans, Alan. <u>Church Architecture in New France</u>. Toronto: Univ. of Toronto Press, 1955. 162 pp.

2996   Hart, John F. 'Barns of Quebec." <u>Geographical Review</u>
(London), 55:3(1965), 424-26.

G 2997   Hatton, Warwick, and Beth Hatton. <u>A Feast of Ginger-</u>
<u>bread from Our Victorian Past</u>. Montreal: Tundra, 1976.
96 pp.

G 2998   Jury, W. Wilfred. <u>Sainte-Marie among the Hurons</u>. Toronto: Univ. of Toronto Press, 1954. 128 pp.

C 2999   Mackay, Alice. 'French Canadian Handicrafts.' <u>CGJ</u>, 6
(Jan. 1933), 27-34.

G 3000   MacLaughlin, Marjorie. 'Landscape Rugs in Quebec.'
<u>CGJ</u>, 1(Dec. 1930), 671-80.

Ga 3001   Moogk, Peter N. <u>Building a House in New France</u>. Toronto: McClelland & Stewart, 1977. 144 pp.

Gc 3002   Morisset, Gerald. 'Old Churches of Quebec.' <u>CGJ</u>, 43
(Sept. 1951), 100-15.

Gc 3003   -- 'Quebec--The Country House.' <u>CGJ</u>, 57(Dec. 1958),
178-95.

A 3004   Palardy, Jean. <u>The Early Furniture of French Canada</u>.
Toronto: Macmillan of Canada, 2nd ed., 1965. 410 pp.

G 3005   Richardson, A. J. H. 'Buildings in the Old City of
Quebec.' <u>Bulletin of the Assoc. for Preservation Tech-</u>
<u>nology</u>, 2:3-4(1970), 3-144.

G 3006   Richardson, A. J. H., and P.-L. Lapointe. 'The Garneau
House.' <u>Bulletin of the Assoc. for Preservation Tech-</u>
<u>nology</u>, 8:1(1976), 28-42.

C 3007   Rowe, R. C. 'The St. Maurice Forges.' <u>CGJ</u>, 9(July
1934), 15-22.

G 3008   Roy, Pierre-Georges. <u>The Old Churches of the Province</u>
<u>of Quebec, 1647-1800</u>. Quebec: n.p., 1925. 324 pp.

C 3009   Séguin, Robert-Lionel. 'Québec Maple Sugar Moulds.'
<u>CanAntC</u>, 9(May/June 1974), 74-77.

Folk Art and Material Culture

C 3010   Spendlove, F. St. George. 'Furniture of French Canada.'
CanAntC, 2(May 1967), 9-15.

Ga 3011 Traquair, Ramsay. _The Old Architecture of Quebec: A
Study of the Buildings Erected in New France from the
Earliest Explorers to the Middle of the Nineteenth
Century_. Toronto: Macmillan, 1947. 324 pp.

Ga 3012 -- _The Old Silver of Quebec_. Toronto: Macmillan, 1940;
rpt. 1973. 168 pp.

Ga 3013 Trudel, Jean. _Silver in New France_. Ottawa: National
Gallery, 1974. 248 pp.

P 3014   Turcot, Henri. 'The French Canadian Homespun Industry.'
Quebec, 4(Sept. 1929), 192-95.

P 3015   Veisse, J. 'French Canadian Blankets.' _CanAntC_, 9(May/
June 1974), 90-92.

G 3016   Wilson, P. Roy. _The Beautiful Old Houses of Quebec_.
Toronto: Univ. of Toronto Press, 1975. 126 pp.

10D   Indian and Inuit

A 3017   Adney, E. Tappan, and Howard I. Chapelle. _The Bark
Canoes and Skin Boats of North America_. Washington:
National Museum, Bulletin 230, 1964. 242 pp.

C 3018   Ahenakew, Edward. 'Tanning Hides.' _Beaver_, Summer 1972,
pp. 46-48.

C 3019   Akitirq, Atoat, and Pauloosie Akitirq. 'Comments on
Carving Soapstone.' _Beaver_, Autumn 1975, pp. 14-17.

B 3020   Arima, Eugene Y. _A Contextual Study of the Caribou
Eskimo Kayak_. Ottawa: National Museum, Ethnology Service Mercury Series 25, 1975. 275 pp.

C 3021   -- 'Itivimiut Sled Construction.' Ottawa: National
Museum, Bulletin 204, 1967, pp. 100-13.

C 3022   -- 'Notes on the Kayak and Its Equipment at Ivuyivik,
P.Q.' Ottawa: National Museum, Bulletin 194, 1964, pp.
221-61.

B 3023   -- _Report on an Eskimo Umiak Built at Ivuyivik, P.Q.,
in the Summer of 1960_. Ottawa: National Museum, Bulletin 189, 1963. 83 pp.

C 3024   Armstrong, Doris, adaptor. _Patterns Based on Northwest
Indian Designs_. Victoria: Indian Arts & Welfare Society, 1955. 16 pp.

G 3025 Baird, Irene. 'Land of the Lively Arts.' Beaver,
        Autumn 1961, pp. 12-21.

C 3026 Barbeau, C. Marius. 'The Modern Growth of the Totem
        Pole on the Northwest Coast.' Proc. of the 23rd Inter-
        national Congress of Americanists, Washington, 1928,
        pp. 505-11.

A 3027 -- Haida Carvers in Argillite. Ottawa: National Mu-
        seum, Bulletin 139, 1957; rpt. 1974. 214 pp.

A 3028 -- Haida Myths Illustrated in Argillite Carvings.
        Ottawa: National Museum, Bulletin 127, 1953. 417 pp.

C 3029 -- 'How to Read a Totem Pole.' Science Illustrated,
        Sept. 1948, pp. 8-9.

C 3030 -- 'Indian Silversmiths on the Pacific Coast.' TRSC,
        (1939), sec. 2, pp. 23-28.

C 3031 -- 'Indian Trade Silver.' Beaver, Dec. 1942, pp. 10-14.

A 3032 -- Totem Poles. Vol. 1. According to Crests and Topics.
        Vol. 2. According to Location. Ottawa: National Museum,
        Bulletin 119, 1950. 880 pp.

C 3033 -- 'Totem Poles: A By-Product of the Fur Trade.' Sci-
        entific Monthly, 55(1942), 507-14.

B 3034 -- Totem Poles of the Gitskan, Upper Skeena River,
        B.C.. Ottawa: National Museum, Bulletin 61, 1929; rpt.
        1973. 275 pp.

B 3035 -- 'Totem Poles: A Recent Native Art of the Northwest
        Coast of America.' Geographical Review, 2(1930),
        258-72.

C 3036 -- 'Totemism, A Modern Growth on the North Pacific
        Coast.' JAF, 57(1944), 51-58.

C 3037 Blackman, Margaret B. 'Mortuary Art from the Northwest
        Coast.' Beaver, Winter 1975, 54-57.

B 3038 Blodgett, Jean. 'The Historic Period in Canadian Eski-
        mo Art.' Beaver, Summer 1979, pp. 17-27.

B 3039 Boas, Franz. Facial Paintings of the Indians of North-
        ern British Columbia. New York: American Museum of Na-
        tural History, Memoir 2, 1900. Pp. 13-24.

Fa 3040 -- Primitive Art. 1927; rpt. New York: Dover, 1955.
        372 pp.

C 3041 Bond, James H. 'Moose Skin Boat.' Beaver, Winter 1959,
        pp. 44-45.

Gb 3042   Brasser, Ted J. A Basketful of Indian Culture Change.
          Ottawa: National Museum, Ethnology Service Mercury
          Series 22, 1975. 121 pp.

C 3043   -- 'Métis Artisans.' Beaver, Autumn 1975, pp. 52-57.

C 3044   Brothers, Ryan. 'Cowichan Knitters.' Beaver, Summer
          1965, pp. 42-46.

C 3045   Brown, Anna. 'Prairie Totems.' CGJ, 23(Sept. 1941),
          148-51.

C 3046   Bruemmer, Fred. 'Sealskin Thong.' Beaver, Summer 1968,
          pp. 45-50.

C 3047   -- 'The Vanishing Kayak.' CGJ, 78(Apr. 1969), 126-31.

C 3048   Buckham, A. F. 'Indian Engineering.' CGJ, 40(Apr.
          1950), 174-81.

C 3049   Burger, Albert. 'On Building a Birch Bark Canoe.'
          Beaver, Summer 1973, pp. 50-53.

C 3050   Burgesse, J. A. 'Montagnais Cross-Bows.' Beaver, Dec.
          1943, pp. 37-39.

P 3051   Burland, Cottie. Eskimo Art. London: Hamlyn, 1973.
          96 pp.

C 3052   Bushman, Leo N. 'Eskimo Art.' Canadian Ethnic Studies,
          1:1(1969), 43-50.

C 3053   Butler, Sheila. 'The First Printmaking Year at Baker
          Lake.' Beaver, Spring 1976, pp. 17-26.

C 3054   -- 'Wall Hangings from Baker Lake.' Beaver, Autumn
          1972, pp. 26-31.

Gc 3055   Cameron, W. Bleasdell. 'Costumes of the Plains Indi-
          ans.' Beaver, Sept. 1943, pp. 33-37.

P 3056   Carl, G. Clifford. 'Treasures from the Northwest Coast.'
          CanAntC, 4(Nov. 1969), 56-57.

C 3057   Carpenter, Carole Henderson. 'Form and Freedom: Art
          and the Northwest Coast.' Canadian Forum, 57(Aug.
          1977), 25-27.

C 3058   Carpenter, Edmund. 'The Eskimo Artist.' Anthropology
          and Art. Ed. Charlotte M. Otten. New York: Natural
          History Press, 1971. Pp. 163-71.

G 3059   Carpenter, Edmund, Frederick Varley, and Robert Fla-
          herty. Eskimo. Toronto: Univ. of Toronto Press, 1959.
          66 pp.

C 3060   Chipman, Paul. 'The Living Stone.' Beaver, Spring 1956,
         13-19.

Ga 3061 Clark, A. McFadyen. The Athapaskans: Strangers of the
         North. Ottawa: National Museum, 1975. 124 pp.

B 3062   Clark, A. McFadyen, and Donald W. Clark. 'Koyukon
         Athapaskan Houses as Seen Through Oral Tradition and
         Through Archaeology.' Arctic Anthropology, 40, Supple-
         ment. Ottawa: National Museum, 1974, 65 pp.

C 3063   Clark, Ian C. Indian and Eskimo Art of Canada. Toronto:
         Ryerson, 1971. 135 pp.

FB 3064 Collins, Henry B., et al. The Far North: 2000 Years of
         American Eskimo and Indian Art. Washington: National
         Gallery of Art, 1973; rpt. Bloomington: Indiana Univ.
         Press, 1977. 289 pp. [Exhibition catalogue.]

A 3065   The Coming and Going of the Shaman. Eskimo Shamanism
         and Art. Winnipeg: Art Gallery, 1979. 246 pp. [Exhibi-
         tion catalogue.]

C 3066   Connelly, Dolly. 'Walrus Skin Boat.' Beaver, Autumn
         1965, pp. 12-21.

F 3067   Covarrubias, Miguel. The Eagle, the Jaguar and the
         Serpent. Indian Art of the Americas. New York: Knopf,
         1954. 314 pp.

C 3068   Crafts from Arctic Canada. An Exhibition Organized by
         the Canadian Eskimo Arts Council. Toronto: Hurtig-
         Somerville, 1974. 64 pp.

C 3069   Craig, Mary. 'The Cape Dorset Prints.' Beaver, Spring
         1975, pp. 22-29.

C 3070   Davidson, Robert. 'Three Sides to a Coin.' Journal of
         the Canadian Conservation Institute, 3(1978), 10-12.

C 3071   Daye, Vera L. 'Micmac Indian Craftsmen.' Atlantic
         Advocate, 54(July 1964), 29-32.

C 3072   Dewdney, Selwyn. 'Ecological Notes on the Ojibway
         Shaman-artist.' artscanada, Nos. 146/147 (Aug. 1970),
         pp. 17-28.

A 3073   -- The Sacred Scrolls of the Southern Ojibway. Toron-
         to: Univ. of Toronto Press, 1975. 199 pp.

Gb 3074 Dickason, Olive P. Indian Arts in Canada. Ottawa: In-
         formation Canada, 1973. 138 pp.

FB 3075 Dockstader, Frederick. Indian Art in North America.
         Toronto: McClelland & Stewart, 1961. 224 pp.

Folk Art and Material Culture

C 3076 Doyon, Madeleine. 'In Memory of One of Our Great Sculptors.' Conservation Canada, 5:1(1979), 12-13. [Charles Edenshaw.]

C 3077 Drew, Leslie. 'Forests of Totems.' Beaver, Winter 1964, pp. 49-55.

A 3078 Duff, Wilson, William Reid, and William Holm. Arts of the Raven. Vancouver: Art Gallery, 1967. 112 pp.

Fc 3079 Durham, Bill George. Canoes and Kayaks of Western North America. Seattle, WA: Copper Canoe Press, 1960. 40 pp.

C 3080 Ebbutt, Frank. 'The Canoe in Western Canada.' CGJ, 3 (Oct. 1931), 287-92.

C 3081 Eber, Dorothy. 'The History of Graphics in Dorset: Long and Viable.' Canadian Forum, 54(March 1975), 29-31.

C 3082 Eckhardt, Ferdinand. Eskimo: Carvers of Keewatin, N.W.T. Winnipeg: Winnipeg Art Gallery, 1964.

C 3083 Emmons, George T. 'Tsimshian Stories in Carved Wood.' American Museum Journal, 15(1915), 363-66.

A 3084 Emmons, George T., and Franz Boas. The Chilkat Blanket, with notes on blanket designs. New York: American Museum of Natural History, Memoir 3, pt. 4, 1900, pp. 329-400.

A 3085 Eskimo Art. Beaver, Autumn 1967. 98 pp.

A 3086 Eskimo Art Issue. North/Nord, 22(Mar./Apr. 1974). 53 pp.

A 3087 The Eskimo World. artscanada, Nos. 162/163(Dec. 1971/ Jan. 1972), pp. 29-121.

B 3088 Fagg, William, ed. Eskimo Art in the British Museum. London: British Museum, 1972. 48 pp.

B 3089 Farrand, Livingston. Basketry Designs of the Salish Indians. New York: American Museum of Natural History, Memoir 1, pt. 5, 1900. Pp. 393-99.

F 3090 Feder, Norman. North American Indian Painting. New York: Museum of Primitive Art, 1967. Unpaged.

C 3091 Feyes, Claire. 'Eskimo Masks.' Beaver, Spring 1959, pp. 56-57.

C 3092 Fieber, Frank. 'Birch-Bark Biting.' Beaver, Spring 1978, pp. 56-57.

C 3093 Foster, W. Garland. 'The Kitsilano Masks.' CGJ, 28 (Feb. 1944), 84-87.

197

C 3094 Frances, Dorothy. 'Indian Crafts.' CanAntC, 8(July/ Aug. 1973), 27-29.

Fc 3095 Fry, Jacqueline D. 'Contemporary Arts in Non-Western Societies.' artscanada, Nos. 162/163(1971-72), 96-101.

B 3096 Galpin, Francis W. 'The Whistles and Reed Instruments of the Northwest Coast.' Proc. of the Musical Assoc. (London), 29(1903), 115-38.

G 3097 Garfield, Viola E., and L. Forrest. The Wolf and the Raven. Seattle: Univ. of Washington Press, 1948. 151 pp.

BY 3098 George, Pat, ed. Igloolik. Ottawa: Education Div., Dept. of Northern Affairs, 1962. 52 pp.

C 3099 Gillial, Rosemary. 'The Shaggy Toys of Port Burwell.' Beaver, Winter 1961, pp. 28-33.

F 3100 Glubbock, Shirley. The Art of the Eskimo. New York: Harper & Row, 1964. 48 pp.

F 3101 -- The Art of the Woodland Indians. Toronto: Collier-Macmillan, 1976. 48 pp.

Gc 3102 Goddard, Pliny E., and Della Kew. Indian Art and Culture of the Northwest Coast. Saanichton: Hancock, 1974. 93 pp.

C 3103 Goetz, Helga. 'An Eskimo Lifetime in Pictures.' Graphics, 27:157(1972), 506-12.

B 3104 -- The Inuit Print. Ottawa: National Museum, 1977. 267 pp.

C 3105 Gordon, Joleen. Edith Clayton's Market Basket: A Heritage of Splintwood Basketry in Nova Scotia. Halifax: N.S. Museum, 1977. 46 pp.

F 3106 Graburn, Nelson H. H., ed. Ethnic and Tourist Arts: Cultural Expressions from the Fourth World. Berkeley: Univ. of California Press, 1976. 412 pp.

C 3107 Green, Edward. 'The Squamish Totems.' Beaver, June 1939, pp. 36-37.

C 3108 Grunfeld, Frederic V. 'Render unto Caesar.' Horizon, 10:4(1968), 64-69. [B.C. totems.]

B 3109 Guemple, D. L. 'The Pacalik Kayak of the Belcher Islands.' Ottawa: National Museum, Bulletin 204, 1967, pp. 124-90.

Pb 3110 Gunn, S. W. A. Haida Totem Poles in Wood and Argillite. Vancouver: Douglas, 1972. 24 pp.

Folk Art and Material Culture

Pb 3111 Gunn, S. W. A. Kwakiutl House and Totem Poles. Vancouver: Douglas, 1972. 24 pp.

Pb 3112 -- The Totem Poles in Stanley Park. Vancouver: Douglas, 1972. 24 pp.

A 3113 Gunther, Erna. Art in the Life of the Northwest Coast Indian. Portland, OR: Portland Art Museum, 1966.

C 3114 -- Northwest Coast Indian Art. Seattle: Century 21 Exposition, Inc. 1962 [Seattle World's Fair Catalogue.]

B 3115 Guy, Camil. The Weymontaching Birchbark Canoe. Ottawa: National Museum, 1974. 55 pp.

A 3116 Haeberlin, H. K., James A. Teit, and Helen H. Roberts. 'Coiled Basketry in British Columbia and Surrounding Region.' 41st Annual Report of the Bureau of American Ethnology, Washington, 1928, pp. 119-484.

C 3117 Hallendy, Norman. Eskimo Graphic Art. Cape Dorset: West-Baffin Eskimo Cooperative, 1969.

C 3118 Hambleton, Josephine. 'The Raven, Frog, and Bear Totem Pole: A Masterpiece of Haida Art.' Ottawa: National Museum, Bulletin 123, 1951, pp. 80-83.

C 3119 Hamilton, Kennin. 'Autobiography of a Canoe.' Beaver, Jan. 1922, pp. 9-11.

C 3120 Harff, Illi-Maria. Eskimo Sculpture. Winnipeg: Winnipeg Art Gallery, 1967.

C 3121 Harrington, Lyn. 'The Cowichan Sweater.' CGJ, 40(Feb. 1950), 94-97.

C 3122 Harrington, Richard. 'Eskimo Stone Carving.' CGJ, 59 (Aug. 1959), 38-47.

A 3123 Hawthorn, Audrey. Art of the Kwakiutl Indians and Other Northwest Coast Tribes. Seattle: Univ. of Washington Press, 1967. 410 pp.

A 3124 -- Kwakiutl Art. Vancouver: Douglas & McIntyre, 1979. 320 pp.

C 3125 -- 'A Living Haida Craft.' Beaver, Summer 1963, pp. 4-12.

A 3126 -- People of the Potlatch. Vancouver: Vancouver Art Gallery with the Univ. of B.C., 1956. 48 pp. & 108 illus.

B 3127 Hawthorn, Harry B. 'The Artist in Tribal Society: the Northwest Coast.' In Royal Anthropological Institute

199

of Great Britain and Ireland. The Artist in Tribal Society. London: Routledge & Kegan Paul, 1961. Pp. 59-70.

B 3128 Hirabayashi, Joanne. 'The Chilkat Weaving Complex.' Davidson Journal of Anthropology, 1(1955), 43-61.

C 3129 Hobson, Robert W. 'Argillite.' Beaver, Summer 1967, pp. 26-31.

FA 3130 Hoffman, Walter J. 'The Graphic Art of the Eskimos.' U.S. National Museum Annual Report, 1895. Washington: Govt. Printing Office, 1897. Pp. 739-968.

C 3131 Holm, Bill. 'Carving a Kwakiutl Canoe.' Beaver, Summer 1961, pp. 28-35.

A 3132 -- The Crooked Beak of Heaven: Masks and other Ceremonial Art of the Northwest Coast. Seattle: Univ. of Washington Press, 1972. 96 pp.

A 3133 -- Northwest Coast Indian Art. An Analysis of Form. Seattle: Univ. of Washington Press, 1965; rpt. Vancouver: Douglas & McIntyre, 1978. 116 pp.

A 3134 Holm, Bill, and William Reid. Indian Art of the Northwest Coast: A Dialogue on Craftsmanship and Aesthetics. Vancouver: Douglas, 1976. 265 pp. Rpt. of Form and Freedom: A Dialogue on Northwest Coast Indian Art. Rice University Institute for the Arts, 1975. [Unpaged exhibition catalogue.]

C 3135 Hopper, Jacqueline. 'Artists in Haida-Gwai.' Beaver, Autumn 1969, pp. 42-46.

B 3136 Houston, James. Canadian Eskimo Art. Ottawa: Queen's Printer, 1966; rpt. 1972. 40 pp.

B 3137 -- 'Eskimo Artists.' Geographical Magazine (London), 34:11(1962), 639-50.

A 3138 -- Eskimo Prints. Toronto: Longman, 1967; 1971. 112 pp.

C 3139 -- 'Eskimo Sculptors.' Beaver, June 1951, pp. 34-39.

C 3140 Howay, F. W. 'The Dog's Hair Blankets of the Coast Salish.' Washington Historical Quarterly, 9(1918), 83-92.

C 3141 Hungry Wolf, Adolf. Traditional Dress Issue. Invermere: Good Medicine Books, 1971. 64 pp.

B 3142 Indian Masterpieces from the Walter and Marianne Koer-
        ner Collection in the Museum of Anthropology, The Uni-
        versity of British Columbia. Vancouver: Univ. of B.C.
        Press, 1976. 48 pp.

A 3143 Inverarity, R. B. Art of the Northwest Coast Indians.
        Los Angeles: Univ. of California Press, 1950. 236 pp.

C 3144 Ipellie, Alootook, and Gabrielle Goliger. 'The Inuit
        Print.' Inuit Today, 7(Mar. 1976), 10-15.

B 3145 Jackson, Marion E. Inuit Sculpture. Ann Arbor, MI:
        Univ. of Michigan Museum of Art, 1979. [Gallery Guide].

C 3146 Jenness, Diamond. 'Eskimo Art.' Geographical Review
        12(1922), 161-74.

C 3147 -- 'Fading Scenes on Quatsino Inlet.' CGJ, 8(Feb.
        1934), 89-97.

C 3148 -- 'The Painted Skins.' Beaver, June 1945, pp. 14-17.

C 3149 Jones, A. R. C. 'The Caribou Carvers of Coppermine.'
        CGJ, 77(Aug. 1968), 58-63.

C 3150 Joss, W. F. 'Eskimo Sleds.' Beaver, Mar. 1951, pp.
        10-13.

C 3151 Kehoe, Thomas F., and Alice B. Kehoe. 'Boulder Effigy
        Monuments in the Northern Plains.' JAF, 72(1959),
        115-127.

C 3152 Keller, Irish. 'Apple Art.' Relics, 5(Apr. 1972), pp.
        16-17.

C 3153 Kildare, Maurice. 'Eskimo Ivory Carving.' Relics, 4
        (Aug. 1970), 16-19, 22.

A 3154 King, Jonathan C. H. Portrait Masks of the Northwest
        Coast of America. [New York]: Thames & Hudson, c. 1979.
        96 pp.

B 3155 Kissell, Mary Louise. 'A New Type of Spinning in North
        America.' American Anthropologist, 18(1916), 264-70.

C 3156 -- 'Organized Salish Blanket Pattern.' American Anthro-
        pologist, 31(1929), 85-88.

C 3157 Knight, Frederica. 'The New Kayak.' Beaver, Spring
        1960, pp. 30-37.

B 3158 'KSAN: Breath of Our Grandfathers. An Exhibition of
        'KSAN Art. Ottawa: National Museum, 1972. 108 pp.

P 3159 'KSAN. Hazelton, British Columbia. Hazelton: 'KSAN
        Association, n.d. 31 pp.

201

B 3160   Lane, Barbara S. 'The Cowichan Knitting Industry.'
         Anthropology in British Columbia, 2(1951), 14-27.

B 3161   Large, R. Geddes. Soogwilis: A Collection of Kwakiutl
         Indian Designs and Legends. Toronto: Ryerson, 1951.
         77 pp.

B 3162   Larmour, W. T. The Art of the Canadian Eskimo. Ottawa:
         Information Canada, 1967. 106 pp.

C 3163   Leechman, Douglas. 'Aboriginal Paints and Dyes in Can-
         ada.' TRSC, 26(1932), sec. 2, pp. 37-42.

  3164   -- 'Arts and the Aborigines.' Queen's Quarterly, 49
         (1942), 252-60.

C 3165   -- 'Beauty's Only Skin Deep.' Beaver, Sept. 1951, pp.
         38-40.

C 3166   -- 'A Ceremonial Palette from Saskatchewan.' CGJ, 48
         (Mar. 1954), 126-27.

C 3167   -- 'Eskimo Sculpture in Stone.' CGJ, 49(Sept. 1954),
         90-99.

C 3168   -- 'The Kootenay Canoe.' Beaver, Spring 1962, pp.
         11-15.

C 3169   -- 'Igloo and Tupik.' Beaver, Mar. 1945, pp. 36-39.

C 3170   -- 'Turtle Mosaic.' CGJ, 39(Dec. 1949), 274-75.

C 3171   -- 'The Uses of Birch Bark.' Beaver, June 1943,
         pp. 30-33.

C 3172   -- 'Wigwam and Teepee.' Beaver, Dec. 1944, pp. 28-31.

C 3173   Leitch, Adelaide. 'Porcupine Crafts.' CGJ, 51(Sept.
         1955), 128-29.

C 3174   -- 'The Snowshoe Makers of Loretteville.' CGJ, 70
         (Feb. 1965), 62-63.

C 3175   Lent, Geneva. 'Masks.' Beaver, Dec. 1938, pp. 53-55.

C 3176   Lewis, Brian W. 'Eskimo Stone Boat.' CGJ, 75(July
         1967), 20-25.

C 3177   -- 'Etuk Makes A Drum.' Beaver, Winter 1968, pp.
         26-29.

B 3178   Lobb, Allan, and Art Wolfe. Indian Baskets of the
         Northwest Coast. Portland, OR: Graphic Arts, 1978.
         119 pp.

C 3179   Loudon, Peter. 'Kwakiutl Totem.' CGJ, 53(Oct. 1956),
         146-51.

A 3180   MacDonald, George S. 'Haida Burial Practices: Three
          Archaeological Examples.' Ottawa: National Museum,
          Archaeology Survey Mercury Series 9, 1973. Pp. 1-59.

C 3181   Macfie, John. 'Crafts of the Cree.' Beaver, Autumn
          1957, pp. 53-57.

C 3182   -- 'Ojibwa Craftsman.' Beaver, Winter 1959, pp. 34-38.

C 3183   MacGregor, James G. 'Stone Gods of the Prairies.'
          Alberta Historical Review, 7(Autumn 1959), 7-11.

C 3184   MacLaren, George E. C. 'The Arts of the Micmac.' N.S.
          Historical Quarterly, 4(1974), 167-77.

C 3185   MacLean, John. 'Birch Bark Records.' Beaver, Mar. 1926,
          pp. 58-59.

C 3186   -- 'Canada's Native Sculptors.' Beaver, Apr. 1924, pp.
          248-49.

C 3187   -- 'The Peace Pipe.' Beaver, Mar. 1925, pp. 80-82.

C 3188   Macpherson, Dorothy. 'Eskimo Handicrafts.' Encyclo-
          paedia Canadiana, pp. 42-45.

Pc 3189 Malin, Edward. A World of Faces. Masks of the Northwest
          Coast Indians. Portland, OR: Timber, n.d. Unpaged.

B 3190   Malin, Edward, and Norman Feder. Indian Art of the
          Northwest Coast. The Cultural Background of the Art.
          Denver Art Museum Quarterly, Winter 1962.

B 3191   Martijn, Charles A. 'Canadian Eskimo Carving in Histor-
          ical Perspective.' Anthropos, 59(1965), 546-96.

B 3192   -- 'A Retrospective Glance at Canadian Eskimo Carv-
          ing.' Beaver, Autumn 1967, pp. 4-19.

C 3193   Mason, S. 'Art of the Eskimos: prints.' Graphic, 32
          (1976-77), 80-87.

B 3194   Mathiassen, Therkel. 'Material Culture of the Iglulik
          Eskimos.' In Report of the Fifth Thule Expedition
          1921-24. Vol. 6, no. 1. Copenhagen: Gyldendalski, 1928.

B 3195   Meldgaard, Jorgen. Eskimo Sculpture. London: Methuen,
          1960. 48 pp.

C 3196   Murdoch, Peter. 'Seeguapik, Artist.' Beaver, Winter
          1956, pp. 24-31.

C 3197   Myers, Marybelle. 'People Who Know How to Dream.'
          North, March/April 1974, pp. 17-21. [Eskimo art.]

C 3198   Nagy, Hendrika G. 'Pottery in Keewatin.' Beaver, Autumn
          1967, pp. 61-66.

Gb 3199 'Native Art in Canada.' Native Perspective, 3:2(1978), 31-87.

B 3200 Northwest Coast Indian Artifacts from the H. R. Mac-Millan Collections in the Museum of Anthropology, the University of British Columbia. Vancouver: Univ. of B.C. Press, 1976. 48 pp.

C 3201 Oldham, Evelyn. 'Renaissance of Coast Indian Art.' CGJ, 84(Nov. 1973), 32-37.

C 3202 Pattee, Lynus R. 'Birch Bark Canoe.' Beaver, June 1942, pp. 24-27.

Gb 3203 Patterson, Nancy-Lou. Canadian Native Art. Don Mills: Collier-Macmillan, 1973. 180 pp.

C 3204 Pelletier, Gaby. Micmac & Maliseet Decorative Traditions. Saint John: N.B. Museum, 1978. 64 pp. [Exhibition catalogue.]

C 3205 -- 'Women's Work Baskets.' Canadian Antiques & Art Review, 1:3(1979), 32-36.

C 3206 Raczka, Paul. 'Indian Dancers.' Beaver, Summer 1978, pp. 25-29. [Costumes.]

FA 3207 Ray, Dorothy Jean. Artists of the Tundra and the Sea. Seattle: Univ. of Washington Press, 1961. 170 pp.

B 3208 Rickard, T. A. 'The Use of Iron and Copper by the Indians of British Columbia.' B.C. Historical Quarterly, 3(1939), 25-50.

C 3209 Ringland, Mabel C. 'Indian Handicrafts of Algoma.' CGJ, 6(Apr. 1933), 185-202.

B 3210 Ritchie, Carson I. A. The Eskimo and His Art. 80 pp. Toronto: Macmillan, c. 1974.

F 3211 Ritzenthaler, Robert. Iroquois False-Face Masks. Milwaukee, WI: Milwaukee Public Museum, 1969. 71 pp.

C 3212 Robertson, John K. B. 'The Sculpture of Tukiki Oshaweetok.' Beaver, Winter 1977, pp. 24-27.

C 3213 Robertson, Syla. 'British Columbia's Dugout Canoes.' CGJ, 43(July 1951), 18-23.

Gc 3214 Robinson, Leigh B. 'To British Columbia's Totem Land.' CGJ, 24(Feb. 1942), 80-93.

B 3215 Roch, Ernst. Arts of the Eskimo: Prints. Toronto: Oxford, 1974. 240 pp.

B 3216 Rogers, Edward S. The Material Culture of the
        Mistassini. Ottawa: National Museum, Bulletin 218,
        156 pp.

C 3217 Ryan, Terrence. 'Drawings from the People.' North, 11:5
        (1964), 25-31.

C 3218 Ryan, Terrance, ed. Dorset 77. Toronto: Feheley, 1977.
        79 pp. [Exhibition catalogue.]

FA 3219 Sacred Circles. Two Thousand Years of North American
        Indian Art. London: Arts Council of Great Britain,
        1976. 252 pp. [Exhibition catalogue.]

A 3220 Sculpture of the Inuit. Toronto: Univ. of Toronto
        Press, 1971. 494 pp.

C 3221 Sherman, Glen. 'Tobacco Pipes of the Western Eskimos.'
        Beaver, Summer 1972. pp. 49-51.

F 3222 Siebert, Erna, and Werner Forman. North American Indian
        Art. London: Hamlyn, 1967. 43 pp.

B 3223 Sinclair, Lister, and Jack Pollock. The Art of Norval
        Morrisseau. Toronto: Methuen, 1979. 200 pp.

C 3224 Smith, Harlan I. 'Restoration of Totem Poles in British
        Columbia.' In Annual Report for 1928. Ottawa: National
        Museum, Bulletin 50, 1928, pp. 81-83.

B 3225 Smith, Harlan I., and Gerard Fowke. Cairns of British
        Columbia and Washington. New York: American Museum of
        Natural History, Memoir 4, 1901. Pp. 55-75.

B 3226 Smyly, John, and Carolyn Smyly. Those Born at Koona.
        Saanichton, B.C.: Hancock, 1973. 120 pp.

B 3227 -- and -- The Totem Poles of Skedans. Saanichton: Han-
        cock, 1973. 119 pp.

A 3228 Société des amis du Musée de l'Homme. Masterpieces of
        Indian and Eskimo Art from Canada. Paris, 1969.
        Unpaged. [Exhibition Catalogue.]

B 3229 Speck, Frank G. 'Art Processes in Birchbark of the
        River Desert Algonquin: A Circumboreal Trait.' Washing-
        ton: Bureau of American Ethnology, Bulletin 128, 1941,
        pp. 231-74.

B 3230 -- The Double-Curve Motive in Northeastern Algonkian
        Art. Ottawa: National Museum, Memoir 42, 1914. 17 pp.

B 3231 -- 'Eskimo Carved Ivories from Northern Labrador.'
        Indian Notes, 4(1927), 309-19.

C 3232 Speck, Frank G. 'Labrador Eskimo Mask and Clown.'
        General Magazine and Historical Chronicle (Univ. of
        Pennsylvania), 37(1935), 159-73.

A 3233 -- Montagnais Art in Birch-Bark, A Circumpolar Trait.
        New York: Museum of the American Indian, 1937. 157 pp.

B 3234 Steltzer, Ulli. Indian Artists at Work. Vancouver:
        Douglas, 1976. 163 pp.

Ga 3235 Stewart, Hilary. Artifacts of the Northwest Coast
        Indians. Saanichton: Hancock, 1973. 172 pp.

Pb 3236 -- Looking at Indian Art of the Northwest Coast. Van-
        couver: Douglas & McIntyre, 1979. 111 pp.

Gb 3237 -- Robert Davidson: Haida Printmaker. Vancouver:
        Douglas & McIntyre, 1979. 120 pp.

Ga 3238 Stones, bones, and skin: Ritual and Shamanic Art.
        artscanada, Nos. 184-187(Dec. 1973/Jan. 1974); rpt.
        Toronto: artscanada, 1977. 200 pp.

B 3239 Stott, Margaret A. Bella Coola Ceremony and Art. Ottawa:
        National Museum, Ethnology Service Mercury Series 21,
        1975. 153 pp.

B 3240 Sturtevant, William C., comp. Boxes and Bowls: Decor-
        ated Containers by Nineteenth-Century Haida, Tlingit,
        Bella Bella, and Tsimshian Indian Artists. Washington:
        Pub. for the Renwick Gallery of the National Collection
        of Fine Arts by the Smithsonian Institution Press, 1974.
        93 pp.

C 3241 Swinton, George. 'Artists from the Keewatin.' Canadian
        Art, 23(April 1966), 32-34.

B 3242 -- 'Eskimo Art Reconsidered.' artscanada, Nos. 162-163
        (Dec. 1971/Jan. 1972), pp. 85-94.

B 3243 -- 'Eskimo Art: Beyond the Mythological Past.' Art News
        77(Jan. 1978), 78-80.

C 3244 -- 'Eskimo Carving Today.' Beaver, Spring 1958, pp.
        40-47.

A 3245 -- Sculpture of the Eskimo. Toronto: McClelland & Stew-
        art, 1965; rev. 1972. 255 pp.

C 3246 Tagoona, Armand. Shadows. Ottawa: Oberon, 1975. 61 pp.

B 3247 Taylor, J. Garth. Netsilik Eskimo Material Culture.
        Oslo: Universitetsforlaget, 1974. 173 pp.

B 3248 Thompson, Judy. Preliminary Study of Traditional
        Kutchin Clothing in Museums. Ottawa: National Museum,
        Ethnology Service Mercury Series 1, 1972. 92 pp.

Folk Art and Material Culture

C 3249 Timberlake, Harold D. 'Eskimo Snow Houses.' CGJ, 76
(Mar. 1968), 102-7.

Gc 3250 Van de Velde, F. Canadian Eskimo Artifacts. Trans.
Yvette Mongeon. Ottawa: Can. Arctic Producers, 1970.
29 pp.

B 3251 Vastokas, Joan M. 'Continuities in Eskimo Graphic
Style.' artscanada, Nos. 162/163(1971-72), pp. 63-83.

C 3252 -- 'The Relation of Form to Iconography in Eskimo
Masks.' Beaver, Autumn 1967, pp. 26-31.

Ga 3253 Veillette, John, and Gary White. Early Indian Village
Churches: Wooden Frontier Architecture in British
Columbia. Vancouver: Univ. of B.C. Press, 1977. 195 pp.

C 3254 Ward, Philip. 'The State of Preservation of the Native
Heritage on the Pacific Northwest Coast.' Journal of
the Canadian Conservation Institute, 3(1978), 4-9.

A 3255 Wardwell, Helen. Objects of Bright Pride. Northwest
Coast Indian American Museum of Natural History. New
York: Center for Inter-American Relations & American
Federation of Arts, 1978. 128 pp.

C 3256 Warner, James A. 'Samuel Ash: Ojibway Artist.' Beaver,
Spring 1977, pp. 56-57.

C 3257 Washburn, Bradford. 'The Practical Igloo.' CGJ, 39
(Dec. 1949), 258-61.

C 3258 Waugh, F. W. 'Canadian Aboriginal Canoes.' Canadian
Field Naturalist, 33(May 1919), 23-33.

A 3259 -- Iroquois Food and Food Preparation. Ottawa: National
Museum, Memoir 86, 1916. 253 pp.

C 3260 Webster, J. H. 'Deerskin Clothing.' Beaver, Dec. 1949,
pp. 44-47.

C 3261 Weekes, Mary. 'Indian Beaded Belts.' Beaver, Sept.
1934, pp. 27-28.

B 3262 Wells, Oliver N. Salish Weaving Primitive and Modern.
Sardis, B.C.: Author, 1969. 36 pp.

P 3263 -- 'Salish Weaving: Return of an Ancient Art.'
Beautiful British Columbia, 11(Summer 1969), 35-39.

3264 Weltfish, Gene. 'Prehistoric North American Basketry
Techniques and Modern Distributions.' American Anthropologist, 32(1930), 454-95.

F 3265 Wherry, Joseph H. Indian Masks and Myths of the West.
New York: Funk and Wagnalls, 1969. 273 pp.

207

C 3266   Whitbred, Donald H. 'The Eskimo Violin.' Canadian
         Forum, 33(July 1953), 82-83.

C 3267   Williamson, Robert. 'The Spirit of Keewatin.' Beaver,
         Summer 1965, pp. 4-13. [Eskimo carvings.]

C 3268   Willis, A. R. 'Talking Sticks.' Beaver, June 1940,
         pp. 48-50.

C 3269   Willoughby, C. C. 'A New Type of Ceremonial Blanket
         from the Northwest Coast.' American Anthropologist,
         12(1910), 1-10.

C 3270   Wilson, Renate. 'Basket Makers of Mount Currie.'
         Beaver, Autumn 1964, pp. 26-33.

C 3271   Wintemberg, W. J. 'The Use of Shells by the Ontario
         Indians.' Annual Archeological Report, Ontario, 1907.
         90 pp.

C 3272   Wyndham-Lewis, Brian. 'Inukshuks and Inunguaks on Foxe
         Peninsula and the North Quebec Coast.' CGJ, 73(Sept.
         1966), 84-87.

B 3273   Zimmerly, David W. Contextual Studies of Material
         Culture. Ottawa: National Museum, Ethnology Service
         Mercury Series 43, 1978. 58 pp.

A 3274   -- Hooper Bay Kayak Construction. Ottawa: National
         Museum, Ethnology Service Mercury Series 53, 1979.
         118 pp.

         10E   Other Cultural Groups

P 3275   'About Backhouses, Little Houses or Whatchacallits.'
         Canadian-German Folklore, 7(1979), 171-73.

A 3276   Bird, Michael S. Ontario Fraktur--A Pennsylvania-German
         Folk Tradition in Early Canada. Toronto: Feheley, 1977.
         144 pp.

C 3277   Doering, J. Frederick. 'Note on the Dyeing of halb
         Leinich among the Pennsylvania-Dutch of Ontario.' JAF,
         52(1939), 124-25.

  3278   Donaldson, Joan. 'An Eisenhauer Portfolio.' artscanada,
         Nos. 230/231(Oct.-Nov. 1979), pp. 20-22.

C 3279   Dragon, R. Museum and Handicraft Program. Saskatoon:
         Ukrainian Women's Assoc., 1955. 16 pp.

C 3280   Fry, Olivia R. Ukrainian Designs. Ceramic Easter Eggs.
           Kelowna, B.C.: Author, 1974. 40 pp.

B 3281   Good, Reginald. Anna's Art. Toronto: Van Nostrand Rein-
           hold, 1976. 48 pp. [Pennsylvania Dutch.]

A 3282   Klymasz, Robert B. Continuity and Change: The Ukrainian
           Folk Heritage in Canada. Ottawa: CCFCS, 1974. 56 pp.

B 3283   -- We Still Live in Our Art. Ottawa: National Museum,
           1971. 18 pp.

C 3284   Kolbenhier, Eric, coll. Ukranian Bukovinian Cross-
           Stitch Embroidery. Windsor, Ont.: Sumner, 1974.
           Unpaged.

C 3285   Lehr, John C. 'Ukrainian Houses in Alberta.' Alberta
           Historical Review, 21(Autumn 1973), 9-15.

B 3286   -- Ukrainian Vernacular Architecture in Alberta. Edmon-
           ton: Alta. Culture Historical Resources Division, 1976.
           43 pp.

Gb 3287 Leonoff, Cyril E. The Architecture of Jewish Settle-
           ments in the Prairies, A Pictorial History. Winnipeg:
           Author, 1975. 48 pp.

C 3288   Mennonite Folk Art of Waterloo County. Waterloo: Univ.
           of Waterloo, 1966. [Exhibition catalogue.]

C 3289   Museum and Handicraft Program Ukrainian Women's
           Association of Canada 1927-1955. Edmonton: Ukrainian
           Women's Assoc., 1955.

A 3290   Musson, Patricia, Lynda Musson Nykor, and Martha
           Kuehner. Mennonite Furniture: The Ontario Tradition.
           Toronto: Lorimer, 1977. 96 pp.

C 3291   N.A.G. 'Ukrainian Easter Eggs.' ZHinochyj Svit, 1:4
           (1950), 6-8.

Gb 3292 Newlands, David. New Hamburg Pottery. Ottawa: National
           Museum, History Division Mercury Series 27, 1979.

C 3293   -- The New Hamburg Pottery, New Hamburg, Ontario 1854-
           1916. Waterloo: Wilfred Laurier Univ. Press, 1978.
           53 pp.

B 3294   Patterson, Nancy-Lou. 'The Iron Cross and the Tree of
           Life: German Alsatian Gravemarkers in Waterloo Region
           and Bruce County Roman Catholic Cemeteries.' Ontario
           History, 68(1979), 1-16.

B 3295   -- 'Mennonite Folk Art of Waterloo County.' Ontario
           History, 60(1968), 81-104.

A 3296   Patterson, Nancy-Lou. Swiss-German and Dutch-German
         Mennonite Traditional Art in the Waterloo Region,
         Ontario. Ottawa: National Museum, CCFCS Mercury Series
         27, 1979. 216 pp.

C 3297   Ruryk, Nancy R., ed. Ukrainian Embroidery Designs and
         Stitches. Winnipeg: Ukrainian Women's Assoc., n.d.
         130 pp.

C 3298   Shewchuk, Maria. 'Ukrainian Folk Embroidery.' ZHinochyj
         Svit, 14:2(1963), 16; 14:3(1963), 16; 14:4(1963), 13.

C 3299   Sichynsky, W. 'Ukrainian Easter Eggs.' Ukrainian Cana-
         dian Veterans' Assoc. Newsletter, 2:4(1954), 3, 5.

B 3300   Sutyla, Charles M. The Finnish Sauna in Manitoba.
         Ottawa: National Museum, CCFCS Mercury Series 24, 1977.
         112 pp.

F 3301   Tamosaitis, Antanas, and Anastasia Tamosaitis. Lithua-
         nian National Costume. Toronto: Lithuanian Folk Art
         Institute, 1979. 256 pp.

A 3302   Tyrchniewicz, Peggy. Ethnic Folk Costumes in Canada.
         Winnipeg: Hyperion, 1979. 229 pp.

P 3303   Verigin, Laura, and Zoe H. Gulley. Practical Doukhobor
         Cook Book/Selected Doukhobor and Quaker Recipes. Ross-
         land, B.C.: Miner, 1957.

Gb 3304 Wiseman, Adele. Old Woman at Play. Toronto: Clarke,
         Irwin, 1978. 148 pp. [Dolls.]

P 3305   Wismer, Helen. 'Folk Art of the Pennsylvania Deutsch.'
         Canadian-German Folklore, 7(1979), 137-44.

For 10A see also items 104, 109, 110, 119, 131, and 321.

For 10B, 21, 2138, 2295, and 2320.

For 10C, 5.

For 10D, 15, 17, 51, 55, 95, 102, 118, 228, 271, 283,
284, 294, 1951, 2411, 2416, 2423, 2424, 2430, 2443,
2448, 2450, 2456, 2464, 2472, 2473, 2483, 2517, 2519,
2520, 2521, 2526, 2534, 2535, 2537, 2547, 2548, 2569,
2571, 2579, 2597, 2610, 2617, 2626, 2636, 2639, 3749,
3754, 3757, 3761, 3770, 3772, 3778, 3780, 3793, 3796,
3798, 3803, 3820, 3835, 3842, 3860, 3861, and 3877.

For 10E, 2691, 2699, and 2758.

11 Biographies and Appreciations

11A Collectors and Scholars

Barbeau, C. Marius

3306 Anon. 'Ex-PM Prompted Dean of Folklore.' Calgary Herald, 9 Apr. 1959.

3307 Barbeau, C. Marius. 'My Life in Recording Songs and Stories of Old Quebec.' Canadian Red Cross/Junior, 37:6(1958), 10-11.

3308 -- 'My Life in Recording Songs and Stories of the Indians.' Canadian Red Cross/Junior, 37:7(1958), 14-15.

3309 Cass-Beggs, Barbara. 'Marius Barbeau--A Personal Recollection.' Come All Ye, 6(1977), 42-44.

*3310 Duff, Wilson. 'Contributions of Marius Barbeau to west coast ethnology.' Anthropologica, 6:1(1964), 63-96.

3311 Fowke, Edith. 'Marius Barbeau (1883-1969).' JAF, 82 (1969), 264-66.

3312 Katz, Israel J. 'Marius Barbeau, 1883-1969.' Ethnomusicology, 14(1970), 129-42.

3313 MacMillan, Ernest. 'Reminiscences of Marius Barbeau.' Musicanada, Apr. 1969, pp. 10-11, 15.

3314 -- 'Marius Barbeau: The Man, His Work.' Canadian Author & Bookman, 37(Winter 1962), 10-13.

3315 Preston, Richard J. 'C. Marius Barbeau and the History of Canadian Anthropology.' In The History of Canadian Anthropology. Ed. Jim Freedman. N.p.: Canadian Ethnology Society, 1976. Pp. 122-35.

*3316 Swayze, Nansi. Canadian Portraits: The Man Hunters. Toronto: Clarke, Irwin, 1960. Pp. 101-40.

Boas, Franz

3317 Lowie, Robert H. 'Franz Boas (1858-1942).' JAF, 57 (1944), 59-70.

Boulton, Laura

*3318 Boulton, Laura. The Music Hunter: The Autobiography of a Career. Garden City, NY: Doubleday, 1969. 513 pp.

Cass-Beggs, Barbara

3319 Dempsey, Lotta. 'Adventurous spirit in song and in person.' Toronto Star, 8 Oct. 1975, p. F2.

Alexander F. Chamberlain

3320 Boas, Franz. 'In Memoriam, A. F. Chamberlain.' JAF, 27 (1914), 326-27.

Cormier, Charlotte

3321 Mungall, Constance. 'Charlotte Cormier, Ethnomusicologist,' in 'Pattern Breakers of New Brunswick.' Chatelaine, July 1977, pp. 33, 50.

3322 Ruebsaat, Rika. 'Interview: Charlotte Cormier.' Canada Folk Bulletin, 2(Jan.-Feb. 1979), 3-13.

Creighton, Helen

3323 Cameron, [Silver] Donald. 'Thanks for the Memories.' Weekend Magazine, 28 Sept. 1974, pp. 11-13.

3324 Creighton, Helen. 'Capturing Folklore on Tape.' Canadian Author & Bookman, 46(Spring 1971), 3-4, 12.

*3325 -- A Life in Folklore. Toronto: McGraw-Hill Ryerson, 1975. 244 pp.

3326 Edward, Barry, and Nancy McGregor. 'Collecting the Lore of Maritime Folk.' Fugue, Dec. 1977, pp. 18-19, 27.

3327 Johnston, Richard. 'Tribute to Helen Creighton.' Canada Music Book, Autumn/Winter 1974, pp. 99-102.

3328 Lennox, Doug. 'Looking Back on a Satisfying Career.' Canadian Composer, No. 12(Apr. 1977), pp. 24-29.

3329 MacGorman, Harry R. 'Lady of the Legends: She Collects Ghosts for Kicks.' Nova Scotia Magazine, 1:1(1969), 15-16.

3340 Sclanders, Ian. 'She's Collecting Long Lost Songs.' Maclean's, 15 Sept. 1952, pp. 14-15, 54-57.

Biographies and Appreciations

Doyon-Ferland, Madeleine

3341 Thomas, Gerald. 'Madeleine Doyon-Ferland, folklorist, dies in January 1978.' Bulletin of the Folklore Studies Assoc. of Canada, 2(May 1978), 4-8.

Fauset, Arthur Huff

3342 Henderson, M. Carole [Carole Henderson Carpenter]. 'Arthur Huff Fauset--A Biographical Sketch.' In Black Gods of the Metropolis by Arthur Huff Fauset. Philadelphia: Univ. of Pennsylvania Press, 1971. Pp. 127-28.

Fowke, Edith

*3343 Donald, Betty. 'Edith Fulton Fowke.' In Profiles. Ed. Irma McDonough. Ottawa: Canadian Library Assoc., 1975. Pp. 69-72. Updated from In Review, 5(Autumn 1971), 5-7.

3344 Fowke, Edith. 'A Personal Odyssey and Personal Prejudices.' Bulletin of the Folklore Studies Assoc.of Canada, 2(Sept.-Nov. 1978), 7-13.

3345 Fulford, Robert. 'The Pleasures of the Folksong Collector: Edith Fowke's Determined Vocation.' Toronto Star, 1 June 1974.

3346 Harrington, Lyn. 'She Merits HER Medal.' Canadian Author & Bookman, 46(Fall 1970), 7, 20.

3347 McFadden, David. 'Twenty Years of Folk Song Collecting.' Quill & Quire, May 1977, pp. 5, 8.

*3348 Weihs, Fred, ed. 'Interview: Edith Fowke.' Canada Folk Bulletin, 1(Nov.-Dec. 1978), 4-12.

Gibbon, John Murray

3349 Anon. 'CPR Fostering Canadian Music.' Calgary Herald, 13 July 1929.

3350 -- 'Developing Canada's Immigrant Culture.' Edmonton Journal, 15 Dec. 1928.

3351 -- 'Ends 40 Years of Activity.' Albertan, 30 June 1945.

Halpern, Ida

3352 Cameron, Silver Donald. 'The Collector: And the music that nearly died lives on.' Weekend Magazine, 6 Dec.

1975. Rpt. in Seasons in the Rain. Toronto: McClelland & Stewart, 1978.

3353 Gothe, Jurgen. 'Ida Halpern Enters Sacred Indian World.' Fugue, Dec. 1977, pp. 15-17, 28.

Hill-Tout, Charles

3354 Barbeau, C. Marius. 'Charles Hill-Tout (1859-1944).' TRSC, 39(1945), sec. 2, pp. 89-92.

Jenness, Diamond

3355 Fowke, Edith. 'Diamond Jenness (1886-1969).' JAF, 83 (1970), 350.

*3356 Swayze, Nansi. Canadian Portraits: The Man Hunters. Toronto: Clarke, Irwin, 1960. Pp. 3-36.

Karpeles, Maud

*3357 Bronson, Bertrand H. 'Maud Karpeles (1886-1976).' JAF, 90(1977), 455-64.

3358 Kennedy, Douglas. 'Obituary: Dr. Maud Pauline Karpeles, O.B.E., 1885-1976.' Folk Music Journal (England), 3 (1977), 292-94.

3359 Wachsmann, Klaus. 'Maud Karpeles (1885-1976).' 1976 Yearbook of the International Folk Music Council, 8 (1977), 9-11.

Lemieux, Germain

3360 Keir, Robert. 'Priest Works to Save Folklore.' Globe and Mail, 4 July, 1966, p. 17.

3361 'Race Against Time.' Ottawa Journal, 8 Nov. 1966.

MacMillan, Ernest C.

3362 Barbeau, C. Marius. 'MacMillan and Canadian Folk Music.' Music Across Canada, July-Aug. 1963, pp. 37, 42.

3363 Johnston, Richard. 'Tribute to Sir Ernest MacMillan.' Canada Music Book, Autumn/Winter 1973, pp. 97-98.

3364 MacKelcan, Fred R. 'Sir Ernest MacMillan.' Queen's Quarterly, 43(1936-1937), 408-14.

Mackenzie, W. Roy

3365 Creighton, Helen. 'W. Roy Mackenzie, Pioneer.' CFMSN, 2(1967), 15-22.

Biographies and Appreciations

*3366   Laws, G. Malcolm, Jr. 'W. Roy Mackenzie, 1883-1957.'
        Foreword in Ballads and Sea Songs from Nova Scotia
        by W. Roy Mackenzie. Rev. ed., Hatboro, PA: Folklore
        Associates, 1963. Pp. i-ix.

Manny, Louise

3367   Daye, Vera L. 'Song for Beaverbrook.' Saturday Night,
        18 Oct. 1949, pp. 32-33.

3668   Murphy, Margaret R. 'The Lady in the Library.' Atlan-
        tic Advocate, 69(July 1979), 21-22.

3669   Sclanders, Ian. 'She Saves the Strangest Songs.' May-
        fair, Dec. 1953, pp. 65-69.

Mills, Alan

3370   Cadoret, Charlotte. 'In Memoriam.' CFMSN, 12:3(1977),
        23-25.

3371   Gesser, Sam. 'Alan Mills--The Voice of Canadian Folk
        Music.' Sing Out!, 10(Dec.-Jan. 1960), 4-7.

Rudnyc'kyj, Jaroslav B.

*3372   Mandryka, M. I. Bio-bibliography of J. B. Rudnyc'kyj.
        Winnipeg: Ukrainian Free Academy of Arts and Sciences,
        1961. 72 pp.

Teit, James A.

3373   Boas, Franz. 'Obituary of James A. Teit.' JAF, 36(1923),
        102-3.

Thomas, Philip J.

3374   Robinson, Martha. 'Search for B.C. folklore provides
        tuneful vocation.' Vancouver Sun, 19 Oct. 1974.

Wintemberg, William J.

*3375   Swayze, Nansi. Canadian Portraits: The Man Hunters.
        Toronto: Clarke, Irwin, 1960. Pp. 143-78.

11B   Folk Artists and Informants

3376   Baird, Ron. 'Man with a Vision.' Beaver, Spring 1962,
        pp. 4-10. [George Clutesi.]

3377   Barbeau, C. Marius. 'Blind Folk Singer.' Dalhousie
        Review, 33(Autumn 1953), 177-86.

3378 Barbeau, C. Marius. 'The Blind Singer.' Kingdom of the Saguenay. Toronto: Macmillan, 1936. Pp. 89-103. [Louis 'L'Aveugle' Simard.]

3379 Carter, Anthony. 'In Memory of Mungo Martin.' Beaver, Spring 1971, pp. 44-45.

3380 Carter, Wilf. The Yodelling Cowboy: Montana Slim from Nova Scotia. Toronto: Ryerson, 1961. 104 pp.

3381 Creighton, Helen. Folksongs from Southern New Brunswick. Ottawa: National Museum, 1971. (Angelo Dornan et al.)

*3382 -- Maritime Folk Songs. Toronto: Ryerson, 1962. [Louis Boutilier, Angelo Dornan, Amos Jollimore, Fred Redden, William Riley, et al.]

3383 -- 'Nathan Hatt of Nova Scotia.' Sing Out, 13(Feb.-Mar. 1963), 23-25.

*3384 -- 'The Songs of Nathan Hatt.' Dalhousie Review, 32 (1953), 59-66.

3385 Doerflinger, William M. 'Satirists of the Sawdust Country.' Shantymen and Shantyboys. Toronto: Macmillan, 1951 (rpt. as Songs of the Sailors and Lumbermen, 1973.) Pp. 253-69. [Larry Gorman, George and John Calhoun, et al.]

3386 Evans, John. 'Jean Carignan, Traditional Fiddler.' English Dance & Song, 32(1970), 125-26.

3387 Fowke, Edith. Booklet with record, O. J. Abbott: Irish and British Songs from the Ottawa Valley. Folkways FM 4051, pp. 1-2.

3388 -- 'O. J. Abbott: The Passing of a Great Traditional Singer.' Sing Out, 12(Summer 1962), 15-17.

3389 -- Booklet with record, Tom Brandon of Peterborough, Ontario, Folk Legacy FSC 10, pp. 1-3.

3390 -- Liner notes, record, LaRena Clark: Canadian Garland. Topic 12T140.

3391 -- Booklet with record, Far Canadian Fields. Leader LEE 4057. [O. J. Abbott, Robert J. Campbell, Captain Charles Cates, Jim Doherty, Mrs. Arlington Fraser, Lennox Gavan, John Leahy, Albert Simms, Emerson Woodcock.]

3392 -- Booklet with record, Songs of the Great Lakes. Folkways FM 4018, pp. 2-3. [Stanley Bâby, C. H. J. Snider.]

Biographies and Appreciations

*3393   Fowke, Edith. <u>Traditional Singers and Songs from Ontario</u>.
        Hatboro, PA: Folklore Associates, 1965. [O. J. Abbott,
        Mrs. Arlington Fraser, Tom Brandon, Mrs. LaRena Clark,
        Dave McMahon, Emerson Woodcock, Jim Doherty, C. H. J.
        Snider, Albert Simms, Stanley James.]

 3394   Gillis, James D. <u>A Little Sketch of My Life</u>. Halifax:
        Allen, 1915.

 3395   Gilmour, Clyde. 'The Moody Minstrel.' <u>Maclean's</u>, 15 May
        1948, pp. 24, 52-55. [Ed. McCurdy.]

*3396   Grover, Carrie. <u>A Heritage of Songs</u>. Bethel, ME: n.p.,
        n.d.; rpt. Norwood, PA: Norwood, 1973. Pp. 1-3.

 3397   Hawthorn, Audrey. 'Mungo Martin, Artist and Craftsman.'
        <u>Beaver</u>, Summer 1964, pp. 18-23.

 3398   'Hector Carmichael, A Maker of Songs.' <u>Cape Breton's
        Magazine</u>, No. 7(1974), pp. 15-17.

 3399   Hresko, Phil. 'Jean Carignan.' Leaflet with record,
        Philo 2001.

*3400   Ives, Edward D. <u>Joe Scott, The Woodsman-Songmaker</u>.
        Urbana: Univ. of Illinois Press, 1979. 473 pp.

*3401   -- <u>Larry Gorman: The Man Who Made the Songs</u>. Blooming-
        ton: Indiana Univ. Press, 1964. 259 pp.

*3402   -- <u>Lawrence Doyle, The Farmer Poet of Prince Edward
        Island</u>. Orono: Univ. of Maine, 1971. 269 pp.

 3403   -- 'The Life and Work of Larry Gorman: A Preliminary
        Report.' <u>Western Folklore</u>, 19(1965), 17-24.

 3404   Lanken, Dane. 'Farewell of a Genius.' <u>Fanfare</u>, 23 Nov.
        1977, p. 3. [Jean Carignan.]

 3405   'Le Crimo Speaks.' <u>Cape Breton's Magazine</u>, No. 1(1972),
        pp. 3-4, 24.

*3406   Mackenzie, W. Roy. <u>The Quest of the Ballad</u>. Princeton:
        Princeton Univ. Press, 1919. [Bob Langille, Dick Hinds,
        et al.]

 3407   MacLeod, Margaret Arnett. 'Bard of the Prairies.'
        <u>Beaver</u>, Spring 1956, pp. 20-25. [Pierre Falcon.]

 3408   -- <u>Songs of Old Manitoba</u>. Toronto: Ryerson, 1960.
        [Pierre Falcon, Louis Riel, et al.]

 3409   Manny, Louise. 'Larry Gorman--Miramichi Balladist.'
        <u>Maritime Advocate and Busy East</u>, 40(Oct. 1949), 5-15.

3410 Manny, Louise. 'Wilmot MacDonald.' Northeast Folklore, 4(1962), 3-4.

*3411 Manny, Louise, and Edward D. Ives. Booklet with record, Marie Hare of Strathadam, New Brunswick, Canada, Folk Legacy FSC 10, pp. 5-6, 9-11.

*3412 Manny, Louise, and J. Reginald Wilson. Songs of Miramichi. Fredericton: Brunswick, 1968. [Larry Gorman, Nick Underhill, Joe Scott, et al.]

*3413 Mercer, Paul, ed. The Ballads of Johnny Burke. St. John's: Nfld. Historical Society, 1974. Introduction.

3414 Murphy, Michael P. 'The Balladeers of Newfoundland.' Atlantic Guardian 13(Sept.-Oct. 1956), 16-23.

3415 -- 'The Balladeers of Newfoundland.' Daily News, St. John's, 27 July 1966, p. 8; 18 Oct. 1966, p. 9; 16 Nov. 1966, p. 6. [Johnny Burke, James Murphy, Michael Power, Johnny Quigley.]

3416 Sellick, Lester B. Canada's Don Messer. Don Mills: BMI Canada, 1955. 170 pp.

*3417 Szwed, John. 'Paul E. Hall: A Newfoundland Song-Maker and His Community of Songs.' Folksongs and Their Makers by H. Glassie, E. D. Ives, and J. F. Szwed. Bowling Green, OH: Bowling Green Univ. Popular Press, 1970. Pp. 147-69.

3418 Vanderburgh, Rosamond M. I am Nokomis, too: the biography of Verna Patronella Johnston. Don Mills: General, c. 1977. 247 pp.

3419 Wareham, Wilfred, and Al Pittman. 'A Tribute: Malcolm (Mack) Masters: 1909-1977.' Culture & Tradition, 3 (1978), 122-24.

*3420 Wells, Evelyn. The Ballad Tree. New York: Ronald, 1950. Pp. 305-8. [Carrie Grover.]

For 11A see also items 6, 20, 27, 94, 192, 223, 294, 925, 937-939, 1169, 1187, and 2633.

For 11B, 469, 906, 925, 981, 1144-1148, 1188, 3853, and 3864.

12 Records

The first section by traditional performers is as complete
as possible; the second section, by professional or semi-
professional performers, is more selective. It includes most
records devoted entirely to Canadian folk music and some that
have a substantial portion of traditional material. Musicians
who have produced many records (e.g., Ward Allen, John Allan
Cameron, Joseph Cormier, Andy Dejarlis, Wilf Doyle, Winston
"Scotty" Fitzgerald, Rudy Meeks, Graham Townsend) are repre-
sented by a sampling only.

All records are 12" LPs unless otherwise marked.

   12A   Field Recordings (Traditional Performers)

3421   Abbott, O. J. Irish and British Songs from the Ottawa
       Valley. Recorded by Edith Fowke. Folkways FM 4051,
       1961.

3422   An Anthology of North American Indian and Eskimo Music.
       Compiled by Moses Asch. Folkways FE 4541, 1973.

3423   Canadian Folk Songs. Columbia World Library of Folk and
       Primitive Music, Vol. 8. Ed. Marius Barbeau from col-
       lections of the National Museum and National Film
       Board, with contributions by Jean Gabus, Museum of Neu-
       châtel, and Ida Halpern. Columbia SL 211, 1954.

3424   Clark, LaRena. Authentic Canadian Folk Symbol. Clark
       Records, LCS 108, 1978.

3425   -- Canada at Turn of the Sod. Clark LCS 110, 1979.

3426   -- Canada's Traditional Queen of Song. Clark LCS 107,
       1978.

3427   -- Canadian Folk Sound with LaRena. Clark LCS 109,
       1979.

   219

3428 Clark, LaRena. Family Legend in Song. LCS 106, 1978.

3429 -- Heritage of Folk Songs. Clark QCS 1311, 1977.

3430 -- LaRena Clark: Canadian Garland. Topic 12T140, 1965.

3431 -- Songs of an Ontario Family. Clark QC 903, c. 1968.

3432 Come Hell or High Water. Songs of the Buchans Miners. Breakwater 1001, 1977.

3433 A Cry from the Earth: Music of the North American Indians. Edited by John Bierhorst. Folkways FC 7777, 1979.

3434 The Doukhobors of British Columbia. Recorded by Barbara Bachovzeff. Folkways FR 8972, 1962.

3435 The Eskimos of Hudson Bay and Alaska. Recorded by Laura Boulton. Folkways FE 4444, 1954.

3436 Far Canadian Fields: Companion to The Penguin Book of Canadian Folk Songs. Recorded by Edith Fowke. Leader LEE 4057, 1975.

3437 Folk Music from Nova Scotia. Recorded by Helen Creighton. Folkways FM 4006, 1956.

3438 Folk Songs of Ontario. Recorded by Edith Fowke. Folkways FM 4005, 1958.

3439 Folksongs of Saskatchewan. Recorded by Barbara Cass-Beggs. Folkways FE 4312, 1963.

3440 Folksongs of the Miramichi. Recorded at the 1959 Miramichi Folk Festival under the direction of Louise Manny. Folkways FE 4053, 1962.

3441 Game Songs of French Canada. Sung by Montreal school children. Recorded by Sam Gesser. Folkways FC 7214, 1956.

3442 Guinchard, Rufus. Newfoundland Fiddler. Breakwater 1002, c. 1978.

3443 Indian Music of the Canadian Plains. Recorded by Kenneth Peacock. Folkways FE 4464, 1965.

3444 Indian Music of the Pacific Northwest Coast. Recorded by Ida Halpern. 2 discs. Folkways FE 4523, 1970.

3445 Iroquois Social Dance Songs. Sung by George Buck, Raymond Spragge, Jacob E. Thomas, and W. G. Spittal. 3 discs. Iroqraft Q.C. 727-28-29.

3446 Lumbering Songs from the Ontario Shanties. Recorded by Edith Fowke. Folkways FM 4052, 1961.

3447 Marie Hare of Strathadam, New Brunswick. Notes by Louise Manny and Edward D. Ives. Folk-Legacy FSC-9, 1962.

3448 Maritime Folk Songs. Recorded by Helen Creighton. Folkways FE 4307, 1962.

3449 Men of the North Are We. Produced by Don and Anne Hill. London, Ont., 1975.

3450 The Music of Cape Breton. Recorded by John Shaw and Rosemary Hutchison. Vol. 1: The Gaelic Tradition in Cape Breton; Vol. 2: Cape Breton Scottish Fiddle. Topic 12T353; 12T354, 1978.

3451 Music of the Algonkians. Recorded by Owen Jones, Jr. Folkways FE 4253.

3452 Nootka: Indian Music of the Pacific Northwest Coast. Recorded by Ida Halpern. Folkways FE 4524, 1974.

3453 Nova Scotia Folk Music from Cape Breton. Recorded by Diane Hamilton. Elektra EKL 23, 1955.

3454 Ontario Ballads and Folksongs. Recorded by Edith Fowke. Prestige/International INT 25014 [1962].

3455 Six Nations Singers. Iroquois Social Music. Music Gallery Editions MGE 16, 1979.

3456 Songs and Dances of Quebec. Recorded by Sam Gesser. Folkways FW 6951, 1956.

3457 Songs and Dances of the Great Lakes Indians. Recorded by Gertrude Kurath. Folkways FM 4003, 1956.

3458 Songs from Cape Breton Island. Recorded by Sidney Robertson Cowell. Folkways FE 4450, 1955.

3459 Songs from the Iroquois Longhouse. Recorded by William N. Fenton at Grand River, Brantford, Ont. Library of Congress AAFS L6, 1942.

3460 Songs from the Outports of Newfoundland. Recorded by MacEdward Leach. Folkways FE 4075, 1966.

3461 Songs of French Canada. Recorded by Laura Boulton, Sam Gesser, and Carmen Roy. Folkways FE 4482, 1957.

3462 Songs of the Great Lakes. Recorded by Edith Fowke. Folkways FM 4018, 1964.

3463 Songs of the Nootka and Quileute. Recorded by Frances Densmore. Library of Congress AAFS L32, 1953.

3464 Sur la Côte Nord: Folklore Music of Northern Quebec. Music Gallery Editions MGE 17, 1979.

3465 Tom Brandon of Peterborough, Ontario. Recorded by
      Edith Fowke. Folk-Legacy FSC-10, 1963.

3466 Ukrainian Christmas Songs. Recorded by Laura Boulton
      in Manitoba. Sung by choral groups. Folkways FW 6828,
      1956.

3467 'When Johnny Went Ploughin' for Kearon' and other
      Traditional P.E.I. Folksongs. Sung by Tommy Banks and
      John Cousins. P.E.I. Heritage Foundation, 1976.

      12B Other Recordings

3468 Allen, Ward. Best of Ward Allen. GRT 9230-1031.

3469 Baillargeon, Hélène, and Alan Mills. Chansons d'Acadie
      (10"). Folkways FW 6923, 1956.

3470 -- and -- Duet Songs of French Canada (10"). Folkways
      FW 6918, 1955.

3471 Baillargeon, Hélène, with Montreal children. Christmas
      Carols of French Canada (Chants de Nöel du Canada
      Français) (10"). Folkways FW 7229, 1956.

3472 Barbeau, C. Marius. My Life in Recording Canadian-
      Indian Folklore. Folkways FG 3502, 1957.

3473 Barde. Direction DLP.-10.010.

3474 The Beatons of Mabou: Marches, Jigs, Strathspeys and
      Reels of the Highland Scot. Rounder 7011.

3475 Bell, Donald. Folk Songs of Canada. CBC SM 168, 1971.

3476 -- Folk Songs from Prince Edward Island. CBC SM 259.

3477 Benoit, Emile. Emile's Dream. Quay CS-7932, 1979.

3478 Blondahl, Omar. Down to the Sea Again. Rodeo RLP 7,
      1956.

3479 -- The Great Seal Hunt of Newfoundland. Rodeo RLP 80,
      1959.

3480 -- Once Again for Newfoundland. Melbourne AMLP 4007,
      1967.

3481 -- The Roving Newfoundlander. Banff RBS 1142, 1959.

3482 -- The Saga of Newfoundland in Song. Rodeo RLP 5,
      1955.

3483 -- Songs of Sea and Shore. Arc A537, c. 1959.

3484 Blondahl, Omar. <u>A Visit to Newfoundland</u>. Rodeo RLP 34, 1958.

3485 '<u>La Bolduc</u>.' Philo 2009, 1975.

3486 Boudreault, Louis. <u>Old Time Fiddler of Chicoutimi, Quebec</u>. Voyageur VRLP 323-5, 1979.

3487 Briand, Elmer. <u>The Cape Breton Fiddle of Elmer Briand</u>. Celtic SCX 56.

3488 Brown, Johnny. <u>Fiddling Old Time & Country</u>. London EB 64.

3489 Bruneau, Philippe. <u>Danses Pour Veillées Canadiennes</u>. Accordion. Philo 2006, 1975.

3490 -- <u>Philippe Bruneau</u>. Philo 2003, 1973.

3491 Cameron, John Allan. <u>Here Comes John Allan Cameron</u>. Apex AL7 1645.

3492 Campbell, John. <u>Cape Breton Violin Music</u>. Rounder 7003, 1977.

3493 <u>Canada's Favourite Folksongs for Kids</u>. Berandol 9031, 1978.

3494 <u>Canadian Folk Songs: A Centennial Collection</u>. Nine records sung by Yves Albert, Hélène Baillargeon, Louise Forestier, Charles Jordan, Tom Kines, Jacques Labrecque, Alan Mills, Diane Oxner, Jean Price, Raoul Roy and Joyce Sullivan. RCA Victor/CBC CS 100, 1967.

3495 <u>The Cape Breton Symphony: Fiddle</u>. Glencoe GMI 1001. 1978.

3496 <u>Cape Breton Violins</u>. Celtic CX 1.

3497 Carignan, Jean. <u>French-Canadian Fiddle Songs</u>. Legacy 120.

3498 -- <u>Hommage à Joseph Allard</u>. Philo 2012, 1976.

3499 -- <u>Jean Carignan</u>. Philo 2001, 1973.

3500 -- <u>Jean Carignan Plays the Music of Coleman, Morrison and Skinner</u>. Philo 2018. 1978.

3501 -- <u>Old-Time Fiddle Tunes</u>. Folkways FG 3531.

3502 -- '<u>Le Violoneux</u>.' Totem TO-9221, 1978.

3503 Carl Tapscott Singers. <u>Songs of Newfoundland</u>. RCA KXL 1-0092, 1975.

3504 Les Chanteurs d'Acadie. <u>Folklore Acadien</u>. Rodeo RLP 30.

3505 Chapman, Jimmy. _Two Sides Down East & Southern_. Banff RBS 1160.

3506 Charlebois, Jeanne d'Arc. _Hommage à Madame Bolduc_. Philo 2014, 1975.

3507 Chisholm, Angus. _The Early Recordings of Angus Chisholm_. Shenachie 14001.

3508 La Chorale de l'Université Saint-Joseph. _Folklore Canadien (Canadian Folksongs)_. Columbia FL 234.

3509 Cremo, Lee. _Champion Fiddler_. Liberty LM 903.

3510 -- _Lee Cremo_. Audat 477-9050.

3511 Christl, Margaret. _Jockey to the Fair_. Woodshed WS 009, 1978.

3512 Christl, Margaret, and Ian Robb with Grit Laskin. _'The Barley Grain for Me' and other traditional songs found in Canada_. Folk Legacy FSC 62, 1976.

3513 CJON Glee Club. _Newfoundland Folk Songs_. Rodeo RLP 83, 1955; and RLP 84, 1956.

3514 Cormier, Joseph. _The Dances Down Home_. Rounder 7004.

3515 -- _Scottish Violin Music from Cape Breton Island_. Rounder 7001.

3516 Dawson, Peter. _Old Country Fiddle Tunes_. Arc AS 835.

3517 Dejarlis, Andy. _Backwoods Fiddle Tunes_. London EBX 4118.

3518 Dobson, Bonnie. _Bonnie Dobson_. Argo ZFB 79, 1972.

3519 _The Dorymen_. Paragon ALS 321.

3520 Doucet, Tom. _I Used to Play Some Pretty Tough Tunes_. Rounder 7010.

3521 Doyle, Wilf. _Traditional Jigs and Reels of Newfoundland_. Rodeo RLP 10, 1956.

3522 Festival Singers of Canada. _Six Canadian Folk Songs_. CBC SM 274.

3523 Fitzgerald, Winston 'Scotty.' _Canada's Scottish Fiddler_. Celtic CX 17.

3524 -- _The Music of Cape Breton_. Canadian Cavalcade 2002.

3525 Gillis, Wilfred. _Arisaig: Violin Music of the Scot_. Celtic CX 45.

3526 The Great Canadian Fiddle. Eleanor, Graham, and Fred Townsend, Maurice Bolyer. Springwater S6, 1976.

3527 Hampson, Sharon, Lois Lilienstein, and Bram Morrison. One Elephant, Deux Elephants. Elephant LFN 78-01.

3528 Hemsworth, Wade. Songs of the Canadian North Woods (10"). Folkways FW 6821, 1955.

3529 Hibbs, Harry. Somewhere at Sea. Caribou CCLP 7004, c. 1971.

3530 Holland, Jerry. Jerry Holland. Rounder 7008, 1976.

3531 Ian and Sylvia. Northern Journey. Vanguard VRS 9154, 1963.

3532 James, Karen. Karen James. Folkways FW 3549, 1961.

3533 Jardine, Kevin. Newfoundland, My Home. Marathon MS 2115, 1972.

3534 Jigs and Reels. Music by Per's Four. Folkways FW 8826, 1960.

3535 Kines, Tom. Folk Songs of Canada. RCA Victor PC/PCS 1014.

3536 -- An Irishman in North Americay. Folkways FG 3522, 1962.

3537 Labrecque, Jacques. Folk Songs of French Canada. Folkways FG 3560, 1957.

3538 Lamb, Grant. Tunes from Home. Voyageur VRLP 312-S.

3539 Landry, Henry. Henry Landry. Philo 2002, 1973.

3540 Levesque, Ernie. Canadian Square Dance. Rodeo RBS 1274.

3541 McCurdy, Ed. Folk Songs of the Canadian Maritimes. Whitehall LP 850.

3542 -- Homeward Bound, A Selection of Canadian Folklore, Rodeo RLP 102.

3543 MacDonald, C. F. Cape Breton Pipe Music. Fiddler Records.

3544 MacDonald, Dan R. Dan R. MacDonald. Celtic CX 28.

3545 MacDonald, Little Jack. The Bard of Scottish Fiddling. Celtic CX 23.

3546 MacInnis, Dan Joe. The Cape Breton Fiddle of Dan Joe MacInnis. Rodeo RBS 1066.

3547 -- Scottish Canadian Fiddle Music. Banff RBS 247.

3548 MacIsaac, Joe. The Sound of Cape Breton. Arc A527.

3549 MacKenzie, Carl. Welcome to Your Feet Again. Rounder 7005, 1977.

3550 MacLean, Joe. Old Time Scottish Fiddle. Banff RBS 1246.

3551 MacLellan, Theresa, and Marie. A Trip to Mabou Ridge. Rounder 7006.

3552 MacLeod, Calum I. Scottish Gaelic Mouth Music. Rodeo RBS 128 and 152.

3553 MacPhee, Doug. Cape Breton Piano. Rounder 7009.

3554 Maple Sugar: Songs of Early Canada. Univ. of Guelph Folk Choir, with Stompin' Tom Connors, Harry Hibbs, Eleanor Moorehead. 2 discs. Springwater Sl/2, 1973.

3555 Meeks, Rudy. Canadian Fiddle Sound. Mariposa 1189M.

3556 -- Fiddles of Shelburne. Mariposa 1364M.

3557 The Men of the Deeps. 'Coal-busting songs by a miners' chorus.' Directed by John C. O'Donnell. Waterloo Music CSPS 898, 1975.

3558 Men of the Deeps 'II'. Waterloo WR7, 1977.

3559 Menard, Joe, Pat, Paul. The Three Best Fiddlers in the North. Bonanza B 29571.

3560 Mills, Alan. Canada's Story in Song. 2 discs. Folkways FW 3000, 1960.

3561 -- Folk Songs of French Canada (10"). Folkways FW 6929, 1952.

3562 -- Folk Songs of Newfoundland (10"). Folkways FW 6831, 1953.

3563 -- Folk Songs of Newfoundland. Folkways FW 8771, 1958.

3564 -- O Canada--A History in Song. Folkways FW 3001, 1956.

3565 -- Songs of the Maritimes. Folkways FW 8744, 1959.

3566 Mills, Alan, and Jean Carignan. Songs, Fiddle Tunes, and a Folktale from Canada. Folkways FG 3532, 1961.

3567 Mitchell, Gerald. Songs of Labrador. Horizon HS 101.

3568 Moorehead, Eleanor. Canadian Queen of the Fiddle. Dominion 93071.

3569 Mooring, Johnny. Champion Fiddler. Banff SBS 5413.

3570 Nolan, Dick. Atlantic Lullaby. Arc A627, c. 1963.

3571 Nolan, Dick. Be True Newfoundlanders. Arc ACS 6024, c. 1968.

3572 -- I'se the B'y What Catches Da Fish. Arc AS 694, 1966.

3573 -- Lukey's Boat. Arc AS 810, c. 1968.

3574 Okun, Milt. I Sing of Canada (10"). Stinson SLP 71.

3575 Old Time Couple Dances. Bob Arbuckle, Verner Mikkelson, and N. Roy Clifton. Folkways FW 8827, 1961.

3576 Orain Cheap Breatainn (Songs of Cape Breton). Celtic CS 38.

3577 Oxner, Diane. Traditional Folk Songs of Nova Scotia. Rodeo RBS 1142. [From the Helen Creighton Collection.]

3578 Peacock, Kenneth. Songs and Ballads of Newfoundland. Folkways FG 3505, 1956.

3579 Phillips, Stu. Visit Old Quebec. Rodeo RLP 20.

3580 Pinsent, Gordon. Roots. Arc ACS 5027, c. 1968.

3581 Poirier, Eddy. Fiddling in the Cape Breton Style. Marathon BT 9001.

3582 Ryan's Fancy. Newfoundland Drinking Songs. Audat 9024.

3583 Robichaud, Gerry. Traditional Dance Tunes from New Brunswick. Fiddler 002.

3584 Rodgers, Frankie. Real Old Time Fiddling. Point P-232.

3585 Roy-Villandre, Adrienne. Canada 100: Indian Folk Songs of Canada. Polydor CP 5002, 1967.

3586 St. John's Extension Choir of Memorial University. Newfoundlanders Sing Songs of their Homeland. RCA Victor CC 1024, 1966.

3587 St. Pierre, Simon. The Joys of Quebec. Revonah 915.

3588 Sally Go Round the Sun. McClelland & Stewart, 1970. [Children's songs.]

3589 Salute to Cape Breton Island. Celtic CX 18. [Fiddle tunes and mouth music.]

3590 Saturday Night Square Dance. Marathon MM 76007, 1973.

3591 16 Great Canadian Fiddlers. Rodeo RBS 1263.

3592 16 Great Folk Songs by Canada's Top Folk Singers. Banff RBS 1133.

3593 Slane, Charlie. 'Miramichi'--Folk Songs of New Brunswick. Miramichi Pioneer Production--C. Slane, 1973.

3594 La Société de la Chorale Bach de Montréal. Mon Canada:
French Canadian Folk Songs. Vox PL 11.860, 1958.

3595 Souvenir Album of Gaelic Mod. Celtic CS 15.

3596 Square Dances with Calls. N. Roy Clifton and Per's
Four. Folkways FW 8825, 1959.

3597 Sullivan, Joyce, and Charles Jordan. Folk Songs of
Canada. Hallmark/Waterloo CS 3, 1955.

3598 Terra Novans. We'll Rant and We'll Roar. TN 1001,
c. 1966.

3599 Tom, Jim and Garth. Songs of Newfoundland. Banff RBS
1252.

3600 Townsend, Eleanor. Lark of the Morning. Condor 977-
1466.

3601 Townsend, Graham. Classics of Irish, Scottish, &
French-Canadian Fiddling. Rounder 7007, 1978.

3602 -- Le Violon/The Fiddle. Rounder 7002, 1978.

3603 Travellers, The. Across Canada with the Travellers.
Hallmark CS-7.

3604 -- A Century of Song. Arc A261, 1967. [Canadian labour
songs.]

3605 Triggs, Stanley G. Bunkhouse and Forecastle Songs of
the Northwest. Folkways FG 3569, 1961.

3606 Walsh, Ray. Favorite Reels and Jigs of Newfoundland.
Arc AS 691, c. 1966.

3607 White, John. Voice of Newfoundland. International Artists 1A 3014, c. 1966.

3608 William McCauley Choir. Canadian Folk Songs. Columbia
FL 226.

3609 -- Nöel à Québec. Columbia FL 207.

3610 Williams, Edison. The Roving Newfoundlander. Audat 477-
9006, 1972.

3611 Wilmot, John. Scottish and Irish Fiddle Tunes. Point
P-234.

3612 Zelkin, Alexander, and Denise Berard. La Belle Province: Quebec. Monitor MFS-714.

13 Films

Few films deal directly with Canadian folklore. Most of the relevant titles, especially those dealing with the native people, portray folkways while a number of others have only limited folklore content. Although the list is fairly extensive, many of the films are, then, only of marginal interest. Some considered particularly valuable for folklore studies are asterisked, and those especially suitable for children are marked Y. Where the title is undescriptive, the subject is indicated in brackets.

All films are in colour unless listed as black and white (B/W), and all are National Film Board productions unless otherwise noted. Length is given to the nearest minute, and producers of independent films are named.

3613　Age of the Beaver. 17 min., 1952.

3614　Age of the Buffalo. 14 min., 1964.

3615　And When Their Time Had Come. 45 min., c. 1972. B/W. Conference of Mennonites in Canada.

Y 3616　Angotee: Story of an Eskimo Boy. 31 min., 1953.

3617　Asivaqtiin (The Hunters). 13 min., 1977.

3618　Attiuk. 29 min., 1963. [Montagnais drum dance.]

3619　Barkerville Days. 14 min., 1974. Ed Cesar. Canadian Filmmakers' Distribution Centre. [B.C. pioneers.]

*3620　Behind the Masks. 37 min., 1973. [Indian masks explained by Levi-Strauss.]

3621　Beluga Days. 15 min., 1968. [Whale hunting.]

3622　Black Creek Pioneer Village. 22 min., 1966. Morland-Thatchford.

3623　Blackfoot People: Siksikai-Kwan. 14 min., 1976. Ed Cesar. Can. Filmmakers' Distribution Centre.

3624 Bluenose Ghosts. 22 min., 1975. N.S. Ministry of Tourism.

3625 Canadians Can Dance. 22 min., 1966. [Canadian National Exhibition, amateur folk dance groups.]

3626 Caribou Hunters. 18 min., 1950.

3627 César's Bark Canoe. 58 min., 1971. [Cree Indian canoe construction.]

3628 The Children of Fogo Island. 17 min., 1968. B/W.

3629 Chinatown-Toronto. 14 min., 1973. Peggy Peacock. Can. Filmmakers Distribution Centre.

*3630 Chinese Folk Cuisine. 45 min., 1978. CCFCS, National Museum of Man.

Y 3631 Christmas at Moose Factory. 13 min., 1971.

3632 Circle of the Sun. 29 min., 1961. [The Sun Dance of the Cree Indians.]

3633 Colors of Pride. 28 min., 1973. Made by Henning Jacobsen for Dept. of Indian and Northern Affairs. Released by NFB. [Canadian Indian art.]

Y 3634 Corral. 11 min., 1954.

3635 Crafts of My Province. 13 min., 1964. [N.B.]

3636 Craftsmen at Work. 16 min., 1946. A Province of N.S. film released through NFB.

3637 Cree Hunters of Mistassini. 58 min., 1974.

3638 The Cree of Paint Hills. 57 min., 1976. CBC.

Y 3639 Cree Way. 26 min., 1977.

3640 Crooked Beak of Heaven. 53 min., 1975. BBC [Northwest Coast Indian traditions.]

3641 Dances of the Kwakiutl. 10 min., 1951. Orbit Films.

3642 The Days of Whisky Gap. 28 min., 1961. B/W. [Prairie pioneer days.]

3643 The Dreamspeaker. 75 min., 1976. CBC. [B.C. Indian lore.]

Y 3644 The Eagle and the Moon. 5 min., 1974. Pictura Films. [An Inuit tale.]

3645 Eskimo Artist--Kenojuak. 20 min., 1964.

3647 Eskimo Arts and Crafts. 22 min., 1944.

3648   The Eskimo in Life and Legend. 23 min., 1960. Encyclo-
       pedia Britannica Educational Corp.

3649   The Eskimo: Fight for Life. 51 min., 1970.

3650   Eskimo Summer. 16 min., 1944.

3651   Estonian National Costumes. 8 min., 1976. CCFCS,
       National Museum of Man. [Dance sequences.]

3652   Fields of Endless Day. 58 min., 1978. James Walker.
       NFB and TV Ontario. [Blacks in Canada.]

3653   Gaels of Cape Breton, 10 min., 1948.

3654   Gitksan. 27 min., 1973. K'SAN, NFB.

Y 3655   Glooscap Country. 14 min., 1962. Province of N.S. film.
       [Micmac legends.]

3656   Good Friday in Little Italy. 13 min., 1971. Peter Rowe.
       Can. Filmmakers' Distribution Centre.

3657   Great Grandmother. 29 min., 1975. [Prairie pioneers.]

3658   Habitant Arts and Crafts. 10 min., 1944.

3659   Haida Carver. 12 min., 1964.

3660   Heritage Kingston. 27 min., 1976. Nicholas Kendall.
       Can. Filmmakers' Distribution Centre.

Y 3661   How the Earth Was Made. 5 min., 1972. Pictura Films.
       [An Iroquois tale.]

3662   How to Build an Igloo. 11 min., 1950.

*3663   The Hutterites. 28 min., 1964. B/W.

*3664   In Search of Utopia--The Doukhobors. 60 min., 1979. B/W.
       L. A. Ewashen, R. Gallon, K. Innes and K. J. Tarasoff.
       Gemini Co-operative.

*3665   In the Land of the War Canoes. 47 min., 1974. B/W. Univ.
       of Washington. [Edited & restored version of E. S.
       Curtis' 1914 film of Kwakiutl life.]

*3666   Indian Arts and Crafts--A Film Series. Commissioned
       by the Native Indian Arts and Crafts Corporation, and
       distributed by North American Indian Films Inc., 177
       Nepean St., Ottawa K2P 0B4.

       A Pair of Moccasins for Mary Thomas. 15 min., 1977.
       Joe Jacobs--Stone Carver. 10 min., 1977.
       A Corn Husk Doll by Deanna Skye. 11 min., 1977.
       A Micmac Scale Basket. 12 min., 1977.

231

A Malecite Fancy Basket. 12 min., 1977.
A Moon Mask by Freda Diesing. 10 min., 1977.
Tony Hunt, Kwakiutl Artist. 10 min., 1977.
Porcupine Quill Work by Bernadette Pangawish. 10 min., 1977.
A Ceremonial Peace Pipe by Guy Siwi. 11 min., 1978.
Robert Bellegarde , Prairie Artist. 12 min., 1978.
Beads and Leather of Manitoba by Cecelia Ross. 10 min., 1978.
Sara Smith, Mohawk Potter. 18 min., 1978.
Birch Bark Biting by Angelique Mirasty. 6 min., 1978.
A Willow Basket by Florine Hotomani. 11 min., 1978.
Wooden Flowers of Nova Scotia, by Matilda Paul. 9 min., 1978.
Iroquoian Pottery by Bill Parker. 14 min., 1978.

Y 3667   Indian Legends. 10 min., 1975. OECA/Foscine.

3668   The Indian Speaks. 40 min., 1967. [Problems of vanishing culture.]

3669   The Islanders. 19 min., 1974. [P.E.I.]

3670   The Jolifou Inn. 10 min., 1955. [Krieghoff pictures.]

3671   The Journals of Susanna Moodie. 15 min., 1972. B/W. Marie Waisberg. Can. Filmmakers' Distribution Centre.

3672   Kaszuby. 29 min., 1975. [Polish culture in Ontario.]

Y 3673   Kumak, the Sleepy Hunter. 15 min., 1955. Dunclaren Productions. Released in Canada by NFB. [Eskimo legend told with puppets.]

*3674   Kung Fu as a Folk Art. 30 min., 1977. CCFCS, National Museum of Man.

3675   Kurelek. 10 min., 1966. [Homesteading.]

3676   Kurelek: The Ukrainian Pioneers. 15 min., 1974. John Griffin. Can. Filmmakers' Distribution Centre.

*3677   The Kwakiutl of British Columbia. 55 min., 1973. B/W. Univ. of Washington. [Edited version of Boas' documentary made in 1930-31.]

3678   Land of the Long Day. 37 min., 1952. [Arctic summer on Baffin Island.]

3679   The Land is the Culture. 36 min., 1976. Union of B.C. Indian Chiefs. Pacific Cinematheque.

3680   Legend. 15 min., 1970. [Beauty and the Beast tale based on West Coast Indian legend.]

3681   Legend of the Magic Knives. 11 min., 1970. Encyclopaedia Britannica. [Legend of chief carver told through
totems and masks.]

Y 3682   The Legend of the Raven. 15 min., 1957. Produced by
Crawley Films for Imperial Oil.

3683   Legends of the Sioux. 20 min., 1975. Lutheran Church
and Indian People.

3684   The Living Stone. 31 min., 1958. [Eskimo sculpture.]

3685   Log Drive. 29 min., 1957. B/W.

*3686   The Longhouse People. 23 min., 1951. [Life and religion
of Six Nations Iroquois.]

Y 3687   The Loon's Necklace. 11 min., 1949. Produced by Crawley
Films for Imperial Oil.

*3688   Luchak's Easter. 28 min., 1976. CCFCS, National Museum
of Man.

Y 3689   Lumaaq: An Eskimo Legend. 8 min., 1975. B/W.

3690   Magnificent Gift. 56 min., 1970. CBC. Visual Education
Centre. [Three hundred years of the fur trade.]

Y 3691   The Man and the Giant: An Eskimo Legend. 8 min., 1975.

3692   Maple Sugar Time. 9 min., 1941.

3693   Margaree People. 27 min., 1974. [Cape Breton.]

Y 3694   Medoonak the Stormmaker. 13 min., 1975. [Micmac
legend.]

3695   Menno's Reins. 60 min., c. 1973. Conference of Mennonites in Canada.

3696   The Moontrap. 84 min., 1964. B/W. [Folk life on Ile
aux Coudres; trapping of whales through traditions
and beliefs.]

3697   Nahanni. 18 min., 1962. [Legend of lost gold mine.]

3698   Nanook of the North. 50 min., 1922. B/W. Revillon
Frères. Released in Canada by McGraw-Hill.

3699   Natsik Hunting. 8 min., 1975. [Seal hunt.]

3700   Netsilik Eskimo Series. Nine half-hour films, released
1967. Filmed in the Pelly Bay region of the Canadian
Arctic.

At the Caribou Crossing Place, Parts 1 and 2.
At the Autumn River Camp, Parts 1 and 2.
At the Winter Sea Ice Camp, Parts 1, 2, 3, and 4.

Jigging for Lake Trout.
At the Spring Sea Ice Camp, Parts 1, 2, and 3.
Group Hunting on the Spring Ice, Parts 1, 2, and 3.
Stalking Seal on the Spring Ice, Parts 1 and 2.
Building a Kayak, Parts 1 and 2.
Fishing at the Stone Weir, Parts 1 and 2.

3701   Norval Morrisseau. 16 min., 1969. Philip Forsythe. Marlin Motion Pictures.

3702   Okan Sun Dance of the Blackfoot. 64 min., 1966. Glenbow Foundation, Calgary.

Y 3703   The Owl and the Lemming--An Eskimo Legend. 6 min., 1971.

Y 3704   The Owl and the Raven--An Eskimo Legend. 7 min., 1973.

Y 3705   The Owl Who Married the Goose--An Eskimo Legend. 8 min., 1974.

3706   The Paradox of Norval Morrisseau. 28 min., 1974.

3707   Paul Kane Goes West. 14 min., 1972.

3708   The People at Dipper. 18 min., 1966. [Indian reserve in Saskatchewan.]

Y 3709   People Might Laugh at Us. 9 min., 1964. [Micmac Indians.]

3710   The People of the Book. 28 min., 1973. [Canadian Jews.]

3711   People of the Potlatch. 21 min., 1944.

3712   People of the Seal. Part 1: Eskimo Summer; Part 2: Eskimo Winter. 52 min. each, 1971.

3713   Pictures Out of My Life. 13 min., 1973. [Pitseolak.]

3714   Pioneer Village at Black Creek. 28 min., 1962. Crawley Films. Released by Metropolitan Toronto and Region Conservation Authority.

3715   Plain People. 28 min., 1976. CBC. Released by NFB. [Mennonites at Elmira.]

*3716   Potlatch: A Strict Law Bids Us Dance. 53 min., 1975. B/W. 'U'mista Cultural Society, Alert Bay, B.C. Distributed by Pacific Cinematheque, Vancouver, and Can. Filmmakers' Distribution Centre, Toronto.

3717   Preparing Foods. 10 min., n.d. [Black Creek, pioneer food preparation.]

3718   Quebec Village. 14 min., 1973. Peggy Peacock. Can. Filmmakers' Distribution Centre.

3719   Race of the Snow Snakes. 8 min., 1972. Made by Ako Productions for Dept. of Indian Affairs and Northern Development. Released by NFB. [Ancient Iroquois game.]

3720   Quillayute Story. 25 min., 1955. Erna Gunther. Titania Productions. [West Coast Indians.]

3721   Reflections of the Past. 36 min., 1974. Slevko Nowytski. Ukrainian Cultural and Education Centre, Winnipeg.

3722   Sacred Circle. 18 min., 1976. Kalli Paakspuu. Can. Filmmakers' Distribution Centre.

3723   St. Lawrence North Series. Produced by Crawley Films for NFB.

Attiuk. 29 min., 1963. [Montaignais Indians' drum dance and seal hunt.]
The 'Jean Richard.' 30 min., 1963. [Building a wooden coastal freighter.]
Whalehead. 30 min., 1963. [Village living on mainland in winter, on islands for summer fishing.]
Winter Sealing at La Tabatière. 30 min., 1963.

*3724   Sananguagat: Masterpieces of 1000 Years. 25 min., 1974. [Inuit art.]

3725   Serpent River Paddlers. 14 min., 1975. Anthony Hall. Can. Filmmakers' Distribution Centre. [Huron Indians.]

3726   The Settlers, Early Pioneer Farmers in the Great Lakes Region. 28 min., 1967. Jack Ruddell. Coronet Instructional Films.

3727   The Songs of Chris Cobb. 8 min., 1958. [A Newfoundland folk composer.]

*3728   Songs of Nova Scotia. 11 min., 1958. B/W. [Helen Creighton's collecting.]

*3729   The Shadow Catcher. 88 min., 1975. T. C. McLuhan. Phoenix Films. [E. S. Curtis.]

3730   Songs and Tales of Yesteryear. 25 min., 1974. Ed. Cesar. Can. Filmmakers' Distribution Centre.

3731   Spence Bay. 14 min., 1976. Brian Kelly. Can. Filmmakers' Distribution Centre.

3732   Spirit in a Landscape: The People Beyond. 57 min., 1975. CBC. Released by NFB, 1976. [Inuit art and culture.]

3733   Standing Buffalo. 23 min., 1968. [Sioux rugmaking.]

3734   Story of 'H.M.S. Shannon.' 8 min., 1958. [Song-story of naval battle in War of 1812.]

3735   These Are My People. 13 min., 1969. B/W. [Iroquois culture.]

3736   They Called Us 'Les Filles du Roy.' 56 min., 1974.

3737   This Is My Grandmother. 12 min., 1976. Lenore Goodings. Can. Filmmakers' Distribution Centre. [Ontario pioneer life.]

3738   This Was the Time. 15 min., 1970. [Haida potlatch, totems.]

3739   Those Born at Massett. 70 min., 1976. B/W. Univ. of Washington. [A Haida stonemoving and feast.]

3740   Time of the Cree. 26 min., 1974. Gail Singer and Bob Rodgers. Can. Filmmakers' Distribution Centre.

3741   Totems. 11 min., 1944.

3742   Treasures of the Ukraine. 45 min. N. E. Tucyk, F. J. Martyniuk, and E. Wachna. National Ethnic Archive, National Film Archive.

3743   The Trout Lake Cree. 57 min. B/W. Gene Gregoret. Universal Education and Visual Arts. [Cree in Alberta.]

3744   Ukrainian Dance. 17 min., 1944.

*3745   Vianoce: A Canadian-Slovak Christmas. 27 min., 1978. CCFCS, National Museum of Man.

3746   Voices from the Landscape. 13 min., 1975. John Brett. Can. Filmmakers' Distribution Centre. [Maritime homesteading.]

Y 3747   Voyageurs. 20 min., 1964. [Fur trade on Canadian rivers; song background.]

3748   Waterloo Farmers. 28 min., 1976. [Amish practices.]

14 Theses and Dissertations

3749 Allhouse, John C. 'The Sculptural Arts of the Pacific Northwest Coast Indians.' M.A. Thesis, Univ. of Oklahoma, 1947. 96 pp.

3750 Arima, Eugene Y. 'A Contextual Study of the Caribou Eskimo Kayak.' Ph.D. Dissertation, Univ. of Toronto, 1972. 301 pp. Published: see #3020.

3751 Arron, Walter J. 'Aspects of the Epic in Eskimo Folklore.' M.A. Thesis, Univ. of New Mexico, 1956. 83 pp.

3752 Beckwith, Martha Warren. 'Dance Forms of the Moqui and Kwakiutl Indians.' M.A. Thesis, Columbia Univ., 1905. 43 pp. Published: see #1367.

3753 Bennett-Knight, Margaret. 'Some Aspects of the Scottish-Gaelic Traditions of the Codroy Valley, Newfoundland.' M.A. Thesis, Memorial University, 1975. 328 pp.

3754 Bessac, S. L. 'The Eskimos' Representational Art in Two Dimensions.' M.A. Thesis, Univ. of California (Berkeley), 1955. 150 pp.

3755 Bosch, James W. 'Kwakiutl Values as Reflected in Mythology.' M.A. Thesis, Stanford Univ., 1952. 163 pp.

3756 Brider, Walter R. 'A Quantitative Approach to Eskimo Folklore.' M.A. Thesis, Indiana Univ., 1966. 44 pp.

3757 Bryers, Joanne E. 'The Grapic Art of the Baker Lake Eskimos from July 1969 to July 1973.' M.A. Thesis, Univ. of Toronto, 1974.

3758 Casey, George J. 'Traditions and Neighbourhoods; The Folklife of a Newfoundland Fishing Outport.' M.A. Thesis, Memorial Univ., 1971. 333 pp.

3759 Chowning, Martha A. 'Raven Myths in Northwestern North America and Northeastern Asia.' M.A., Thesis Univ. of Pennsylvania, 1952. 179 pp.

3760 Class, Loretta M. 'In-group and Out-group Attitudes as Expressed in Haida Folktales.' M.A. Thesis, Univ. of Washington, 1968. 71 pp.

3761 Coe, Jayne R. 'Adaptation of the Designs of the Haida, a Northwest Coast Indian Group, to Contemporary Situations.' M.A. Thesis, Washington State Univ., 1968. 84 pp.

3762 Coldwell, Joyce. 'Treasure Stories and Beliefs in Atlantic Canada.' Ph.D. Dissertation, Memorial Univ., 1977. 302 pp.

3763 Cox, Gordon S. A. 'Some Aspects of the Folk Music Complex of a Newfoundland Outport.' M.A. Thesis, Memorial Univ., 1976. 213 pp.

3764 Dailey, Robert C. 'Medical Practices Among the Plains Indians; A Study in Culture Pattern.' Ph.D. Dissertation, Univ. of Toronto, 1957. 291 pp.

3765 Darby, Herbert K. 'A Survey of the Lexicon of Fishing, Farming and Carpentry in the French Community of Cape St. George, Port-au-Port Peninsula, Newfoundland.' M.A. Thesis, Memorial Univ., 1977. 164 pp.

3766 Davis, Reginald C. 'Canadian Folksongs for American Schools.' M.M. Thesis, Univ. of Rochester, 1950. 180 pp.

3767 Dillon, Virginia. 'The Anglo-Irish Element in the Speech of the Southern Shore of Newfoundland.' M.A. Thesis, Memorial Univ., 1968. 164 pp.

3768 Doucette, C. M. Laurel. 'Skill and Status: Traditional Expertise Within a Rural Canadian Family.' M.A. Thesis, Memorial Univ., 1977. 167 pp. Published: See #2026.

3769 Dundes, Alan. 'The Morphology of North American Indian Folktales.' P.D. Dissertation, Indiana Univ., 1962. 219 pp. Published: Folklore Fellows Communications, 195 (1964), 134 pp.

3770 Ennals, Peter M. 'The Development of Farm Barn Types in Southern Ontario during the Nineteenth Century.' M.A. Thesis, Univ. of Toronto, 1968.

3771 Fauset, Arthur Huff. 'Abstract of Thesis on Folklore of Negroes in Nova Scotia.' M.A. Thesis, Univ. of Pennsylvania, 1924. 38 pp.

3772 Fichtner, Mary A. 'Rattle Types of the Pacific Northwest Coast Indians.' M.F.A. Thesis, Univ. of Iowa, 1960. 248 pp.

3773 Fisher, Anthony D. 'The Perception of Instrumental Values Among the Young Blood Indians of Alberta.' Ph.D. Dissertation, Stanford Univ., 1966. 223 pp.

3774 Fortier, Sylvia M. 'A Study of Valued Behavior in Ojibwa Mythology.' M.A. Thesis, Catholic Univ., 1963. 33 pp.

3775 Fraser, Mary. 'Folkore of Nova Scotia.' Ph.D. Dissertation, Catholic Univ., 1929. Published: see #268.

3776 Gedalof, Robin. 'An Introduction to Canadian Eskimo Prose in English.' M.A. Thesis, Univ. of Western Ontario, 1977. 74 pp.

3777 Gellatly, Marjorie G. 'Fourteen Northwest Coast Indian Songs Transcribed into Musical Notation.' M.A. Thesis, Univ. of Washington, 1932. 79 pp.

3778 Glatthaar, Trisha C. 'Tom Price (c. 1860-1927): The Art and Style of a Haida Artist.' M.A. Thesis, Univ. of British Columbia, 1970. 160 pp.

3779 Gray, Pamela. 'Traditional Newfoundland Foodways: Origin, Adaptation, and Change.' M.A. Thesis, Memorial Univ., 1977. 232 pp.

3780 Gunther, Erna. 'Design Units on Tlingit Baskets.' M.A. Thesis, Columbia Univ., 1920. 31 pp.

3781 Hallowell, A. Irving. 'Bear Ceremonialism in the Northern Hemisphere.' Ph.D. Dissertation, Univ. of Pennsylvania, 1926. 175 pp. Published: American Anthropologist, 28(1926), 1-175.

3782 Halpin, Marjorie M. 'The Tsimshian Crest System: A Study based on Museum Specimens and the Marius Barbeau and William Beynon Field Notes.' Ph.D. Dissertation, Univ. of British Columbia, 1973. 469 pp.

3783 Haywood, Charles. 'A Bibliography of North American Folklore and Folksong.' Ph.D. Dissertation, Columbia Univ., 1951. 1292 pp. Published: see #43.

3784 Henderson, M. Carole [Carole Henderson Carpenter]. 'Many Voices: A Study of Folklore Activities in Canada and Their Role in Canadian Culture.' Ph.D. Dissertation, Univ. of Pennsylvania, 1975. 502 pp. Published: see #169.

3785 Hennigh, Lawrence. 'Control of Incest in Eskimo Folktales.' M.A. Thesis, Univ. of Washington, 1965. 99 pp.

3786 Hickerson, Joseph C. 'Annotated Bibliography of North American Indian Music North of Mexico.' M.A. Thesis, Indiana Univ., 1961. 464 pp.

3787 Higgins, John C. 'The Lumberjack in American Literature; His Life and Customs, His Slang, His Ballads and Shanties and His Folk-Epic of Paul Bunyan.' M.A. Thesis, Univ. of South Carolina, 1935.

3788 Hoe, Ban Seng. 'Structural Changes in Two Chinese Communities in Alberta, Canada.' Ph.D. Dissertation, Vanderbilt Univ. 1974. 410 pp. Published: see #2688.

3789 Hoffman, Bernard. 'Historical Ethnography of the Micmac Indians of the Sixteenth and Seventeenth Centuries.' Ph.D. Dissertation, Univ. of California (Berkeley), 1955. 105 pp.

3790 Inglis, Joyce G. 'The Interaction of Myth and Social Context in the Village of Cape Mudge.' M.A. Thesis, Univ. of British Columbia, 1965. 163 pp.

3791 Ives, Edward D. 'The Satirical Song Tradition in Maine and the Maritime Provinces of Canada, with Particular Reference to Larry Gorman.' Ph.D. Dissertation, Indiana Univ., 1962. 470 pp.

3792 Jitodai, Kinuye. 'Bibliography of the Arts and Crafts of Northwest Coast Indians.' M. Lib. Thesis, Univ. of Washington, 1954. 74 pp. Published: see #51.

3793 Johnson, Jean D. 'The Relationship between the Traditional Graphic Art and the Contemporary Graphic Art of Canadian Eskimo.' M.A. Thesis, Univ. of Washington, 1975.

3794 Jones, Rosalie M. 'The Blackfeet Medicine Lodge Ceremony: Ritual and Dance Drama.' M.S. Thesis, Univ. of Utah, 1968. 162 pp.

3795 Jorgensen, Grace M. M. 'A Comparative Examination of Northwest Coast Shamanism.' M.A. Thesis, Univ. of British Columbia, 1970. 221 pp.

3796 Kaufmann, Carole N. 'Changes in Haida Indian Argyllite Carvings, 1820-1910.' Ph.D. Dissertation, Univ. of California, 1969. 225 pp.

3797 Kennedy, Norman J. 'The Growth and Development of Music in Calgary.' M.A. Thesis, Univ. of Alberta, 1952.

3798 Kidwell, Vivian M. 'Some Suggested Applications of Indian Motifs to Modern Design.' M.A. Thesis, Washington State Univ., 1931. 76 pp. [Northwest Coast.]

3799 Kirshenblatt-Gimblett, Barbara. 'Traditional Story-telling in the Toronto Jewish Community: A Study in Performance and Creativity in an Immigrant Culture.' Ph.D. Dissertation, Indiana Univ., 1972. 521 pp.

3800 Klymasz, Robert B. 'Ukrainian Folklore in Canada: An Immigrant Complex in Transition.' Ph.D. Dissertation, Indiana Univ., 1971. 342 pp.

3801 Koppert, Vincent A. 'Some Myths of the Nootka Indians.' M.A. Thesis, Catholic Univ., 1928. 44 pp.

3802 Lerman, Norman H. 'An Analysis of Folktales of Lower Fraser Indians, British Columbia.' M.A. Thesis, Univ. of Washington, 1952. 188 pp.

3803 Lester, Joan A. 'A Study of the Iconography of Certain Supernaturals in the Arts of the Kwakiutl Indians.' M.A. Thesis, Univ. of California (Los Angeles), 1963. 288 pp.

3804 Lillos, Brian M. 'Selective Studies in Musical Analysis of Beaver Indian Dreamer Songs: A Structural Approach to Ethnomusicology.' M.A. Thesis, Univ. of British Columbia, 1973.

3805 Lowie, Robert H. 'The Test-Theme in North American Mythology.' Ph.D. Dissertation, Columbia Univ., 1908. Published: JAF, 21(1908), 97-148.

3806 Luccock, Norma. 'Songs of Ethnic Canada (An Interdisciplinary Teachers' Guide for Grades 1-7, based on the Folksongs of Four Canadian Ethnic Groups).' M.M.Ed. Dissertation, Univ. of British Columbia, 1979.

3807 Luomala, E. Katherine. 'Turtle's War Party: a Study in Comparative Mythology.' M.A. Thesis, Univ. of California, 1934. 79 pp.

3808 MacKinnon, Kathleen L. 'A Short Study of the History and Traditions of the Highland Scot in Nova Scotia.' M.A. Thesis, St. Francis Xavier Univ., 1964.

3809 Macmillan, Cyrus J. 'The Folk Songs of Canada.' Ph.D. Dissertation, Harvard Univ., 1909. 1120 pp.

3810 MacOdrum, Maxwell M. 'Survivals of the English and Scottish Popular Ballads in Nova Scotia: A Study of Folk Song in Canada.' M.A. Thesis, McGill Univ., 1924.

3811 Mannion, John. 'Irish Imprints on the Landscape of Eastern Canada in the Nineteenth Century: A Study in Cultural Transfer and Adaptation.' Ph.D. Dissertation, Univ. of Toronto, 1970. 485 pp. Published: see #2267.

3812 Maranda, Lynn. 'Coast Salish Gambling Games.' M.A. Thesis, Univ. of British Columbia, 1972. 184 pp.

3813 Mark, Lindy Li. 'The Structure of Inland Tlingit Music.' M.A. Thesis, Northwestern Univ., 1955. 133 pp.

3814 Martens, Helen. 'Hutterite Songs: The Origins and Aural Transmission of Their Melodies from the Sixteenth Century.' Ph.D. Dissertation, Columbia Univ., 1969. 306 pp.

3815 Mathewson, Dorothy R. 'French-Canadian Folk Songs.' M.A. Thesis, McGill Univ., 1924.

3816 Mealing, F. Mark. 'Our People's Way: A Study in Doukhobor Hymnody and Folklife.' Ph.D. Dissertation, Univ. of Pennsylvania, 1972. 789 pp.

3817 Melnyk, John A. 'A Typology of Ukrainian-Canadian Folklore.' M.A. Thesis, Univ. of Manitoba, 1972.

3818 Méndez-Domínguez, Alfredo A. 'Eskimo Moral Systems as Reflected in the Mythology: A Construction of a Logical Model.' M.A. Thesis, Univ. of Minnesota, 1956. 127 pp.

3819 Mercer, H. Paul. 'A Bio-Bibliography of Newfoundland Songs in Printed Sources.' M.A. Thesis, Memorial Univ., 1979. 382 pp. Published: see #69.

3820 Moder, Frances G. 'A Study of Ojibwa Art and Literature.' M.A. Thesis, Indiana Univ., 1927. 98 pp.

3821 Morrison, Monica S. 'A "Small Boy in Small Town": An Individual's Response to the Study of His Own Life.' M.A. Thesis, Memorial Univ., 1977. 237 pp.

3822 Munro, John B. 'Language, Legends, and Lore of the Carrier Indians.' Ph.D. Dissertation, Univ. of Ottawa, 1945. 320 pp.

3823 Murray, Hilda E. L. 'The Traditional Role of Women in a Newfoundland Fishing Community.' M.A. Thesis, Memorial Univ., 1972. 319 pp. Published: see #2288.

3824 Nelson, Mary F. 'Voice of the Mythical Being.' M.A. Thesis, Univ. of Idaho, 1968. 57 pp. [Haida & Tsimshian.]

3825 Nettl, Bruno. 'American Indian Music North of Mexico: Its Styles and Areas.' Ph.D. Dissertation, Indiana Univ., 1951. 239 pp. Published: see #1455.

3826 Noseworthy, Ronald G. 'A Dialect Survey of Grand Bank, Newfoundland.' M.A. Thesis, Memorial Univ., 1971. 269 pp.

3827   Paddock, H. 'The Dialect of Carbonear.' M.A. Thesis, Memorial Univ., 1966. 159 pp.

3828   Panyity, Patricia H. 'Stylistic Devices in Ojibway Folk Tales.' M.A. Thesis, Univ. of California (Berkeley), 1949. 48 pp.

3829   Paquin, Robert. 'Child Ballads in French and English Canada: A Comparative Study.' Ph.D. Dissertation, Univ. of London, 1976. 273 pp.

3830   Pocius, Gerald. 'The Place of Burial: Spatial Focus of Contact of the Living with the Dead in Eastern Areas of the Avalon Peninsula of Newfoundland.' M.A. Thesis, Memorial Univ., 1976. 498 pp.

3831   Posen, I. Sheldon. 'Songs and Singing Tradition at Children's Summer Camps.' M.A. Thesis, Memorial Univ., 1974. 216 pp.

3832   Pratt, E. L. 'The Hutterian Brethren in Alberta.' M.A. Thesis, Univ. of Manitoba, 1949.

3833   Randall, Betty U. 'Elaboration of the Cinderella Theme.' M.A. Thesis, Columbia Univ., 1947. 197 pp. [Northwest Coast & Grimm Brothers.]

3834   Reichard, Gladys A. 'Literary Types and Dissemination of North American Myths.' M.A. Thesis, Columbia Univ., 1920. 46 pp.

3835   Richardson, James B., III. 'The Double-Curve Motif in the Decorative Art of the North-Eastern Algonkian: Diffusion and Origin.' M.A. Thesis, Syracuse Univ., 1963. 121 pp.

3836   Ricketts, MacLinscott. 'The Structure and Religious Significance of the Trickster-Transformer-Culture Hero in the Mythology of the North American Indians. Ph.D. Dissertation, Univ. of Chicago, 1964. 2 vol. 653 pp.

3837   Robertson, Margaret. 'The Newfoundland Mummers' House-Visit.' M.A. Thesis, Memorial Univ., 1979. 239 pp.

3838   Robinson, Sarah A. 'Spirit Dancing among the Salish Indians, Vancouver Island.' Ph.D. Dissertation, Univ. of Chicago, 1963.

3839   Rogers, Ruth A. 'French Canadian Folk Music.' M.M. Thesis, Northwestern Univ., 1947. 115 pp.

3840   Rohner, Ronald P. 'Ethnography of a Contemporary Kwakiutl Village: Gilford Island Band.' Ph.D. Dissertation, Stanford Univ., 1964. 332 pp. Published: see #2572.

3841 Sargent, Margaret N. [Margaret S. McTaggart]. 'The Native and Primitive Music of Canada.' Mus. Bac. Thesis, Univ. of Toronto, 1942. 54 pp.

3842 Scott, Margaret A. 'Bella Coola Ceremony and Art.' M.A. Thesis, McGill Univ., 1969. 151 pp.

3843 Scott, John R. 'The Function of Folklore in the Interrelationship of the Newfoundland Seal Fishery and the Home Communities of the Sealers.' M.A. Thesis, Memorial Univ., 1975. 248 pp.

3844 Shaham, Milton A. 'Distribution of Eskimo Mythical Elements.' M.A. Thesis, Univ. of Pennsylvania, 1932. 104 pp.

3845 Small, Lawrence. 'The Interrelationship of Work and Talk in a Newfoundland Fishing Community.' Ph.D. Dissertation, Univ. of Pennsylvania, 1979. 230 pp.

3846 -- 'Patterns in Personal Experience Narratives: Storytelling at Cod Harbour--a Newfoundland Fishing Community.' M.A. Thesis, Memorial Univ., 1972. 279 pp.

3847 Sommmer, Frank H., III. 'Kwakiutl Iconography. Prehistoric Origins and Development.' Ph.D. Dissertation, Yale Univ., 1950. 430 pp.

3848 Spradley, James P. 'The Kwakiutl Indian Guardian Spirit Quest. An Historical Functional and Comparative Analysis.' M.A. Thesis, Univ. of Washington, 1963. 128 pp.

3849 Stone, Kay F. 'Romantic Heroines in Anglo-American Folk and Popular Literature.' Ph.D. Dissertation, Indiana Univ., 1975. 390 pp.

3850 Stuart, Wendy B. 'Gambling Music of the Coast Salish Indians.' M.A. Thesis, Univ. of British Columbia, 1972. 114 pp. Published: see #1489.

3851 Svennungsen, Lowell R. 'Music and Myth: The Ancient Greeks and Kwakiutl Indians.' M.A. Thesis, Univ. of Montana, 1969. 60 pp.

3852 Swackhammer, Robert M. '"I'm A Professional, but I'm Not on Records": The Reflection of a Performer's Self-Image in His Repertoire.' M.A. Thesis, Memorial Univ., 1979.

3853 Tallman, Richard. 'The Tall Tale Tradition and the Teller: A Biographical Contextual Study of a Storyteller, Robert Coffil of Blomidon, Nova Scotia.' Ph.D. Dissertation, Memorial Univ., 1974. 552 pp.

3854 Teicher, Morton I. 'Windigo Psychosis: A Study of a Relationship between Belief and Behaviour among the Indians of Northeastern Canada.' Ph.D. Dissertation, Univ. of Toronto, 1956. 400 pp. Published: see #1964.

3855 Thomas, Gerald. 'Stories, Storytelling and Storytellers in Newfoundland's French Tradition: A Study of the Narrative Art of Four French Newfoundlanders.' Ph.D. Dissertation, Memorial Univ., 1977. 823 pp.

3856 Thomas, Gregory E. G. 'The British Columbia Ranching Frontier 1858-1896.' M.A. Thesis, Univ. of British Columbia, 1976. 259 pp.

3857 Thompson, John B. 'The Evolution of an English-speaking Community in Rural French Canada, 1820-1867.' M.A. Thesis, McGill Univ., 1968.

3858 Thompson, Stith. 'European Borrowings and Parallels in North American Indian Tales.' Ph.D. Dissertation, Harvard Univ., 1914. 488 pp. Published: see #856.

3859 Tsuchijama, Tamie. 'A Comparison of the Folklore of the Northern, Southern and Pacific Athabaskans: A Study in Stability of Folklore Within a Linguistic Stock.' Ph.D. Dissertation, Univ. of California, 1947. 201 pp.

3860 Vanderburg, Joanne. 'Chilkat and Salish Weaving.' M.A. Thesis, Univ. of Washington, 1953. 119 pp.

3861 Vastokas, Joan M. 'Architecture of the Northwest Coast Indians of America.' Ph.D. Dissertation, Columbia Univ., 1966. 369 pp.

3862 Verrall, Edith A. 'The Use of Videotaping in Folklore Fieldwork: Some Problems in the Transcription of a Children's Game.' M.A. Thesis, Memorial Univ., 1975. 356 pp.

3863 Waldman, Debbie. 'Transcultural Folksong Survival: Active and Passive Bearers of the French-Canadian Folksong Tradition in Woonsocket, R.I., and Adjacent Towns.' M.A. Thesis, Brown Univ., 1976.

3864 Wareham, Wilfred. 'Social Change and Music Tradition: The Role of Singing in the Life of a Newfoundland Singer.' M.A. Thesis, Memorial Univ., 1972. 270 pp.

3865 Waterman, Thomas T. 'The Explanatory Element in the Folk-tales of the North-American Indians.' Ph.D. Dissertation, Columbia Univ., 1914. 54 pp. Published: JAF, 27 (1914), 1-54.

3866 Waterton, Eric. 'Gambling Games of the Northwest Coast.' M.A. Thesis, Univ. of British Columbia, 1969. 131 pp.

3867 Wenker, Jerome. 'A Computer-Aided Analysis of Anglo-Canadian Folktunes.' Ph.D. Dissertation, Indiana Univ., 1978. 2 vols., 298 pp.; 690 pp.

3868 Weyer, Edward M., Jr. 'The Eskimos: A Study in Adaptation to Environment.' Ph.D., Yale Univ., 1930. 494 pp. Published: see #2631.

3869 Wickwire, Wendy. 'Songs of the Canadian Interior Salish Tribes: An Anthology and Ethnography.' M.A. Thesis, York Univ., 1978. 128 pp.

3870 Widdowson, John D. A. 'Aspects of Traditional Verbal Control: Threats and Threatening Figures in Newfoundland Folklore.' Ph.D. Dissertation, Memorial Univ., 1972. 605 pp. Published: see #2343.

3871 Wilson, H. Rex. 'The Dialect of Lunenburg County, Nova Scotia.' Ph.D. Dissertation, Univ. of Michigan, 1958. 287 pp.

3872 Wilson, J. Reginald. 'Ballad Tunes of the Miramichi.' M.A. Thesis, New York Univ., 1961. 148 pp.

3873 Winger, Bjorn. 'A Classification of Motifs in Eskimo Folk Literature.' A.M. Thesis, Indiana Univ., 1930. 177 pp.

3874 Witmer, Robert E. 'The Musical Culture of the Blood Indians.' M.M. Thesis, Univ. of Illinois, 1970. 314 pp.

3875 Wooley, Ruth E. 'A Comparative Study of Some French-Canadian Tales.' M.A. Thesis, Indiana Univ., 1927. 92 pp.

3876 Wycoco, Remedios S. 'The Types of North-American Indian Tales.' Ph.D. Dissertation, Indiana Univ., 1951. 293 pp.

3877 Zahniser, J. Jay. 'The Killer Whale Motif of the Northwest Indians.' M.A. Thesis, Univ. of Pittsburgh, 1956.

See also items 38, 44, 71, and 1014.

Index of Authors and Editors

Index

Index

Index

Index

Index

MacMillan, Ernest C., 987, 988, 1336, 1337, 3313, 3314.
McNab, Mary, 1182.
McNamara, Charles, 2264.
McNeil, Bill, 2086.
MacNeil, Neil, 292.
MacNeish, June H., 1942.
MacNutt, W. Stewart, 2087.
MacOdrum, Maxwell M., 1183, 3810.
MacPhail, Margaret, 2265.
Macpherson, Dorothy, 3188.
MacPherson, Flora, 1995.
Macpherson, Ken, 2909.
MacQuarrie, Gordon F., 1184.
McQueston, C., 1450.
McRae, Earl, 1730.
MacRae, Marion, 2939.
McTaggart, Margaret S., 989, 1003, 1483, 3841.
MacWhirter, Margaret G., 360.
Mage, Julius, 2719.
Magee, Eleanor E., 63.
Maillard, A. S., 2545.
Main, J. R. K., 2088.
Maine, Dal, 1786.
Major, Kevin, 2266.
Malin, Edward, 3190.
Malloff, Marjorie, 2720.
Mallon, Mick, 1451.
Mandelbaum, David G., 2546.
Mandryka, M. I., 64, 3372.
Mannion, John J., 2267, 3811.
Manny, Louise, 465, 1185-1189, 3409-3412.
Mansfield, Grace Y., 1134.
Maranda, Lynn, 4812.
Margaret, Len, 2268.
Marie-Ursule, Soeur, 561.
Mark, Lindy Li, 4813.
Marks, William, 1787.
Marlatt, Daphne, 2721.
Marsh, D. B., 1452.
Marsh, Winifred P., 2547.
Marshall, Ingeborg, 2548.
Martens, Helen, 1523, 3814.

Martijn, Charles A., 3191, 3192.
Martin, Eva, 1190.
Martin, J. Lynton, 2269, 2940.
Martin, John P., 466.
Martin, Peggy, 1788.
Martin, Pol, 2379.
Martin, Virgil E., 2722.
Mascayano, Ismael, 892.
Mason, Joe, 2270.
Mason, Leonard, 2549.
Mason, Patricia F., 756.
Mason, S., 3193.
Masta, Henry L., 293, 757.
Matejko, Joanna, 2723.
Mathewson, Dorothy R., 3815.
Mattie, Wesley C., 2847, 2848.
Mattfield, Julius, 65.
Matthews, J. S., 2271.
Matthews, John, 1191.
Matthews, Ralph, 2272.
Matthews, Washington, 1731.
Matthews, William, 66.
Mathiassen, Therkel, 3194.
Maud, Ralph, 294.
Maxwell, Janet, 67.
Maxwell, Percy A., 2273.
May, John, 2274.
Mayer, Theresa, 673.
Mayrand, Pierre, 2849.
Mead, Margaret, 2550.
Mealing, F. Mark, 206, 1524, 2724, 3816.
Mechling, William H., 758, 759.
Medwidsky, Bohdan, 1525.
Melançon, Claude, 760.
Melchen, Elizabeth V., 2275.
Meldgard, Jorgen, 3195.
Melnyk, John A., 3817.
Melvin, Grace, 232.
Melzack, Ronald, 761-763.
Mendelson, Michael, 68.
Mendez-Domineguez, Alfredo A., 3818.

262

Index